The Gospel of Luke

Introduction and Theology

Colourpoint Educational

Raymond Banks

All rights reserved. No part of this publication may be reproduced, stored in a retrieval system or transmitted in any form or by any means, electronic, mechanical, photocopying, scanning, recording or otherwise, without the prior written permission of the copyright owners and publisher of this book.

6 5 4 3 2 1

© Raymond Banks and Colourpoint Books 2006

Designed by: Colourpoint Books, Newtownards
Printed by: ColourBooks Ltd

ISBN 10: 1 904242 29 4
ISBN 13: 978 1 904242 29 1

Except where otherwise stated, the Scripture quotations contained herein are from The New Revised Standard Version of the Bible, Anglicized Edition, copyright © 1989, 1995 by the Division of Christian Education of the National Council of the Churches of Christ in the United States of America. All rights reserved.

Cover picture: Corbis

Colourpoint Books
Colourpoint House
Jubilee Business Park
21 Jubilee Road
Newtownards
County Down
Northern Ireland
BT23 4YH
Tel: 028 9182 0505
Fax: 028 9182 1900
E-mail: info@colourpoint.co.uk
Web-site: www.colourpoint.co.uk

The author

Raymond Banks
Raymond Banks BD (Hons), PGCE, is Head of Religious Studies at Regent House Grammar School, Newtownards and has taught the synoptic Gospels to Advanced Level for several years.

Contents

Preface 4
Abbreviations 5
Map of Palestine at the time of Jesus 6

An Introduction to the Gospel of Luke

1 Background to the Gospel of Luke 7
2 Selected narratives in Luke's Gospel 48
3 The words and deeds of Jesus 194

The Theology of the Gospel of Luke

4 Christianity according to Luke 229
5 Religious themes in Luke's Gospel 266
6 Theological significance of Jesus' words and deeds ... 290

Glossary 312
Index 316

Author Preface

This text has been written specifically to assist teachers and students to meet the requirements of CCEA's* GCE Religious Studies AS and A2 courses on the Gospel of Luke. The first section of the book covers the AS course ('An Introduction to the Gospel of Luke') and the remainder the A2 course ('The Theology of the Gospel of Luke'). In each case the order of the chapters matches that of the categories listed in the relevant section of CCEA'S Specification. This order, of course, is not prescriptive and teachers are therefore free to deal with the topics within each section in whatever order they choose. Along with my book *The Early Church: The Christian Church to AD 325* (also published by Colourpoint), this text will provide a complete resource for two assessment units of CCEA's GCE Religious Studies.

As with my previous book, this text represents a collation of the work of many others before me, to whom I gladly acknowledge my debt, as well as my own understanding of the Gospel of Luke. Again, thanks are due to all at Colourpoint Books for the benefit of their professional experience, expertise and assistance during the completion of the book. Above all, special thanks are due to my wife Jennifer and to my sons Christopher and Andrew for, yet again, their understanding and support as I spent many, many hours apart from them while preparing this text. To them I gratefully dedicate this book.

R Banks
May 2006

* Northern Ireland Council for the Curriculum, Examinations and Assessment

Abbreviations

OLD TESTAMENT

Gen	Genesis	Song	Song of Solomon
Ex	Exodus	Isa	Isaiah
Lev	Leviticus	Jer	Jeremiah
Num	Numbers	Lam	Lamentations
Deut	Deuteronomy	Ezek	Ezekiel
Josh	Joshua	Dan	Daniel
Judg	Judges	Hos	Hosea
Ruth	Ruth	Joel	Joel
1/2 Sam	1/2 Samuel	Am	Amos
1/2 Kings	1/2 Kings	Ob	Obadiah
1/2 Chr	1/2 Chronicles	Jon	Jonah
Ezra	Ezra	Mic	Micah
Neh	Nehemiah	Nah	Nahum
Esth	Esther	Hab	Habakkuk
Job	Job	Zeph	Zephaniah
Ps	Psalms	Hag	Haggai
Prov	Proverbs	Zech	Zechariah
Eccl	Ecclesiastes	Mal	Malachi

NEW TESTAMENT

Mt	Matthew	1/2 Thess	1/2 Thessalonians
Mk	Mark	1/2 Tim	1/2 Timothy
Lk	Luke	Titus	Titus
Jn	John	Philem	Philemon
Acts	Acts of the Apostles	Heb	Hebrews
Rom	Romans	Jas	James
1/2 Cor	1/2 Corinthians	1/2 Pet	1/2 Peter
Gal	Galatians	1/2/3 Jn	1/2/3 John
Eph	Ephesians	Jude	Jude
Phil	Philippians	Rev	Revelation
Col	Colossians		

OTHER BOOKS

1/2 Macc	1/2 Maccabees	Tobit	Book of Tobit
Ps Sol	Psalms of Solomon	Wisdom	Book of Wisdom

MISCELLANEOUS

cf	compare	ff	and following (pages, verses, etc)

Palestine at the time of Jesus

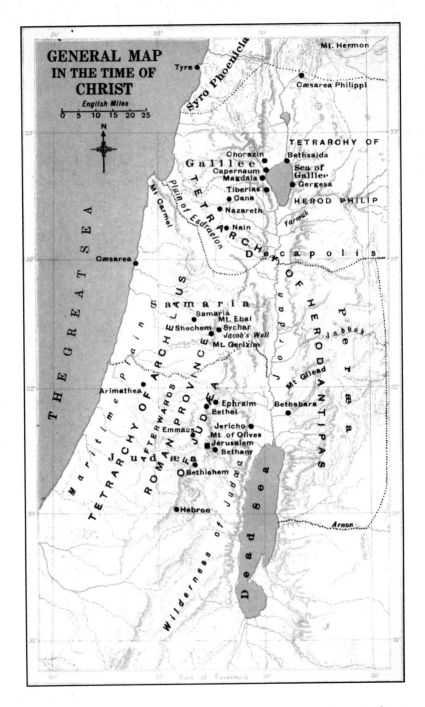

From Stirling, Rev John F, *Philip's Atlas of the New Testament,* London: George Philip & Son

Background to the Gospel of Luke

DATE

IT IS NOT KNOWN when the Gospel of Luke was written. The latest possible certain date is in the AD 180s, when Irenaeus quotes the Gospel in his *Against Heresies* (3.13.3; 3.15.1). Whether our Gospel of Luke was known by writers earlier in the second century (Polycarp, the *Didache*, Basilides, Valentinus, Marcion and Justin) is uncertain.

Three main dates – early, middle and late – have been proposed.

Early (AD 60s)

The following arguments are used to support an early date.

- It is generally agreed that Luke and Acts, in that order, were written by the same author (see Authorship, p11ff). Acts must have been written by AD 62 since it ends abruptly with Paul's imprisonment in Rome and does not record the following important events that occurred after this:

    – the martyrdom of James, brother of Jesus and leader of the Jerusalem church, in AD 62 (Acts 12:17; 15:13; 21:18)

    – the martyrdom of Paul in the mid to late 60s and the Emperor Nero's persecution of Christians in AD 64 with which Paul's death is associated. The lack of reference to the martyrdoms of these two key figures in the book of Acts is all the more significant since the author records the martyrdoms of Stephen (7:59–60) and James, one of the twelve disciples (12:1–2).

– the fall of Jerusalem to the Romans in AD 70. The silence of Acts regarding this is significant in the light of Luke's emphasis on Jerusalem and of the fact that among the Gospels Luke records the most specific prophecy of this event (21:20; also 13:35; 19:43; 21:24). Indeed, Acts includes the fulfilment of a prediction by a lesser prophet (11:27–28). Further, reference to the fall of Jerusalem would have been particularly appropriate in parts of the narrative (Acts 6, 7, 21–23).

- The early/primitive content of Acts is apparent in various ways:

  – its undeveloped theology (teaching, beliefs) is seen in the primitive titles it uses for Jesus (eg Servant – 3:13,26, etc; the Christ/Messiah – 2:31; 8:5, etc) and in its almost 'adoptionist' Christology, in which Jesus is portrayed as a man whom God adopts and uses (eg 2:22; 10:38).

  – Acts focuses on issues that were especially relevant before the fall of Jerusalem, for example the basis on which Gentiles (non-Jews) could be admitted to the Church and have fellowship with Jewish Christians (eg chs 10–11,15; also a concern in Paul's early letters, eg Galatians, Romans).

  – the ignorance and indifference of the Roman authorities concerning Christianity (eg 18:12–17), as well as the emphasis on Jewish persecution of the Church (eg ch 4; 9:23), best reflects circumstances before the Neronian persecution of AD 64.

Thus, Acts was written in the early AD 60s and the Gospel of Luke shortly before this.

However, in response to the above arguments it has been noted that it is speculative to state what the author would or should have included in his record. He may indeed have been aware of Paul's martyrdom (Acts 20:25,38; 28:30 – "two whole years") but did not refer to it since his purpose was not to provide a biography of Paul but to present the progress of the Gospel from Jerusalem to Rome. Also, lack of reference to the fall of Jerusalem may be due to the fact that this event was of more interest to Jews than Christians and that by AD 70 Christianity had moved beyond its Palestinian origins to largely Gentile areas. Further, the primitive features of Acts may reflect the author's accurate account of early Christianity rather than the date of his composition.

Outline and assess the arguments for an early dating of the Gospel of Luke.

Middle (late first century)

The following arguments are used to support a date in the late first century, usually in the AD 80s.

- The author's knowledge of the fall of Jerusalem in AD 70 as a past event is apparent in comparison with Matthew and Mark. Compare the passages in the table below.

Matthew 24:15	Mark 13:14	Luke 21:20
"So when you see the desolating sacrilege standing in the holy place …"	"But when you see the desolating sacrilege set up where it ought not to be …"	"When you see Jerusalem surrounded by armies, then know that its desolation has come near."

While in Matthew and Mark Jesus predicts a desecration of the Jerusalem *temple* (based on Dan 9:27; 11:31; 12:11), in Luke there is a more specific reference to a military siege against the *city*, such as occurred in AD 70. Later in the same passage only Luke reports Jesus as saying that the city will be trampled on by the Gentiles (21:24) and omits the reference to "winter", which may reflect his awareness that the siege of the city was during April–September (cf Mt 24:20/ Mk 13:18/ Lk 21:23ff). Also, Luke alone has Jesus predicting that Jerusalem's enemies would set up ramparts around the city, destroying it and its inhabitants (19:41–44). Other passages in Luke may also indicate knowledge of this event (see Lk 13:35/ Mt 23:38 and Lk 23:28–31 – only in Luke). Since it is generally believed that Luke (and Matthew) used Mark's Gospel as a source, it appears that Luke has rewritten Mark's more general wording in the light of his knowledge, limited though it may have been, of the Roman destruction of Jerusalem. Luke has modified the original prediction of the desecration of the temple to show its fulfilment in the events of AD 70 and to make Jesus' cryptic words from Daniel more understandable to his Gentile readership.

- Luke was dependent on Mark's Gospel and the latter is usually dated in the late 60s or early 70s. The circulation of Mark and Luke's use of it would require a date for Luke in the 80s. Indeed, the author refers to previous accounts he has investigated before composing his own (1:1–4), which would suggest a later rather than an earlier date for Luke.

- Paul is portrayed in Acts as an idealised, even heroic, figure in the early Church. Such a portrayal of a controversial person who was not one of the Twelve would have required some time to develop.

- Luke's theology shows signs of lateness and development, particularly in relation to eschatology (concept of the end times) and ecclesiology (concept of the Church). Thus, the emphasis of early Christian eschatology on the imminent return of Jesus has been replaced by ongoing 'salvation history' (eg cf Lk 22:69 with Mk 14:62; see Eschatology, pp39–40).

There is also a developed picture of the Church in Acts, evident in its concern for organisation and leadership (eg 8:16–17; 14:23; 20:17,28). Overall, then, there are signs of early catholicism, features which would become dominant in the second-century Church and beyond.

Thus, Luke was written in the late first century, probably in the 80s.

However, in response to the above arguments a number of points have been made. Regarding Luke's alleged knowledge of the fall of Jerusalem, it is a fact that there is no direct reference to this event anywhere in either Luke or Acts. It has been argued that Luke's description of the siege of Jerusalem is based not on awareness of the event but on standard Old Testament language for the destruction of cities, particularly the fall of Jerusalem to the Babylonians in the sixth century BC (eg Jer 6:3,6; 52:4ff; Hos 13:16). Further, Luke shows no awareness of certain elements of the siege and destruction, such as cannibalism and fire. It has been proposed too that Luke's shift from the focus on the *temple* (in Mt/Mk) to the *city* is due to a pro-temple tendency in Luke's writings generally, rather than to knowledge of the events of AD 70. Again, that Jesus could have predicted the fall of Jerusalem is not historically impossible – another Jesus (son of Ananias) did so in AD 62, according to the first-century Jewish historian Josephus (*Jewish War* 6.5.3 300–301). In relation to the claims that Luke's theology is late, this needs to be balanced with evidence of early theology (see p8), such as expectation of an imminent End (eg 3:9; 12:9–46) and the absence of a uniform hierarchy of Church leadership. Finally, it is a matter of speculation how much time would have to elapse for Luke to make use of Mark and for Paul's influence to grow.

Late (second century)

The following arguments are used to support a date in the second century.

- Luke made use of Josephus' *Antiquities of the Jews* (eg Lk 3:1–2/ *Ant* 14.13.3 330, 15.14.1 92; Acts 5:36/ *Ant* 20.5.1 97–98). Josephus' work was written around AD 94 and Luke would have had access to it in the early second century.

- Acts has theological similarities with the mid second-century writings of Justin Martyr, suggesting that Luke's writings are post first-century.

- The second-century heretic Marcion (about AD 140) used an earlier edition of Luke's Gospel which was later expanded to produce our Luke.

However, there is no clear evidence of Luke's dependence on Josephus. Indeed, there are significant differences where the two overlap (see The census/registration of Luke 2, and Theudas and Judas, pp43–45). Also, the supposed affinities between Luke and Justin can be better explained by Luke's influence on Justin. As for Marcion, it is more likely that he altered our Luke, as indeed the early Church Fathers maintained – if they were wrong the Marcionites would soon have corrected them. A second-century date is improbable because of Luke's apparent ignorance of Paul's letters. His portrayal of churches such as in Ephesus (Acts 20) seems to reflect a time of writing before the Emperor Domitian's apparent persecution of Christians (AD 96). Furthermore, the fact that the Ephesian church had a collective episcopal leadership (Acts 20:17,28) may imply that Acts was written before the establishment of the government of this church and others in this region by a single bishop, by the time of Ignatius (early second century).

In conclusion, our study of the dating of Luke's Gospel has shown that there is uncertainty over when it was written. However, most scholars are persuaded by the arguments for the middle dating and hold that Luke was probably written in the AD 80s.

> **Task**
>
> *Outline and assess the arguments for the dating of the Gospel of Luke in the late first century and in the second century.*

AUTHORSHIP

To identify the author of the Gospel traditionally attributed to Luke we must examine both *external* and *internal* evidence, the former relating to information outside the text of Luke–Acts and the latter to information within the text.

External evidence

The oldest existing copy of Luke's Gospel (Papyrus Bodmer XIV, known as P75), dated AD 175–225, attributes the Gospel to Luke. From the late second century (eg the Muratorian canon, AD 170–180; the anti-Marcionite prologue to Luke, about AD 175; Irenaeus' *Against Heresies* 3.1.1 and 3.14.1, AD 180s) the unanimous and undisputed belief of the early Church was that the author was Luke, the doctor and companion of Paul (see Col 4:14; 2 Tim 4:11; Philem 24). However, the value of this evidence has been challenged on the grounds that it is based merely on inferences from the New Testament writings rather than on historical knowledge. Yet, it has been doubted whether inference alone could account for the unanimous and exclusive identification of Luke as author by the early Church. And why, if the author was unknown, was the Gospel not attributed to an apostle, rather than a minor figure in the New Testament?

The Gospel of Luke

Task

Outline and evaluate the external evidence for the authorship of Luke's Gospel.

Internal evidence

The Gospel of Luke is anonymous inasmuch as the author does not identify himself in the text, in the way, for instance, that Paul does in his letters. It has been generally assumed that the Gospel remained anonymous until the second century when its authorship was attributed to Luke by early Church Fathers. However, Martin Hengel has argued, on the basis of ancient book distribution practice and the early need to distinguish between the Gospels, that the traditional authorship titles of the Gospels would have existed from the start[1]. Hence the early uncontested view that Luke was the author. And Martin Dibelius has maintained it is improbable that while the person to whom the book was dedicated was identified (Theophilus: Lk 1:3; Acts 1:1), the author was not[2]. Rather, the author's name would have been on a separate tag.

It is generally agreed that the author of Luke also wrote Acts – both books are dedicated to the same person (see above), Acts refers to the "first book" (1:1) and both books have similar vocabulary, style and themes. Does the internal evidence provided by these texts support the early external evidence that Luke, the doctor and companion of Paul, was their author? From Luke–Acts we get the following picture of their author:

A post first generation Christian

He[3] distinguishes himself from the initial eye-witnesses of the ministry of Jesus and indeed from those who had previously drawn up similar accounts (Lk 1:1–2). This is consistent with what we know of Luke in the New Testament.

A Gentile

The author refers to *their* language when speaking of the Aramaic of the residents of Jerusalem (Acts 1:19). The quality of the author's Greek, the general lack of Semitic words and the universalism (see Salvation, p35) in Luke–Acts also imply that he was a Gentile. It appears from Colossians 4:10–14 that Luke was a Gentile, since he is distinguished from those "of the circumcision" (ie the Jews; though some maintain that this refers only to those Jews who regarded circumcision as necessary for salvation).

---

[1] Hengel, Martin, *Studies in the Gospel of Mark* (English translation), London: SCM, 1985, pp64–84

[2] Dibelius, Martin, 'The Speeches in Acts and Ancient Historiography' (English translation, trans M Ling) in *Studies in the Acts of the Apostles*, ed H Greeven, London: SCM, 1956; German original, 1951

[3] The masculine pronoun is used because the social/cultural context of the time indicates that the author was probably male.

A companion of Paul

In several places in Acts the author presents himself as a travelling companion of Paul. In these 'we' passages (Acts 16:10–17; 20:5–15; 21:1–18; 27:1–28:16) he uses the first person plural (we) rather than the usual third person (he, she, they, etc). While some hold that this was a fictional literary device to create the impression of first-hand knowledge[1], its limited use and the occurrence of the first person singular in the prefaces to both Luke and Acts count against this. Nor is it likely that the author has simply introduced someone else's material, first person plural and all, so that the 'we' does not include the author. Apart from the editorial incompetence involved, the style of these passages is the same as the surrounding context. The author, of course, would not be among those named in these passages and Luke is not named here or elsewhere in Acts. Further, it seems probable from the last 'we' passage that the author was present with Paul during his imprisonment in Rome (28:16–31). This is consistent with Paul's reference to Luke as a companion in his prison letters (Philem 24; see also Col 4:14), assuming that these letters were written during Paul's Roman imprisonment.

However, the author's implicit claim to be a companion of Paul has been widely rejected due to apparent historical and theological inconsistencies between the Paul of Acts and Paul as we find him in his own writings – his letters. Historically, for example, Paul's own account of his conversion and travels, in his letter to the Galatians, does not fit easily with what we read in Acts. Paul says that he did not confer with any person at the time of his conversion, yet in Acts Ananias assisted him on that occasion (Gal 1:15–16; Acts 9:10–19). Further, Paul's reference to his post-conversion visit to Arabia cannot be easily reconciled with the account of his travels in Acts (Gal 1:15–17; Acts 9:10–26). It is particularly difficult to square both the number and nature of his visits to Jerusalem – two in Galatians and three in Acts (Gal 1:15–2:10; Acts 9:26ff; 11:27–30; ch 15; also 18:22; 21:17, but these appear to be later than the Galatian visits). Theologically too, significant differences have been perceived between the Paul of Acts and the Paul of the letters[2] in the areas of natural theology (Rom 1:18–21; Acts 17:22–30), the Law (eg 1 Cor 8–10; Gal 5:2–4; Phil 3:5–8; Acts 15:22–35; 16:3; 21:17–26; 23:6), Christology (eg Phil 2:5ff; Acts 13:17–41; 26:22–23; Acts has an almost adoptionist Christology and little concept of atonement or union with Christ) and eschatology (Paul's imminence has gone while Acts is seen as being concerned with ongoing Church life and order). Further, it has been argued that the portrait of Paul is different in Acts compared with Paul's letters[3] (Acts has Paul as a miracle-worker, a persuasive speaker and as unconcerned about equality with the Jerusalem apostles). Finally, the author of Luke–Acts shows no clear knowledge of Paul's letters.

---

[1] eg Haenchen, Ernst, *The Acts of the Apostles* (English translation), Oxford: Basil Blackwell, 1971

[2] eg Vielhauer, P, 'On the "Paulinism" of Acts' in *Studies in Luke–Acts*, eds LE Keck and JL Martyn, London: SPCK, 1966, p37ff

[3] Haenchen, *The Acts of the Apostles* (op cit), p112ff

In light of these points it is held that the author of Luke–Acts was not a genuine companion of Paul. However, not all are persuaded that Luke's Paul is irreconcilable with what we find in Paul's letters[1]. Different contexts, emphases and perspectives, as well as incomplete information, may account for the apparent divergence and still allow that the author of Luke–Acts was a companion of Paul.

A doctor

The New Testament refers to "Luke, the beloved physician" (Col 4:14) and it has been argued that the author of Luke–Acts used medical language comparable to that of Greek medics such as Hippocrates and Galen[2]. However, it has also been shown that the language used does not require a medical author since it is found also in the writings of non-medical authors[3] (eg the Septuagint and Josephus). Yet, there is no doubt that compared with Mark, Luke often gives detail which might be of interest to a medical person. For example, Peter's mother-in-law had a "high fever" (4:38) rather than a "fever" (Mk 1:30) and the leper was "covered" with leprosy (Lk 5:12/ Mk 1:40; cf also Lk 6:6/ Mk 3:1; Lk 8:43/ Mk 5:25–26; and Lk 22:50/ Mk 14:47). While such detail does not demonstrate that the author of Luke–Acts was a doctor, it is at least consistent with it.

In conclusion, although the external evidence unanimously identifies Luke as the author of Luke–Acts, the internal evidence is inconclusive. Fortunately, the interpretation of the Gospel does not depend on the identification of its author. Throughout the present book, the author will be referred to as Luke as a matter of convenience.

Tasks

a Outline the picture we get of the author of Luke–Acts from the internal evidence.

b Discuss how this picture relates to the external evidence for authorship.

---

[1] eg Bruce, FF, 'Is the Paul of Acts the Real Paul?' in *Bulletin of the John Rylands Library* 58, 1976; Carson, DA, Moo, DJ, and Morris, L, *An Introduction to the New Testament*, Leicester: Apollos/IVP, 1992, pp187–190

[2] Hobart, WK, *The Medical Language of St Luke*, Dublin: Hodges, Figgis, 1882; reprinted Grand Rapids, Michigan: Baker, 1954

[3] Cadbury, HJ, *The Style and Literary Method of Luke*, Cambridge, Massachusetts: Harvard University Press, 1920

SOURCES

That Luke relied on various sources is clearly implied in his preface (1:1–4) which, uniquely among the Gospels, gives us an insight into how the work was composed. It is not certain, though, precisely what those sources were. Most New Testament scholars hold that behind Luke there are three main sources – the Gospel of Mark, non-Marcan material which he shares with Matthew (called Q), and material which is found in Luke alone (called L).

Mark

The close similarity in wording and order between the first three Gospels (Matthew, Mark and Luke) has led to them being called the 'synoptic' Gospels, since they can be 'viewed together' in parallel columns in a Gospel 'synopsis'[1]. This close similarity has convinced most scholars that there is literary dependence among them, that is, at least one has made use of one or both of the others. The general view is that Mark was written first[2] (Marcan priority) and that both Matthew and Luke independently relied on Mark. However, a minority of scholars argue that Mark was the last of the synoptics to be written and, therefore, was used by neither Matthew nor Luke[3].

Assuming the majority view of synoptic relationships, it appears that Luke made use of over 50 per cent of Mark (though estimates vary), arranged by Luke in five blocks and accounting for about 35 per cent of his Gospel (see the table below).

	Luke	Mark
1	3:1–4:15	1:1–15
2	4:31–6:19	1:21–3:19
3	8:4–9:50	4:1–9:40
4	18:15–21:33	10:13–13:32
5	22:1–24:12	14:1–16:8

- Luke omits two sections of Mark – a major (6:45–8:26, at Lk 9:17) and a minor (9:41–10:12, at Lk 9:50) omission. Whether these omissions were accidental or deliberate and why they occurred are a matter of debate.

---

[1] eg Throckmorton Jr, BH, *Gospel Parallels*, Nashville: Nelson, 1992 (NRSV text); Aland, K, *Synopsis Quattuor Evangeliorum*, Stuttgart: Deutsche Bibelgesellschaft, 1963, 15th edition, 1996 (Greek text)

[2] Stein, RH, *Studying the Synoptic Gospels*, Grand Rapids, Michigan: Baker, 2001, p49ff

[3] eg Farmer, WR, *The Synoptic Problem: A Critical Analysis*, New York: Macmillan, 1964

- Some of Mark's passages have been expanded by Q and L (Lk 3:7–14,23–38; 4:2–13; 5:1–11; 19:1–28; 22:28–33,35–38; 23:6–16,27–31,39–43,47–49).

- Luke appears to rearrange Mark's order on several occasions for literary and theological reasons (compare the following with the Marcan order: Lk 3:19–20; 4:16–30; 5:1–11; 6:12–19; 8:19–21; 13:18–19; 22:21–23,54–71).

- There are changes to Mark's language (eg omission of Mark's very frequent use of the Greek word *euthus* meaning 'immediately', and of his Aramaic words such as *Boanerges* and *Golgotha*), style (eg changes to the introductions and conclusions of narrative units) and a reduction in chronological and geographical detail.

- The characterisation of Jesus and the disciples in Luke is somewhat different than in Mark. The disciples appear in a more favourable light (eg cf Mk 4:13,38/ Lk 8:11,24) and Jesus is less emotional (eg cf Mk 1:41,43/ Lk 5:13–14 and Mk 10:14,21/ Lk 18:16,22).

- Luke's own special interests have also influenced his use of Mark, for example his emphasis on Jesus praying (see Prayerful, pp29–30, and Prayer, p38–39).

Tasks

a What three main sources did Luke apparently make use of?
b Outline Luke's use of Mark.

Q

Material shared by Matthew and Luke but not found in Mark is termed Q, probably from the German word *quelle* meaning 'source'. While there is no external evidence that such a source actually existed, the close similarity between the common material has convinced most scholars that it must have. Some scholars hold that this shared material can be explained by Luke's dependence on Matthew, thus dispensing with the need for the Q hypothesis[1]. However, most see this as unlikely since, among other things, it would require that while Luke normally followed Mark's order closely, he did not do so with Matthew and also that he consistently ignored Matthew's additions to Mark. Still, there are many unknowns regarding Q, such as whether it was written or oral or both, whether it overlapped with Mark and material unique to Matthew ('M') and Luke ('L'), whether Matthew or Luke preserves its original order and/or wording, whether it existed in different editions, and to what extent Matthew and Luke have edited it, to mention just a few. Despite these uncertainties, some scholars[2]

---

[1] eg Farmer, *The Synoptic Problem,* (op cit); Goulder, MD, *Luke: A New Paradigm,* Sheffield: JSOT Press, 1989

[2] eg Kloppenborg, JS, *The Formation of Q: Trajectories in Ancient Wisdom Collections,* Philadelphia: Fortress, 1987

claim to have identified separate stages in the evolution of Q (Q1, Q2, Q3) and the corresponding history of the communities that produced it!

Most scholars are agreed, however, that the Q material is among the oldest in our Gospels. In Luke it amounts to over 240 verses, about 21 per cent of the Gospel (see the table below on the contents of Q).

	Luke	Matthew
Preaching of John the Baptist	3:7–9	3:7–10
Temptation of Jesus	4:2–12	4:2–10
Sermon on the Mount/Plain	6:20–23,27–49	5:2–12,39–48; 7:1–5,12,15–20,24–27; 10:24–25; 15:14
Healing of centurion's servant	7:1–10	8:5–13
John the Baptist and Jesus	7:18–35	11:2–19
Would-be disciples	9:57–60	8:19–22
Mission speech to disciples	10:2–16	9:37–38; 10:7–16,40; 11:21–23
Jesus' thanksgiving to the Father	10:21–24	11:25–27; 13:16–17
Lord's Prayer	11:2–4	6:9–13
Ask, search, knock	11:9–13	7:7–11
Jesus and Beelzebul	11:14–23	12:22–30
Return of unclean spirit	11:24–26	12:43–45
Sign of Jonah	11:29–32	12:38–42
Light of the body	11:33–36	5:15; 6:22–23
Against the Pharisees	11:37–52	23:4–7,13–36
Fearing people and God	12:2–12	10:19–20,26–33; 12:32
On worry	12:22–34	6:19–21,25–33
Readiness for the master's return	12:39–46	24:43–51
Family divisions	12:51–53	10:34–36
Signs of the times	12:54–56	16:2–3
Settling out of court	12:57–59	5:25–26
Parables of mustard seed and yeast	13:18–21	13:31–33
Narrow door	13:24–30	7:13–14,22–23; 8:11–12; 25:10–12
Lament over Jerusalem	13:34–35	23:37–39
Parable of the banquet	14:15–24	22:1–10

Cost of discipleship	14:26–27	10:37–38
Parable of lost sheep	15:3–7	18:12–14
Two masters	16:13	6:24
Law and Prophets	16:16–17	5:18; 11:13
Sin and forgiveness	17:1–4	18:6–7,15,21–22
Day of the Son of Man	17:23–27, 33–37	24:26–28,37–41
Parable of the pounds	19:11–27	25:14–30

It is uncertain at times what passages in Luke should be regarded as real parallels with Matthew. For instance, some similar material is found in different contexts and/or is worded quite differently. Thus, there are various estimates among scholars concerning the number of verses that belong to Q. Most Q material in Luke is located in two interpolations to his Marcan material – a major (9:51–18:14) and a minor (6:20–8:30) interpolation. It will be observed that Q mainly contains sayings of Jesus with little narrative/story material (eg temptation of Jesus, healing of centurion's servant) and no passion or resurrection narratives. Also, there appear to be doublets of the same material, with one version coming from Mark and one from Q, for example 8:16 (from Mk 4:21) and 11:33 (from Q: Mt 5:15).

Tasks

a Explain what Q is and problems with the alternative hypothesis.
b Outline the uncertainties concerning Q.
c Discuss the character of Q and its apparent use in Luke.

L

Material unique to Luke's Gospel – that which is not from Mark or shared with Matthew – is designated 'L'. This is a convenient label for Luke's special source. As with Q, there is no external evidence of L's existence. Scholars therefore speculate as to whether L represents a single source or multiple sources, whether it was written or oral or both, whether it overlaps with Q, whether some of it was directly composed by Luke, and so on. Certainly much of Luke's Gospel is unique – L amounts to over 40 per cent of the entire work (see the table below on the contents of L).

Infancy narratives	chs 1–2
Preaching of John the Baptist	3:10–14
Genealogy of Jesus	3:23–38

Jesus at Nazareth	4:17–21,23,25–30
Miraculous catch of fish	5:1–11
Raising of widow's son at Nain	7:11–17
Jesus anointed by a woman	7:36–50
Women helpers	8:1–3
Rejection by Samaritans	9:51–56
A would-be disciple	9:61–62
Return of the Seventy	10:17–20
Parable of the good Samaritan	10:29–37
Martha and Mary	10:38–42
Context of Lord's Prayer	11:1
Parable of friend at midnight	11:5–8
True blessedness	1:27–28
Parable of the rich fool	12:13–21
Readiness for the master's return	12:35–38
Slave's reward	12:47–48
Jesus bringing fire	12:49
Teaching on repentance, including parable of barren tree	13:1–9
Healing of crippled woman	13:10–17
Herod's murderous intent	13:31–33
Healing of man with dropsy	14:1–6
Guests and hosts	14:7–14
Cost of discipleship	14:28–33
Parable of lost coin	15:8–10
Parable of lost son	15:11–32
Parable of shrewd manager	16:1–9
Rebuke of Pharisees	16:14–15
Rich man and Lazarus	16:19–31
Worthless slaves	17:7–10
Healing of ten lepers	17:11–19
Coming of God's kingdom	17:20–21
Day of the Son of Man	17:28–32
Parable of widow and judge	18:1–8
Parable of Pharisee and tax collector	18:9–14
Zacchaeus	19:1–10

Reply to Pharisees	19:39–40
Lament over Jerusalem	19:41–44
Destruction of Jerusalem and coming of the Son of Man	21:18,21b,22,23b,24,25b, 26a,28,34–36
One who serves	22:27
Jesus has prayed for Peter	22:31–32
Two swords	22:35–38
Jesus before Herod	23:6–12
Pilate's declaration of Jesus' innocence	23:13–16
On the way to the cross	23:27–31
Prayer for forgiveness	23:34
Two criminals crucified	23:39–43
Jesus' death	23:46,47b–49
Women's preparation of spices	23:56
Jesus' appearance on Emmaus Road	24:13–35
Jesus' appearance to disciples in Jerusalem	24:36–49
The ascension	24:50–53

We can see that Luke's unique material contains some of Jesus' best known parables (eg good Samaritan, lost son, rich fool, Pharisee and tax collector) and several miracle stories, which may represent different sources. The four 'hymns' of the infancy narrative (1:46–55,68–79; 2:14,29–32) may constitute still another source. And in L we see some of Luke's characteristic themes and concerns, for example Samaritans, women (particularly widows), tax collectors, wealth and poverty, prayer, and Jerusalem (see L material in Characteristics, p26ff). Indeed, Luke's ethical and pastoral concerns are clear throughout L. It has been observed too that, unlike Matthew and Mark, Luke's special material has much in common with John's Gospel – for example Martha and Mary, questions about the messianic status of John the Baptist, and common material in their passion and resurrection narratives such as Pilate's triple declaration of Jesus' innocence and post-resurrection appearances in Jerusalem. The majority view is that both Gospels independently drew on common material rather than one being dependent on the other. Certainly, the verbal and sequential differences between the passion narratives in Luke and Mark suggest that Luke had access to other source material. Further, there has been speculation that some of L may have come from the "eyewitnesses" referred to in the preface (1:2). Thus, for example, Mary (2:19,51) may have supplied information for the infancy narrative and the visit to Nazareth, Joanna and Manaen (8:3; Acts 13:1) on Herod Antipas, and Cleopas (24:18) on the Emmaus Road events. However, while this is possible, it remains hypothetical.

Proto-Luke

For the Proto-Luke theory – that Luke originally consisted of Q and L into which Marcan material was later inserted – see pages 241–244.

> **Tasks**
>
> a Explain what L is and the uncertainties concerning this source.
> b Comment briefly on its content and extent.
> c Outline possible origins of some of the L material.
> d What is the Proto-Luke theory?

PURPOSES

To discover why Luke's Gospel was written we must begin with the author's own statement of his purpose for writing, in the preface to his work (1:1–4). Luke addresses his book to a certain "most excellent Theophilus" with the express purpose, he is told, that "you may know the truth concerning the things about which you have been instructed" (v 3–4). If the name Theophilus (one 'loved by God' or 'loving God') is not merely a symbolic designation for Christian readers generally, Luke was writing primarily for an individual, possibly of some social standing ("most excellent"; Acts 23:26; 24:2; 26:25), who at the least had heard something about Christianity and may well have been a Christian convert ("instructed/informed", author's translation). Luke's stated aim in providing an account of what "Jesus did and taught" (Acts 1:1) was that he might be assured of the "truth" (Greek *asphaleia:* 'certainty, reliability') of what he had heard about Jesus and, indeed, Christian beginnings (if the Gospel preface also relates to Acts). It has been suggested that Theophilus may have been a former 'God-fearer'[1] – a Gentile partly converted to Judaism, frequently mentioned in Acts – who was having second thoughts about his connection with the Church, hence Luke's concern to show that Christianity is for Jew and Gentile (see p35). Alternatively, Theophilus may still have been a God-fearer who was torn between Christianity and Judaism[2]. Thus, Luke presents Christianity as the fulfilment of Judaism in God's plan (see Theology, pp26–27). Whether Theophilus was an interested inquirer or a (recent?) convert to Christianity, Luke writes to confirm and reinforce the Christian message. While Luke dedicates his work to Theophilus, possibly because he was its patron, its content clearly assumes a wider readership and its author would have viewed it as relevant to all who required a reliable account of the beginnings of Christianity. Attempts to identify Luke's audience or community more specifically have not resulted in any consensus.

---

[1] eg Bock, DL, *Luke 1:1–9:50*, Grand Rapids, Michigan: Baker Books, 1994, p15
[2] eg Nolland, J, *Luke 1–9:20*, Nashville: Nelson, 1989, pxxxii

Task

Discuss what the preface of Luke can tell us about why this Gospel was written.

Beyond Luke's general statement of his purpose for writing, various suggestions have been made concerning possible motives for the composition of the Gospel, which may be broadly categorised as follows.

Historical

Luke's preface (1:1–4) seems to indicate that Luke was writing consciously as a historian, providing an historical "account/narrative" (1:1, author's translation; Greek *diegesis*) of the origins of Christianity in the life of Jesus (Gospel) and the early Church (Acts). He acknowledges previous attempts by others and presents his own as based on careful research and eyewitness testimony, to demonstrate the reliability of the historical basis that exists for Christian faith. Indeed, similarities have been noted between Luke's prefaces, in his Gospel and Acts, and those in the writings of ancient historians such as Herodotus, Thucydides and Josephus (see Luke as a historian, p40ff). Also, more than the other evangelists, Luke is careful to note the historical context – secular and religious – of his account (see 1:5; 2:1–2; 3:1–2; Acts 11:28; 18:2).

Theological

However, Luke's history is not mere history, in the sense of simply reporting or chronicling events. Rather, he clearly has a *theo*logical (*theos:* God) and religious view of history. He is writing not just about events, but about "the events that have been *fulfilled* among us" (1:1). Luke presents his account of Jesus and the early Church as part of the flow of biblical history – salvation history, related to and indeed the fulfilment of Israel's history and Scriptures, in accordance with the plan of Israel's God (eg chs 1–2, especially 1:32,54–55,68–75; 2:29–32,34,38; also 4:16–21; 24:25–27,44–47; see Theology, pp26–27). Thus, one of his purposes in writing his Gospel is to show the theological continuity between the events he records and Israel's history and hopes, and the ongoing purpose of God underlying both.

A specific theological motivation for Luke's Gospel, according to Hans Conzelmann, was to deal with a crisis in the late first-century Church[1]. The expected imminent return of Jesus had not occurred and so Luke revised his sources to remove this expectation and replaced it with an ongoing salvation history which would conclude

---

[1] Conzelmann, Hans, *The Theology of St. Luke*, Faber & Faber: London, 1960; reprinted London: SCM, 1982; German original, 1953

in the distant future (eg cf Mk 14:62 and Lk 22:69; see Eschatology, pp39–40). Luke sought to provide an explanation for or solution to the problem of the 'delay of the *parousia*', as it is often called (*parousia* is Greek for 'coming, presence'). However, it appears that the expectation of an imminent End is not entirely absent from Luke (eg 12:39–40,42–46). Luke may therefore have written to correct two extremes – an over-emphasis on either the delay or the imminence of Jesus' return[1]. Alternatively, while Luke was conscious of the delay, he still saw the return of Jesus as an imminent possibility in his own day[2].

Sociological

PF Esler sees Luke's purpose in sociological terms, as an attempt to justify or legitimate the Church of his day in the face of Jewish opposition (reflected for example in 4:28–30)[3]. Luke explains both its origins in and departure from Judaism, resulting in its now largely Gentile membership. Luke's sociological legitimation of the Church was an attempt to reassure its members in the face of claims and criticisms of its parent religion[4]. Indeed, there appears to be a growing consensus among scholars[5] that Luke's theological picture of the beginnings of Christianity was in the main governed by this sociological motive – to explain and legitimate the connection between a Jewish Messiah and the now Gentile Church – hence Luke's emphasis on Jewish rejection of the Messiah and the consequent Gentile mission (eg 4:16–30; 7:9; 8:19–21; 11:27–28; 13:22–30; 14:15–24; 24:47).

Political

Luke–Acts may have been composed as a political apology, defending the new Christian movement before the Roman authorities. Thus, the emphasis on the Jewish origins of Jesus – for example his birth and circumcision – and the portrayal of Christianity in Acts as a 'sect' of Judaism (cf 5:17; 15:5; 24:5,14; 26:5; 28:22) could be read as an argument for Christianity being given the same legal tolerance that Rome accorded to Judaism. While it was a new sect, it stemmed from an ancient religion. Further, Luke's emphasis on the innocence of Jesus during the account of his trials and execution, especially in the eyes of the Roman governor Pilate and his centurion (23:4,14–15,22,47), would have underlined that Christianity's founder was not a political threat to Rome, despite Rome's execution of him. Again, the attitude of the Roman authorities to the early Christians in general, and to Paul in particular in Acts

---

[1] Wilson, SG, *The Gentiles and the Gentile Mission in Luke–Acts*, Cambridge: CUP, 1973, ch 3
[2] Tuckett, CM, *Luke: New Testament Guides*, Sheffield: Sheffield Academic Press, 1996, pp42–43
[3] Esler, PF, *Community and Gospel in Luke–Acts*, Cambridge: CUP, 1987
[4] Maddox, R, *The Purpose of Luke–Acts*, Edinburgh: T&T Clark, 1982
[5] According to Bock, DL, 'Luke' in *The Face of New Testament Studies: A Survey of Recent Research*, eds S McKnight and GR Osborne, Apollos/IVP: Leicester / Baker: Grand Rapids, Michigan, 2004, p35

(eg 13:7,12; 16:35–39; 18:12–17; chs 24–25), implies that the Church was politically harmless. If Theophilus himself was a Roman official (he is addressed in the same way as Roman governors: Lk 1:3; Acts 23:26; 24:2; 26:25), a political motive in writing would be very likely.

However, while this may have been a secondary aim it is possible to overstate its importance. Luke clearly holds Pilate responsible for Jesus' execution (Acts 4:25–28) and portrays Roman leaders as weak on occasion (not least Pilate; also Acts 16:35–39; 24:25–27)[1]. It has even been argued that the political apology was in the other direction, Luke defending Rome before the Church[2]. Far from being a political defence of Christianity, Luke's presentation of Jesus has also been viewed as a political threat[3]!

Polemical

Luke–Acts has been understood as an attack (Greek *polemos*: 'battle') on Gnosticism[4]. This heresy flourished in the second century, was believed by early Christian Fathers to have originated with Simon Magus (Acts 8) and, among other things, denied the real humanity of Jesus. Some of Luke–Acts, for example Luke's emphasis on the physical reality of Jesus' resurrection (Lk 24:39,43) and his portrayal of Simon Magus, is seen as a corrective to Gnostic views. However, not only is there uncertainty about the origins and nature of Gnosticism[5], there is nothing in Luke's writings that specifically demands an anti-Gnostic aim. However, it is generally acknowledged that Paul's warning about future teachers who would prove divisive for the Church (Acts 20:29–31) tells us something about the situation of Luke's day, which his writings sought to address.

Evangelistic

It has been maintained that Luke–Acts was composed to present the 'gospel' (Greek *euangelion:* 'good news'), the message that God's kingdom and salvation have come for all people in Jesus Christ. It has been argued, for example, that Luke, in both his volumes, was seeking to evangelise and convert educated Romans[6]. IH Marshall believes Luke's purpose was primarily evangelistic and that he wrote to assist the Church in its ongoing work of evangelism[7].

---

[1] Brown, RE, *An Introduction to the New Testament,* Garden City, New York: Doubleday, 1997, p271
[2] Walaskay, PW, *"And So We Came to Rome": The Political Perspective of St Luke,* Cambridge: CUP, 1983
[3] Cassidy, RJ, *Jesus, Politics and Society: A Study of Luke's Gospel,* Maryknoll, New York: Orbis, 1978
[4] Talbert, CH, *Luke and the Gnostics: An Examination of the Lucan Purpose,* Nashville: Abingdon, 1966
[5] Banks, R, *The Early Church: The Christian Church to AD 325,* Newtownards: Colourpoint, 2003, p155ff
[6] O'Neill, JC, *The Theology of Acts in its Historical Setting,* London: SPCK, 1970
[7] Marshall, IH, *Luke: Historian and Theologian,* Exeter: Paternoster, 1970 (last chapter especially)

Theodicy

Luke's work has been viewed also as a theodicy – an attempt to explain and defend God's justice and faithfulness (Greek *theos*: 'God'; *dike*: 'justice'). Luke maintains that God has fulfilled his promises to Israel (eg Lk 4:17ff; 24:21,25–27,44), even though most Jews rejected Jesus as Messiah[1]. Luke may have been addressing the concerns of Jewish Christians in the aftermath of the Jewish revolt against the Romans and the consequent destruction of Jerusalem and its temple in AD 70, explaining that their suffering was a participation in Israel's sufferings due to her rejection of the Messiah[2]. Nevertheless, God's faithfulness to Israel would be demonstrated in her eventual restoration.

Pastoral

Luke's role as a pastor is apparent in the text, as he seeks to guide and support the faith and lifestyle of Christian readers. Indeed, it has been suggested that other perceived purposes of Luke serve this primary pastoral concern[3]. Thus, any of the proposed purposes noted above which have a pastoral aspect are relevant here – for example historical, theological and sociological aims. Specifically, if Theophilus was already a Christian then the opening words of the Gospel and Acts reveal Luke's pastoral aim to reassure his Christian readers of the sound historical and theological basis that exists for what they have heard (see Historical and Theological, pp22–23). Luke's concern may have been to support his fellow Christians as they faced opposition, Jewish and Gentile, for their belief that God's salvation was for all[4]. Also, emphases such as spirituality, wealth, the place of women and, indeed, discipleship in general (see Salvation, p34ff, and Discipleship, p276ff), reflect Luke's pastoral and ethical concern.

In conclusion, while a variety of suggestions have been made as to the purposes behind the composition of Luke (and Acts), many of these are based on inferences from the text and may or may not have been conscious aims on the part of the author. However, the author's own explicit statement of his purpose for writing (1:1–4; see start of Purposes, p21, and Discipleship, p276ff) indicates that his general aim was to confirm the Christian message by providing a reliable account of its beginnings. Other more specific suggestions as to purpose appear to be subsidiary to this main aim and indeed increase in probability insofar as they are relevant to it.

---

[1] DeSilva, DA, *An Introduction to the New Testament*, Leicester: Apollos/IVP, p310
[2] Tiede, DL, *Prophecy and History in Luke–Acts*, Philadelphia: Fortress, 1980
[3] Martin, RP, *New Testament Foundations, Vol 1*, Exeter: Paternoster, 1975, pp249–250
[4] Green, JB, *The Gospel of Luke*, Cambridge/Grand Rapids, Michigan: Eerdmans, 1997, pp21–22

> **Tasks**
>
> a Outline and discuss the main suggestions concerning the purposes for the composition of Luke.
>
> b Comment on how Luke's own statement of his purpose may act as a control on other suggestions.

CHARACTERISTICS

The distinguishing characteristics of Luke's Gospel are apparent in its prominent themes, special emphases and distinctive theology. These features are noticeable especially in Luke's unique material (L) and also in the modifications that he has apparently made to his sources, particularly Mark. Identifying possible changes to the hypothetical source Q is speculative, not least because it is not clear whether Luke or Matthew has more accurately preserved its original form/s. However, Luke's concerns are to be found also in the traditional material that he has passed on without significant alteration. The book of Acts provides secondary confirmation of the Gospel's special interests where these are prominent there also.

Theology

Theology is the study of *God* (Greek *theos*) and the theological, indeed theocentric (God-centred), character of Luke's Gospel is clearly apparent[1]. "God" (122 times in Luke) rarely appears directly (3:22; 9:35), yet clearly guides and governs events in the narrative. For Luke, God is the "Master/Sovereign Lord" of all things (author's translation; Greek *despotes,* used only by Luke among the four evangelists: 2:29; also Acts 4:24).

Luke has a particular stress on "God's purpose" (7:30; also in Acts, eg 2:23; 4:28), the plan of God being central to him, more so than in the other synoptics[2]. Jesus knows that God's "will" must be done (22:42). Indeed, his betrayal to his enemies had been "determined" by God (22:22). The priority of the divine agenda for Luke is seen in his frequent use of a word meaning 'it is necessary/must' (author's translation; Greek *dei* – about 40% of the NT occurrences of this word are found in Luke–Acts, eg Lk 2:49; 4:43; 9:22; 17:25; 22:37; 24:7,26,44). The sense that God's purpose is being realised is evident too in the recurring theme of fulfilment or accomplishment (eg 4:21; 9:31; 18:31; 21:24; 22:37; 24:44). In fact, at the very outset of the Gospel the reader is made aware that the book's contents are related to some previous expectations which

---

[1] Brawley, RL, *Centering on God: Method and Message in Luke–Acts,* Louisville: Westminster/John Knox, 1990

[2] Squires, JT, *The Plan of God in Luke–Acts,* Cambridge: CUP, 1993

they have "fulfilled" (1:1, although a different meaning is possible). Specifically, this idea is related to the Scriptures of Israel – God's ancient purpose, revealed to the Old Testament prophets, was actualised in the ministry of Jesus. Thus, Luke quotes or refers to the Old Testament at the beginning of the ministries of both John the Baptist (3:4–6) and Jesus (4:16–21), and also at the end of Jesus' ministry (22:37; 24:25–27, 44–47). The story of Jesus is shown, then, to be rooted in the story of Israel and both are presented as the outworking of the one purpose of God. This link is made repeatedly in the opening two chapters – the infancy narrative – so that the reader is led to view the following narrative from the perspective of God's purpose (eg 1:16–17,32–33,54–55,67–79; 2:4,11,25–38).

That the story of Jesus is the realisation of the divine purpose is highlighted also by the appearance of angels (particularly in the opening and closing chapters) and the emphasis on the activity of the Holy Spirit (particularly in the infancy narrative and at the beginning of Jesus' ministry). And while the divine plan meets resistance, not least in Satan and the religious leaders (eg 4:2–13; 7:30; 8:12; 22:3,31), there are many who serve God's purpose (eg Mary, Elizabeth, John the Baptist, the disciples). Paradoxically, from Luke's perspective even opponents of God's purpose mysteriously serve it (22:22; Acts 2:23; 4:27–28).

History

Luke, most notably among the evangelists, is concerned with presenting the story of Jesus in the context of contemporary world history. In his preface he implicitly refers to his work as an account or narrative, using a word (*diegesis*) often employed by contemporary historians. In the opening chapters of his narrative he relates his account of Jesus to its historical context three times (1:5; 2:1–2; 3:1–2). JA Fitzmyer has noted how Luke connects his narrative to Roman, Palestinian and Church history[1]. Links are made with Roman history in references to the Emperors Augustus (2:1) and Tiberius (3:1; Claudius is mentioned in Acts 11:28; 18:2). Indeed, Luke is the only New Testament writer to name Roman emperors. Luke also refers, for example, to Quirinius (2:2), Pilate (3:1, etc), Felix (Acts 23:24), Festus (eg Acts 24:27) and to Herodian rulers (eg 1:5; 3:1; 23:6ff). And Luke alone of the evangelists provides a sequel, on the history of the early Church (Acts).

We see Luke's historical interest also in the scope of his work. While he is certainly selective, he has still provided a comprehensive account of Christian beginnings. The Gospel of Luke is the longest book in the New Testament and its sequel Acts is the next longest. Both works account for about 28 per cent of the New Testament, while the 13 letters attributed to Paul make up about 24 per cent[2].

---

[1] Fitzmyer, JA, *The Gospel According to Luke I–IX*, New York: Doubleday, 1981, pp174–179
[2] Green, JB, *New Testament Theology: The Theology of the Gospel of Luke*, Cambridge: CUP, 1995, p2

The Gospel of Luke

Among the Gospels Luke provides us with the fullest infancy and journey narratives, a unique childhood story of Jesus and, also uniquely, an account of Jesus' ascension (the latter is however absent from some early manuscripts). Luke the historian, then, was clearly concerned with producing a comprehensive account of Christian beginnings rooted in both religious and secular history (see Luke as a historian, p40ff, and Salvation history, p229ff).

Geography

As well as having a sense of time, Luke also possesses a sense of place – arguably more so than the other Gospels. Special emphasis is given in particular to *Jerusalem*. In fact, Luke alone among the evangelists begins and ends his Gospel in Jerusalem (1:8–9; 24:53). Twice in the infancy narrative Jesus is brought to Jerusalem (2:22,41–42). At the beginning of his ministry the climactic temptation of the three, unlike in Matthew, is also in Jerusalem (4:9; Mt 4:1–11). The one journey that Jesus makes to Jerusalem in Mark is more detailed and focused in Luke (9:51–19:44). It begins with a reference to Jerusalem as its destination (9:51–53) and along the route the reader is reminded more than once of this (13:22; 17:11; 18:31; 19:11,28,41). Before the journey began Moses and Elijah had talked with Jesus about his "departure" (Greek *exodos*) which he would "fulfil/accomplish" in Jerusalem (9:31, author's translation), and Luke's passion narrative (chs 22–23) provides the details. In addition, unlike the other synoptics the resurrection narrative (ch 24) focuses on Jerusalem as the location of the resurrection appearances. Indeed, Jerusalem is an important narrative link binding this last chapter of Luke with the first chapter of Acts (it is mentioned five times in each chapter). Thus, Jerusalem is the place where both Jesus' journey and ministry ends (13:33ff) and the Church's journey and mission begins (24:47; Acts 1:8). The Gospel of Luke's movement in Jesus' ministry from Galilee to Samaria to Jerusalem (4:14; 9:51–52; 19:28) is reversed in Acts from Jerusalem to Samaria to Galilee (eg 1:8; 8:5; 9:31) and beyond, to the end of the earth. All this emphasis on Jerusalem may reflect Old Testament influence, where it is from Jerusalem that God's word and salvation would go out to the end of the earth (eg Isaiah 2:3; 49:6). Luke's journey motif is apparent also in his fondness for a word meaning 'go, depart' (author's translation; Greek *poreuomai*), found about 50 times in his Gospel (especially in the journey narrative, eg 9:51–53) and about 40 times in Acts (compared with about 30 times in Matthew and once in Mark). We should note too the regular occurrence of "the way" (author's translation; Greek *hodos*, eg 3:4; 9:3,57; 10:4; 18:35; 24:32,35).

Task

Outline what is characteristic about Luke in the following areas:
a) theology   b) history   c) geography

Christology

While Luke's portrait of Jesus has much in common with the other Gospels, particularly the other synoptics, there are a number of characteristic features of his Christology to note. We shall consider specifically the character, titles and death of Jesus in Luke's perspective.

The character of Jesus

Luke particularly characterises Jesus as:

Compassionate

After quoting Dante's description of Luke as "the scribe of the gentleness of Christ", Fitzmyer refers, among other things, to the mercy, love and delicacy of Luke's Jesus, seen not least in parables of mercy unique to Luke, such as the good Samaritan (10:29–37), the lost son (15:11–32) and the Pharisee and the tax collector (18:9–14)[1]. Notable too is the focus on people as individuals in these and other parables found in Luke alone. Indeed, this concern for individuals may tell us something about Luke himself since it is a feature of his narrative generally (eg Zechariah, Elizabeth, Mary, Mary and Martha, Zacchaeus, and Cleopas and his companion).

Dispassionate

Despite our previous point, it is noticeable how Luke reveals less of the emotions of Jesus than Mark does. In material he shares with Mark, Luke (and often Matthew too) lacks Mark's references to Jesus' compassion (5:13/ Mk 1:41; but Lk 7:13), sternness (5:14/ Mk 1:43), anger (6:10/ Mk 3:5), indignation (18:16/ Mk 10:14), love (18:22/ Mk 10:21) and distress (22:40/ Mk 14:33–34). Further, while all four Gospels record Jesus' demonstration in the temple, only Luke omits Jesus' dramatic overturning of the traders' tables (19:45ff). Again, unlike the other synoptics, Luke does not record Jesus' cursing of the fig tree.

Sociable

Luke likes to show Jesus dining socially in various contexts. He alone has three instances of Jesus dining with Pharisees in their homes (7:36ff; 11:37ff; 14:1ff). Other similar examples unique to Luke include hospitality at the homes of Martha and Mary (10:38ff) and Zacchaeus (19:5ff) and with the two in Emmaus (24:30).

Prayerful

Prayer is a prominent theme in Luke generally (see Prayer, pp38–39) and specifically so in the life of Jesus. On several occasions common to the synoptics only Luke has Jesus praying – at Jesus' baptism (3:21), after the healing of a leper (5:15–16), before the choosing of the Twelve (6:12–13), before Peter's confession of Jesus as Messiah (9:18), and on the mountain of transfiguration (9:28–29). We

---

[1] Fitzmyer, *The Gospel According to Luke I–IX* (op cit), pp257–258

also see Jesus at prayer before he teaches the Lord's Prayer (11:1), on behalf of Simon Peter's faith (22:31–32), intensely on the Mount of Olives on the eve of his crucifixion (22:44, if original), and on the cross (23:34, if original).

Innocent

Luke, more than the other evangelists, stresses the innocence of Jesus in his passion narrative. At the Jewish trial, absent from Luke are the false witnesses and charge of blasphemy present in the other synoptics. The three accusations made by the Jewish leaders against Jesus (23:2) are more than matched by Pilate's four declarations of Jesus' innocence (23:4,14–15,22). Also, unlike the other Gospels, Jesus' innocence is confirmed by Herod (23:15), one of the criminals crucified with Jesus (23:41) and the centurion at the cross (23:47). Executed by the Romans as he was, the innocence of Jesus would have been an important apologetic emphasis for Luke's Roman readership, not least for Theophilus who himself may have been a Roman official (1:1–4; see Political, pp23–24).

Outline, with textual examples, Luke's particular characterisation of Jesus.

The titles of Jesus

Luke shares with the other evangelists a number of titles of Jesus and his distinctive use of them should be noted[1]. The variety of designations for Jesus in Luke reveals his diverse, multifaceted Christology which may not be reduced to a single category.

Lord

This is clearly Luke's favourite title for Jesus. It is notable that while the other synoptics never refer to Jesus as 'the Lord' (Greek *ho kurios*) as they narrate the story of Jesus, Luke frequently does. This happens at least 14 times and never in his Marcan material (7:13,19; 10:1,39,41; 11:39; 12:42; 13:15; 17:5–6; 18:6; 19:8; 22:61). However, since this title was more commonly used of Jesus after his resurrection (eg 24:34; Acts 2:36), Luke normally does not have the disciples use it formally of Jesus in his Gospel (but see 1:43 and 2:11 in the infancy narrative). While Jesus is often addressed as "Lord" (eg 5:8,12), it may be that on at least some of these occasions *kurios* is being used as a courtesy title (eg translated "Sir" in Acts 16:30; Jn 4:11ff), rather than with any religious meaning. The title is also frequently used in Luke to refer to God

---

[1] Titles in Luke's Gospel not considered here include Son of Man and Son of David, since Luke's use of them is not distinctive.

(1:6,9,11,15, etc) and there is evidence that Jews used the term *kurios* for God in pre-Christian Palestine[1]. Thus, Luke presents Jesus as having authority along with God, seated at his right hand (20:41–44; Acts 2:33–36). Yet, he is distinct from God who alone is called "Father" and "Master/Sovereign Lord" (author's translation; Greek *despotes*; see Theology, pp26–27) in Luke.

Master

Seven times in Luke Jesus is addressed with a term (*epistates*: master) found nowhere else in the New Testament (5:5; 8:24,45; 9:33,49; 17:13). On all but one of these occasions the word is used by his disciples (the exception being the ten lepers in 17:12–13). In parallel passages the other synoptics have different titles, for example during the storm on the lake Luke has "Master, Master" (8:24), Mark has "Teacher" (4:38) and Matthew has "Lord" (8:25).

Saviour

Among the synoptics only Luke has this title. It is applied once to God (1:47) and once to Jesus (2:11), both found in the infancy narrative. It is never applied to Jesus during his ministry, but was particularly appropriate after his exaltation to God's right hand (Acts 5:31; 13:23). Along with the related terms 'salvation' and 'save', we have here a central theme of Luke (for details, see Salvation, p34ff).

Prophet

In several passages unique to Luke, we find Jesus presented as a prophet, a messenger of God. Jesus compares himself to the Old Testament prophets Elijah and Elisha (4:25–27), and his raising of the widow of Nain's son (7:11–17) recalls similar incidents in the ministries of both these prophets (1 Kings 17:17–24; 2 Kings 4:18–37). The passage in Luke, in fact, concludes with Jesus being acclaimed as a "great prophet" (7:16). In contrast, later in the same chapter Jesus' prophetic status is questioned by a Pharisee (7:39). Further, Jesus refers to himself as "a prophet" (13:33) and is described by the two on the road to Emmaus as "a prophet mighty in deed and word" (24:19). In addition to these unique passages, Luke also portrays Jesus as a prophet in material he shares with other evangelists (eg 4:24; 9:8–19; 22:64).

Messiah/Christ

Messiah (Hebrew) and Christ (Greek) both mean 'anointed one'. This term was used especially, though not exclusively, of Jewish kings (eg 1 Sam 16:1–3; 24:6–7; see also Lk 23:2). Luke's distinctive use of this title is found in the idea that the Messiah suffers (24:26, 46) and in the expressions "the Lord's Messiah" (2:26) and "God's Messiah" (author's translation; 9:20; 23:35). Luke also closely connects the anointing of Jesus with the descent of the Spirit at his baptism (3:21–22; 4:18,21; Acts 10:37–38).

---

[1] Fitzmyer, *The Gospel According to Luke I–IX* (op cit), p202

Son of God

While this title is found in the other Gospels, there are unique occurrences of it in Luke. It is related to Jesus' virgin conception (1:31–35) and forms the climax of Jesus' genealogy (3:23–38; Matthew's genealogy of Jesus goes back to Abraham – 1:1–17). Further, only in Luke do we find Jesus as a 12-year-old with an awareness that God is his Father (2:48–49). Likewise, Luke alone has Jesus address God as "Father" while on the cross (twice – 23:34,46).

Teacher

Among the Gospels this title is most frequent in Luke and is a term of address used by those who are not disciples of Jesus (eg 7:40; 9:38; 10:25; 11:45). While the other synoptics also present Jesus as a teacher of parables, Luke does so more and has more unique parables too (at least 15).

Outline, with textual examples, Luke's distinctive use of titles for Jesus.

The death of Jesus

It has been argued that Luke has no theology of the cross[1], that is, that Luke does not present Jesus' death as an atonement, a sacrifice for sins, nor as specifically related to forgiveness of sins (unlike, for example, Mark and Paul). The saying about the Son of Man giving his life "a ransom for many" (Mk 10:45/ Mt 20:28) is absent from Luke, though a non-ransom version of it is found in 22:27. Also, it is particularly notable that the evangelistic sermons/speeches in Acts attach no saving significance to Jesus' death, creating a contrast between the Paul of Acts and the Paul we find in his own letters.

However, in Luke's account of the institution of the Lord's Supper Jesus' body is "given for you" and the blood (or the cup) "that is poured out for you" is the new covenant (22:19–20). If this is an original part of Luke (this is uncertain), then we have here a sacrificial understanding of Jesus' death, which is also regarded as introducing the new covenant. Further, a similar view of Jesus' death is found in Acts 20:28, where we read of the Church being obtained or bought with blood. We may note too Luke's emphasis on the necessity of the Messiah's suffering in accordance with the Scriptures (eg 24:7,26,44). It is in the name of this suffering and resurrected Messiah that "forgiveness of sins" is to be proclaimed to all nations (24:44–47). Again, quotations from Isaiah 53 (v 12 in 22:37; v 7–8 in Acts 8:32–33) may indicate that Luke considered Jesus to be Isaiah's suffering Servant figure

---

[1] eg Conzelmann, *The Theology of St. Luke* (op cit), p201

who died for the sins of others (Isa 53:4–6, 8, 10–12). Certainly, Luke regarded the cross to be Jesus' conflict with "the power of darkness" (22:53). We should also remember that, like the other evangelists, Luke sees the passion, along with the resurrection, as the climax to the story of Jesus. The long journey to Jerusalem, predictions of the passion, Jesus' conversation with Moses and Elijah about his departure (Greek *exodos*) which he would "accomplish/fulfil" in Jerusalem (9:31, author's translation) – all this preceding narrative has prepared the reader for the most significant events. For Luke, the salvation of God that Jesus brings reaches its climax in his death and resurrection.

In conclusion, it appears that while Luke does not present the saving significance of Jesus' death as specifically or as clearly as other New Testament writers, such a perspective is not entirely absent from his writings. It seems that Luke was more concerned with the *who* of salvation than explaining its *how*, a task to which Paul gave himself instead[1].

> **Task**
>
> *Discuss and evaluate the claim that for Luke Jesus' death has no saving significance.*

The Holy Spirit

The prominence of the Holy Spirit in Luke and Acts[2] is particularly apparent when compared with the other synoptics. While Mark has 6 references to the Spirit and Matthew has 12, there are 17 (nearly all unique) throughout Luke's Gospel, mostly at the beginning of new stages in the narrative[3]. The infancy narrative contains 7 of the 17 occurrences – Jesus is conceived through the Spirit (1:35), John the Baptist (in the womb) and his parents are filled with the Spirit, resulting in inspired, prophetic speech (1:15,41,67), and we read of three activities of the Spirit in relation to Simeon (2:25,26,27). At the start of Jesus' public ministry the Spirit descends on him at his baptism (3:22; see also v 16), after which, full of the Spirit, he is led by the Spirit in the desert (not "into the desert" as in the other synoptics) where he is tempted (4:1). He then returns to Galilee in the power of the Spirit (4:14), where he formally announces the beginning of his ministry with the words of Isaiah 61: "The Spirit of the Lord is upon me ..." (4:18). Indeed, Luke attributes the effectiveness of Jesus' ministry in general to his baptismal anointing with the Spirit (4:18–21; Acts 10:37–38). Finally, near the start of Luke's journey narrative, we read of Jesus rejoicing in the Spirit (10:21), of how the Father gives the Spirit (Matthew has "good things"– 7:11) to

---

[1] Bock, 'Luke' (op cit), p361

[2] eg Shelton, JB, *Mighty in Word and Deed: The Role of the Holy Spirit in Luke–Acts*, Peabody, Massachusetts: Hendrickson, 1991

[3] Fitzmyer, *The Gospel According to Luke I–IX* (op cit), pp227–228

those who ask him (11:13), of blasphemy against the Spirit, and of the Spirit's help at trial (12:10–12).

The emphasis on the Spirit at the start of Jesus' life, ministry and journey to Jerusalem serves as an indication that God's purpose and initiative underlies and legitimates these events. The Gospel ends with Jesus saying that the disciples should wait for what his Father has promised, for power from on high (24:49). This expectation is fulfilled in the opening chapters of Luke's sequel with the coming of the Spirit on the day of Pentecost (Acts 2). John the Baptist's claim that Jesus would baptise with the Spirit is now realised (Lk 3:16; Acts 1:4–5). In his two volumes Luke parallels the mission of Jesus and the Church – as Jesus in the Gospel commenced and continued his life and ministry in the power of the Spirit (eg 1:35; 3:22; 4:1,14,18ff), this is also the case of the Church in Acts (eg 1:4–5,8; ch 2).

Outline and discuss Luke's emphasis on the Holy Spirit.

Salvation

More than one Lucan scholar has considered salvation to be the central and coordinating theme of Luke's writings[1]. Certainly, Luke uses the *vocabulary* of salvation more than any other New Testament author. In the Gospel alone we have "salvation" six times (*soteria/soterion*: 1:69,71,77; 2:30; 3:6; 19:9), "Saviour" twice (*soter:* 1:47; 2:11) and "save" at least 17 times (*sozo:* sometimes translated as 'heal', 'made well', etc – 6:9; 7:50; 8:12,36,48,50; 9:24; 13:23; 17:19; 18:26,42; 19:10; 23:35,37,39). The words translated "salvation" and "Saviour" occur nowhere in Matthew and Mark.

As for the *source* of salvation, for Luke it is ultimately "of God" (3:6; cf 1:46,69,71; 2:30; 18:26) and is at the heart of "God's purpose", a key theme of Luke (eg 7:30; see Theology, pp26–27). The *agent* of God's salvation is clearly Jesus, born "a Saviour" (2:11) and, in fact, called God's salvation (2:27–30). He is the Son of Man who came "to seek out and to save the lost" (19:10), the one who mediates the divine salvation to others (4:18–21; 6:9–11; 7:48–50; 8:36,39–40,44, 48,50,54–55; 17:14,19; 18:42–43; 19:9–10), by means of God's Spirit (3:22; 4:14,18ff; Acts 2:22; 10:38) or "God's finger" (11:20, author's translation). As we have seen, it is not certain that Luke attaches saving significance specifically to Jesus' death, at least in the Gospel (cf Acts 20:28); rather, it is in his ministry (the Gospel) and as the risen, exalted Lord (Acts) that he particularly displays God's saving power. The *nature* of salvation in Luke is seen in its close relation to the main theme of Jesus' ministry in the synoptic Gospels, namely, the kingdom (or reign) of God. To be in God's kingdom is to be saved and vice versa (8:1,9–12; 13:23–29; 18:24–30). Indeed, it has been proposed that salvation in

---

[1] eg Marshall, *Luke: Historian and Theologian* (op cit), p92f; Green, *The Gospel of Luke* (op cit), p22, 24

Luke–Acts means "participation in the reign of God"[1]. Luke stresses that this saving reign of God was present in Jesus' ministry (11:20; possibly also 10:9,11; 16:16; 17:21; note too Luke's frequent "today", author's translation, eg 2:11; 4:21; 5:26; 19:9; 23:43), but is aware, like the other synoptics, that it awaits a future completion (eg 11:2; 23:42).

Specifically, the *effects* of the arrival of God's saving reign in Jesus' ministry are both negative and positive. Salvation is deliverance from sin (eg 1:77; 3:3; 5:20ff; 7:47–50; ch 15; 19:7–10; 24:47), from demons (exorcisms, eg 4:41; 11:20), from disease and disability, as well as their social isolation (see especially 4:18–19; 7:21–22; also, for example, 8:43–48; 17:11–19; 18:42), from political oppression (1:69–75; 2:38; possibly Acts 1:6–7) and from death (8:49ff; 7:11ff). In fact, practically all these things are presented as the adverse effects of Satan's kingdom or reign (4:5–6; 8:12; 11:14–22; 13:11–13,16; 22:3–4; Acts 10:38), which the in-breaking of God's reign in Jesus' ministry was now reversing. Positively, Luke particularly characterises this salvation and its effects as "good news" (*euangelizomai*: 'to announce good news' – ten times in the Gospel, eg 2:10; 4:18,43; and frequently in Acts), as "forgiveness of sins" (eg 1:77; 3:3; 5:20ff; 7:47–50; 24:47; expressed in Jesus' table fellowship with sinners, eg 15:2; 19:5–7), as "peace" (most often in Luke's Gospel in the NT, eg 2:14; 7:50; 8:48; 19:38; 24:36; yet 11:51ff) and as "joy" (eg 2:10–11; 10:17; 15:7,10; 24:41,52; and the corresponding verb, eg 10:20; 13:17; 15:5,32; 19:6).

The universal *scope* of salvation is an important theme for Luke. While the opening chapters of the Gospel, and elsewhere, clearly root the story of Jesus in Israel's history and Scriptures, and while Luke has a particular fondness for Jerusalem and its temple, he puts particular emphasis on the universality of God's salvation. As a Gentile himself (see A Gentile, p12), he wants his Gentile readership to see that the Messiah of Israel is also the Saviour of the world. Thus, though in each Gospel Isaiah 40:3 is quoted in relation to John the Baptist, it is only Luke who continues the quotation to include the words "and all flesh shall see God's salvation" (3:4–6, author's translation/ Isa 40:3–5, Greek OT; cf Mt 3:3/ Mk 1:3/ Jn 1:23). We may note too peace "on earth" at the Saviour's birth (2:14); Simeon's declaration that Jesus ("your salvation") was prepared in the presence of "all peoples" as a light for revelation to "the Gentiles" (2:30–32); how Jesus' genealogy goes back to Adam (the father of the human race) rather than, as in Matthew, to Abraham (the father of the Jewish race; Lk 3:38/ Mt 1:2); Luke's unique reference to the blessing of Gentiles rather than Israelites in the time of Elijah and Elisha (4:25–27); how people from north and south as well as east and west (Matthew only mentions the latter) will be in God's kingdom (Lk 13:28–29/ Mt 8:11–12); how "the Gentiles" will trample on Jerusalem until their time is fulfilled (21:24, only in Luke); and, finally, the disciples' mission to "all nations" (24:47).

---

[1] Powell, MA, 'Salvation in Luke–Acts' in *Word & World* 12/1, St Paul, Minnesota: Luther Seminary, 1992, p5

The Gospel of Luke

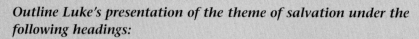

> **Task**
>
> *Outline Luke's presentation of the theme of salvation under the following headings:*
>
> a) vocabulary b) source c) agent
>
> d) nature e) effects f) scope

However, while its scope is universal, the *focus* of salvation in Luke is clearly on outcasts, on the socially marginalised and disadvantaged, on those who at the least were considered unimportant and in fact were often despised. Luke has a particular concern for the following groups:

The Samaritans

Samaria lay between Galilee to the north and Judea to the south (see map, p5). The origins of the Samaritans are unclear but, by the time of Jesus, the Jews had come to view them as racially mixed and religiously corrupt, and therefore not as proper Jews. This situation, amounting to hostility on occasion, is reflected in the Gospels (Mt 10:5; Lk 9:51–56; 17:16–18; Jn 4:9,20–22; 8:48). However, in three passages unique to his Gospel, Luke presents Jesus as having a positive attitude towards them. James and John are rebuked by Jesus for wanting the destruction of a Samaritan village that would not welcome him (9:51–56), and in the other two passages a Samaritan is the 'hero' or 'good guy' – the parable of the good Samaritan (10:29–37) and the healing of the ten lepers (17:11–19; note "saved" in v 19, author's translation). This contrasts with the other synoptics where Mark makes no reference to Samaria or the Samaritans and where Matthew's one reference is negative (10:5). Luke's concern for the Samaritans continues in the book of Acts (eg 1:8; ch 8).

The poor

Luke's concern for the poor and criticism of the rich are evident throughout his Gospel. The tone is set in the infancy narrative when Mary contrasts God's blessing of the "lowly" and "hungry" with his depriving of the "powerful" and "rich" (1:52–53). Here too the poverty of Jesus' own beginnings is apparent (2:7,22–24/ Lev 12:8). Later, Luke presents Jesus as homeless during his ministry (9:58). Only in Luke does Jesus begin his ministry using the words of Isaiah 61 as a summary of his mission: "The Spirit of the Lord is upon me, because he has anointed me to announce good news to the poor" (4:18, author's translation; also 7:22). The Sermon on the Plain begins with beatitudes on the "poor" and "hungry" (6:20–21; contrast v 24–25), which appear in Matthew with a spiritual and religious reference (5:3, 6). Luke alone records the story of wealthy Zacchaeus who gives half of his possessions to the poor (19:1–10), an indication that "salvation" had come to his house (v 9–10). We note also parables on the theme of wealth and poverty unique to Luke – the rich fool (12:13–21), the shrewd manager (16:1–9) and, particularly relevant, the rich man and Lazarus (16:19–31; also note 6:30; 14:12–14,21; 18:22; 21:1–4).

Women

In the generally male-dominated world of the first century women had a low status, a fact reflected in the Gospels (eg Jn 4:27). However, Luke in particular among the evangelists presents Jesus' concern for women and their importance in his ministry. This is clear from the outset in the infancy narrative (chs 1–2) where Elizabeth (John the Baptist's mother), Mary and the prophetess Anna feature. By contrast, in Matthew's infancy narrative (chs 1–2) the focus is on Joseph rather than Mary. Indeed, throughout his Gospel, Luke includes at least 12 women not referred to in the other Gospels – Elizabeth (1:5–7,13,24–25,36,40–45,56–61), Anna (2:36–38), the widow of Zarephath (4:26), the widow of Nain (7:11–17), the sinner who anointed Jesus (7:36–50), Joanna (8:3), Susanna (8:3), the woman in the crowd (11:27), the crippled woman (13:10–17), the daughters of Jerusalem (23:27–28), and two women who are the main characters of parables (the lost coin, 15:8–10; the widow and the judge, 18:1–8). Luke also has a unique story about Martha and Mary (10:38–42) and, of course, material about women found in other Gospels (eg 4:38–39; 8:43–48; 21:1–4; 23:49, 55–56; 24:10–11). Especially notable is Luke's emphasis on widows which includes several unique passages (see the references above, including Anna), as well as material found in Mark (Lk 20:47; 21:1ff).

While Luke has a concern for women, there is also a recurring female–male parallelism. This is observable in the infancy narrative (Zechariah and Mary, 1:10–20,26–38; Simeon and Anna, 2:25–38) and throughout the Gospel (eg the widow of Zarephath and Naaman the Syrian, 4:25–27; the demon-possessed man and Simon's mother-in-law, 4:31–39; the centurion and the widow of Nain, 7:1–17; a man with 100 sheep and a woman with ten coins, 15:4–10).

Children

Due to their minority, children too were regarded as unimportant. Luke's concern for them is seen at the start of his Gospel in the infancy narrative, where his focus on the births and childhoods of both John the Baptist and Jesus (note the summaries at 1:80; 2:40,52) underlines the fulfilment of God's purpose. And it is Luke alone who provides a boyhood story of Jesus (2:41–52). We may note too that Luke has three unique references to 'only' children (7:12; 8:42; 9:38; the latter two have synoptic parallels but with no mention that they are sole children).

Tax collectors

In the synoptics tax collectors are often bracketed with sinners, that is those who openly rejected the norms of Jewish culture and religion (references in Luke include 5:30; 7:34; 15:1). Their collaboration with the Gentile occupying power (the Romans) and their reputation for gaining personal wealth by overcharging (eg Lk 3:12–13; 19:2, 8) resulted in them being treated as outcasts. Luke's focus on them as being within the scope of God's salvation is apparent in various unique passages. They are specifically mentioned as being among those who received John's baptism (3:12–13; also 7:29–30). In addition, Luke alone has two stories in which tax collectors are 'heroes' – the parable of the Pharisee and the tax collector (18:9–14), and Zacchaeus (19:1–10, in which the theme of salvation is central: v 9–10). Even in the account of the call of Levi/Matthew which he shares with the other synoptics, there is a greater emphasis on tax collectors (cf Lk 5:27,29 with Mt 9:9–10 and Mk 2:14–15).

Sinners

Overlapping with the previous category to some degree is Luke's special concern to show that God's salvation is for the immoral. Like the other synoptics he presents Jesus as coming to call not the righteous but sinners (5:32). However, Luke alone has Peter's confession of his own sinfulness (5:8), the story of the sinful woman who anointed Jesus (7:36–50), two passages in which tax collectors are specifically characterised as sinners (18:13; 19:7–8), and Jesus' promise of Paradise to one of the "criminals" crucified along with him (23:39–43; the other synoptics call them "bandits"). The moral recklessness and subsequent repentance of the central character in Luke's unique parable of the lost son (15:11–32; note v 1–2 for the context) is also relevant here[1].

> Show how the focus of salvation in Luke is on the marginalised, with reference to the following groups:
>
> a) the Samaritans   b) the poor   c) women
> d) children   e) tax collectors   f) sinners

Spirituality

Luke's special interest in the spiritual life and religious experience is evident in his emphasis on prayer, worship and joy.

Prayer

We have already noted how Luke focuses on the prayer life of Jesus more than the other Gospels (see The character of Jesus, pp29–30). Luke also contains three unique parables of Jesus on prayer: the friend at midnight (11:5–8), the widow and

---

[1] Shepherds (2:8–20) have a reputation for immorality in sources later than the New Testament but not specifically so in first-century sources. Yet, Luke's aim in presenting them as the first to hear of the Saviour's birth might be to show God's concern for the lowly (eg 1:52).

the judge (18:1–8) and the Pharisee and the tax collector (18:9–14), as well as other teachings of Jesus on prayer (eg 6:28; 11:1–4, 9–13; 20:47; 22:40,46).

Worship

Three Greek verbs relating to worship feature in Luke. They are variously translated in Bible versions, so the traditional translation is provided in brackets:

- *aineo* (praise): this word is unique to Luke among the evangelists (2:13,20; 19:37).
- *doxazo* (glorify): this word is found more often in Luke than the other synoptics (eg 2:20; 4:15; 5:25–26).
- *eulogeo* (bless): again, this word occurs most frequently in Luke among the synoptics (eg 1:64; 2:28; 24:53).

The language of worship and praise is used of God (although see 4:15), especially for his blessings given in the ministry of Jesus. On the theme of worship there are also four canticles/songs found only in Luke (1:46–55,68–79; 2:14,29–32).

Joy

This is a prominent theme in Luke, more so than in the other synoptics. The Gospel begins and ends with "great joy" (2:10; 24:52) and rejoicing occurs throughout, especially at news of the births of John and Jesus (1:14,44,47; 2:10), at the blessings of Jesus' ministry (eg 8:13; 10:17,20; 13:17; 15:5,7,10,32; 19:6,37) and at Jesus' resurrection (24:41).

With reference to the text, show how spirituality is an important theme in Luke.

Eschatology

Luke's treatment of the 'last things' (Greek *eschatos*: 'last'), such as the return of Jesus and final judgement, appears to have a focus different to that found in the other synoptics. While there is still an expectation of the future *parousia* (Greek: 'coming') of Jesus, the importance of the present is stressed. Thus, there is not the emphasis on the imminence/nearness of the *parousia* that we find in Matthew and Mark. For example, while the other synoptics have Jesus speaking before the Jewish council of his future coming on/with the clouds of heaven, this is omitted in Luke and replaced with a reference to Jesus' imminent position at the right hand of (the power of) God (cf Mt 26:64/ Mk 14:62/ Lk 22:69). Again, only Luke states that Jesus told a parable to correct the belief that God's kingdom was to appear immediately (19:11ff). These passages, and others (eg Mt 24:4/ Mk 13:5/ Lk 21:8 and Mt 16:28/ Mk 9:1/ Lk 9:27), as well as the fact that Luke wrote a history of the Church,

The Gospel of Luke

have been viewed as evidence of a lesser emphasis on imminent eschatology, in comparison with his fellow synoptics. Rather, Luke's focus is on the present and this is seen, for instance, in his fondness for the words "today" (author's translation; eg 2:11; 4:21; 5:26; 13:32–33; 19:5,9; 23:43 – all unique to Luke; see also p35) and "daily" (author's translation; 9:23; 11:3; 16:19; 19:47; 22:53). Nevertheless, it is not true that there is no expectation of an imminent and sudden End in Luke (see 3:7,9,17; 12:35–40; 18:7–8; 21:27,31–32,36), but there is an awareness of an interval before the return of Jesus (12:41–48; 19:11–27).

Compare Luke's eschatology with that of the other synoptics.

Our study of the characteristics of Luke's Gospel has noted its distinctive presentation of God, history, geography, Jesus, the Holy Spirit, salvation, spirituality and eschatology. The next task should be completed to review our main findings.

Provide a summary outline and broad overview of the main distinctive characteristics of Luke's Gospel.

LUKE AS A HISTORIAN

We have already noted Luke's concern with presenting his narrative of Jesus in its historical context, relating it to the history of Rome, Palestine and the Church (see History, pp27–28). He situates his story of Jesus not only in secular history but particularly in 'salvation' or 'sacred' history, that is, in the flow of biblical history. Thus, at the outset, in the infancy narrative, Luke introduces Jesus against the background of – indeed as the climax of – Israel's history and hopes. Among the evangelists Luke appears to have the greatest historical consciousness and has been called "the first Christian historian"[1]. However, scholarly opinion on the role and value of Luke as a historian ranges from viewing Luke as a writer of edifying fiction[2] to regarding him as an accurate and reliable historian[3]. Consideration of Luke as a historian requires discussion of a

---

[1] Dibelius, 'The Speeches in Acts and Ancient Historiography' (op cit), p123f; Marshall (*Luke: Historian & Theologian* (op cit), p49) disagrees and notes that Luke was preceded by Mark.

[2] eg Haenchen, *The Acts of the Apostles* (op cit)

[3] eg Hemer, C, *The Book of Acts in the Setting of Hellenistic History*, Tubingen: Mohr, 1989

number of both general and specific issues related to his Gospel, the book of Acts and beyond.

In the preface to his Gospel (1:1–4) Luke certainly presents himself as a serious historian whose "account/narrative" (author's translation; *diegesis,* a term used by contemporary historians) of Jesus is based on eyewitness tradition (v 2) and careful research (v 3), with the stated aim of convincing Theophilus of the "truth/certainty" (v 4, author's translation) of what he has heard. A similar concern with historical reliability is apparent in the preface to Acts, in relation to Jesus' resurrection (1:3, "many convincing proofs"). Furthermore, comparison of the prefaces and contents of Luke–Acts with Jewish and Graeco-Roman historiography (history writing) of the time suggests that in terms of genre (type of literature) Luke's writings should be classed as history[1]. However, it has been argued that the claims in Luke's preface should not be given too much weight since such statements were a matter of literary convention in ancient writings. Rather, Luke's claims should be judged by his actual performance – by the historical quality of the contents of his writings, where they can be tested.

The quality of any historian's work depends to a large degree on the quality of his sources. The general view is that Luke made use of Mark's Gospel and the hypothetical sources Q and L in the composition of his Gospel (see Sources, p15ff). There is no certainty about the sources of Mark's Gospel, although some internal evidence is consistent with the early Church tradition that the apostle Peter was a source. It is generally held that before any of our Gospels were written, there was a period of oral tradition of at least 40 years, when the stories and sayings of Jesus were passed on as small, independent units. The 'forms' that these units of tradition developed (eg parables, prophetic sayings) during the oral period can tell us about their use in the early Church (eg preaching, apologetics) and these uses in turn modified the original material. 'Form criticism' is concerned with this process (see p246ff). Some feel that by the time the material was written down in Mark it had undergone so many changes in the oral period, including the invention of new material attributed to Jesus, that its historical value is limited. Others, however, acknowledge that some modification of the original material inevitably occurred, but that invention of new material or significant transformation of existing tradition is incompatible with the controls that surviving eyewitnesses would have provided. Whatever view one has of the historical reliability of Luke's major source, we have seen that Luke has not simply reproduced it. He has instead edited or 'redacted' ('redaction criticism' is concerned with this practice) Mark, in relation for example to order of contents, language, style, and characterisation of both Jesus and the disciples (see Sources, p15ff, for examples). Thus, scholars' assessment of the nature of Luke's sources and his use of them has led to varying conclusions about his role and value as a historian. Some hold that

---

[1] eg Aune, D, *The New Testament in Its Literary Environment*, Philadelphia: Westminster, 1987, pp77–157. However, contemporary literary comparisons have led some to regard Luke as a biography and others to view Luke–Acts as a novel.

the historical value of Luke's Gospel has been significantly undermined because of changes made by the Church to traditions about Jesus in the oral period and changes made by Luke's editorial activity. Others, however, argue that such alterations were not substantial enough to have an adverse effect on the historical accuracy of Luke.

A further issue concerning Luke's historiography relates to his motives for writing. We have noted that he was not a mere reporter or chronicler of past events, but rather that his account was shaped by certain definite theological, apologetic and pastoral goals (for details see Purposes, p21ff). Thus, Luke was not writing as a neutral, impartial, disinterested historian who was concerned merely with the facts, but as someone whose selection and interpretation of the material at his disposal was driven by various agendas. Some hold that this means Luke's writings are consequently tendentious and distorted representations of the past, and are therefore historically suspect. Others, however, note that all history writing, modern as well as ancient, to a greater or lesser degree reflects the interests and concerns of the historian, and that the ideal of pure or uninterpreted history is an unattainable myth. The historical validity of a work is not necessarily compromised by the fact that the historian has motives for writing. Again, it is at the level of actual performance that the historian's work may be assessed.

Luke, like biblical writers generally, had a religious view of history which involved belief in supernatural beings, forces and experiences such as God, Satan, angels, demons, visions, prophecy and miracles. Many who hold to a modern scientific world-view of reality, in which the laws of nature are predictable and unalterable, regard such beliefs as primitive superstitions and fantasies which were generally held in the pre-scientific period of history, when the religious world-view was dominant. Thus, much in Luke–Acts is viewed as lacking historical credibility. However, it could be argued that such rejection of the supernatural is partly based on an outdated view of science which has moved on from Newtonian mechanics to quantum theory and beyond (see p309). Indeed, postmodernism rejects modernity's exclusive reliance on naturalism and rationalism, noting the limitations of scientific methodology and allowing for the presence of mystery in the universe. In any case, it is clear that a historian's ideological presuppositions, whether for or against supernaturalism, will influence his assessment of the historical value of Luke's writings.

In addition to the general considerations we have noted thus far, there are a number of specific issues relevant to Luke's role as a historian which require our attention. These are important issues since, as mentioned before, it is in the area of actual performance that a historian's work may be assessed.

Internal consistency

It has been argued that there are inconsistencies within Luke–Acts which reflect poorly on Luke's historical accuracy. While in the Gospel, Jesus' ascension to heaven occurs on the same day his tomb was found to be empty (24:51; cf Acts 1:1–2), in

Acts his ascension doesn't happen until 40 days later (Acts 1:3, 9; 13:30–31). However, while Jesus' ascension *seems* to occur on Easter day in Luke's Gospel, there is actually no reference to its timing in Luke 24, which may in fact be a compressed summary of events recounted in more detail in Acts. The repetition may have a literary motive – the creation of a link between Luke and Acts.

Another inconsistency is seen in Jesus' commissioning of his disciples to preach to all nations (Lk 24:46–47; Acts 1:8), and the disciples' apparent ignorance of and indeed resistance to this in Acts (10,11). Objections to the Gentile mission are not resolved by reference to Jesus' words, which are often regarded as an invention to justify the Church's universal mission. However, it may be that the disciples were aware of Jesus' words but mistakenly assumed that the mission was for Jews in every nation (as in Acts 2), hence the controversy over the Gentile mission later in Acts[1].

Finally, there appear to be inconsistencies in the three accounts of Paul's conversion in Acts (9:1–19; 22:1–16; 26:9–18). In one account Paul's companions hear the voice (9:7) and in another they don't (22:9). Also, in one account, Jesus commissions Paul on the Damascus Road (26:15–18), while in the others the commission is communicated later through Ananias (9:10–16; 22:12–16). However, it may be that both 9:7 and 22:9 affirm that Paul's companions heard the voice but that the latter verse indicates they did not understand it (cf Jn 12:28–30). Indeed, the Greek grammar of 22:9 may support such an interpretation[2]. Again, the differences in the accounts concerning Paul's commission may be due to Paul's (or Luke's) compression of the details for the sake of brevity – the essential fact of his divine commission to the Gentile mission is found in each account.

The census/registration of Luke 2

For many this is the most problematic issue in Luke's writings as regards his historical accuracy. In the opening verses of Luke 2 it is stated that the Roman Emperor Augustus issued a decree that a census or registration should be taken of all the world, that this was the first census and was taken while Quirinius was Governor of Syria, and that all went to their own towns to register, including Joseph and Mary who travelled to Bethlehem from Nazareth. The historical problems related to this passage and the proposed solutions are numerous and complex[3], and here we can only outline the key points.

Firstly, we have no other evidence of an empire-wide census in Augustus' time. However, censuses did occur under Augustus in many provinces and Luke's wording may reflect the general situation.

---

1 Bock, DL, *Luke 9:51–24:53*, Grand Rapids, Michigan: Baker, 1996, p1940

2 Marshall, IH, *The Acts of the Apostles*, Leicester: IVP, 1980, p355

3 See, for example, R Brown, *The Birth of the Messiah*, London: Chapman, 1977, pp547–556; IH Marshall, *The Gospel of Luke: A Commentary on the Greek Text*, Exeter: Paternoster, 1978, pp99–104; and Bock, *Luke 1:1–9:50* (op cit), pp903–909.

Secondly, Quirinius became Governor of Syria in AD 6, ten years after the death of Herod the Great, yet according to Luke (and Matthew) Jesus was born in Herod's time. Further, the first-century Jewish historian Josephus refers to a census under Quirinius in AD 6 which resulted in riots under Judas the Galilean (referred to by Luke in Acts 5:37). So, it seems that Luke has mistakenly connected the birth of Jesus with the census under Quirinius, when in fact he was born some ten years earlier in the time of Herod the Great. However, several suggestions have been made of possible resolutions to this apparent historical discrepancy. Quirinius may have been Governor of Syria (or had some other authority) at the time of Jesus' birth, as well as later in AD 6; the census may have been initiated by a governor of Syria at the time of Jesus' birth but the resulting taxation came later with Quirinius in AD 6; and the word translated "first" (*prote*) in Luke 2:2 could be translated 'earlier' or 'before' (as, for example, in Jn 1:15,30; 15:18) so that Luke's census is earlier than that of Quirinius or simply occurred before he was governor. Josephus' lack of reference to a census previous to AD 6 is not necessarily decisive. While many scholars remain unconvinced by these (and other) attempts to absolve Luke of historical error on this matter, others argue that they are real possibilities which should prevent hasty judgements on Luke's historical accuracy.

Thirdly, a Roman census would not require Joseph to return to his ancestral home since it would relate to place of residence. However, those with property in another district were required to register there and Joseph may have had property in Bethlehem. Further, the Romans sometimes permitted registration to be carried out according to local custom, and for the Jews ancestry was important in the context of a census. Mary may have been required to make the journey too as his wife or Joseph may have wanted her with him to be sure of being present at the birth. Finally, it is argued that a Roman census would not have been taken in Herod's Jewish domain. However, Roman censuses in vassal kingdoms were not unknown and it may be that the relationship between Augustus and Herod had become difficult at this time.

Theudas and Judas

In Acts 5:36–37 Luke has the Pharisee Gamaliel address a closed session of the Jewish council in which he refers to two Jewish revolutionaries, Theudas and "after this" (author's translation) Judas the Galilean, who both perished and whose followers dispersed. The historical problem is that the first-century Jewish historian Josephus also appears to refer to this Theudas (*Ant* 20.97ff), but dates him in the mid AD 40s, long after the events of Acts 5. Further, Gamaliel then places the Judas incident "after" Theudas, yet it occurred in fact quite some time before, in connection with the census of AD 6 (see above). Thus, it seems that Luke, who would have had no access to what was said in the closed session of the council, has put historically confused and anachronistic words in the mouth of Gamaliel. However, it is not impossible that some details of the private proceedings were made public by a member of the council.

Also, it is possible that Josephus rather than Luke is historically inaccurate here, or that another, unknown, Theudas is mentioned in Acts 5[1].

Palestinian geography

Luke, as a foreigner, has been accused of having an imperfect knowledge of the geography of Palestine[2]. For example, he refers to Galilee as Judea (eg cf Lk 4:44/ Mt 4:23/ Mk 1:39; see map, p5). However, it appears that Luke uses the term 'Judea' with broad and narrow meanings, referring at times to the whole land of the Jews (1:5; 4:44; 6:17; 7:17; 23:5; Acts 10:37) and at times to a more restricted area (1:39,65; 2:4; 3:1; 5:17; 21:21). Further, the Greek of Luke 17:11 is too obscure to know precisely how Luke understood the geographical relationship between Judea, Samaria and Galilee.

Paul

One of the main reasons why many view Luke as an unreliable historian is that despite the author's claim to be a companion of Paul, the Paul of Acts is considered to be inconsistent with the Paul we find in this man's own writings – his letters. There appear to be historical differences, particularly relating to events surrounding his conversion and his visits to Jerusalem (when Acts is compared with Galatians). Also, it has been argued that there are theological differences, specifically concerning natural theology, the Law, Christology and eschatology. Finally, the portrait of Paul himself in Acts as a miracle worker, a persuasive speaker, and one unconcerned about equality with the Jerusalem apostles, is viewed as incompatible with Paul's self-portrait in his letters. However, not all scholars hold that the Paul of Acts is irreconcilable with Paul in his letters. Neither Paul nor Acts provides us with complete information concerning Paul's travels. Also, some apparent inconsistencies can be resolved by noting the different contexts, emphases and perspectives of seemingly contradictory passages (see A companion of Paul, pp13–14).

The early Church

It has been observed that Luke to some extent presents an idealistic, simplified, even romanticised, picture of the history and growth of the early Church as it progresses from Jerusalem to Rome, from its Jewish beginnings to its Gentile mission. It is argued that disagreements, when reported, are minimised or trivialised (eg Acts 6:1–6) and that Luke frequently presents a rosy picture of the Church's unity and growth (eg Acts 2:41–47; 4:4,21,32–35; 5:12ff; 6:7; 9:31; 12:24; 16:5; 19:20; 21:20).

---

[1] eg Marshall, IH, *The Acts of the Apostles*, Leicester: IVP, 1980, pp121–123
[2] eg Conzelmann, *The Theology of St. Luke* (op cit)

However, it is possible to exaggerate this point. Luke, of course, is being selective, providing typical incidents in the history of the early Church, rather than a complete account of its beginnings. Also, he does not have an entirely idealised view of things – he reports disagreements (eg Acts 15:36–41), lapses (Acts 5:1–11) and persecutions in the early chapters and throughout Paul's missionary journeys.

The speeches in Acts

The book of Acts contains several speeches/sermons which are attributed to the early Christian leaders Peter, Stephen and Paul. However, the historicity of these speeches has been denied, with many scholars regarding them as Lucan compositions[1]. In support of this view it is noted that the speeches have a stereotypical pattern, that their language and style are similar to each other and indeed similar to Luke's in the narrative sections of Acts, and that they contain Luke's theology rather than specifically Paul's or Peter's. Luke's practice is often said to be similar to that of the ancient historian Thucydides (fifth century BC) who acknowledged that in relation to speeches he could not always report exactly what was said by others and so he gave the general sense of what was probably said on various occasions (*History of the Peloponnesian War* 1.22.1). However, other scholars deny that the speeches are Lucan creations and argue that, while they are not verbatim accounts, they are accurate Lucan paraphrases based on traditional reports[2].

In conclusion to our study of Luke as a historian, we should note the importance of not judging Luke by the demanding standards of modern historiography. Rather, Luke's role as a historian should be seen against the background of the ancient historiography of his day which, while not as rigorous or scientific as today, was nevertheless aware of the difference between fact and fiction and of the importance of historical accuracy[3].

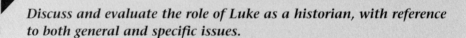

Discuss and evaluate the role of Luke as a historian, with reference to both general and specific issues.

---

[1] eg Dibelius, 'The Speeches in Acts and Ancient Historiography' (op cit)

[2] eg Bruce, FF, *The Speeches in the Acts of the Apostles*, London: Tyndale, 1942; and 'The Speeches in Acts – Thirty Years Later' in *Reconciliation and Hope*, ed R Banks, Grand Rapids, Michigan: Eerdmans, 1974

[3] eg note the second-century (AD) historian Lucian's 'How to Write History' in *Lucian*, trans AM Harmon, Cambridge, Massachusetts: Loeb Classical Library, Harvard University, 1959

Practice essay titles

1 (a) Outline your knowledge and understanding of the authorship of Luke's Gospel. (30)

(b) Comment on the claim that the author offers a full life story of Jesus. Justify your answer. (15)

2 (a) Outline your knowledge and understanding of the sources used by the author of Luke's Gospel. (30)

(b) Explore the view that the dating of this Gospel is a problem. Justify your answer. (15)

3 (a) Outline your knowledge and understanding of the main purposes of the writer of Luke's Gospel. (30)

(b) Explore in particular the claim that the writer had a special interest in the downtrodden and oppressed. Justify your answer. (15)

Selected narratives in Luke's Gospel

STRUCTURE

A STUDY OF THE structure of Luke's Gospel is concerned with how Luke has arranged or organised the contents of his Gospel – indeed, he introduces his work by describing it as an "orderly" account (1:3). We will consider two main views of how Luke has structured his Gospel. For how Luke has arranged his source material, see Sources, p15ff.

A geographical structure

It is generally agreed that Luke's Gospel has a broadly geographical outline, taken from Mark's Gospel which appears to have been one of his main sources. The account begins in the southern province of Judea, where Jesus is born and where he prepares for his ministry (public service of God), moves on to the northern province of Galilee, and then has a long journey back south to Jerusalem, where his ministry climaxes in his passion and resurrection. We see this in the following outline:

1:1–4	Preface/Prologue
1:5–2:52	Birth and childhood of John the Baptist and Jesus
3:1–4:13	Preparation for Jesus' ministry: baptism and temptation
4:14–9:50	Jesus' ministry in Galilee

9:51–19:44	Journey to Jerusalem
19:45–21:38	Jesus' ministry in Jerusalem
chs 22–23	Passion of Jesus
ch 24	Resurrection of Jesus

It has been noted that in Luke's second book, Acts, this geographical progression is in roughly the reverse direction (Acts 1:8). Thus, Acts begins in Jerusalem where Luke's Gospel ends, and moves out through Judea and Samaria (cf Acts 8 and Lk 9:52; 17:11) to the ends of the earth; Acts ends in Rome while Luke's Gospel begins with references to Roman authority (2:1; 3:1). The result is that at the centre of this inverse parallelism Luke's geographical focus is on Jerusalem (end of Luke, start of Acts), and here too we find his theological focus – the resurrection and ascension of Jesus[1].

A historical structure

Luke's account of Jesus is broadly chronological in that it begins with events surrounding his birth, infancy and childhood, continues with his adult ministry and concludes with his death, resurrection and ascension. However, it has been argued that Luke has consciously structured his Gospel and Acts according to a 'salvation history' scheme, in which Jesus is in the 'middle of time'[2]. Thus, world history is divided into three distinct historical periods[3] – the period of Israel (from creation to John the Baptist: 1:5–3:1; note 16:16), the period of Jesus (from John's baptism to Jesus' ascension: 3:2–24:51), followed by the period of the Church (from Jesus' ascension to his return: Lk 24:52–Acts 28:31 and beyond). However, it is not clear from the text, including 16:16, that Luke himself thought in such sharply defined phases of salvation history as these. Indeed, it could be argued that the text shows more clearly that he viewed salvation history as having two main phases – the age of promise/prophecy (the Old Testament) and the age of fulfilment (Luke–Acts, eg Lk 1:1,54–55,69–73; 3:3–6; 4:16–21; 24:25–27,44; Acts 2:16).

Explore Luke's claim that his Gospel is an "orderly" account.

---

1 Details may be found, for example, in CL Blomberg, *Jesus and the Gospels*, Leicester: Apollos/IVP, 1997, pp142–144.

2 Conzelmann, *The Theology of St. Luke* (op cit). The 'middle of time' reflects the German title of Conzelmann's book.

3 The following is Fitzmyer's modification of Conzelmann and others in Fitzmyer, *The Gospel According to Luke I–IX* (op cit), p185.

INFANCY NARRATIVE (1:5–2:52)

The first two chapters of Luke's Gospel, apart from the introductory preface (1:1–4), are often referred to as Luke's 'infancy narrative(s)' (1:5–2:52). The very Old Testament atmosphere and Jewish Greek of Luke's infancy narrative contrast with the formal, literary Greek of the preface before it and the common Hellenistic Greek after it.

The infancy narrative, which is mostly about the births of John the Baptist and Jesus, may be broadly outlined as follows.

1:5–25	The birth of John the Baptist foretold
1:26–38	The birth of Jesus foretold
1:39–45	Mary visits Elizabeth
1:46–55	Mary's song of praise
1:56–66	The birth, circumcision and naming of John the Baptist
1:67–80	Zechariah's song of praise
2:1–21	The birth, circumcision and naming of Jesus
2:22–40	The presentation of Jesus in the temple
2:41–52	The boy Jesus in the temple

Some have argued that the content and structure of Luke's infancy narrative have been influenced by certain Old Testament narratives (eg 1 Sam chs 1–3: the infancy narrative of Samuel). However, it is more obvious that Luke has arranged his material in an effort to draw parallels between John and Jesus, the two key characters in these opening chapters of his Gospel. While there is disagreement over the extent and symmetry of this parallelism, it is nevertheless broadly evident in the text. The following (modified) scheme by JB Green illustrates the point[1].

John		Jesus
1:5–7	The introduction of parents	1:26–27
1:8–23	The foretelling of the birth	1:28–38
1:24–25	The mother's response	1:39–56
1:57–58	The birth	2:1–20
1:59–66	Circumcision and naming	2:21–24
1:67–79	Prophetic response	2:25–39
1:80	Growth of the child	2:40–52

---

[1] Green, *The Gospel of Luke* (op cit), p50

Indeed, this John–Jesus parallelism continues into the third and fourth chapters (eg both are in the desert, both are written of in Isaiah, both preach the good news) and beyond (7:18–35). Yet, as will be noted below, this is not an equal or balanced parallelism; while the similarities indicate that both John and Jesus serve the one purpose of God, the differences highlight the superiority of Jesus, of whom John is but the forerunner. It may be that Luke has stressed Jesus' superiority over John because of the continuing existence of John's disciples in Luke's time (cf 3:15; 5:33; 7:18ff; Acts 13:24–25; 18:25; 19:1–7). We may note too that this is but one example of Luke's general fondness for parallelism, seen, for example, in his unique parables (eg the two sons in the lost son, and the Pharisee and the tax collector), unique narrative episodes (eg Mary and Martha), and also in the book of Acts – such as the comparison between Peter and Paul, and the contrast between Barnabas on the one hand and Ananias and Sapphira on the other.

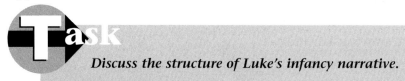

Discuss the structure of Luke's infancy narrative.

As we turn now to a study of the individual passages within the infancy narrative, the relevant verses in Luke should be read in conjunction with the corresponding notes below.

The birth of John the Baptist foretold (1:5–25)

Luke begins his infancy narrative at the time of Herod King of Judea and in the Jerusalem temple, where the angel Gabriel tells Zechariah the priest that his barren wife Elizabeth will bear him a son, whom he is to name John. The passage may be outlined as follows.

v 5–7	John's parents
v 8–10	Zechariah's offering
v 11–17	Gabriel's announcement
v 18	Zechariah's question
v 19–20	Gabriel's judgement
v 21–22	Wondering worshippers
v 23–25	Elizabeth's pregnancy

John's parents are introduced as similar to Old Testament characters such as Abraham and Sarah who were also aged and childless (Gen 16:1–2; 18:10–12), and John's miraculous birth to a barren mother parallels the births of the significant

Old Testament figures Isaac (Gen 21:1–7), Samson (Judg 13) and Samuel (1 Sam 1). The miraculous nature of these births indicates that they are due to God's initiative and activity – thus, John's coming was God's doing and in God's time. The whole passage has a form similar to these and other biblical accounts of annunciation (announcement) of coming births and of commissioning of individuals to a future mission or role. The account, for example, has several features in common with the annunciation of Samson's birth (Judg 13:2–5 – barren woman, angel, abstinence from wine and strong drink, dedication to God from birth, future role). The angel identifies himself as Gabriel, who spoke about the end times in the Old Testament book of Daniel (8:16; 9:21), and describes John's role and mission as turning Israel to God and preparing a people for the Lord. He likens John's mission to that of the prophet Elijah, whose coming to renew Israel at the end times is promised in the closing verses of our Old Testament (Mal 4:5–6). The main purpose of Luke's account here is therefore to indicate the significance of John the Baptist, whose birth was due to God's initiative and whose mission was to prepare Israel for the Lord.

Several of Luke's characteristic themes and emphases are introduced for the first time in this opening section of his Gospel – for example, the temple (where the infancy narrative and the Gospel both conclude), prayer (v 10,13), joy (v 14), being filled with the Holy Spirit (v 15; as were both John's parents also: v 41,67), good news (v 19), and women (Elizabeth); see Characteristics, p26ff, for details of Luke's development of these themes.

Tasks

a **Outline the Old Testament background of the annunciation to Zechariah.**

b **What is the main purpose of this passage?**

c **What characteristic Lucan themes are introduced here?**

The birth of Jesus foretold (1:26–38)

Luke immediately parallels his opening passage by having Gabriel announce another coming birth. This time the message is given to Mary, an engaged virgin in Nazareth, who is told that she will bear a son, whom she is to name Jesus. The passage may be outlined as follows.

v 26–27	Jesus' mother
v 28–33	Gabriel's announcement
v 34	Mary's question
v 35–37	Gabriel's explanation
v 38	Mary's submission

That Luke is paralleling the announcements of the coming births of John and Jesus is clear from the many similarities between the two accounts – time reference, introduction of the couple, abnormal conditions for conception, visit by Gabriel, distressed response, instruction of named individual not to fear, announcement of coming miraculous birth (including name, status and role of child, as well as involvement of the Spirit), problematic question in response, and answer by Gabriel including a sign (Zechariah's silence; Elizabeth's pregnancy). We shall see that this parallelism between John and Jesus continues throughout the infancy narrative and, indeed, beyond. However, it is an unequal parallelism in that Luke presents Jesus as superior to John. Thus, we also note differences in this direction between the two passages we have compared – the conception of Jesus is a greater and unprecedented miracle, Jesus will be "great" without any limiting statement being added to this, Jesus' role is greater as God's Son and everlasting king, the activity of the Spirit is more significant in relation to Jesus, and the unbelief of John's father contrasts with the submission of Jesus' mother, as does the angelic greeting that each receives. So, the similarities between the two passages indicate the common place in the purpose of God of both John and Jesus, while the differences point to the superior status and role of Jesus, for whom John will prepare the way.

While in Matthew's Gospel it is Joseph who receives the angelic message (1:20–21), in Luke's Mary is the recipient, showing his characteristic concern for women; although Zechariah, rather than Elizabeth, receives Gabriel's message. Gabriel stresses that the choice of Mary to be the mother of the Messiah is due to the gracious initiative of God ("favour/grace", author's translation, v 28,30). Of the synoptics only Luke has the word *charis* ('favour/grace'), which is used also of Jesus in the infancy narrative (2:40,52). Mary's question was not taken by Gabriel as a sign of unbelief, unlike Zechariah's (v 18–20). Rather, she is presented as an exemplary disciple who submits to the word of God (v 38; cf 8:21).

Unlike Matthew (1:21), Luke does not develop the meaning of the name 'Jesus' (Greek form of Joshua: 'the Lord/Yahweh saves'). The emphasis is rather on Jesus as Son of God (twice: v 32,35) and as the royal son/descendant of David who will reign for ever over Israel (v 32–33; also v 27). The language of verses 32 and 33 clearly reflects 2 Samuel 7, where David will be "great" (v 9) and his "throne" and "kingdom" will last "for ever" (v 16), as will those of his offspring who will also be a "son" of God (v 12–14). This Old Testament concept of the king of Israel as God's son in 2 Samuel 7 (also, for example, in Ps 2:7; 89:20,26–27) implies that we should understand "Son of God" in this royal sense in Luke 1:32 and 35. Indeed, elsewhere in Luke–Acts the royal title "Messiah/Christ" (author's translation; meaning 'anointed') is closely associated with "Son of God" (Lk 4:41; 22:67,70; Acts 9:20–22). However, "Son of God" may have other meanings in different contexts, not least the idea of a special relationship with God (eg 10:22). We should note too the close link in our passage (v 35) between Jesus as Son of God and the activity of the Holy Spirit, an association found elsewhere in Luke (3:22; 4:1,3,9,14; 10:21–22). In fact, Gabriel's words seem to imply that the virgin conception of Jesus – the activity of God's creative Spirit (Gen 1:2; Ps 104:30) in the absence of a human father – means that Jesus is God's son rather than Joseph's son (cf 3:23,38; 2:48–49).

The mention of the Spirit here is, of course, characteristic of Luke generally, and particularly in his infancy narrative. The idea, at the start of Luke's Gospel, of the Spirit and power having "come upon" Mary to begin Jesus' life (1:35), corresponds to the start of Acts (1:8), where similarly the Spirit and power will "come upon" the apostles and others to begin their witness to Jesus. Indeed, the opening chapters of both Luke and Acts are linked in other ways, including the common themes of prayer, praise and fulfilment of prophecy. That the power of the "Most High" will "overshadow" Mary also recalls God's presence and protection in the (Greek) Old Testament (eg Ex 40:35; Ps 91:4) and anticipates his presence at the transfiguration (9:34).

Different views have been expressed on the matter of the historicity of the virgin conception of Jesus. Some deny its actual occurrence, noting that in the New Testament it is only explicitly found in Matthew (1:18–25) and Luke, generally accepted as two of the later books of the New Testament. Further, comparisons are sometimes made with ancient pagan myths of the conceptions of rulers and other significant figures due to the union of their mothers with the gods (eg Plato's birth to his human mother and Apollo). Thus, it is argued that the story of Jesus' virgin conception is a late Christian invention reflecting increasing devotion in an attempt to give Jesus divine parentage and status. However, those who regard the story as factual, note the independent nature of the two accounts, argue that they are based on earlier tradition, and point to the improbability of such direct pagan influence on the early Christians and especially on the very Jewish world of the Gospel infancy narratives. Often one's view of the issue is influenced by general beliefs regarding the possibility and nature of supernatural and miraculous events[1]. The theological message of the virgin conception, however, is that the coming of the king of Israel, the Son of God, is not a human initiative or achievement. Rather, his coming is God's doing, in God's time – he is in fact God's gift. Yet his origins are also human, for the Son of the Most High is also the son of lowly Mary.

Tasks

a *Compare and contrast the announcements of the future births of John and Jesus.*

b *Comment on the presentation of the following in the annunciation to Mary:*

   (i) Mary (ii) Jesus (iii) the Holy Spirit

c *Discuss the historicity and theology of the virgin conception of Jesus.*

---

[1] See p42; and for a more detailed discussion of the historicity of the virgin conception of Jesus see Marshall, *The Gospel of Luke* (op cit), pp73–75.

Mary visits Elizabeth (1:39–45)

Having just heard from the angel that her relative Elizabeth was in her sixth month of pregnancy, Mary quickly travelled from her home in Nazareth to Elizabeth's home in Judea. Mary's greeting triggered a response from both Elizabeth and her unborn child. The passage may be outlined as follows.

v 39–40	Mary's journey
v 40	Mary's greeting
v 41	The baby's response
v 41–45	Elizabeth's response

This meeting of the two expectant mothers links the two main characters of the infancy narrative – their children, John the Baptist and Jesus. As throughout the infancy narrative, John's inferiority to Jesus is apparent, since John leaps for joy and Elizabeth calls Jesus "my Lord" (cf Ps 110:1/ Lk 20:41–44). John appears to demonstrate his prenatal filling with the Holy Spirit (see v 15) by leaping with joy (cf Gen 25:22–23), joy being a theme of the infancy narrative (eg 1:14,47,58; 2:10) and beyond in Luke; even before John's birth he anticipates his later ministry of bearing witness to the Messiah (eg 3:15–17). Like her unborn child (v 15) and her husband (v 67), Elizabeth is "filled with the Holy Spirit" who inspires her to recognise and loudly proclaim the blessedness of Mary ("among women" only she will bear God's Son; cf 11:27) and of her child, who is no less than the "Lord". Mary is commended too for her faith in the Lord's message, in contrast to Zechariah's unbelief (v 20) – another instance of her exemplary discipleship (also v 38).

Outline Luke's characterisation of the two mothers and their unborn children in the passage above.

Mary's song of praise (1:46–55)

Immediately after Elizabeth's words to Mary we have Mary's song of praise to God, for what he has done for her and to others. The passage may be outlined as follows.

| v 46–49 | God's acts for Mary |
| v 50–55 | God's acts to others |

The Gospel of Luke

Also known as the Magnificat, after the Latin translation of its opening Greek word, Mary's song is the first of four generally recognised songs/canticles in the infancy narrative (see also v 67–79; 2:13–14,28–32). It has been speculated that these songs may have been added later to the infancy narrative, since they are mostly not specifically related to their contexts. Thus, if Mary's song were removed, verse 56 would naturally follow verse 45. However, the wording of the song provides several links with its broader context (eg in a literal translation cf v 46/58 – both have the same Greek verb, meaning 'magnify, make great'; cf also 47/44; 48/38; 48/42,45). Various views exist concerning the source of the songs. For instance, while some hold that Mary composed the song as the text implies, other suggestions are that Luke created it or that it is a Jewish or Jewish-Christian hymn which Luke may have adapted. Further, some Latin manuscripts attribute the song to Elizabeth rather than to Mary in verse 46, as do some early Church Fathers. Nevertheless, the best manuscript evidence favours the traditional view.

While the song is comparable with many Old Testament hymns of praise (eg Ex 15; Judg 5), it is linked especially to Hannah's prayer (1 Sam 2:1–10) by similar circumstances (miraculous conception of a significant child) and common themes (eg joy in, and holiness of, the Lord; reversal of fortunes of poor/weak and rich/powerful). Like such Jewish hymns, it is marked too by poetically parallel lines (eg v 46–47; 52–53) and an emphasis on God's acts – note the frequent verbs, relating to God's past deeds. Old Testament links are apparent too with Israel as the Servant of the Lord in Isaiah (v 54; Isa 49:3), descent from Abraham (v 55; Gen 12:1–3), and possible echoes of the Exodus from Egypt (v 51; Ex 6:1,6). Thus, as throughout the infancy narrative, the focus is on the fulfilment of Israel's national hopes and history in the coming of John and Jesus.

Mary's song immediately follows and parallels Elizabeth's blessing. Structurally, although the song moves from God's dealings with Mary to his dealings with others, these two parts remain united by common terms such as "servant" (v 48,54), "lowliness/lowly" (v 48,52) and "mercy" (v 50,54; if v 50 is viewed as the conclusion to the first section). Two complementary characterisations of God are held in balance as the song proceeds – God the warrior, who acts mightily for his people and against their enemies (v 49,51–53), and the God of the covenant, who in mercy remembers his people of old (v 48,50,54–55). The song also contains several Lucan themes, familiar in the infancy narrative and beyond, such as praise, joy, reversal of poverty and wealth (compare especially with Jesus' Beatitudes: 6:20–26), and the expression "from now on" (v 48), which sees the birth of the Messiah as a significant turning point (note other such occurrences in 5:10; 12:52; 22:18,69; Acts 18:6).

Task

Outline your knowledge and understanding of Mary's song, with particular reference to its:

a) Old Testament background   b) structure
c) view of God   d) themes

The birth, circumcision and naming of John the Baptist (1:56–66)

After Mary's song Luke tells us that she stayed with Elizabeth for about three months, until John was born (v 36,56), and then returned home. Luke now narrates this birth, though Mary is not specifically mentioned in the narrative.

| v 56–58 | John's birth |
| v 59–66 | John's circumcision and naming |

The prophecies and expectations of Gabriel's annunciation of John's birth to Zechariah (v 11–20) now begin to be "fulfilled in their time" (v 20) – Elizabeth gives birth to a son (v 13,57), Zechariah names him John (v 13,62–63), many rejoice at his birth (v 14,58), and Zechariah's speech is restored on the day these things occur (v 20,64). Also, Elizabeth's relatives and friends, as well as Luke himself, confirm earlier statements that these events are the Lord's doing (v 13,15,25,58,66). Indeed, the responses of the people to the events are typical reactions in Luke to the miraculous and supernatural – amazement (v 63; eg 8:25; 9:43) and fear (v 65; eg 1:12; 8:25). Further, Elizabeth's view that the social and cultural shame of her barrenness had been removed with her pregnancy (v 25) is now confirmed in the very public celebration of John's birth (v 58). Again, even though the people are apparently unaware of Gabriel's words concerning the significant future of this child (v 15–17), due to the events surrounding his birth they voice an expectation of something unusual ahead for him (v 66). Like Mary elsewhere in the infancy narrative (2:19,51), the people ponder "in their heart" (v 66, author's translation), but their musings are about John and others will follow them in this (3:15; all these verses have "in her/their heart(s)" in Luke's Greek).

The circumcision of John on the eighth day reinforces the Jewish context of the infancy narratives, since this was the sign of God's covenant with Abraham and his descendants, echoing the closing words of Mary's song (v 55; Gen 17:11–12). John's circumcision also highlights another theme of the infancy narrative, namely the compliance of both sets of parents with the Law of the Lord (1:6; 2:21–24,27,39,41). However, the emphasis in the passage falls on the naming of the child, which occurred at the birth in earlier biblical history (eg Gen 21:3–4) but on the day of circumcision in later Judaism. While the initial decision to name the child after the father does not appear to have been a requirement of contemporary Jewish culture, it was possibly seen as a fitting gesture to the elderly and now handicapped priest. Elizabeth insisted on the name 'John'. In the Old Testament it was most often the mother who named the child, at times assisted by neighbouring women (v 59: "they"; Ruth 4:17). This choice of name and its confirmation by Zechariah is stressed to underline its divine origin and the fulfilment of Gabriel's words (v 13). Unlike the Old Testament (eg Gen 25:26), Luke does not draw attention to the meanings of the names of the children of his infancy narrative, but the appropriateness of the name John ('Yahweh has been gracious/shown favour') may have been noted by informed readers (v 28,30). As soon as Zechariah confirms the divinely-given name, Gabriel's prophecy is fulfilled and Zechariah's first use of his restored speech is, fittingly, to bless God (in the Greek; also 2:28; 24:53), the praise of God being a regular Lucan theme.

> **Tasks**
>
> a Outline the links between this passage and other parts of the infancy narrative.
>
> b Discuss the significance of John's circumcision and naming.

Zechariah's song of praise (1:67–80)

After the naming of his son, Zechariah praises God for the coming of the salvation long promised for his people and prophesies concerning the future ministries of John and Jesus.

v 67	Introduction
v 68–75	Zechariah's praise
v 76–79	Zechariah's prophecy
v 80	Conclusion

Zechariah's song is also known as the Benedictus after the Latin translation of its opening word and, like the other songs in the infancy narrative, is thought by some to be a later addition, with verse 80 originally following verse 66. However, there are links with the broader context – for example, the opening word in the Greek recalls Zechariah's blessing of God a few verses earlier (v 64), and the prophecy about John echoes verses 16 and 17 and answers the question of the people which immediately precedes the song (v 66). As with Mary's song, there has been speculation about its origins. For instance, while some hold that it came from Zechariah as the text states, others argue that Luke composed it or that it was a Jewish/Jewish-Christian hymn or a hymn from followers of John the Baptist which Luke adapted.

Luke introduces the song by telling us that Zechariah was "filled with the Holy Spirit", as were his unborn child (v 15) and wife (v 41) before him. This undoubtedly accounts for Luke's use of the term "prophesied" (author's translation) to describe Zechariah's words, indicating that his speech was a message inspired by God through his Spirit (cf Acts 2:17–18; 11:27–28). As a response to the birth of the promised child, the passage is paralleled by the response of the shepherds and the angels (2:8ff) and Simeon's song (2:28–32) after Jesus' birth. In addition, as with the other songs of the infancy narrative, this is a pause in the story for reflection on the religious meaning of these events. Though the song has two distinct parts, they are united by common terms and themes, for example visit (v 68,78 – same Greek verb in each verse), salvation (v 69,77 – a Lucan emphasis), prophets (v 70,76), and mercy (v 72,78). The first section locates the birth of John as part of the salvation history and hopes of Israel, as a fulfilment of God's covenantal promises to Abraham through the prophets of old. The nationalistic, even political, tone in this first part of the passage (Israel, house of David, Abraham, saved from our enemies), is similar to what we found in Mary's song (v 54–55). However, it is clearly linked with religious and ethical concerns (v 74). While the past tenses of the opening verses have led some to regard this first section of the song as being originally about Jesus' birth, it seems rather that for Zechariah the process of salvation had already begun in events thus far.

With its second part the song moves from speaking about God to directly addressing the newborn child (v 76). Already knowing that Jesus would be "the Son of the Most High" (v 32), now we read of John's inferior role as "a prophet of the Most High" who will but prepare the way for the Lord (cf v 17; 3:3–6; 7:24–27). John's role in relation to "salvation" and "forgiveness of ... sins" – two important Lucan themes – will be recalled at the beginning of his ministry (3:3–6). Zechariah then concludes his song with reference to Jesus as the "dawn from on high". While Luke's Greek word here (*anatole*: 'rising') was used in the Greek Old Testament for the "Branch" from David's line who would be king (eg Jer 23:5), the context in Zechariah's song seems to reflect the Messiah's role as a bringer of light (cf Simeon's song: 2:29–32), especially in Isaiah (eg 9:1–7; 60:1–3). Immediately following the song Luke provides a summary statement of John's growth (as he will do twice for Jesus: 2:40,52), in terms similar to those used of two special Old Testament children, Samson (Judg 13:24–25) and Samuel (1 Sam 2:21). This summary statement acts as a link between John's infancy and the beginning of his ministry as an adult in chapter 3. He is absent from the second chapter of Luke's infancy narrative, which deals exclusively with Jesus.

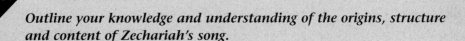

Outline your knowledge and understanding of the origins, structure and content of Zechariah's song.

The birth, circumcision and naming of Jesus (2:1–21)

The focus now moves from John the Baptist to Jesus.

v 1–5	The registration/census
v 6–7	Jesus' birth

v 8–12	An angel's announcement
v 13–14	The angels' song
v 15–20	Reactions
v 21	Jesus' circumcision and naming

The parallels between the birth accounts of John and Jesus are not as numerous as those we have noted between the annunciation accounts, yet there are similarities. There are similar descriptions of the timing and occurrence of the births, and references to joy, amazement and reflection of heart, as well as to the circumcisions and divinely chosen names. However, obvious differences serve to underline the superiority of Jesus, whose birth account is notably longer, has more public and heavenly dimensions (shepherds and angels), and attaches far greater significance to the identity and impact of the child. It has been argued more generally that Luke 2 appears to be unaware of Luke 1 since, for example, Jesus' parents are introduced as if for the first time (v 4–5/ 1:26–27), there is no sense of Jesus' virgin conception (v 27,33,41,43,48/ 1:27,34–37; later scribes altered the 'offending' wording in ch 2), and Mary appears to be unaware of Jesus' status as Son of God (v 49–50/ 1:32,35). But this may be reading too much into the wording of Luke 2 which, as we have noted and will note again below, has clear links with the previous chapter.

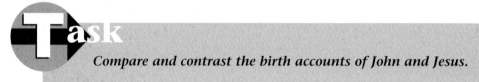

Compare and contrast the birth accounts of John and Jesus.

The setting of Jesus' birth within the context of a decree by Emperor Augustus is not just another example of Luke's general interest in relating early Christianity to Roman history (eg 3:1), but may also indicate that even a pagan ruler may unknowingly serve the God of Israel's purpose (cf Cyrus: Isa 45), namely by making Bethlehem the Messiah's birthplace as expected (Mic 5:2/ Mt 2:3–6). The compliance of Joseph and Mary with the imperial decree may also serve a possible apologetic goal of Luke in showing that Jesus did not come from a politically revolutionary family. Reference should be made here to our earlier discussion of the historical problems associated with Luke's registration/census – no other evidence of an empire-wide census in Augustus' time, the governorship and census of Quirinius coming some 10 years after Jesus' birth, no Roman requirement to return to ancestral homes, and the improbability of a Roman census in Herod's domain (see pp43–44). The important theological point in this passage, however, is Luke's desire to highlight the Davidic origins of Jesus' birthplace (v 4,11; though Jerusalem was normally so described, eg 2 Sam 5:6–9), a continuation of the Davidic theme of the previous chapter (1:27,32,69). As well as reaffirming that Mary had not previously given birth, the reference to Jesus as "firstborn" also prepares the reader for his presentation in the temple (v 22–23) and implies his inheritance rights as the adopted son of his Davidic father, Joseph (1:32).

The customary bands of cloth (eg Ezek 16:4; Wisdom 7:4–6) were wrapped around the newborn to keep his limbs straight. That he was laid in a "manger", that is, an animals' feeding trough, has led to the assumption that animals were present (influenced too by Isa 1:3), though this is not stated by Luke. Nor indeed may there have been an "inn", since Luke's word may refer to a 'guest room' (as in 22:11), and he uses a different word for a commercial inn (10:34). Rather, it may be that there was no space in the single-room peasant house in which they were lodging and use had to be made of the manger in the animals' section of the room. The one destined for a throne (1:32–33) begins his life in a trough, and Luke will later report similar accommodation problems in Jesus' ministry (9:58). The humble circumstances of Jesus' family background and beginnings is a recurring theme of the infancy narrative.

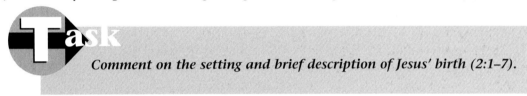

Comment on the setting and brief description of Jesus' birth (2:1–7).

Parallel to Zechariah's response to the birth of John is the response of shepherds and angels to the birth of Jesus. While the mention of shepherds near Bethlehem is fitting, since this is the town of the shepherd David (1 Sam 16:1,4,11), it seems that the shepherds are here representative of the humble, ordinary people for whom God's salvation has come. Thus, as indicated already in Mary's song, it is the "lowly" rather than the "powerful" whom God has lifted up (1:48,52). The angelic announcement of the Saviour's birth is not made to Augustus or Quirinius (v 1–2), but to ordinary shepherds on the nightshift near Bethlehem. The anonymous "angel of the Lord", who may be the Gabriel of the annunciations (1:19,26), is accompanied by the "glory of the Lord" shining into the night (cf 1:78–79) – a dramatic display of the presence of God (eg Ex 16:10) which Luke will mention again (9:30–31; Acts 7:55). As with the other angelic appearances, the human reaction is one of fear (1:12–13,30).

The angel's message contains Luke's characteristic themes. He "bring[s] ... good news" (the verb occurs frequently in Luke–Acts), reflecting Isaiah's language (eg 40:9; 52:7; 61:1–2/ Lk 4:17–19), and describes it as "great joy" (also in 24:52) in contrast to the "great fear" (as Luke's Greek has it) of the shepherds in the previous verse (v 9). Also typical of Luke is the emphasis on "today" (author's translation; cf eg 4:21; 19:9; 23:43) for, unlike the future focus of previous angelic announcements, the promises of God's coming salvation are now being fulfilled in the present with the birth of Jesus.

In keeping with the nationalistic tone of the infancy narrative thus far, these events are said to be happening in David's town and are "for all the people", which in Luke refers mostly to Israel. Two of the three titles used by the angel for the child, Saviour and Lord, are favourites of Luke, and we have already noted his distinctive use of the third – Messiah/Christ (for discussion of the three titles, see pp30–31). As with the two previous angelic announcements, the message concludes with a confirmatory sign, with which the reader is already familiar (v 12,7; cf 1:20,36–37).

The angel is joined by many more "angels" (v 15), the multitude of the heavenly "host/army" (author's translation) being God's courtiers (eg 1 Kings 22:19; Neh 9:6). Their song of praise to God parallels other similar responses to God's acts in the infancy narrative (the songs of Mary and Zechariah), but the number and nature of the singers on this occasion highlights its importance – the Saviour has been born and a heavenly choir celebrates!

Their song, called the Gloria in Excelsis after the Latin of its opening words, consists of two broadly parallel lines with corresponding word pairs: glory/peace, highest (heaven)/earth, and God/people ("those whom he favours"). Similar words of praise will be uttered by another "multitude", again unique to Luke, at Jesus' entry to Jerusalem, except that the peace will be in heaven rather than earth (19:37–38). "Highest" (author's translation; eg 1:32,35,76; 6:35) and "peace" (eg 1:79; 2:29; 7:50) are, of course, favourite words of Luke's.

The peace on earth brought by the Saviour's birth (though contrast 12:51!) corresponds to the *shalom* (Hebrew: 'prosperity, wellbeing') that the prophets associated with the messianic age (eg Isa 9:6–7; Mic 5:2,4–5). The word "earth" may suggest the beginnings of a vision broader than the nationalistic emphasis of the infancy narrative thus far, but the peace is immediately limited to "people of [God's] goodwill/favour" (according to the best manuscripts). Luke's readers will soon see that this includes those beyond the nation of Israel (v 30–32). The language used in these verses is similar, maybe intentionally so, to that used of the Emperor Augustus – his divine birthday was viewed by politicians in Asia Minor as the beginning of "good news" for the world and he was described as a "saviour" and "lord" who had brought "peace" in his domain[1]. This may have been read as a political challenge by some (eg 23:2; Acts 17:7); certainly Luke's claim is that it is the reign of Christ rather than Caesar that brings these benefits.

After the angels leave, Luke reports a number of reactions to the unfolding events – the responses of the shepherds, hearers of their message, and Mary. All these reactions appear to be presented to the reader as exemplary – the speed with which the shepherds sought the Saviour, as well as their spreading of the news (the first evangelists) and their praise of God; the amazement of those who heard (cf 1:65; 4:22, etc); and Mary's inner reflection (cf v 51; 1:66; also Gen 37:11; Dan 7:28). The circumcision and naming of the child parallels what we have read of John (see comment on 1:59ff, pp57–58) and reminds us that Jesus came as a descendant of Abraham and as a member of God's covenant people, Israel.

---

[1] See Fitzmyer, *The Gospel According to Luke I–IX* (op cit), pp393–394

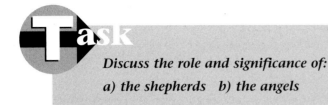

Discuss the role and significance of:
a) the shepherds   b) the angels

The presentation of Jesus in the temple (2:22–40)

The rest of the infancy narrative returns to the setting with which it began – the temple in Jerusalem. Before the final episode (2:41–52), Jesus' parents visit the temple for their purification and to present the infant Jesus to the Lord. While there, they meet Simeon and then Anna, two devout prophets who see in Jesus what they had long been waiting for – the fulfilment of God's promises concerning Israel.

v 22–23	Presentation of Jesus
v 24	Purification of parents
v 25–35	Simeon meets the family
v 36–38	Anna meets the family
v 39	Family's return to Nazareth
v 40	Growth of Jesus

Throughout this section Luke repeatedly draws attention to how Joseph and Mary observed the Law of the Lord (v 22–24,27,39; also v 21,41–42). Thus, as with John's parents (1:6), they are characterised as devout Jews and, yet again in the infancy narrative, the continuity of Jesus and early Christianity with Judaism is underlined. For the only time in the infancy narrative Luke 'quotes' (neither citation is an exact quotation) the Old Testament to explain the two purposes for which the family have travelled to Jerusalem. Firstly, Luke links Jesus' presentation to the Lord with the Old Testament requirement that first-born males be consecrated to the Lord (Ex 13:2,12,15). The words "holy to the Lord" (v 23) recall Gabriel's words concerning Jesus (1:35). Though Luke doesn't mention it, this consecration was a means of financial support for the Jewish priesthood, since five shekels were paid to redeem first-born sons from the priesthood when they were a month old (Num 18:7,14 –16). Luke's description of the event as the presentation of Jesus to the Lord may reflect the story of Samuel (1 Sam 1:22,24,28). The second purpose of the visit was the need to offer a sacrifice for the purification of the mother after childbirth. The regulations for this in Leviticus 12, which Luke partially quotes, state that a woman was ceremonially unclean for 40 days after the birth of a son, after which time she must bring an offering to the sanctuary. Luke refers to "their" purification, even though it was only Mary's, and some think that this may reflect Luke's ignorance or Greek influence, where both mother and child were considered impure. However, the pronoun (which was changed variously by later scribes) may indicate that Luke viewed this broadly as a family concern. The sacrifice that was offered underlines the poverty of Jesus' family (v 24/ Lev 12:8).

Explain the Old Testament background of the two purposes of the family's visit to Jerusalem.

With Simeon and Anna Luke introduces one of his characteristic male–female pairings, such as Zechariah and Mary earlier in the infancy narrative (see Women, p37). Echoing recurring themes of these opening chapters of Luke, they are characterised as two elderly, devout Jews who symbolise the hopes of Israel and praise God for the fulfilment of those hopes in the birth of Jesus. Along with the angels and inspired songs in these chapters, they represent both divine legitimation and interpretation of the birth of Jesus. Their devotion to God and link with the temple recalls Zechariah and Elizabeth (1:5ff). And their "looking for" (author's translation; the same Greek word is used in v 25 and v 38; also in 23:51) the "consolation of Israel" (Simeon) or the "redemption of Jerusalem" (Anna) not only reflects the language of Isaiah (Isa 40:1; 51:3; 52:9), but also frames this whole section of Luke within the broader context (v 39 follows naturally from v 22–24).

The three references to the Spirit in connection with Simeon represent an important emphasis throughout the infancy narrative and also present him in prophetic terms, since the Spirit is "upon him" (author's translation; as in Isa 61:1/ Lk 4:18) and has imparted a revelation to him. This inspired message was that he would see the "Lord's Messiah" (see also 2:11; 9:20; 23:35) before he died. To fulfil this, while it was God's "law" that had brought Jesus and his parents to the temple, God's "Spirit" brought Simeon there – either way, their meeting was a divinely inspired realisation of God's purpose.

Simeon's song of praise, also known as the Nunc Dimittis after its opening words in Latin, parallels other similar songs in the infancy narrative. Containing six lines arranged in three pairs, it highlights typical Lucan themes. Its opening word in the Greek – "now" – stresses that God's plan is coming to pass in the present. Again, only Luke among the four Gospels has God termed "Master" (author's translation; Greek *despotes*; also in Acts 4:24), of whom Simeon is the "servant". We note too the Lucan themes of "peace" (eg 1:79; 2:14) and "salvation" (here, Jesus is called God's salvation). And Luke's dual concern to relate Jesus to both "Israel" and the "Gentiles" forms the climax of the song. Indeed, for the first time in an otherwise very Jewish infancy narrative we have an explicit statement of one of Luke's leading themes – the universal scope of God's salvation (hinted at earlier in v 14). The song's language – relating to salvation for all, light for the Gentiles and glory for Israel – is heavily influenced by several passages in Isaiah which concern the Servant of the Lord and Israel's role as a light to the nations (eg Isa 42:6; 46:13; 49:6; 52:10; 60:1–3). Now Israel's Messiah takes up her mission and brings light to the Gentiles (eg 1:78–79; Acts 26:22–23), as indeed his followers will do also (Acts 13:47).

Simeon's song is followed by the amazement of the parents (a common response to divine activity in these chapters and beyond), and his almost priestly blessing of them (eg Num 6:23), which once again recalls the story of Samuel (1 Sam 2:20). Simeon then has words for Mary which contrast sharply with the positive tone of his song. Her child will be the cause of mixed fortunes for many in Israel (cf Isa 8:14–15; 28:16) and will expose the inner thoughts of many (cf 12:1–3). Indeed, Mary is cryptically told that a sword would pierce her own soul (cf Ps 37:15). This may refer to the loss of her son to his higher calling (v 48–50; 8:19–21; 11:27–28; Jn 2:4) or specifically to her witnessing of his crucifixion (Jn 19:25–27). Simeon's words thus set up for the reader both positive and negative expectations for the story of Jesus that lies ahead.

The female counterpart to Simeon is Anna, whose credentials as a reliable witness are stressed by Luke. She is a prophet, recalling female messengers of God in Israel's history such as Deborah and Miriam, and anticipating similar messengers in Luke's sequel (Acts 2:17–18; 21:9). Further, her Jewish pedigree is underlined (father and tribe), as is the dignity of her old age. Luke particularly draws attention to her status as a widow (a Lucan emphasis). Whether she was a widow until she was 84 (after seven years of marriage) or for 84 years, she is presented as the ideal devout widow who never remarried but rather devoted herself to prayer and fasting, such as the apocryphal/deuterocanonical Judith (Judith 8:4–8; 16:22) and early Christian widows (I Tim 5:3ff). Her devotion to worship, prayer and the temple reflects yet more Lucan themes. Like Simeon she praises God (though the details are not given) after meeting the family and, like the shepherds, she speaks to others about Jesus – specifically to those expecting the redemption of Jerusalem (one of six references to the city in this chapter, and also a Lucan theme).

The passage concludes with a reference to the family's return to their home town. There is also a summary of the child's growth (another will appear in v 52), similar to the earlier note on John the Baptist's development (1:80), and reminiscent of Samson (Judg 13:24) and Samuel (1 Sam 2:21,26; 3:19). The summaries of the growth of John and Jesus (1:80; 2:40) are paralleled by Luke's later summaries of the growth of God's word in the book of Acts (6:7; 12:24; 19:20; the same Greek verb is used in both sets of references).

Task

Discuss the function of the Simeon and Anna stories within the infancy narrative and show how they contain characteristic Lucan themes.

The boy Jesus in the temple (2:41–52)

The climactic passage in Luke's infancy narrative, like the previous one some 12 years earlier, finds Jesus and his parents in the temple in Jerusalem. Here the boy Jesus amazes Jewish teachers with his understanding and puzzles his parents with words about God his Father.

v 41–42	Family visit to Jerusalem for Passover
v 43–44	Parents' return journey without Jesus
v 44–46	Parents' search for Jesus
v 46–47	Jesus and the teachers
v 48–51	Jesus and his parents
v 52	Jesus' growth

If we take the preceding verse (v 40) as the beginning of this section, then it starts and ends (v 52) with a reference to Jesus' development, which acts as a frame for the story. Also, both these verses contain two key themes of the story – Jesus' "wisdom" (see v 47) and his relationship to God (God's "favour/grace", author's translation; see also v 48–49; and Mary in 1:30). Luke alone of the evangelists has a boyhood story of Jesus and indeed an interest in the age of Jesus; as well as this reference to Jesus being "twelve years old", we read of his circumcision after "eight days" (2:21) and that he was "about thirty years" (3:23) when he began his ministry. This story, in fact, along with its summary statements about Jesus' growth, serves as a link between his birth/infancy (chs 1–2) and his baptism which marks the beginning of his ministry (ch 3). Luke's inclusion of a boyhood story of Jesus may, among other things, have met an early Christian curiosity about the 'hidden years' of Jesus' life. From the second century on we have legendary accounts of Jesus' miraculous childhood activities, such as in the apocryphal *Infancy Gospel of Thomas* where we read, for instance, of Jesus bringing clay sparrows to life, fatally cursing boys who offended him and astonishing a teacher with his knowledge. Luke's story, by comparison, is more restrained and less fanciful. Gentile Luke may have known of stories of childhood prodigy and precocity common in Graeco-Roman biographies (eg Plutarch on Alexander the Great; Suetonius on Augustus) and Jewish writings (eg Josephus on Moses and Samuel; Philo on Moses), and which were usually associated with the age 12. Of particular relevance are Josephus' comments (late first century) that Samuel already held the office of prophet by the age of 12 (*Ant* 5.10.4) and that the three-year-old Moses had an "understanding" beyond his "stature/years" (*Ant* 2.9.6; cf Lk 2:47,52). While some regard Luke's unique boyhood story of Jesus as a legend modelled on this common child-prodigy literature and similar to apocryphal childhood stories of Jesus, others note that Luke's story is comparatively more restrained and that he presents his work as based on careful historical research (1:1–4).

Yet another example of the religious devotion of Jesus' parents (cf v 21–24, 27,39) is found in their annual trip to Jerusalem for Passover (as required by Deut 16:1–8,16), reminiscent of the annual pilgrimage of Samuel's parents (1 Sam 1:3,7,21; 2:19). Luke's reference to Jesus being 12 probably indicates that he was starting to move from childhood to maturity, though rabbis connected this more with the age 13. That this may have been Jesus' Bar Mitzvah – when a Jewish boy became a 'son of the commandment' and accepted adult responsibilities – is unclear since the evidence for this is from a later period. After the week-long festival was over, Jesus' parents did not realise that he was not among their fellow travellers until they camped at the close of the first day. They found him back in the temple among the Jewish teachers, of whom he appears almost as a pupil (v 46) and then as a teacher himself (v 47). The focus on Jesus' "understanding" recalls the references to Jesus' "wisdom" in the introduction and conclusion of the passage and may imply that Jesus is the long-expected Messiah (Isaiah 11:1–2).

Tasks

a Explain how the introduction and conclusion of this passage highlight its key themes.

b What factors may have influenced Luke to include a boyhood story of Jesus in his Gospel?

c Discuss the possible significance of Jesus' age in this passage.

Jesus "amazed" the Jewish teachers (indeed "everyone", author's translation), introducing the theme of his superiority over them. He also "astonished" his parents, not because of his wisdom but due to his apparent disregard for them. Mary's rebuke (v 48) begins a dialogue on the central and climactic theme of this episode – whose son is Jesus? Who is the true father of Jesus? While Luke regularly calls Joseph one of the "parents" of Jesus in this passage (v 27,41,43; though later scribes 'corrected' him!) and Mary refers to Joseph as "your father" when speaking to Jesus, Jesus immediately replies by calling God "my Father". Jesus will again speak of God in such personal terms in this Gospel (10:22; 22:29; 24:49) and when speaking to his disciples will refer to God as "your Father" (6:36; 12:30,32), but never as 'our Father' including himself, since his is a unique divine sonship (10:22).

In this passage we have Jesus' first words and first active part in Luke, and the dramatic pronouncement of the whole episode. His parents "did not understand", in contrast to the amazing "understanding" of Jesus. And Mary's lack of understanding of Jesus' words is hard for the reader to understand, since in the narrative Gabriel had told her that Jesus was the son, not of Joseph, but of God (1:32–35). This theme of Jesus' divine sonship will be continued in the next chapter (3:22–23,38 – Jesus' baptism and genealogy) and beyond (eg 4:3,9 – Jesus' temptation). Jesus certainly

The Gospel of Luke

expected them to know that he had to be in his "Father's house" or about his "Father's interests" (author's translation) or "with the ones of" (author's translation) his Father.

Mary was now possibly beginning to see the fulfilment of Simeon's disturbing prophecy (v 35), as she is told that Jesus' divine sonship has priority over his human sonship – he is son of God before he is son of Mary (cf 8:19–21; 12:51–53; 14:26). She is beginning to lose her son to his divine mission. Indeed, that priority is given to his relationship with God is a "must", a favourite word of Luke's (Greek *dei*, eg 4:43; 9:22), indicating a strong sense of divine vocation and destiny even as a youth. In fact, it has been argued that this whole passage is a foreshadowing of the climactic events of Jesus' ministry and life at the other end of this Gospel – later Jesus will again travel from Galilee to Jerusalem for Passover (9:51ff; 22:7ff), will again question the teachers in the temple and amaze them and others with his answers (eg 20:1–3,17,23,26,39–40; 21:37–38; 22:53), will again stress the 'must' of his divine vocation (eg 22:37; 24:7,25–27,44), and will again be missing for three days (23:54–24:1ff). Also, there will again be a lack of awareness by two on a journey from Jerusalem (24:13ff). Impressive though these coincidences appear to be at first sight, close study of the similarities reveals that Luke himself does not consciously exploit them.

Lest anyone misread Jesus' behaviour and words in the temple as disrespect for or insubordination to his parents, Luke rounds off the passage with a reference to his obedience to them back in Nazareth (cf 18:20). We also have the final of several instances of inward reflection in Luke's infancy narrative, as Mary "treasured all these things in her heart" (cf v 19; 1:29,66). As Luke brings his infancy narrative to a close, this may be his way of inviting the reader also to keep all these events in mind as the story continues into the main body of the Gospel.

Tasks

a Discuss how the passage characterises Jesus' relationship to:
    (i) the Jewish teachers   (ii) his parents   (iii) God
b Assess the claim that this incident foreshadows Jesus' later life and ministry.

Selected narratives

> 1 (a) Outline your knowledge and understanding of the structure of Luke's Gospel. (30)
>
> (b) Comment on the claim that in his infancy narrative Luke compares and contrasts John the Baptist and Jesus. (15)
>
> 2 (a) Outline your knowledge and understanding of Luke's account of either the presentation of Jesus in the temple or the 12-year-old Jesus in the temple. (30)
>
> (b) Explore the claim that the canticles or songs of Luke's infancy narrative are not specifically related to it. (15)

JOHN THE BAPTIST

Before we move on to Luke's journey narrative, we need briefly to consider Luke's presentation of John the Baptist beyond the infancy narrative. In addition to the material on John in the first chapter of the infancy narrative, which we have already considered, the following passages should be noted.

John's preaching and imprisonment (3:1–20)

Luke picks up the story of John again after previously leaving him in the desert until his public appearance to Israel (1:80). The time (note the six-fold dating in v 1–2) for this public appearance has arrived. John, now about 30 years old (cf v 23), is still in the desert and there receives a message from God in the way that Old Testament prophets had before him (cf v 2 with, for example, Jer 1:1–2; Hos 1:1; Joel 1:1). He now begins the prophetic ministry that was anticipated in the infancy narrative (1:16–17,76–77) – verses which also anticipated his preparatory role, now underlined by Luke's quotation of Isaiah 40:3–5 (v 4–6). These words from Isaiah, originally about the return of the Jews from exile in Babylon through the desert to Israel, are given a fresh application to John since the language is appropriate (voice calling in the desert, prepare). While all the evangelists quote this passage in relation to John, only Luke extends it to include two of his favourite themes: "salvation" for "all flesh" (v 6; Greek OT).

John's preaching is summarised as "a baptism of repentance for the forgiveness of sins" (v 3). Luke will later describe Christian baptism in almost the same terms (Peter in Acts 2:38). Repentance is turning from sin to God and is illustrated by three examples (v 7–14: crowds, tax collectors and soldiers). This repentance involved baptism (Greek *baptisma*: 'immersion, dipping, washing') and resulted in "forgiveness of sins", a Lucan theme connected with John's ministry in the infancy narrative (1:76–77). Various suggestions have been made about the background and origins of John's baptism, such as ritual washings practised in the Old Testament and later Judaism, particularly as found among the Qumran community which produced the Dead Sea Scrolls. The Qumran community (probably Essenes), which was located in the same general area as John, practised an initiatory immersion into membership of the community, followed by regular immersions to maintain purity. While some have argued that John was influenced by Jewish proselyte baptism, which Gentile converts to Judaism had to undergo, it is not certain that this practice existed before AD 70. Since John's baptism is both like and unlike these various ritual washings at different points, it is probably best to see his baptising ministry against a general Jewish background of ritual washing for physical and moral cleansing – especially the latter, in light of John's ethical emphasis on repentance (cf Isa 1:16–17; Zech 13:1). One unusual aspect of John's practice was that the baptism was performed by him rather than self-administered, as was normally the case in Judaism.

Three groups ask John what they should do (v 7–14, of which v 10–14 are unique to Luke) and in each case John requires practical evidence of repentance, relating to money and the poor (key themes in Luke). In addressing the "crowds" John uses the illustration of trees bearing fruit to underline the need for evidence of repentance and tells his Jewish hearers not to rely merely on their racial descent from Abraham (v 8; cf 1:54–55,72–73). The urgency of this repentance is stressed by John's references to the imminent judgement of God throughout the passage – the coming wrath, the axe "even now" at the root of the trees, the winnowing-fork already in hand, and the fire (twice: v 9,17). The demand to share clothing and food with the needy recalls the message of Old Testament prophets (eg Isa 1:10–20; Ezek 18:5–9) and anticipates the teaching of Jesus, especially in Luke (eg 12:33; 16:19ff; 18:22). "Even" tax collectors came, says Luke, reflecting their despised status as those who financially exploited their position and collaborated with the Roman enemy. Yet in unique, positive references to them, here and elsewhere (18:9–14; 19:1–10), Luke stresses his concern for them. John requires financial honesty of the tax collectors in their dealings with others, as he does next with the soldiers who may have assisted them in their collection of revenue. The poor wages of the soldiers may have tempted them, like the tax collectors, to make dishonest financial gain from the public.

Luke alone of the synoptics notes the sense of expectancy among the people and their speculation about John being the Messiah/Christ (v 15; see p31). John's response (v 16–17) clearly implies that while he is not the Messiah, the coming one is. Thus, the unequal John–Jesus parallelism of the infancy narrative is continued. John contrasts the baptisers and their baptisms. The coming one (Jesus) is "more powerful" than John, who is not worthy to untie his sandals (ie to be his servant; Mt 3:11 has "carry his sandals"). While John baptises in/with water, Jesus will baptise in/with the Holy Spirit and fire. In the sequel to his Gospel Luke sees the fulfilment of this on the day of Pentecost and beyond (Acts 1:5; 2:1ff; 11:15–16). The word 'fire' is not mentioned in these later references since it may refer to the Spirit's refining and purifying work (cf eg Isa 4:4; Mal 3:1–3). However, in the context of Luke 3, "fire" is used twice of God's judgement (v 9,17; cf 12:49ff, yet 9:54ff). Thus, John may be saying that Jesus will perform two contrasting baptisms – the repentant will receive the Holy Spirit (a Lucan emphasis, not least in the preceding infancy narrative) and the unrepentant God's wrath. These two activities of Jesus are immediately illustrated with the use of current farming practices – as the threshed wheat is tossed into the wind (winnowing) to separate the grain from the chaff, so Jesus will separate the righteous and unrighteous to their different fates. Luke adds by way of summary that John issued many other exhortations to the people, using a favourite verb meaning 'to announce good news' (v 18). If the verb does not mean simply 'preach, proclaim' here, then Luke may want to link the ministries of John and Jesus (cf 4:18,43).

Luke concludes his account of John's ministry by referring to his imprisonment by "Herod the tetrarch" (author's translation), that is Herod Antipas, tetrarch of Galilee (v 1), to be distinguished from his father King Herod the Great, during whose reign Jesus was born (1:5). Luke vaguely says that John had rebuked him "because of Herodias, his brother's wife". Mark tells us that the brother was Philip (cf Lk 3:1) and that Antipas had married his wife (Mk 6:17–18), in breach of Jewish Law (Lev 18:16; 20:21). Luke alone mentions that John also rebuked him for all the evil things he had done. Thus, John is portrayed as prophets of old who had challenged immoral rulers (especially Elijah: 1 Kings 21:17ff), and the negative response of a ruler to God's word is contrasted with the positive response of the lowly (v 10–14; cf 1:52). The record of John's imprisonment at this point, rather than later as in the other synoptics, clearly separates the ministry of John from that of Jesus, which begins in the next verse with Jesus' baptism (v 21). While it is implicit that John baptised Jesus, Luke does not mention John's involvement, unlike the other Gospels.

Tasks

a How does Luke characterise John as he introduces his ministry (v 2)?

b Comment on the relevance of Luke's quotation from Isaiah to John's ministry (v 4–6).

c Outline the main elements of John's message.

d Discuss John's comments concerning the one who was to come (v 15–18).

e Comment on Luke's account of John's imprisonment (v 19–20).

The disciples of John and Jesus contrasted (5:33–39)

While the disciples of John and of the Pharisees (a strict Jewish religious sect) often fasted (Luke alone adds "and make prayers", author's translation; cf 11:1), Jesus' disciples did not[1]. Jesus explains that his ministry is like a wedding, in which he is the groom and his disciples the guests. Feasting and not fasting is appropriate on such an occasion. In the Old Testament God is pictured as Israel's groom, an image associated on occasion with the age of salvation in the end times (eg Isa 54:5–6; 62:4–5). However, in one of the earliest hints of the cross, Jesus says that the groom will be taken away and then fasting will be appropriate. While some hold that Jesus would not have spoken so early of his death, others note that already Jesus was experiencing hostility (4:28–30; 5:21,30). Jesus then used a parable (Greek *parabole*: 'comparison'; see Parables, p194ff) containing two illustrations which make the same point – the "new" (Jesus' ministry) is incompatible with the "old" (John the Baptist, the Pharisees). Thus, the old must give way to the new (v 38; cf 16:16).

Explain how this passage throws light on the differences between the ministries of John and Jesus.

John's question (7:18–23)

From his prison (assumed from 3:20; cf Mt 11:2ff), John sent two of his disciples to "the Lord" (a favourite title in Luke) to ask about Jesus' identity. Is Jesus the one who is to come or should they wait for another? The question is repeated to highlight the issue of Jesus' identity. John had spoken earlier of a coming one (ie the Messiah; 3:15ff) who was about to act in judgement (3:16–17). However, the reports of Jesus' ministry that were coming to John from his disciples (v 18) did not fit John's expectations. Jesus' ministry was one of salvation rather than condemnation (eg the events of ch 7 immediately preceding this). Jesus answers John's question with deeds (v 21) and words (v 22–23) which recall words from Isaiah (29:18–19; 35:5–6; 61:1) and the 'sermon' with which Jesus introduced and outlined his ministry (Lk 4:16–21/ Isa 61:1–2). Thus, Jesus answers John's question in the affirmative by providing evidence which confirms that he is the coming one, evidence consistent with Isaiah's picture of the coming age of salvation. His healing of the afflicted and his proclamation of good news to the poor indicate his identity. It is John's concept of the coming one that requires adjustment. This passage ends with a pronouncement or punch line (v 23), as do the others about John in this chapter (v 28; v 35) – a benediction on anyone (John or otherwise) who is not offended (Greek *skandalizomai*) by Jesus.

---

[1] See p51 for more information on the continued existence of John's disciples.

> **Task**
>
> *Explain how John's question and Jesus' response reveal a misunderstanding by John of Jesus' identity and mission.*

John's identity (7:24–30)

After John's disciples leave, Jesus asks the crowds three questions ("What did you go out to look at/see?", three times) focusing on John's identity. The first two answers are provided and dismissed by Jesus, and may represent contrasting options – a weak, insignificant person (reed shaken by the wind), or a wealthy member of the social elite (finely clothed, royal palaces). Jesus' third answer is the one he affirms. John is a prophet, as stated in the infancy narrative (1:76) and implied in the introduction to his ministry (3:2), that is, a messenger of God. But, says Jesus, John is "more than a prophet". He is the eschatological prophet (prophet of the end times) spoken of by Malachi, who would prepare the way for the Lord, the Elijah who would come before the great and terrible day of the Lord (Mal 3:1; 4:5; Jesus quotes a combination of Mal 3:1 and Ex 23:20). This preparatory role of John, along with the Elijah motif, was introduced in the infancy narrative (1:17,76) in language from Malachi and Isaiah, and reappeared at the beginning of John's ministry (3:4–6). The punch line with which Jesus ends this passage, before Luke's editorial comment (v 29–30), gives high praise to John (cf 1:15) but also accords a higher status to even the least person in God's kingdom. This may imply that John belonged to the old order rather than God's kingdom brought by Jesus (cf 5:33–39 16:16), or that whatever one's estimation of John or any prophet, being in God's kingdom is the greatest thing. Luke's editorial aside (v 29–30), which some take rather to be Jesus' own words, contrasts the responses to John of the Jewish religious leadership and the people ("even the tax collectors", author's translation; cf 3:12). While the people who heard Jesus' praise of John had "justified/vindicated" God (author's translation; the same Greek verb is used in v 35) by being baptised by John, the Pharisees and lawyers (scribes, experts in Jewish Law) had rejected "God's purpose" – a key theme in Luke – by not accepting his baptism.

> **Task**
>
> *Outline the attitudes of Jesus, the people and the religious leaders to John as portrayed in this passage.*

Responses to John and Jesus (7:31–35)

In this passage Jesus deals with contemporary responses to John and himself by telling a parable (v 31–32), explaining its application (v 33–34), and concluding with a punch line (v 35). Since this passage immediately follows Luke's comments about the negative response of the Jewish leaders to John (v 29–30), the "people of this generation" (v 31) will be understood by the reader to refer particularly to them. The application of the parable implies that the ascetic John (cf 1:15; 5:33; Mk 1:6), who will not change in accordance with the people's expectations, is represented by the children who would not dance to the tune of their peers. The more indulgent Jesus (cf 5:29–30), who likewise would not change to suit the wishes of others, is represented by the children who would not weep in response to the wailing of others. The difference in the lifestyles of John and Jesus and their respective disciples is thus highlighted again (cf 5:33–39). It is apparent too that John was being criticised for not doing the very thing that Jesus was being criticised for doing and vice versa! John's asceticism was viewed as evidence of demon possession and Jesus' lack of asceticism was viewed as overindulgence and keeping the wrong company. In the concluding punch line (v 35) "wisdom" stands for God (cf Prov 8:1–9:6) and is "justified/vindicated" (author's translation) by all her children, including those who "justified/vindicated God" by accepting John's baptism (v 29, author's translation), as well as John and Jesus themselves[1].

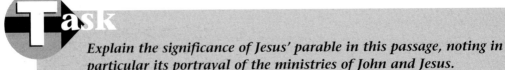

Explain the significance of Jesus' parable in this passage, noting in particular its portrayal of the ministries of John and Jesus.

Jesus is John? (9:7–9,18–20)

For the first time in Luke we are told that Herod Antipas, who had imprisoned John (3:19–20), had also beheaded him (Mt 14:3–12 and Mk 6:17–29 provide the details). Now Herod is perplexed because some were saying that Jesus was actually John back from the dead – in Mark's account Herod shares their view (Mk 6:16). A similar belief seems to be behind the disciples' answer to Jesus' question about popular views of him (v 18–19). This belief, along with his association with great prophets of the past (v 7–8,19), demonstrates that John was generally perceived as being a significant prophetic figure[2].

What can we learn about popular perceptions of John from these passages?

---

[1] Since the focus of our study at present is John the Baptist, the significance of Jesus' reference to himself in this passage as "the Son of Man" will be considered later.

[2] On the basis of this popular view of Jesus, Enoch Powell, a former MP for South Down, speculated that John rather than Jesus had risen from the dead, and that the Gospels were in fact records of John's ministry which were later corrupted! See RT France, *Matthew*, Tyndale New Testament Commentaries, Leicester: IVP, 1985, p233 footnote.

John and God's kingdom (16:16)

A direct translation of the part of this verse relating to John reads, "The Law and the Prophets were until John; from then the good news of the kingdom of God is proclaimed …". This important text (paralleled in Mt 11:12–13) concerns the place of John the Baptist in the history of salvation. The era of the Law and the Prophets (basically the Hebrew Bible/OT; cf eg 16:29,31; Acts 13:15) has given way to the new era of God's kingdom, yet, paradoxically, the former still apply (16:17,29,31). Which of these two eras does John belong to? The language is ambiguous. Some (eg Conzelmann) take "until" in an inclusive sense so that John belongs to the old era, while others (eg Marshall) view "until" exclusively and place John in the new era. While John, as the forerunner of Jesus, clearly has a preparatory role (1:17,76; 3:3–6,15–17; 7:27) and is associated with the old rather than the new (5:33–39), yet he too "proclaimed the good news" (compare our text and 3:18; a favourite verb of Luke's) and is placed by Luke at the beginning of the good news (Acts 1:21–22; but cf 10:37). The ambiguity arises partly because John appears to be a transitional figure, almost bridging the two eras, as the last prophet of the old era and the first evangelist of the new. John stood at the turning point of the ages, concluding one and introducing the other (compare "from then", author's translation, with the "from now" of 1:48; 5:10; 12:52; 22:18,69). The age of promise and prophecy (the Law and the Prophets) was giving way to the age of fulfilment and salvation (God's kingdom; cf 4:16–21; 24:25–27,44ff). Now the good news of the arrival of God's saving reign in Jesus was being proclaimed.

Discuss the place of John in the history of salvation according to Luke 16:16.

John's authority (20:1–8)

The final passage in Luke's Gospel about John the Baptist concerns the legitimacy of his baptism, that is, of his ministry. Jesus' dramatic action in the temple (19:45–46), as well as his teaching there (19:47–20:1), are apparently perceived by the temple authorities as a challenge and a threat to their position as the legitimate leaders of the temple and Judaism. He turns their question about the source of his authority for such activity into a question about the source of John's authority – divine or human? In putting the issue like this Jesus was implying that both his ministry and John's had the same authorisation; thus, if the leaders accepted that John had divine sanction, then they must similarly view the one for whom John prepared the way. The self-serving response of the temple leaders draws attention, again in Luke, to John's prophetic role (eg 1:76; 7:26) and to popular rather than official approval of him (eg 7:29–30).

The Gospel of Luke

> **Tasks**
>
> a Outline the perceptions of Jesus, the religious leaders and the people concerning John in this passage.
>
> b Briefly summarise the key points of Luke's presentation of John the Baptist in the passages we have surveyed (including relevant material in the infancy narrative).

JOURNEY NARRATIVE (9:51–19:44)

After the infancy narrative (chs 1–2), preparation for Jesus' ministry (3:1–4:13, his baptism and temptation) and the section on Jesus' ministry in Galilee (4:14–9:50), we have a large section of Luke's Gospel known variously as the journey or travel narrative or as Luke's central section. This section is broadly about Jesus' journey to Jerusalem, beginning up north in Galilee (9:51) and continuing for ten chapters until Jesus finally arrives down south in the city of Jerusalem (19:44–45). Some place the end of this section at other points (eg 18:14; 19:27; 19:48); however, it is clear that Jesus is not actually in the city until 19:45 (cf 19:11,28,41). Luke reminds his readers along the way that Jerusalem is the destination of the journey (13:22,31–35; 17:11; 18:31; 19:11,28,41), the city being an important theme generally for Luke. The journey motif, also important in Acts, is underlined by regular use of journey words such as a verb meaning 'go, depart' (*poreuomai*; 9:51–53,57; 13:31–33; 17:11; 19:28,36) and the expression "the way/road" (*hodos*; 9:57; 10:4; 18:35; 19:36) – words favoured by Luke throughout his Gospel. However, it is obvious that Luke does not follow a direct, straight-line journey with a specific travel itinerary and clear indications of time and place. When an attempt is made to plot the journey along these lines, then it becomes rather convoluted. For example, the journey begins up north in Galilee and Samaria (9:51ff), apparently reaches Bethany near Jerusalem by the end of the next chapter (10:38ff; cf Jn 11:1,18–19; 12:1ff), and is back up north again several chapters later (17:11). Thus, while there is a general movement in the direction of Jerusalem, the emphasis is on the destination rather than the route. It is in Jerusalem that Jesus will reach his goal and destiny – his cross, resurrection and ascension to heaven (9:51; 13:31–35; 18:31–33; cf 9:31,43–45). The focus of the journey is therefore theological rather than geographical or chronological.

The journey narrative is long, accounting for approximately 40 per cent of Luke's Gospel, though estimates vary depending on one's method of calculation. More than a third of it is unique to Luke, with roughly the same proportion being parallel with Matthew, while less than a third of it is paralleled in Mark. Luke follows Mark's order until this section begins and then picks it up again near its end (18:15ff). While miracles are rare, there is an emphasis on Jesus' teaching, including 17 parables – most

Selected narratives

of which are unique to Luke. It is not obvious that Luke has structured his journey narrative according to any particular logical scheme. Since the section is so long it is unlikely that Luke has consciously arranged its material chiastically for its hearers and readers – that is, creating an inverse parallelism so that, starting at each end and moving in towards a significant centre, the material is arranged in thematically parallel sub-sections. Despite many attempts to discern the structure of the journey narrative along these lines Luke's text does not neatly fit into such schemes. However, as we go through the narrative we will note smaller structural arrangements of material grouped around common themes.

Tasks

a Discuss how appropriate it is to call this section of Luke the 'journey' narrative.

b Outline the main features of this section of Luke.

A Samaritan village (9:51–56)

Luke's journey narrative begins with an episode noting Jesus' resolve to go to Jerusalem, his consequent rejection by Samaritan villagers, and his rebuke of his disciples James and John for requesting God's judgement on the Samaritans. The journey narrative thus begins as it will end (19:41–44), with the theme of Jesus' rejection – the same way, in fact, that his ministry began (4:16–30). Since it is the start of the journey narrative there is repeated reference to the theme of travel and movement (v 51–53,56) and particularly to its destination – Jerusalem (twice, v 51,53; cf 9:31). Twice also we read of Jesus' determination to go to Jerusalem, in language reminiscent of the resolve of Old Testament prophets ("set his face"; see Isa 50:7; Ezek 21:2). Luke describes Jesus' destination not only as a place, but also as an event – he will be "taken up" (Luke's Greek noun is found only here in the NT). Luke's use of the corresponding verb in Acts 1 implies that this is a reference to Jesus' ascension to heaven – beyond, yet assuming, his death and resurrection (v 2,11,22). This language, as elsewhere in the opening verses of the journey narrative, recalls the story of Elijah (2 Kings 2:11; cf Lk 9:30–31) who was "taken up" (author's translation) to heaven. Jesus' ministry in Luke began with similar parallels between himself and Elijah (4:24ff). Jesus' disciples are described in similar terms to John the Baptist, as "messengers sent before his face … to make ready for him" (author's translation; cf v 52 and 1:17,76; 3:4; 7:27).

The historical origins of Samaritans, who have continued right up to the present, are unclear due to the nature of the available sources. However, by the time of Jesus there was clearly traditional animosity between them and the Jews, reflected in this passage and elsewhere in the New Testament (eg Jn 4:9; cf Mt 10:5–6). They were a religious group (or groups) who lived in the central hills area of Samaria between Galilee to the north and Judea to the south (see map, p5). The geographical focus of their worship was Mount Gerizim, near the ancient town of Shechem, while that of the Jews was Jerusalem (cf Jn 4:20–22). Their Scriptures were more limited than the Jewish Bible, consisting of a slightly different form of its first five books (the Samaritan Pentateuch). Thus, while they were not considered to be in the same category as Gentiles, neither were they regarded as truly Jewish. The first-century Jewish historian Josephus refers to violent hostility between Samaritans and Jews because the latter passed through Samaritan territory en route from Galilee to Jerusalem. Particularly relevant to our current passage in Luke, Josephus also instances a fatal attack by certain Samaritan villagers on Jewish pilgrims (*Ant* 20.6.1 118). To avoid this, Galilean Jews often bypassed Samaria by crossing the Jordan and travelling down its east side. In our passage Jesus and his disciples decided to go directly through Samaria (cf Jn 4:3–4).

The desire of his disciples James and John (see 5:9–10; 6:13–14; 9:28ff) to call down fire on the unwelcoming Samaritans reflects, then, the traditional Jewish dislike of the Samaritans and is yet another echo of the Elijah story in this passage, also involving fire from heaven on Samaritans (2 Kings 1:1–16; some later scribes added the words "even as Elijah did" to Lk 9:54). Jesus "turned" (frequently in Luke, introducing a definite statement or act: 7:9,44; 10:23; 14:25; 22:61; 23:28) and "rebuked" James and John (as often with demons in Luke, eg 4:35,41). Later scribes sought to provide the content of Jesus' rebuke by adding to verses 55 to 56 (see relevant footnote in, for example, NRSV, NIV). His disciples were not following his previous instructions about dealing with the unwelcoming (9:5) and, in fact, were acting like John the Baptist in still another way by expecting Jesus to bring down the fire of God's judgement quickly (3:17; yet 12:49ff; 17:29ff). On two more, likewise unique, occasions in this journey Jesus will show a positive attitude to Samaritans (10:25–37; 17:11–19; cf Acts 1:8; 8:5–26; 9:31). One of the lessons that his disciples must learn on this educational journey, and indeed a central theme of Luke, is that God's kingdom is for all people. The single-mindedness of Jesus and the universality of salvation, then, are the key themes of this opening episode in Luke's journey narrative. And the journey continues (v 56).

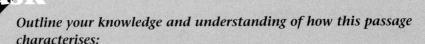

Outline your knowledge and understanding of how this passage characterises:

a) Jesus   b) the Samaritans   c) James and John

Would-be followers of Jesus (9:57–62)

As Jesus and his disciples travel on (v 57a), we meet three individuals who would join Jesus on his journey – two are volunteers and the middle one a recruit. Two of the three are paralleled in Matthew (8:18–22; in Galilee rather than en route to Jerusalem).

Selected narratives

The theme of the passage is discipleship, the word "follow" in relation to Jesus being found in each of the three incidents (cf 5:11,27–28; 9:23; 18:22,28). It is also concerned with the "kingdom of God" (twice: v 60,62). Near the start of Jesus' journey and just before a section on mission, this passage presents the demands of discipleship and of God's kingdom.

The first person volunteers to join Jesus' journey wherever it might lead. Jesus' response seeks to bring some realism to this apparent enthusiasm by indicating that even the wild animals have a better lot than he does. As at the beginning of this Gospel there was no place for him, other than an animals' feeding trough (2:7), so now he is homeless and must rely on the hospitality of others (cf 9:4; 10:5–7). There is also always the possibility of rejection, as just before this in Samaria (v 52–53; cf 9:5; 10:10–11). Thus, following Jesus on this journey means forgoing the normal material comforts of life (cf 8:14; 12:22; 14:33; yet 12:29–30).

Some have taken "Son of Man" (v 58) not to be a self-reference by Jesus, but as a general term for any man or human being. Certainly, this was a Jewish way of referring to men or humans generally (eg the parallelism in Num 23:19 and Ps 8:4, where the second line in each case has 'son of man' in the Hebrew). Indeed, in some sayings of Jesus in the Gospels it appears that "Son of Man" may well be understood in this general sense (eg Mk 2:27–28; Mt 9:6,8). However, a general reference in our passage does not suit the context nor Jesus' teaching elsewhere (eg 12:24ff), nor the plain fact that most people were not homeless! Rather, "Son of Man" is used here and in most other places in the Gospels as a self-reference by Jesus. This was his favourite self-designation, used by him frequently in the Gospels, but never by others to refer to him. The Old Testament background to Jesus' use of the term appears to be Daniel 7:13–14, where Daniel in a vision sees "one like a son of man" (author's translation; representing God's people: Dan 7:18,22,25,27) receiving an everlasting kingdom from God so that all people should serve him. At least some of Jesus' "Son of Man" sayings specifically reflect the Daniel passage (eg Lk 21:27). Unlike the main titles of Jesus in the Gospels (eg Messiah/Christ, Son of God), "Son of Man" is not used by anyone as a focus for or explanation of Jesus' identity (cf eg Lk 1:32; 2:11; 3:22; 22:67–70; 23:3). However, the term is used specifically and exclusively of Jesus, highlighting his unique qualities and functions, particularly in relation to his ministry (eg 5:24, first use in Luke; 9:58; 19:10), passion and resurrection (eg 9:44; 18:31–33) and future coming (eg 18:8; 21:27).

The remaining two examples of would-be disciples are a parallel pair – both begin with the idea of following Jesus, have Jesus addressed as "Lord" (ironically), have a request that "first" family matters be dealt with, and end with a statement by Jesus stressing the priority of the "kingdom of God". The request to be allowed first to bury one's father seems reasonable and in Jewish literature was a sign of respect for one's parents and relatives generally (eg Gen 23:1–6; Tobit 4:1–4; 6:14; 14:11–13). Possibly the father had not yet died and was terminally ill, or was perfectly well and the request was another way of saying that the son would not join Jesus until his father's life was over and his obligation to him was finished. If the latter, then a very long delay may have been in view. Jesus' response begins with a difficult statement (v 60). It may be a rhetorical way of saying that such things should be left to take care of themselves, or more likely that the burial of the physically dead should be left to the spiritually dead, those without the life of God's kingdom (cf 15:24,32). For Jesus no earthly reason or excuse has priority over the demands of God's kingdom (cf also v 61; 14:15–24). While the man wanted to "go" and bury his father, Jesus told him rather to "go" and proclaim the kingdom of God. In this way he would be following Jesus (4:43), as had the twelve disciples (9:1–2,6) and, in the very next section of Luke, as would the Seventy (10:1,9,11).

Like the first potential disciple, the last one is a volunteer and also, like the first, Jesus replies with some almost parabolic reference to ordinary life and experience. As with the second example, the volunteer wants first to delay because of family matters. His desire to say goodbye to his family before following Jesus recalls Elisha's desire to do the same before following Elijah, in a passage which also involves ploughing (1 Kings 19:19–21). That Elisha's request was granted implies that with Jesus we have a greater than Elijah (cf 4:24ff) and that with the kingdom of God we have a more urgent demand. Jesus' reply, as with the previous case, shows that God's kingdom has priority over family allegiances (cf 14:26). The use of ploughing imagery to illustrate the need for single-minded dedication, commonly used by ancient writers, echoes the story of Lot's wife who also "looked back" with fatal consequences (Gen 19:26; Lk 17:28–32). As the farmer must keep his eye fixed ahead to plough a straight furrow, so Jesus' disciples cannot be distracted, looking over their shoulders at families left behind, if they would join Jesus on his journey to proclaim God's kingdom. Such are not "fit" (used of salt in 14:35) for the demands of the kingdom. Yet, it is clear from Luke that this statement is not absolute (compare Peter's denial of Jesus, 22:31–34).

We do not know how these three would-be disciples responded to Jesus' demands. The focus of the passage is on Jesus' teaching rather than on them. Luke may have left the matter of response open-ended as a challenge to his readers.

Twice in this passage Jesus speaks of the "kingdom of God". This was the central theme of Jesus' teaching in the synoptic Gospels, often given as a summary of his message (eg Mk 1:14–15/ Mt 4:17; Lk 4:43; 8:1). While the precise term is not found in the Old Testament, the concept certainly is (eg Ps 145:10–13; Isa 52:7; Dan 2:44). The term "kingdom of God" is found in the mid first-century BC Jewish writing Psalms of Solomon, which hopes for a son of David to come as king and drive the Gentiles (Romans) from Jerusalem (Ps Sol 17–18). In the Gospels, God's kingdom appears to be primarily his reign rather than his realm, that is, it has more to do with God's sovereign activity than what he rules over, a dynamic rather than a spatial concept. Also, it is apparent that while Jesus thought of God's reign as coming in the future (eg Lk 9:27; 11:2; 13:28–29; 21:29–30; 22:16,18), he also conceived of it as being in some sense already present in his ministry (eg Lk 10:9,11; 11:20; 12:32; 16:16;

17:20–21), or at the very least imminent. It seems that while God's reign was being established already in the ministry of Jesus, it would yet come fully and climactically in the future. Luke's infancy narrative portrays Jesus' future in royal terms, as one whose kingdom will never end (1:32–33). At the start of his ministry Jesus is faced with the temptation to gain "the kingdoms of the world" by worshipping their master, the devil (4:5–8). Indeed, Jesus presents his ministry, with its exorcisms and healings, as the conquest of Satan's kingdom by God's kingdom (10:9,17–20; 11:14–23; 13:11–13,16). The "good news" of the kingdom, of which Luke is so fond of writing, is that God's reign in Jesus brings release from the adverse effects of Satan's reign (eg 4:17–19,43). While Jesus is the agent of God's reign during his ministry (19:38; 22:29), Luke's unique emphasis is that Jesus' role as king is particularly associated with his ascension to God (eg the parable of the minas, 19:11–27; cf Acts 2:30–36). This heavenly reign of Jesus will become apparent at his return (19:15; 23:42). More of the nature and demands of God's kingdom, particularly in Jesus' parables and teaching on discipleship, will unfold as we proceed through Luke's journey narrative.

Tasks

a Outline the teaching of Jesus in this passage on discipleship.
b Discuss the theme of the "kingdom of God" as presented in Luke.

The mission of the Seventy (10:1–24)

In this passage Jesus gives instructions to seventy (or seventy-two) whom he sends ahead of himself (v 1–12), issues woes to unrepentant cities (v 13–15), indicates the representative nature of the mission (v 16), receives and responds to a report on the mission (v 17–20), gives thanks to his Father (v 21–22), and speaks of the blessedness of the disciples (v 23–24).

This is the second mission that Jesus sends disciples on in Luke. The first mission was that of the twelve disciples, which is also found in the other synoptics (Lk 9:1–6/ Mt 10:1,7,9–11,14/ Mk 6:7–13). Only Luke, however, has this second mission and the relationship of it to the first is confused because the descriptions of each overlap in the Gospels and, further, sayings of Jesus in Luke 10 are in different contexts in Matthew. Some argue that there was in fact only one mission out of which Luke created two, because he found varying reports of it in two different sources, namely Q and Mark. Also, on his last night with the Twelve, Jesus recalls his previous mission instructions to them in words which he had actually spoken to the Seventy (22:35/ 10:4). However, others hold that there were indeed two missions, noting that Jesus appears to have sent disciples ahead on various occasions (cf Lk 9:52). Overlap in the wording of mission instructions does not necessarily indicate that there was originally only one mission, since such instructions would have been inevitably similar on additional missions.

The Gospel of Luke

It is uncertain whether Luke wrote of seventy or seventy-two (v 1,17). Either number may have had symbolic meaning. Moses had 70 elders as assistants (Num 11:16ff), possibly implying that Jesus is the new Moses and his disciples the new leaders of Israel. There were 70 members in the Sanhedrin (the Jewish ruling council), apart from the high priest – again maybe representing a challenge for the leadership of Israel. Also, the number 70 may symbolise the Church's later universal mission (in Acts), since it was thought that there were the same number of nations in the world (eg Gen 10). However, the number 72 could have the same symbolism, since the Greek version (LXX/Septuagint) of Genesis 10 has 72 nations. According to legend there were 72 translators of the LXX (translated to make the Hebrew Bible universally accessible), and in the later Jewish work 3 Enoch (17:8; 18:2–3; 30:2) there are 72 princes and languages in the world. However, it is not clear that Luke sees any symbolic meaning in either number since it is not explicitly developed in the text.

> **Tasks**
>
> a Discuss the relationship of the mission of the Seventy to the mission of the Twelve.
>
> b What possible symbolism may be suggested by the number of the missionaries?

The Seventy are "others", probably in distinction from the Twelve (9:1ff), sent ahead of Jesus, as were the messengers in Samaria (9:52) and John the Baptist (1:17,76; 3:4; 7:27) previously. Jesus urges prayer due to the fewness of the workers to reap the great spiritual harvest. He also underlines the danger of the mission by likening the Seventy to lambs (as Israel in, for example, Isa 40:11) among wolves (cf Lk 9:52–53). The urgency of the mission requires that they travel light and avoid being held back by stopping to greet others (v 4; cf 9:3,61–62; 12:33; 22:35ff; 2 Kings 4:29).

Jesus then deals with the reception of the missionaries, first in whatever "house" (v 5–7) and then in whatever "town" (v 8–12) they enter. In a house, the greeting of "peace" reflects the Hebrew greeting *shalom*, containing the idea of wellbeing and prosperity (1 Sam 25:6), and in Luke is associated with the blessing of God's salvation (eg 1:79; 2:14,29; 7:50; 8:48). The peace is almost objectified and externalised, since if there is a peaceable person (literally 'son of peace') in the house then it will rest on him, if not then it will return to the greeter. Hospitality is but the wages that the missionary "labourer" (v 2,7) deserves (cf 1 Tim 5:18; 1 Cor 9:14). However, abuse of such hospitality by moving from house to house would only discredit the mission (v 7; 9:4) and in second-century Christianity was seen as the mark of a false apostle/prophet (*Didache* 11–13). Jesus then explains what should happen in the towns, both welcoming and unwelcoming towns. In welcoming towns (v 8–9) the missionaries should accept their hospitality, heal their sick and announce the arrival of God's kingdom (on the latter, see pp80–81). While there is a debate whether the relevant verb in verse 9 means that the kingdom is approaching or has actually arrived, the latter must be so in some sense, since healing here is an evidence that Satan's reign is being overturned and replaced by God's reign (see also 17–20; 4:18–19; 11:14–23; 13:11–13,16). The Seventy then, as the Twelve before them (9:1–2), are sharing in Jesus' mission (eg 9:11) of proclaiming God's kingdom by both word and deed. To the unwelcoming towns (v 10–12) the same message is proclaimed, but unaccompanied by the kingdom's blessing of healing. Rather, in a very public act of rejection (v 10–11) similar to prophetic acts of judgement (eg Isa 20:2–4), the town's dust is to be wiped off the missionaries' feet (also in 9:5), an instruction that would be followed by later missionaries in Acts (13:51; cf 18:6). A similar act was performed by Jews who had travelled through Gentile territory in order to remove defilement, but now those who reject God's kingdom are not in the new Israel.

Jesus' final words about unwelcoming towns (v 12/ Mt 11:24) lead into a more general statement about other similar towns (v 13–15/ Mt 11:21–23). The general point is that on "that day", "the judgement" will be more bearable for towns regarded as more wicked, than towns that have rejected God's kingdom. Thus, Jesus held the traditional Jewish expectation of a coming day of God's judgement – "the day of the Lord" (eg Am 5:18ff; Ob 15–16). Therefore, John the Baptist (3:9,17) and Jesus' disciples (9:54) were not wrong to expect judgement, but were mistaken about its timing (cf 17:24ff). The town of Sodom became a symbol for wickedness (Gen 19; Isa 1:9; Lam 4:6) and was known, among other things, for its inhospitality to God's messengers (Gen 19), which makes it particularly appropriate in our present text. A "woe", an expression of grief or pity for those facing God's judgement (eg Lk 6:24–26; Am 5:18 [LXX]), is uttered against the Galilean towns Chorazin and Bethsaida, as Jesus reflects on his earlier ministry in that region (4:14–15,43; 9:10–11). If the "deeds of power", demonstrating the kingdom's presence (eg v 9), performed in these towns had been performed in the unrighteous Gentile towns of Tyre and Sidon (eg Isa 23), they would have repented long ago, expressing this in the traditional way (eg Jon 3:6). Repentance is turning to God and his ways and both the verb used here, and its related noun, are used most frequently by Luke among the Gospels. This leading theme of John the Baptist's ministry (3:3,8) thus continued into Jesus' ministry (eg 5:32; 13:3,5; 15:7,10). Capernaum, another Galilean town, which had witnessed much of Jesus' ministry (4:23,31ff; 7:1ff), is also singled out for rebuke. In language reminiscent of Isaiah's denunciation of the king of Babylon (Isa 14:13–15), "heaven" is contrasted with "Hades". In Greek mythology Hades was the name of the god of the underworld. In the LXX the word is used to translate *sheol*, referring to the underworld, the place of the dead generally (eg Ps 16:10/ Acts 2:27,31). By the first century Hades was considered increasingly to be a place of punishment (Lk 16:23ff; Rev 20:13–14).

Jesus' final statement before the mission (v 16) is about its representative nature. The Seventy represent Jesus as he in turn represents God (cf Mt 10:40; Jn 13:20).

The Gospel of Luke

Therefore, rejection of the messenger is rejection of the one who "sent" (Greek *apostello;* v 1,3,16; 4:18,43) the messenger, a theme continued in Acts (eg 9:1,4–5; cf 2 Cor 5:20).

> **Task**
>
> Outline your knowledge and understanding of Jesus' instructions to the missionaries, particularly concerning their reception and rejection.

We are not told of the mission itself. Rather, the focus is on Jesus' instructions, since these would undoubtedly have been relevant for the ongoing missionary activity of the Church of Luke's day. However, Luke includes a report of the mission (v 17–20), a unit framed by opening and closing references to joy (a Lucan theme), submission of demons/spirits, and names (v 17,20). The missionaries (v 17), along with Luke (v 1) and Jesus (v 2), refer to Jesus as "Lord" (see pp30–31). This is appropriate in a context where Jesus' "authority" is stressed (v 19; 9:1), for it is in the "name" of Jesus (an important theme in Acts, eg 2:36; 3:6; 4:12; 5:41; 9:14) that demons have submitted to them (cf 9:49). The Old Testament refers to various evil spiritual beings, including demons (Deut 32:17; Ps 106:37; cf also eg Lev 17:7; Isa 13:21). While the word 'demon' (Greek *daimonion*) was used in the wider Gentile world to refer to any divinity or god (as in Acts 17:18), whether good or bad, in Judaism the term was used of evil, harmful beings. It was widely held in the ancient world that various ailments and conditions were the result of demon possession, which could only be remedied by the expulsion of the demon (exorcism). Certainly, in Luke as in the other synoptics, Jesus is presented as an exorcist (eg 4:33ff,40ff; 8:27ff; Acts 10:38), and his exorcisms are viewed as evidence that Satan's reign is being overturned with the arrival of God's reign in his ministry. "Satan", the Hebrew for 'adversary, enemy' (eg Num 22:22), was a heavenly accuser of Job (Job 1–2) and, in later Judaism, the leader of evil powers (cf 11:15, where he is the "ruler of demons"). Until this point Luke has called him "the devil" (Greek *diabolos*: 'slanderer'; 4:1ff; 8:12). It is probable that Jesus' saying to the Seventy about seeing Satan falling from heaven (cf also v 15) refers to his observation of exorcisms performed by the Seventy during their mission, though it may refer metaphorically to his conflict with the devil at his temptation (4:1ff). However, the saying has also been seen as relating to a pre-cosmic fall of Satan and his angels from heaven (eg Jude 6; Gen 6:1–4; indirectly in Isa 14:12ff; Ezek 28:11ff). Others hold that Jesus' words may indicate that he had a prophetic vision (eg Jer 1:13) of Satan's final downfall at "the judgement" (v 12–15). Certainly, for Luke neither Jesus' ministry nor his death, resurrection and ascension, was the end of Satan (Acts 5:3; 13:10; 26:18). Jesus has given the Seventy authority over all Satan's power ("the enemy") and over snakes (cf Mk 16:18; Acts 28:3–6) and scorpions (cf Deut 8:15), so that nothing will harm them. Jesus' final remark (v 20) in response to the report echoes its opening words. A greater cause of joy than the submission of the demonic spirits is the fact that the missionaries' names are written in heaven, the latter idea being found in the Old Testament and beyond (eg Ex 32:32–33; Dan 7:10; Heb 12:23). That they are God's people, is a greater honour than their ability to conquer demons in Jesus' name.

Discuss the significance of Jesus' response to the report of the mission.

Jesus then (v 21: "At that same hour") gives thanks to his Father. The theme of joy continues (v 17,20), as does the link between Jesus and the Spirit (3:22; 4:1,14,18) – the "Holy" Spirit (contrast v 20). Jesus addresses God as "Father" (the word is found five times in v 21–22) and highlights the unique relationship between the Father and "the Son" (cf 1:32,35 and comment there; 2:49; 3:22; 9:35; see p32), in language more characteristic of John's Gospel than the synoptics. The Son takes the initiative to "reveal" to some who the Father is. Indeed, this is the reason for Jesus' grateful prayer, because while the Father has "hidden" the mysteries of the kingdom (cf 8:9–10) from the wise and intelligent, he has "revealed" them to infants (cf 2:46ff). Thus, Luke's theme of the reversal of normal conventions resurfaces (eg 1:51–53; 2:34; 9:46ff).

Finally, "turning" (see comment on 9:55, p78) to his disciples, Jesus speaks of their blessedness as those who have received God's revelation (v 23–24). Old Testament prophets who spoke of the coming age of salvation (cf 1:70ff; 3:4ff; 4:17ff; 24:25ff,44ff), and royalty, people of apparently greater importance and status (as v 21), vainly longed to experience what Jesus' disciples now see and hear – the manifestation of God's saving kingdom (v 17; 2:30). Thus, they are truly "blessed" (cf 1:42,45; 6:20ff).

Comment on the relevance of Luke 10:21–24 to the mission of the Seventy.

The parable of the good Samaritan (10:25–37)

In this passage, Jesus' conversation with an expert in Jewish Law (v 25–28) leads into the parable of the good Samaritan (v 29–37). These two parts of the passage are connected by key terms (in the Greek: 'do', v 25,28/37; 'neighbour', v 27/29,36) and also by a parallel structure.

The Gospel of Luke

v 25/29	The lawyer's motive
v 25/29	The lawyer's question
v 26/30–36	Jesus' answer: counter-question
v 27/37	The lawyer's answer
v 28/37	Jesus' concluding instruction

Jewish "lawyers" (eg 7:30), also called "teachers of the law" (5:17) and "scribes" (eg 5:21,30; 6:7; 9:22) in Luke, are part of the wider Jewish leadership who are often hostile to Jesus. This lawyer, while respectfully addressing Jesus as "Teacher", puts him on trial (v 25; cf 11:16). He wants to know how he can "inherit" (simply obtain, or have a present right to) "eternal life" (cf 18:18). "Eternal" (*aionios*) life is the life of the "age" (*aion*) to come (18:30), which will commence with resurrection (Dan 12:2; Lk 20:34–36). Jesus directs the lawyer to the Law (basically the OT, especially the Torah – its first five books), and by doing so affirms its religious authority (cf 4:4,8,12). The lawyer's reply quotes a version of the Shema (Hebrew: 'hear'; Deut 6:4–5), so important in Jewish worship, and the neighbour command (Lev 19:18). The two commands deal respectively with Israel's relationship to God and to others. Love is required in both – with one's whole being in relation to God and as oneself in relation to neighbours. In another conversation with a lawyer in the other synoptics, Jesus identifies these as the two greatest commandments (Mk 12:28ff/ Mt 22:34ff), and so commends this lawyer for his reply.

However, the lawyer wants to discuss the meaning of the word "neighbour" in the second command. Luke says this was motivated by a desire for self-vindication. Possibly, he wanted to justify his need to ask a question to which he clearly knew the answer by focusing on a point of interpretation. Alternatively, in accordance with his own practice, he perhaps felt that some kind of limit should be put on the extent of this term; after all, in Leviticus 19 the command refers primarily to fellow Israelites (also resident aliens, Lev 19:33–34). Surely love for Gentiles (particularly the occupying Romans), Samaritans (see comment on 9:52ff, pp77–78) and sinners is not required?

Jesus replies to this point of scriptural interpretation by providing a parable, as other contemporary Jewish rabbis did when explaining scriptural passages. In this realistic (possibly even real) story he deals with the broader issue of the meaning and application of Leviticus 19:18, rather than just the narrow focus of the lawyer's question[1]. The parable has several points of comparison with 2 Chronicles 28:5–15, which may have influenced its details. The story begins with a "certain man" (author's translation; cf eg 12:16; 14:16; 15:11), whose anonymity is preserved throughout the story, possibly to discourage sectarian classification. His "going down" from Jerusalem to Jericho was a

---

[1] On the allegorical interpretation of this parable as a coded summary of the history of salvation, ignoring its context, see p203.

geographical necessity, since the former is about 2,500 feet (762 metres) above sea level and the latter about 800 feet (244 metres) below sea level. The road, about 17 miles long, wound its way through a lonely desert area with caves that could be used by robbers as hide-outs. Left half dead by the robbers, his only hope was help from other travellers. In turn, two personnel from the nearby Jerusalem temple "saw" the man and "passed by on the other side". Only priests were descended from Aaron and thus were senior to the Levites, who assisted the priests in the temple (eg Ex 28:1; Num 1:47–53; ch 18). Various suggestions have been made as to why these religious leaders did not help the man. The idea that they did not want to become ritually unclean by contact with a possible corpse, thus interfering with their temple duties (eg Lev 21:1ff, of priests), does not sit easily with the fact that they were travelling away from, rather than towards, Jerusalem. Also, later Judaism required that even priests should bury neglected corpses and this may have applied in Jesus' time. It may be, rather, that fear of ambush and attack by robbers prevented them assisting the man. However, the parable does not raise the issue of their motives, and focuses instead on their failure to act. The religious establishment (cf v 25) is therefore cast in a negative light.

The lawyer and others may have expected the third and climactic traveller in the parable to be an ordinary Jewish layperson, giving the story an anti-clerical edge. Indeed, some speculate that perhaps this was how the original version of the parable went. However, the shocking cultural twist of the parable is that its hero is a Samaritan, a traditional enemy of the Jews (see comment on 9:51ff, pp77–78). This is one of several unique examples in Luke of Samaritans being positively characterised (see 9:51ff; 17:11ff). The parable's subversion of cultural convention is further highlighted by the intentional contrast that is drawn between the responses of the Jewish leaders and the Samaritan. While all three travellers "saw" the robbers' victim, only the Samaritan "was moved with pity/compassion" (author's translation; cf 7:13). This feeling of pity was expressed in practical assistance which the story details at some length, causing the narrative pace to slow down so that its focus falls climactically on the Samaritan's care for the man in need. The parable itemises seven successive compassionate acts by the Samaritan (v 34–35): (i) he went to the wounded man, thus putting himself at risk from possible ambush and attack; (ii) bound his wounds, possibly using ripped pieces of his own clothes as bandages; (iii) poured on olive oil (to soothe) and wine (to cleanse); (iv) put him on his own animal; (v) brought him to an inn; (vi) took care of him overnight, since ancient inns were not like modern hospitals; and (vii) paid the innkeeper the equivalent of two days' wages for a labourer to cover further care while he was away, including the promise of further payment on his return for any additional expense (which may have left him open to extortion). The resulting picture is of a traditionally disliked Samaritan who went to considerable effort and personal expense out of concern for a needy stranger, contrasted with the apparent heartless abandonment of the dying man by two Jewish religious leaders, in turn. The details of the Samaritan's possessions may imply that he was a merchant on a business trip, which would explain his unusual presence in 'enemy territory' and should also prevent a hasty negative verdict on the parable's authenticity.

At the close of the parable, Jesus asks the lawyer a question which changes the focus of the lawyer's original question about the neighbour commandment from 'Who is the neighbour that I should love?' to 'Who is a loving neighbour?' Clearly, the parable answers the lawyer's question by showing that anyone in need is one's neighbour, regardless of race or religion, as demonstrated by the love of even a Samaritan for a stranger in religiously hostile territory. However, more important for Jesus than the hair-splitting and self-serving interpretation of a biblical text which apparently concerned the lawyer, is the issue of what loving one's neighbour means in practical terms. The lawyer agrees with the inescapable facts of the parable that it was "the one" (he maybe couldn't bring himself to say 'Samaritan'; cf 15:30) who showed "mercy" who was being neighbourly. The lawyer's word "mercy", along with the Samaritan's "pity", matches the "love" of the neighbour commandment. Jesus finishes the conversation by telling the lawyer to "do" as the Samaritan had done v 37b), echoing his uses of the same word in his initial question (v 25) and concluding answer (v 37a; the Greek verb means 'doing').

Tasks

a **Show how the two parts of this passage, the lawyer's question and the parable, are essentially connected.**

b **Explain the relevance of the parable to the command to love one's neighbour (10:27).**

c **Outline and discuss the parable's contrasting responses to the wounded man.**

Martha and Mary (10:38–42)

As Jesus receives hospitality in the home of Martha, a contrast is drawn between the host and her sister Mary. While Martha is anxiously distracted by preparing to serve her guest, Mary sits at his feet listening to his words. Martha's irritation spills over into criticism of both Jesus and Mary. The main point of the story is found in its climactic conclusion, a statement by Jesus in which he commends Mary, rather than Martha, for getting her priorities right. The story thus provides a lesson on discipleship – Jesus' followers must not allow themselves to be distracted from listening to his teaching by lesser, though legitimate, duties.

This uniquely Lucan passage begins with two themes already stressed in the journey narrative – travelling (9:51–53,56–57; 10:1) and, in particular, hospitality (9:53; 10:5–12), since here we have an example of a positive reception of Jesus. As already noted (see p29), this is but one of several examples in Luke of Jesus teaching while an invited guest in someone else's home (also 5:29ff). While Luke refers merely to "a certain village",

John identifies Bethany (11:1,18; 12:1) as the sisters' place of residence. Since Bethany is near Jerusalem (19:29), it appears that Jesus' journey to Jerusalem (eg 9:51ff) is not to be viewed as progressing directly to its destination (eg 17:11).

The contrasting characterisation of the two sisters is at the heart of the story. While Mary is sitting, Martha is busy. Mary's position, "at the Lord's feet" links with similar positioning elsewhere in Luke (7:38,44–46; 8:35,41; 17:16) and indicates submission, especially that of a disciple before her teacher (cf Acts 22:3). This latter role is reinforced by Luke's characteristic designation of Jesus as "the Lord" (v 39,41) and the description of Mary as "listening to his word" (author's translation; cf 6:47; 8:11ff,21). That Luke approvingly portrays Mary as a disciple of a rabbi, regarded as a male role in a culture where females were expected to be like domestic Martha, demonstrates his generally positive view of women (cf 8:1–3; see p37). Thus, his characterisation of Mary is as culturally subversive and boundary-breaking as the characterisation of the Samaritan in the preceding passage. On the other hand, Martha is portrayed not as sitting but as "serving" (author's translation; both the noun *diakonia* and the related verb *diakoneo* are used in v 40). "Distracted" by her preparations for her guest, she is annoyed at both him and her sister. "Lord, don't you care ..." (author's translation) echoes the desperation of the disciples in the storm (Mk 4:38), and the demand that Jesus tell her sibling to act anticipates a later request (12:13). A similar contrast between two types of women is drawn by Paul, using language also found in our passage (1 Cor 7:34–35).

Jesus responds (v 41–42) to Martha's complaint with feeling, indicated by his double use of her name (cf 8:24; 13:34; 22:31) and challenges her to re-prioritise. Jesus does not find fault with the fact that she was performing her duties as a host, which was a cultural expectation (cf 7:36,44–46). Rather, the problem is that she has allowed anxiety about lesser things to distract her from Jesus' "word" (v 39, author's translation; cf Deut 8:3), the very thing Jesus had warned against in the parable of the sower (see 8:11,14) and will warn against again (12:22,29–31; 21:34). Martha's distraction by "many things" is contrasted with the necessary "one thing" (though some manuscripts have "few things are needed, or only one"), which in the context must refer to Jesus' teaching. This is the "better part" which Mary has chosen and will not be taken from her, by Martha's demands or otherwise. So, while this passage has been traditionally used to argue for the religious superiority of the contemplative life over the active, its sharper focus is rather on the priority of hearing God's word over concern for lesser things, legitimate though they may be.

Tasks

a *What key Lucan themes are found in this passage?*
b *Contrast Luke's characterisation of the two sisters.*
c *How do Jesus' words help us understand the purpose of the passage?*

The Gospel of Luke

The Lord's Prayer (11:1–4)

A section concerning Jesus' teaching on prayer (11:1–13) begins with what is traditionally known as the Lord's Prayer, though it would be more appropriately called the Disciples' Prayer. A different and more well-known version of the prayer is found in Matthew, in a different context (the Sermon on the Mount, Mt 6:9–13), with which many later scribes harmonised Luke's version. While some hold that Jesus taught two versions of the prayer on different occasions, many scholars believe that Luke's shorter version is the more original and that Matthew's version reflects liturgical expansion, that is, additions have been made over time which have been influenced by its use in congregational Christian worship (eg compare the opening address to God). However, while accepting that Luke's version of the prayer is probably closer to its original form, many also hold that Matthew's actual wording is nearer to that of Jesus' Aramaic (in which language the prayer's rhythm and rhyme are apparent). As for the content of the prayer, it is apparent that it is similar in places to other Jewish prayers, which may well have existed at the time of Jesus (especially the *Shemoneh Esreh/Eighteen Benedictions* and the *Qaddish*). In fact, it is notable that there is nothing exclusively Christian about the prayer.

The context for the prayer in Luke presents us with one of his characteristic themes – Jesus at prayer (see Prayerful, pp29–30). The disciple's address of Jesus as "Lord", and his request for teaching, continues the theme of discipleship from the previous passage (10:38ff). The request to have teaching on prayer just as John's disciples had (see comment on 5:33, p72) may represent a desire for distinctiveness, for a type of praying which distinguishes Jesus' disciples from John's group and other Jewish sects. As well as functioning as an identity marker, a common prayer would socialise the group, acting as a communal symbol. Jesus thus provides his disciples with a prayer to repeat (v 2a), though in Matthew it may be more a model or pattern to follow (6:9).

Structurally, the opening address ("Father") is followed by five petitions/requests, the first two relating to God ("your") and the remaining three concerning the disciples ("us"). In this way, Jesus taught his disciples to be concerned first with God (his name and kingdom) before their own concerns (food, forgiveness, trial). The same order of priority is found in the Ten Commandments (Ex 20:1–17) and in the two greatest commandments (Mt 22:36–40).

Address

The disciples are taught to address God as "Father", as Jesus himself did (10:21–22; 22:42; 23:34,46). The Aramaic word that Jesus used (*abba*; see Mk 14:36) was preserved in the worship of Greek-speaking churches (Rom 8:15; Gal 4:6), so meaningful had it become in terms of their relationship to God – a relationship both exemplified and taught by Jesus himself. While God is described as the father of Israel in the Old Testament (eg Deut 32:6; Isa 63:16) and later Jewish writings, it was rare for Jews to address God as such (eg Wisdom 14:3; Sirach 23:1,4), preferring as they did more formal, less intimate terms. However, a family metaphor is used for the disciples' relation to God – they are his children and he is their father. In ancient societies in general and in Jewish culture in particular, this family relationship would have suggested ideas of authority and obedience, but also of provision and dependence. The latter appear to be to the fore in the prayer (see also v 11–13). In prayer, Jesus' disciples are to view God as a caring and merciful father. Some prefer a neutral term other than the gender-specific "Father", since God is asexual or genderless in Judaeo-Christian thought (eg Jn 4:24) and, therefore, the language is metaphorical or analogous rather than literal. However, the masculine term reflects ideas associated with the patriarchal culture of biblical times which will be lost with the use of more abstract, impersonal, gender-inclusive terms such as 'parent'.

First petition

Jesus teaches his disciples that their first concern in prayer should be God's "name", which in biblical thought refers to his reputation, effectively to God himself (eg Isa 52:5–6). God is asked that his name be "hallowed", that is, that it be 'sanctified', as the verb is usually translated (eg Acts 20:32; 26:18). The idea is that God should be set apart as holy (the related adjective is usually translated 'holy', as in v 13). This recalls the commandment concerned with the reverent use of God's name (Ex 20:7) and, particularly, God's promise in Ezekiel to "sanctify" his "great name" through his restored people, who "profaned" his "holy name" (36:20–32). Ezekiel's prophecy thus gives this petition an eschatological edge, as it looks forward to the restoration of God's people in the last days. This petition is reflected also in the Jewish prayers known as the *Qaddish* (see p90), which includes the words "Magnified and hallowed be his great name ...", and the *Shemoneh Esreh*, which says "You are holy and your name is holy ...".

Second petition

The mention of God's kingdom or reign brings us to the central theme of Jesus' preaching. The request to let the kingdom come focuses on its future aspect, when God's reign, already begun in the ministry of Jesus, will come in all its fullness (see comment on 9:60, pp79–81, for details). Again, similar petitions are found in contemporary Jewish prayers, particularly the *Qaddish*: "May he establish his kingdom in your lifetime and in your days, and in the lifetime of all the household of Israel, quickly and at a near time". In this manner, Jesus expresses a current Jewish hope for God to manifest his sovereignty on earth. In place of this second petition, a few later manuscripts and writers have, "Your Holy Spirit come upon us and cleanse us."

Third petition

The prayer now moves from requests relating to God to the needs of the disciples. The request for a daily provision of food (the Greek word can have a broader meaning than "bread") is an acknowledgement of the disciples' daily dependence on

God's fatherly provision of a basic necessity (see 12:22–24,29–31). Such dependence on God was apparently required of the Twelve during their mission (see 9:3). However, as is clear from the mission of the Seventy, God's provision of food for the travelling preachers came through human hospitality and was even to be viewed as earned payment, as well as the divine gift that is implied here (10:7–8). Here, the emphasis is on the disciples' daily need of food ("each day"), recalling the daily provision of manna in the wilderness for Israel (Ex 16:9–21), rather than unusual, miraculous provision of abundant food, as in the feeding of thousands by Jesus (9:12ff). The word usually translated 'daily' (*epiousios*) is not found anywhere in ancient literature outside the Lord's Prayer and is, therefore, of uncertain meaning. Other suggested meanings include 'essential, necessary for existence', and 'for the future or the coming day'. It may relate to a similar word (*epiousa*) used by Luke in Acts with the meaning 'the following, next [day]' (7:26; 16:11; 20:15; 21:18; 23:11), which can refer to 'tomorrow' or 'the day ahead'. It may be too that, particularly in light of the eschatological tone of the prayer, the request relates to the future messianic feast in the coming kingdom of the previous petition (see 14:15). While later Christians saw some reference to the bread of the Eucharist/Communion, probably described as 'breaking of bread' in Acts (eg 2:42; 20:7), the context of the Lord's Prayer in the Gospels implies no other meaning than ordinary food.

Fourth petition

Forgiveness of sins is an important theme in Luke (1:77; 3:3; 5:20ff; 7:47–49; 12:10; 17:3–4; 24:47). Here, divine forgiveness and human forgiveness are closely related in the two parts of this request. While the relation has been understood in cause–effect terms, God's forgiveness of the disciples being conditional on their forgiveness of others, it may be just an appeal from the lesser to the greater – even the disciples are forgiving, so much more can God be expected to forgive. Yet, it is clear from the teaching of Jesus elsewhere that the unforgiving will not be forgiven by God and that, conversely, the forgiving will be forgiven by God. After Matthew's account of the Lord's Prayer, this is the one petition that Jesus develops in stark terms (Mt 6:14–15; see also Mt 18:23–35), an idea also found in Luke (6:36–38) and, indeed, in Jewish literature before Jesus (Sirach 28:2). The idea of sin as a debt, found in the second part of the petition (Matthew has this in both parts), is present elsewhere in Jesus' teaching (7:41–43,47–48; Mt 18:23–35).

Fifth petition

The final petition of Luke's version of the Lord's Prayer literally reads, "And do not bring us into temptation/trial." The final word (*peirasmos*) and its related verb (*peirazo*) can refer to both temptation (attraction or enticement to sin) and trial (testing, especially by God). The request expresses a fear of failure, either by yielding to sin (compare the previous petition) or not passing the test, and asks God to prevent such failure occurring (cf 22:31–32,40,46). In the Old Testament God often tested his people (eg Gen 22:1; Ex 16:4; Ps 26:2–3); sometimes Satan was permitted by God to test his people (Job 1–2; Lk 22:31–32); and, of course, Jesus experienced this in his ministry (Lk 4:2,13, where the NRSV translates the verb as "tempt" and its related noun as "test"; also 22:28). The possibility of failure of faith during trial/temptation was highlighted in Jesus' parable of the sower (8:13), and was a threat to the disciples on their journey with Jesus in the face of opposition and persecution (eg 10:3,10; 21:12ff,34–36). The petition may refer to the expected final tribulation or trial before the arrival of the new age (compare NRSV's rendering here and in 22:40,46; see also 21:9ff; Rev 3:10), but the absence in the Greek of the article ('the') before "trial" makes such a specific reference unlikely.

Tasks

a **Comment on the relation between the two versions of the Lord's Prayer.**

b **Explain the significance of the context of the prayer in Luke.**

c **Outline the prayer's structure.**

d **Discuss the significance of how God is addressed.**

e **Briefly explain the meaning of its petitions.**

The parable of the friend at midnight (11:5–10)

Jesus continues to teach his disciples to pray. Having taught them *what* to pray, he now teaches them *how* to pray. In this passage a parable is followed by its application (v 9–10), as indeed in the passage which follows (v 11–13).

In this uniquely Lucan parable, the would-be host has no food because bread was baked and eaten on the same day. To avoid the cultural embarrassment of not being able to provide hospitality for an unexpected visitor, he hopes that his "friend" (the word occurs four times) will have some extra bread (three loaves being suitable for an evening meal) to "lend" him, despite the unsociable hour. However, this would cause too much of an upheaval for his friend. To open the barred door would probably create noise that would wake his family. Indeed, he and his children are already in bed, on a mat in a single-roomed peasant house.

Jesus concludes the parable with a hint of its relevance to prayer (v 8), which he will spell out clearly in the application which follows (v 9–10). Two words of Jesus in verse 8, which the NRSV translates as "his persistence", provide the key to the meaning of the parable. However, there's a problem with each of these words! The word translated "persistence" (*anaideia*) literally means 'shamelessness, boldness' (cf Sirach 25:22) and in the parable the would-be host is not persistent. Also, to whom does the word "his" refer – to the man in bed or to the would-be host? Some argue that the reference is to the man in bed, and that Jesus is saying that even though he won't be moved to help because of friendship, he will to avoid the cultural and social shame of not offering assistance (cf Prov 3:28). Consequently, the meaning of the parable in this view is that God will answer the disciples' prayers since his honour is at stake if he doesn't. However, the relevant noun in verse 8 means 'shamelessness' rather than 'avoidance of shame'.

Others argue that the reference is to the would-be host's shamelessness and boldness, having the nerve and gall to wake a whole family, and probably a whole village in the process (since the houses were close together), to get what he needed. The point of the parable then would be that the disciples should be bold and confident in their prayers to God, which fits the clear application of the parable which Jesus goes on to make, as Luke presents it (v 9–10). It is notable, however, that the parable has shifted its focus from the asker at the beginning to the giver at the end, implying a secondary comparison between the man in bed and God, as well as the primary comparison between the would-be host and the disciples. While this might imply an unflattering picture of God (reluctant to help), it is interesting to note that it is often the case in Jesus' parables that the character who seems to represent God (or Jesus) is unlikeable (eg 12:39–40; 18:1ff; 19:20ff)! However, comparison can also reveal contrast, or an argument from lesser to greater (v 13; 18:6ff).

The application of the parable (v 9–10), found in a different context in Matthew (7:7ff), is clearly linked to it by "So I …" (v 9). With three verbs (ask, search, knock), Jesus encourages his disciples to pray by assuring them that God will certainly answer.

Tasks

a *Outline the parable of the friend at midnight and discuss the different views of its meaning.*

b *What is the main point of the parable's apparent application in 11:9–10?*

Fatherhood and prayer (11:11–13)

The section concerning Jesus' teaching on prayer (11:1–13) concludes with a little parable (v 11–12) and its application (v 13), structured in the same way as the previous passage (v 5–8, 9–10). The passage is linked to the immediately preceding verses by their common use of the word "ask" (v 9–13, once in each verse). Our passage is paralleled in Matthew (7:9–11), in a different context and with slightly different wording, to which later scribes harmonised Luke's version. A comparison is drawn between human fathers and the heavenly Father[1], using a lesser-to-greater argument.

---

[1] In the interests of gender-inclusiveness the NRSV has not translated the word for 'father', replacing it with "anyone" (v 11), and has thus weakened the force of the human–divine fatherhood analogy. (Matthew does not have 'father' in his parallel passage, using a less gender-specific term.) Also, the Greek word for 'son' has been rendered with the gender-neutral term "child" in verse 11. The use of even the gender-inclusive term 'parent' in verse 11 may have gone some way to preserving the clarity of the analogy.

If even human fathers, who are evil (ie sinners), give good gifts (fish, egg) rather than harmful alternatives (snake, scorpion; cf 10:19) to their children when they ask, "how much more" will the heavenly Father (cf v 2) give the "Holy Spirit" to those who ask him. An unequal comparison is implied in that, unlike the heavenly Father, human fathers are sinners and what the heavenly Father gives is greater (compare "good gifts" and "Holy Spirit"). In Matthew, the heavenly Father gives "good things" rather than the 'Holy Spirit', the latter possibly reflecting Luke's emphasis on the Spirit (though cf Lk 11:20/ Mt 12:28). The gift of the Spirit from the Father occurs beyond Luke in Acts and was, indeed, given in response to prayer (Lk 24:49; Acts 1:14; 2:1ff,33; 4:31). In the parable, while some have suggested some similarity in appearance between the requested foods and their respective alternatives (including between a rolled-up scorpion and an egg), with the implication of cruel deception on the part of the father, this was probably not in view. The emphasis of the passage is on the goodness and generosity of God in response to prayer. Appropriately, and acting as a literary frame for the passage, Jesus' teaching on prayer in this section ends as it began, with the theme of God's fatherhood (v 2,13).

Explain the significance for prayer of this passage's analogy between human and divine fatherhood.

An exorcism controversy (11:14–23)

This passage marks an abrupt change from Jesus teaching his disciples (v 1–13) to a section (v 14–36) where Jesus is addressing "the crowds" (v 14,27,29). Our present passage begins with an exorcism by Jesus (v 14), leading to mostly negative responses from "the crowds" (v 14–16). This is followed by a reply from Jesus (v 17–23) in which he argues that it is illogical to attribute his exorcisms to Satan – they are, on the contrary, evidence of the presence of the kingdom of God.

Jesus' exorcism of a demon, resulting in the healing of a physical handicap, is one of several such instances in Luke (on demon-possession, see comment on 10:17, pp84–85). While the crowds are generally "amazed", two negative responses to the exorcism are singled out (v 15–16) – Jesus' exorcisms are attributed to Satan (to which Jesus responds in v 17–23) and there are demands for a sign from heaven (to which Jesus responds in v 29–32). Both responses are concerned with the source of Jesus' activity and, thus, the legitimacy of his ministry. The first respondents see Jesus as an agent of Satan, acting on his authority and by his power, and therefore reject his ministry as illegitimate (for Satan, see comment on 10:18, pp84–85). The second group are not as negative, but still require divine authentication of Jesus' ministry. Satan's name "Beelzebul" (v 15,18–19), spelt variously in the manuscripts, may reflect the name of an ancient Canaanite god (*Baal-zebul*). The Latin form *Beelzebub* recalls the name of a god (*Baal-zebub*: 'Lord of the flies') of a Philistine town (2 Kings 1:2–3), which itself is probably a derogatory form of *Baal-zebul* (possibly meaning 'Baal of the Exalted Dwelling'). In Luke, he is further described as "the ruler of the demons" (11:15).

Jesus replies to the first response of the crowd to his exorcism with two counter-arguments (v 17–19). First, he shows how illogical it is to claim that his exorcisms were performed by Satan's power, since the ruler of demons would be destroying his own "kingdom" (v 17–18). Second, Jesus exposes their inconsistency – if his exorcisms are from Satan, why do they not pass the same verdict on those by other Jewish exorcists (v 19; cf Acts 19:13)? Their own exorcists will condemn their views on the Satanic origins of exorcisms, now or on Judgement Day (cf v 31–32). If Jesus is here accepting the validity of other exorcisms, then it seems to undermine the uniqueness of his own and of the associated claim that they demonstrate the arrival of God's kingdom in his ministry (v 20). However, it is possible that Jesus is simply making a rhetorical or hypothetical point to expose the inconsistency of his opponents (cf 1 Cor 15:29).

After demonstrating the implausibility of the claim that his exorcisms were from Satan, Jesus interprets them to be, on the contrary, acts of God. It is "by the finger of God", an Old Testament expression for God's activity (eg Ex 8:19; 31:18; Deut 9:10; Ps 8:3), that he exorcises, thus demonstrating the arrival of God's kingdom (as 9:1–2; 10:9,11,17ff; for God's kingdom, see comment on 9:60, pp79–81). Jesus then illustrates his point with a little parable (v 21–22). Satan, or one of his demons, is likened to a "strong man" guarding his castle, which probably represents the demon-possessed. Jesus, as God's agent, is likened to the "stronger man" (author's translation) who attacks and overpowers the "strong man" (the exorcism). In this way, the whole passage presents Jesus' ministry as a conflict between two kingdoms and their respective kings, Satan and God. Jesus' exorcisms of demons are victorious assaults on Satan's kingdom and signs of the arrival of God's superior kingdom. Those who are not with Jesus, including those who claim he is an agent of Satan (v 15), are against him and are, ironically, on Satan's side. Not siding with Jesus by gathering God's people into his kingdom (cf 3:17; Isa 11:12), they are rather scattering them (v 23).

Tasks

a Outline your understanding of the response of the crowds to Jesus' exorcism.

b Explain the relevance of Jesus' reply to the crowds in verses 17 to 23.

The return of the unclean spirit (11:24–26)

Jesus continues with the theme of exorcism in a passage paralleled in Matthew 12:43–45. The picture of an expelled, unclean spirit/demon (4:33) looking for a resting place in waterless areas may reflect the association of such beings with desolate places (eg 4:1–2; Isa 34:14; Baruch 4:35). That it returns to find its previous residence (ie victim) "swept and put in order" implies a contrast between the chaos resulting from demon-possession and the orderliness left by exorcism (cf v 14; 8:27,29,35). The spirit's return with "seven" (possibly implying completeness) more evil spirits indicates the demon's determination to re-inhabit its host permanently, by more effectively resisting further attempts at exorcism. The result, then, is that the demon-possessed person's condition is now even worse. Jesus may be implying that the work of other exorcists (v 19) is ultimately ineffective or, more likely, that any exorcism is only a temporary release from Satan's power, without a positive and continuing acceptance of God's kingdom in its place.

What is Jesus' main point in this passage?

True blessedness (11:27–28)

In a passage unique to Luke, a woman's exclamation of the blessedness of Jesus' mother (cf 1:41–42,45,48) is modified by Jesus to indicate a greater blessedness, that of hearing and obeying God's word (see 8:11,15,19–21). More important, then, than physical relation is the doing of God's will (3:8). Thus, while the woman's response to Jesus is more positive than others "in the crowd", its focus is still misplaced.

The sign of Jonah and the judgement (11:29–32)

Jesus' condemnation of his "generation" (also 7:31; 9:41) as evil for seeking a sign recalls earlier demands from the crowds, after an exorcism, for divine authentication of his ministry. Jesus regarded the exorcism itself as sign enough that God was at work through him (v 20). The only sign they will receive is "the sign of Jonah", which in Matthew's parallel passage (12:38–42) is an analogy between Jonah's time in the belly of the fish and the Son of Man's time in the heart of the earth. However, Luke has no explanation of what the sign is. It may refer to "the proclamation of Jonah" concerning its future judgement and the subsequent repentance of the Ninevites (Jonah 3), which Jesus mentions later in this passage (v 32). So, the sole sign that Jesus' contemporaries will get is his preaching of repentance before the coming judgement in the fall of Jerusalem and beyond (eg 2:34; 13:1–5; 21:5ff). Another view of the sign of Jonah relates it to his rescue from the sea by God, of which the Ninevites were aware according to later Jewish interpretation. Indeed, God's vindication of Jesus in his resurrection and exaltation became an important theme in Acts, and this yet future event suits the future tenses in verses 29 to 30. It has also been argued that since Jonah was sent to preach to Gentiles, the sign here concerns the future Gentile mission of the Church, as recorded in Acts.

Verses 31 and 32 contain parallel statements of Jesus in which he pictures his fellow Jews being condemned by Gentiles at the final judgement, a shocking reversal of Jewish expectations (cf 10:12–15). The reason given is that the Gentiles responded positively to God's message – the Queen of the South to the wisdom of Solomon (I Kings 10:1–13/ 2 Chr 9:1–12) and the Ninevites to the proclamation of Jonah – yet Jesus' generation had responded negatively to his ministry (15–16), even though it had brought to them something greater than Solomon or Jonah. The irony is clear – Gentiles accepted God's lesser messengers, while Jews rejected his greater messenger.

a What did Jesus mean by "the sign of Jonah"?

b Explain the significance of what will happen at the judgement, according to this passage.

Lamps and light (11:33–36)

Jesus' sayings here, all linked by the common theme of light, are in the form of little parables. Since no interpretation or application is provided with them, their meaning is debated. In the first statement (v 33; cf 8:16; Mt 5:15) Jesus may be saying that his message is not hidden, but rather openly declared (cf 1:78–79; 2:32), and that the disciples should continue to make it known. However, the other sayings (v 34–36) seem to be about the reception of the message, rather than its transmission. Whether the body has light or darkness in it depends on the condition of the eyes, says Jesus (v 34). This implies that the quality of a person's inner life is determined by the soundness of his or her spiritual perception. In the context, this saying is linked to Jesus' unreceptive hearers (v 29) by the word 'evil' (*poneros*; rendered as "not healthy" by the NRSV in v 34). Jesus then challenges his hearers (v 35) to examine themselves to check whether the "light" that they think they have is not, in fact, darkness (eg v 39ff). The last statement (v 36) is problematic because it seems to be an example of tautology (saying the same thing twice, using different words), so that in effect Jesus is saying, "If you're full of light, you're full of light." However, the point may be that those who are presently enlightened (recalling the imagery of v 34) will experience the same at the future judgement (note the future tense in v 36b). The section concludes by returning to the lamp imagery with which it began, serving as a device to frame the passage.

What main points may Jesus be making in these sayings about light and darkness?

Jesus rebukes Pharisees and lawyers (11:37–54)

A change of audience and location now occurs as Jesus leaves the crowds outdoors to dine with Jewish religious leaders indoors. After the introductory setting (v 37–38) the passage divides into two main parts, with Jesus criticising first the Pharisees (v 39–44) and then the lawyers (v 45–52), each part containing three woes. Finally, the action moves outdoors again, where both sets of Jewish leaders engage in hostile cross-examination of Jesus (v 53–54).

Material similar to much of this passage is found elsewhere in the Gospels in different contexts (especially Mt 23; also Mk 7:1ff/ Mt 15:1ff and Mk 12:38–39/ Lk 20:46) and the relationships between the various passages is debated.

Criticism of the Pharisees (v 37–44)

The Pharisee's invitation of Jesus to dine with him is another example of Luke's fondness for having Jesus teach while a dinner guest in someone's home (see p29) and, indeed, is one of three uniquely Lucan occasions when Jesus dines in a Pharisee's home (also 7:36ff; 14:1ff). The Pharisees were a lay (ie not priestly) religious group who were concerned with the proper observance in society of Jewish Law, including traditions additional to biblical (OT) laws. When linked with "lawyers" (also known as "scribes" and "teachers of the law") in Luke, the Pharisees are consistently characterised as opponents of Jesus (eg 5:21,30; 6:7; 7:30).

In our present passage, the Pharisee's surprise at Jesus' failure to wash before dinner reflects Pharisaic concern with ritual purity, rather than hygiene (see Mk 7:1–5). The general background for this concern is found in the Old Testament distinction between what is 'clean' and what is 'unclean' and required cleansing (eg Lev 11–15). Though no Old Testament law required ritual washing before meals, a growing concern with ritual defilement through contact with various sources of uncleanness, particularly in a Gentile context, resulted in increasing regulations relating to purity among some Jewish groups. To the Pharisee, Jesus was not only breaching the conventions of the host–guest relationship (by not respecting the host's expectations), but was also offending against ritual purity. Luke introduces Jesus' response to the Pharisee's surprise by characteristically describing Jesus as "the Lord", thus implying that the teaching which follows has a greater authority than that of the Jewish leaders whom Jesus denounces. Jesus' immediate response (v 39–41) criticises Pharisaic concern with the "outside" (ritual purity) while neglecting the "inside" (moral purity). The Pharisees' inner greed and wickedness (cf 16:14) contrasts hypocritically with their obsession with outer purity. They have foolishly ignored the fact that God made the inside too. Everything would be clean for them if they would give to the poor "what is within" (author's translation). The meaning of the phrase in verse 41 is unclear, possibly referring to the contents of the cup and dish in verse 39 or to the need to give from within, from the heart. It has also been suggested that, in verse 41, Luke mistranslated an underlying Aramaic word meaning 'cleanse' by confusing it with a similar word meaning 'give alms'. In this case, the instruction would have been to cleanse the inside in order to make everything clean, which is basically what the apparently parallel passage in Matthew states (23:26). The instruction to give to the needy, contrasts with the previously mentioned greed (v 39), breaks down the social boundaries which Pharisaic purity laws had fixed and, of course, reflects a general Lucan concern for the poor (eg 12:33; see The poor, pp36–37).

Then follow three woes on the Pharisees (v 42–44), matched by three on the lawyers (v 45ff; in Mt 23 the two groups are the combined object of the woes). Woes were exclamations of grief or pity for those facing God's judgement (see comment on 10:13, p83). The first woe condemns the Pharisees for being concerned about tithing (giving a tenth of) herbs (18:11–12; Deut 14:22ff; Lev 27:30ff; Num 18:21ff), while at the same time neglecting justice and God's love (cf 10:25–27 and the following parable). Thus, as with the previous criticism (v 39–41), Jesus denounces the Pharisees for their wrong priorities in relation to the Law. The second woe criticises the Pharisees' love of social recognition and honour (contrast "love of God" in the previous verse) in public places, a criticism later levelled at the scribes also (20:46). The final woe against the Pharisees is particularly damning (v 44). Contact with a corpse resulted in ritual impurity (eg Num 19:11ff), so despite their obsession with purity laws, the Pharisees themselves were ironically an unmarked source of impurity. They themselves were impure and so they compromised the purity of their followers. The irony of purists being sources of impurity is stark.

Tasks

a **Who were the Pharisees and why was washing before meals important to them?**

b **Explain the four criticisms that Jesus made of the Pharisees.**

Criticism of the lawyers (v 45–50)

The "lawyers" were experts in Jewish Law and thus associates of the Pharisees (see previous section). Consequently, one of them regards Jesus' attack on the Pharisees as an attack on them too. This brings from Jesus three more woes, specifically directed against the lawyers. First, they are condemned for overburdening people with their various legal demands and traditions, while at the same time showing no pastoral concern to help them (cf Acts 15:10). The second woe concerns the fatal end of Old Testament prophets (cf 6:22–23; Acts 7:52; Neh 9:26). Jesus regards the lawyers' (and others) erection of these prophets' tombs not as a sign of respect to their memory but rather as an endorsement of their murder (Matthew's version of this is not as stark – 23:29–31). The point seems to be that because of their rejection of the teaching of the prophets, the tombs they erect are, in effect, memorials of rejection rather than respect. Jesus' next statement (v 49) could be a quotation from a writing (the "Wisdom of God") which currently remains unknown, or he may be simply personifying God's wisdom (as in, for example, Prov 8) rather than referring to the title of a book. Matthew's parallel passage attributes similar words directly to Jesus (23:34). The point of the 'quotation' is that God's messengers ("apostles" may also have this general sense) would suffer fatal rejection. Jesus then states that God holds his "generation" (cf v 29) accountable for the murders of all the prophets, from Abel (Gen 4) to Zechariah (probably the one identified as son of Jehoiada, 2 Chr 24:20–22) – the first and last murders in the Hebrew Bible (which ends with 2 Chronicles). In Matthew's parallel, it is the deaths of the "righteous" rather than of the "prophets" that Jesus' generation is held accountable for (23:35; Abel was not a prophet, in the usual sense of the term). It may be that the fall of Jerusalem to the Romans (AD 70) is the time in view when "this generation" was held accountable for its rejection of God's messengers (eg 13:33ff; 21:20ff). The final woe (v 52) corresponds to the final woe against the Pharisees (v 44) since both assert that the reverse of the intended goal has occurred. The lawyers are meant to be knowledgeable about God's will and to impart that knowledge to others, but have in fact hindered both (in Matthew the saying relates to God's kingdom rather than knowledge, 23:13).

In sum, Jesus criticises the religious leadership of Israel for being concerned more about appearance than sincerity, legality than morality, status than service, duty than compassion and, in a tragic irony, for being a hindrance rather than a help to the people. Such a comprehensive indictment provokes the combined hostility of the Pharisees and scribes/lawyers, who now interrogate Jesus and hope that his teaching will provide an opportunity to bring him down (v 53–54).

Outline your understanding of Jesus' three criticisms of the lawyers.

Hypocrisy (12:1–3)

Jesus is outdoors again (11:53ff) and, with a crowd of many thousands present, he teaches his disciples. He warns them first to beware of the "hypocrisy" of the Pharisees, that is, their insincere practice of religion (cf 11:39–41,43). This is pictured as "yeast" because of its hidden and corrupting influence (cf 1 Cor 5:6). In a probable reference to the coming Judgement Day, Jesus implies that this concealed insincerity will be exposed (v 2; 8:17) and broadcast (v 3). Hypocrisy is therefore a possibility for the disciples too, and they must guard against it. In Matthew (10:26–27) similar sayings are given as exhortations to the disciples to proclaim Jesus' teaching openly. In the light of this, and of the immediate context's references to persecution and confession of Jesus before others, some understand these sayings in Luke in the same sense as they are given in Matthew, regarding 12:1 as the conclusion of the previous passage.

Fear (12:4-7)

Describing his disciples as his "friends" (cf 11:53-54), Jesus urges them not to fear persecution by humans (cf v 11), but rather to fear judgement by God. Human persecution is limited to the body, but God has the authority to cast into hell. The word for 'hell' here is *Gehenna*. This was the Old Testament Valley of Hinnom (eg Josh 15:8; 18:16), south of Jerusalem, where children were sacrificed in fire to the god Molech (eg Jer 19:4-6; 32:34-35), and which therefore became associated with God's future judgement (eg Jer 7:30ff; 19:6ff; and later Jewish literature). It also became a site for the incineration of rubbish and dead criminals. To discourage fear of persecution Jesus also speaks of God's knowledge of the disciples (v 6-7), referring to sparrows and hair to illustrate the point. Five sparrows are sold in the market for a mere two pennies. One *assarion* (Greek: 'penny') was but one-sixteenth of a denarius, the latter being a day's wage (Mt 10:29 has "two sparrows sold for a penny"). Yet, despite their insignificant value not one sparrow is forgotten by God, and the disciples are worth more than many sparrows – a characteristically lesser-to-greater argument (eg 11:13). Also, even the number of insignificant hairs on their heads is known to God (cf 21:18).

Public acknowledgement and denial of Jesus (12:8-12)

Following on from a passage about fear of persecution, Jesus now says that public acknowledgement of him by the disciples will result in their heavenly acknowledgement at the judgement. Conversely, public denial of Jesus now will result in their heavenly denial then (cf 9:26). It may be that the formal setting of a trial is in view here (as v 11). That this statement of Jesus is not absolute, is seen in the case of Peter (22:31-34). While it has been argued that "the Son of Man" appears to be a different person than Jesus here (v 8), it is clear in the parallel passage (Mt 10:32) and generally in the Gospels that Jesus is the Son of Man (on this title, see p79). Some see a contradiction of Jesus' first statement (v 8-9) at the beginning of his next saying (v 10a), but it may be that Jesus is thinking in more general terms in the latter, rather than specifically of public identification with him. While speaking against the Son of Man will be pardonable at the judgement, blaspheming (Greek *blasphemeo*: 'slander, defame') against the Holy Spirit will not. The latter may relate to apostasy (falling away from the faith; eg v 9) or to attributing Jesus' work to Satan (11:15). Indeed, this last point is closely associated with blasphemy against the Spirit in Matthew (12:32) and, particularly, Mark (3:29-30). Finally in this passage, the disciples should not worry about either the manner or content of their defence before authorities, since the Holy Spirit will instruct them what to say in those circumstances (cf 21:12–15). Already in Luke we have seen examples of Spirit-inspired speech (1:41ff,67; 2:27ff), and in his sequel Luke will provide instances of the fulfilment of this promise (Acts 4:8ff; 6:10ff).

> **Tasks**
>
> a Outline your understanding of Jesus' teaching on hypocrisy in 12:1–3.
> b What does Jesus say about fear in 12:4–7?
> c Comment on Jesus' teaching about speech in relation to:
> (i) himself (ii) the Holy Spirit (iii) the authorities

The parable of the rich fool (12:13–21)

Jesus' instruction of his disciples is interrupted by someone in the crowd (cf v 1). Rabbis were often consulted to sort out disputes (v 13, "Teacher") and the man's demand that Jesus intervene with his brother (cf 10:40) about family inheritance may imply that simple application of the normal regulations (eg Num 27:1–11; Deut 21:16–17) was not possible. Jesus refuses to intervene, but turns the incident into a general lesson about the dangers of greed and the folly of equating life with possessions. This lesson and the parable that Jesus then gives to illustrate it (unique to Luke) reflect Luke's wider concern with issues of wealth and poverty (see pp36–37).

The parable itself is similar to a passage in the second-century-BC Jewish writing Ecclesiasticus or Sirach, which reads, "There is a man who is rich because of his effort and self-denial and this is his reward: he says, 'I have found rest and now I will live off my goods', he does not know how long it will be before he leaves it all to others and dies" (author's translation, Sirach 11:18–19). Jesus' statements immediately before (v 15) and after (v 21) the parable imply that its main character was guilty of both greed and godlessness (accepting that the context of the parable is authentic and not a Lucan creation). On the one hand, he appears as a prudent businessman who makes sensible plans for expansion. On the other, there appears to be a self-centred neglect of God and of the poor in his deliberations. He thinks only of himself and of his possessions, underlined by the numerous self-references of verses 17 to 19. His plans are abruptly interrupted by God, who in addressing him as a "fool" draws attention to his moral or religious folly, in the Old Testament sense of the term (eg Jer 4:22; Ps 14:1). The rich man's "many years" (v 19) contrast sharply with God's "this very night" (v 20), when "they" (literally) are demanding his "life" (or "soul", as the NRSV twice translates the same word in v 19). "They" may refer to angels (cf 16:22) or, more likely, is an indefinite way of referring to God. The climactic, divine question with which the parable ends (v 20) focuses on the temporary nature of possessions. Jesus' general application of the parable (v 21) contrasts living for earthly and heavenly wealth (cf v 33–34).

The Gospel of Luke

Task

Explain how the parable of the rich fool relates to its context (v 13–15,21).

Anxiety about food and clothing (12:22–32)

After dealing with the interruption from the crowd (v 13ff), Jesus returns primarily to the instruction of his disciples (v 22; cf v 1), but he continues with the theme of earthly possessions (note "therefore" in v 22). The main point of the passage, paralleled in Matthew 6:25–33, is that the disciples are not (negatively) to worry about food and clothing (v 22–30), but are (positively) to strive for God's kingdom instead (v 31–32).

Jesus had earlier drawn attention to Martha's worrying (10:41) and has just told his disciples not to worry about defending themselves before authorities (v 11). Now he again advises against anxiety (v 22,25–26,29), this time in relation to the basic necessities of food and clothing – vital concerns for a subsistent society and for itinerant preachers, such as he and his disciples were. Jesus provides a number of reasons why they should not be anxious about these things:

> Life/the body is more important than food/clothing (v 23).
> God feeds even the birds and clothes even the flowers (v 24,27–28).
> Worry cannot change even a little thing (v 25–26).
> The nations/Gentiles strive after all these things (v 30).
> The disciples' Father, God, knows their needs (v 30).
> Instead, they should be striving for God's kingdom – his gift to them (v 31–32).
> Necessities will be given to them (v 31).

Most of the passage focuses on Jesus' appeal to nature, using a characteristic lesser-to-greater argument to convince the disciples of God's care for them. God feeds even unclean birds of prey, such as ravens (Lev 11:13ff; Ps 147:9), and the disciples are much more valuable (cf v 7). Using a greater-to-lesser argument, Jesus says that not even Solomon in his royal splendour (v 31; 1 Kings 10) could match the beauty of the lilies. Jesus then reverts to arguing in the reverse direction – if God clothes the short-lived, dry field-grass which is used as oven fuel, "how much more" (cf 11:13) will he clothe them, "little-faiths" as they are (v 28, literally). Jesus' saying about the powerlessness of anxiety to lengthen human life even a little (v 25; though the word may refer to height as in 19:3) is particularly appropriate in this context, in light of the rich fool's inability to prevent his unexpected death, despite the (false) sense of security provided by abundant food and possessions (v 19–20). A contrast is drawn between the materialistic priorities of the nations or Gentiles (v 30) and what ought to be the priority of the disciples – the kingdom of God (v 31; see pp 79–81). While this kingdom should be their goal, it is also a gift to them from the Father (v 32; 22:29). Therefore, the "little flock" of disciples should not fear (cf Isa 41:14; 40:11).

Task: *Outline your understanding of the reasons Jesus gave to prevent his disciples worrying about food and clothing.*

Heavenly treasure (12:33–34)

Continuing the theme of possessions which has been running since verse 13, Jesus contrasts the transience of earthly wealth with the permanence of heavenly treasure (paralleled in Mt 6:19–21). The "possessions" (cf v 15) of the disciples are to be sold and the money given to the poor (cf 11:41; 14:33; 18:22; 19:8). In so doing, they would be exchanging their temporary earthly "purses" (10:4; 22:35–36) for ones that would not "grow old" (author's translation) and for an unfailing, heavenly treasure (cf v 21). Thus, in giving they would be gaining. And, unlike earthly wealth, heavenly treasure is burglar-proof and pest-proof! Finally, Jesus notes that one's devotion will follow what one values. The unfailing treasure of God's kingdom is what they must set their hearts on (v 31–32).

Task: *Explain Jesus' contrast between earthly and heavenly wealth.*

Readiness for the master's return (12:35–48)

The unifying theme of this passage is summed up in verse 40: "You also be ready, because the Son of Man is coming at an hour you do not expect" (author's translation) This idea of preparedness for a future return of Jesus, found elsewhere in Luke (17:20–37; 18:8; 21:27ff), is developed here by the use of three parables about (i) a returning master and alert slaves (v 36–38), (ii) a thief and a householder (v 39–40), and (iii) a returning master and faithful/unfaithful slaves (v 42–48). Consequently, the theme of the end times, which until now has been in the background of this chapter (v 2–3,5,8–10), is now brought into the foreground.

The passage opens with two metaphors (v 35) and a simile (v 36–38), each stressing the need for readiness. The disciples are first told, literally, to have their "loins girded" (author's translation; recalling Ex 12:11), since long robes had to be tucked into one's belt in preparation for activity such as a journey (eg 1 Kings 18:46). This is paraphrased in the NRSV as a command to be "dressed for action" (v 35a; it translates the same verb as "fasten (his) belt" two verses later). The second metaphor ("have your lamps burning", author's translation) likewise requires readiness (cf Mt 25:1ff). The extended simile (v 36, "be like …") is the first of the three parables in this section. The "waiting" (v 36) and "alert" (v 37) slaves are twice described as "blessed" (v 37–38) for being ready to open the door "as soon" as their master comes and knocks, even if it is during the night (v 38). That the "master" in this (and the third) parable represents Jesus is suggested, not only by the analogy of verse 40, but also by the fact that Jesus himself is so described in the passage (the "Lord" of v 41–42 = the "master" of the parables in the Greek). The unexpected and culturally subversive role-reversal of slave and master in this little parable (v 37) reflects a theme introduced in the infancy narrative (1:52–53), and anticipates Jesus' picture of himself as a servant at the table of his disciples (see 22:27). The image of the slaves having a meal after their master's return looks ahead to the heavenly or messianic banquet of Jewish expectation (eg Isa 25:6–8; 65:13–14; Lk 13:29; 14:15).

The second little parable (v 39) with its application (v 40), paralleled in Matthew 24:43–44, also points to the need for constant readiness due to the uncertainty of the timing of the Son of Man's coming. Peter's interruption (v 41) raises a question about the intended audience of "this parable" (possibly referring to all of v 35–41). The question is not answered, maybe intentionally so – to leave open its possible relevance to any hearer (or reader). However, the context indicates that the disciples are specifically in view (v 22,32), and it may be that Peter is wondering if the parable is specifically for the Twelve, as the leadership of the disciples, or for all disciples. The parable that follows Peter's question may imply that the Twelve ("manager" over "slaves") are in view, and would have had particular relevance later for Church leaders.

The parable (v 42–48/ Mt 24:45–51) envisages not just a master and his slaves, as in the first parable, but a master and a "manager/steward" (author's translation) whom he appoints over his other slaves – a common practice in larger first-century households. This manager may prove to be "faithful" and "prudent", by ensuring that the other slaves receive their regular rations. If he is found to be so when his master comes, then he is "blessed" (cf v 37–38) and will be promoted to greater responsibility. But if, due to the delay in his master's coming, he begins to mistreat the other slaves and becomes self-indulgent, then when his master returns at an unexpected time (cf v 39–40), he will be cut to pieces and placed with the "unfaithful". Since, unlike Matthew's parallel passage, this slave is called a "manager/steward" and the future tense is used of his appointment (v 42), it has been suggested that the parable has been modified to make it 'look forward' to Church leaders (cf Titus 1:7). However, neither of these observations demands such a conclusion. While bad slaves were often punished brutally by their masters in antiquity, the punishment of the slave in the parable seems excessive (v 46) and may be coloured by its metaphorical referent, the final day of judgement. There may even be a veiled reference to the eventual fate of Judas Iscariot (cf Acts 1:17,25). The mention of the master's delay in coming is intended to refer to, and increasingly reflected the Church's awareness of, the time interval before Jesus' return. And the challenge to the disciples is not to allow the delay to lead to unfaithful service of their master, lest they be caught out by his coming at an unexpected time (as v 40). Applications for other details of the parable, such as the steward's specific task (v 42) and reward (v 44), are probably not intended but should be taken simply as narrative colouring.

The distinction between sins committed knowingly and ignorantly (v 47–48, unique to Luke) reflects Old Testament regulations (eg Num 15:27–31). This distinction, along with the idea of proportionate accountability (v 48b), may be understood as a general principle for all followers of Jesus. Having said that, some have suggested that more specific distinctions are in view – such as between Jews and Gentiles, Jewish leaders and their people, Church leaders and members, and Christian believers and unbelievers. The parable implies varying degrees of both reward (v 44; cf 19:16ff) and punishment (v 46–48) at the final judgement.

> **Task**
>
> *Explain how the three parables in this section relate to its unifying theme (v 40).*

Division, not peace (12:49–53)

Jesus uses two metaphors (fire and baptism) in relation to the purpose of his mission (v 49–50). "Fire", an Old Testament symbol for God's punishment (eg Jer 43:12; Mal 4:1), refers to the judgement which Jesus is bringing to the earth (see 3:9,16–17; 9:54; 17:29–30), and which he is eager to see. "Baptism" may also figuratively refer to God's judgement, with which Jesus will be overwhelmed or deluged (eg Job 9:31; Ps 42:7; Isa 8:7–8) in his death (see the parallel saying in Mk 10:38 and its context, v 32ff; also Mk 15:33–34). Until this is "completed" (the same Greek verb is used in 18:31; 22:37a), Jesus is "stressed" or "dominated" (author's translation) by the thought.

These metaphors and Jesus' denial that he has come to bring peace "on the earth" (v 51, author's translation; cf v 49), stand in tension (at the least) with other statements in Luke, particularly the angels' song in 2:14 (also 1:79; 7:50; 8:48; Acts 10:36ff). However, "division" (v 51) results because his message is rejected (eg 2:34; 3:17; 7:49–50; 10:5–6). "From now on" (see comment on 1:48, p56) families will be divided by their response to Jesus (v 52–53; echoing Mic 7:6), since the demands of God's family and kingdom have a greater claim (see 8:19–21; 9:59–62; 14:26; 18:28–30). Thus, while Jesus' statements in this passage are worded as if he were speaking of the purpose of his mission, they can be understood as referring more to its effects (v 51–53 are paralleled in Mt 10:34–36).

> **Task**
>
> *According to this passage, how did Jesus view the purpose/effects of his mission?*

The Gospel of Luke

Interpreting the time (12:54–56)

While the reader may have assumed that Jesus had been primarily addressing his disciples up to this point (v 22,32), it now appears (v 54) that he has been speaking also to "the crowd" which was also present (v 1), at least from verse 49. However, the ambiguity of Jesus' audience (v 41) arises from its mixed character (v 1) and clear lines cannot always be drawn. In this passage (cf Mt 16:2–3), we are specifically told that the wider audience is in view. Jesus rebukes them for being able to read nature to make accurate weather forecasts – a cloud from the west bringing rain from the Mediterranean (I Kings 18:44–45) and a south wind bringing heat from the desert – but not being able to understand the significance of "this time" (author's translation; cf 11:16,29ff). As cloud and wind are signs of imminent weather conditions, so Jesus' ministry signifies the arrival of God's kingdom (7:18–23; 11:20). Such inconsistency on the part of the crowds brings from Jesus the charge of hypocrisy (cf v 1).

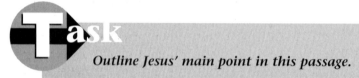

Outline Jesus' main point in this passage.

Settling with one's accuser (12:57–59)

By asking the crowds to judge for themselves what is right, Jesus basically repeats the theme of the question in the previous verse (v 56). Using a legal illustration probably related to the non-payment of debt, Jesus urges that an effort be made to settle with one's accuser or creditor, to avoid an indefinite sentence to a debtors' prison (cf Mt 18:28–30,34). The *lepton* (Greek: 'penny') was just one twenty-eighth of a day's wage (a denarius). In Matthew, this little parable appears in the context of being reconciled to a "brother who has something against you" (5:23–26, author's translation), but in Luke the context is failure to interpret the significance of Jesus' ministry (v 54–56). Thus, while not every detail of the parable is to be regarded as significant, the accuser appears to represent God, to whom the people must urgently be reconciled because of their debt (ie sin, eg 7:41–43; 11:4), or otherwise face certain and indefinite judgement.

What was the message of this parable to its original audience?

Repentance or destruction (13:1–9)

A long section in which Jesus teaches his disciples and the crowds outdoors (beginning at 12:1) is now brought to a climax with a dialogue (13:1–5) and a parable (13:6–9) which issue a call to repentance, an important Lucan theme (see comment on

10:13, p83). The passage is unique to Luke. The dialogue stresses that repentance is a *universal* need ("all" is used four times) and the parable that it is an *urgent* need – the fig tree is on borrowed time.

The dialogue concerns two tragedies, one involving Galileans and the other Jerusalemites. The first was raised by some in the crowd, possibly as an attempt at self-justification in the light of Jesus' warning of judgement immediately preceding this passage. Certainly, Jesus' reply seems to rebuke them for taking the traditional view that when people suffer they are being judged by God (cf Job 4:7–9; Jn 9:1–2). The first tragedy probably refers to an incident when Galilean pilgrims were offering Passover sacrifices (other sacrifices were slaughtered by the priests) at the temple in Jerusalem. For some reason, Pilate (cf 3:1) had the pilgrims cut down. While no other source refers to this event, similar violent Roman acts against the Jews are known to have occurred, often in connection with uprisings and protests against Roman occupation or religious insensitivity. While it may be that some in the crowd wanted to hear Jesus' political views on the Roman occupation, or even to trap him on the issue of Jewish revolutionaries, there is no indication of this in the text. Jesus himself provides an example of another, otherwise unknown, tragedy, this time apparently a natural rather than a human disaster. Siloam was a reservoir at the south-east end of the city and the tower may have been part of Pilate's building program to enhance the city's water supply (*Ant* 18.60).

Jesus' response to both these tragedies has the same form – a *question* concerning whether the tragedy indicates that the victims were more sinful than others, a *denial* that this was so, and a *warning* that his hearers will similarly perish, unless they repent. The conclusion that should be drawn from such events by Jesus' audience is therefore not that other people are worse than them, since they have been judged by God, but that "all" need to repent because "all" are facing God's judgement.

The parable of the barren fig tree develops the theme of repentance and is similar to Isaiah's song about an unproductive vineyard, threatened with destruction and representing Israel (Isa 5:1–7). Since the nation as a whole is often compared to a vineyard (eg Ps 80:8ff), it has been suggested that the narrower focus on a fig tree may represent a threat to Israel's leaders (11:37ff; 12:1). However, the parable probably had a national application (eg Jer 24:1–8; Mic 7:1). The basic message is that, like the owner of the fig tree, God has been patiently (v 7) looking for the fruit of repentance (see 3:7–9; 6:43–45; 8:14–15) in Israel, and has given it extra time (v 8). However, time is running out (cf v 56; 3:9,17) and urgent repentance is essential to prevent root and branch judgement (v 9,34–35; 11:50–51; 21:5ff,20). Certain details of the parable have probably no significance beyond their narrative function within the story (eg references to the gardener, the three years and one year). A similar story of barren trees, but lacking the period of grace, occurs in the ancient tale of Ahiqar which originated in pre-Christian times.

> ## Tasks
>
> a What main point did Jesus make in this passage with reference to two tragedies?
>
> b What is the message of the parable of the barren fig tree?

The healing of a crippled woman on the Sabbath (13:10–17)

The mention of Jesus teaching in a synagogue and, controversially, healing on the Sabbath day (ie the seventh day = our Saturday) recalls Jesus' earlier ministry in Galilee (4:14–16,31–37,44; 6:6–11) and anticipates similar activity later in his journey (14:1–6). The synagogue was a Jewish place of prayer and, especially, of the reading and explanation of the Jewish Scriptures (eg 4:16ff; Acts 13:14ff). In this uniquely Lucan passage, a deformed woman is present in the synagogue whose condition may have been what is known as spondylitis ankylopoietica (fusion of the spine) or skoliasis hysterica (hysterical or muscular paralysis). That she has had her condition for 18 years makes the former more likely. The passage attributes her condition to a "spirit" (v 11) and to "Satan" (v 16) and so it seems she is presented as another example of demon possession (see comment on 10:18, pp84–85; 11:14). Rather than going to the woman, Jesus calls her over to where he is, in front of the congregation, with the result that her restoration is visible to all. His act of healing involves speech and touch (compare 4:40; 5:13; 8:54) and his choice of words ("set free") recalls his mission manifesto, given in another synagogue at the start of his ministry (4:18–19), as well as reflecting her satanic bondage (v 16). Her reaction of praise to God is one example of a recurring Lucan theme (see p39).

The story might have suitably ended at this point, but the "synagogue leader" (author's translation; cf 8:41), responsible for ensuring that the Scriptures were read and taught, complains angrily that the Sabbath commandment (Ex 20:8–11/ Deut 5:12–15) is not being observed. Either because he does not want directly to confront Jesus or because he wants to reassert his authority as leader of the synagogue, or both, he addresses the congregation rather than Jesus. As far as he is concerned, healing is "work" which is not permitted on the Sabbath; it is undoubtedly clear to him that if the woman has been in this condition for 18 years, then she is not an urgent case and can wait until the Sabbath is over. Characteristically and significantly, Luke at this point refers to Jesus as "the Lord", thereby identifying him as the authoritative teacher, not least in relation to the Sabbath (cf 6:6), rather than the leader of the synagogue. Jesus then exposes the hypocrisy of the Jewish leaders generally (v 15; 12:1; also 12:56), who "untie" their oxen or donkeys (both included in the Sabbath work prohibition, Deut 5:14) for a drink on the Sabbath, but object when the woman is "untied" (author's translation; the same Greek verb is used in v 15–16) from satanic bondage. While the synagogue leader had used the word "ought"

(Greek *dei*) in relation to the Sabbath command (v 14), Jesus uses it in relation to the woman's release from Satan (v 16, Greek *dei*). In the matter of religious duty and obligation, then, the woman's need has priority for Jesus, for why should the leaders give priority to animals over "a daughter of Abraham" (cf 3:8; 16:22ff; 19:9)? Indeed, it is the descendants of Abraham, the father of the Jewish race, whom Jesus has come to bless (1:54–55,72–75). Jesus' release of this woman from Satan's grip (v 12,16) is a conquest of Satan's kingdom by God's kingdom (cf 11:20). This understanding of the woman's healing is reinforced by Luke's linking of it with the immediately following parables about God's kingdom (v 18, "therefore").

"All" Jesus' opponents are shamed (echoing the Greek version of Isa 45:16) while "all" (author's translation) the synagogue crowd are rejoicing (a favourite Lucan theme) at "all" the wonderful things he is doing (cf eg Ex 34:10; Deut 10:21). Ironically then, the synagogue leader who intended to shame Jesus and the congregation for a perceived breach of the Sabbath, is shamed himself, along with his like-minded colleagues, for their hypocritical application of the Sabbath command, which put legal observance before human need. The contrast of the characterisation in the story is stark, as the anger and hypocrisy of the synagogue ruler is set against the woman's praise, the crowd's joy and Jesus' wonderful deeds.

Tasks

a Discuss the passage's understanding of the woman's ailment and cure.

b Explain Jesus' problem with the Jewish leaders' view of the Sabbath.

c Comment on the characterisation in the story.

The parables of the mustard seed and the yeast (13:18–21)

These two little parables (paralleled in Mt 13:31–33 and Mk 4:30–32) are introduced by Jesus as illustrations of the "kingdom of God", the central theme of Jesus' ministry (see comment on 9:60, pp79–81). The male–female pairing (v 19 has *anthropos*, which in the cultural context probably refers to a man) may reflect Luke's fondness for gender balance in parables and stories (eg 15:3–10), but also represents the cultural reality of gender-specific tasks of the time. While both parables are generally about the growth of God's kingdom, more specifically they make the point that the kingdom will grow to a substantial size despite its small beginnings, such as the healing of the crippled woman with which this passage is linked (v 18). The "tree" (Mark calls it a "shrub" and Matthew uses both terms) that eventually grows from the proverbially small mustard seed could reach a height of about four metres, with branches on which birds nest. The latter echoes several Old Testament passages referring to the extent of kingdoms, including Israel's (Ezek 17:22–24; Ps 104:12; Dan 4:20–22). The birds in such passages refer to all the peoples of the earth, but it is not clear if such symbolism is intended in Jesus' parable. That Jesus did not use a much taller "tree" to make his point more effectively, such as the cedars of Lebanon (as in Ezek 17:22ff) where birds would be more likely to nest, may be due to his preference for the very small mustard seed as an illustration of the tiny beginnings of God's kingdom. If the mustard seed is very small, the amount of flour used by the woman was very large, being able to feed over 100 people. Thus, in both cases, the difference between a small beginning and a big end is stressed. Some have taken the reference to the yeast being "hidden" (v 21, literally) as illustrating the concealed nature of the kingdom, but this may be a case of overinterpreting the parable. The same may be said of attempts to interpret the yeast negatively in line with its Jewish use as a symbol of corruption (see comment on 12:1, pp101–102). On this view, the yeast symbolises either the growth of evil before the end, or the immoral background of the kingdom's typical members (tax collectors, sinners). However, the latter option appears to be too subtle and the parable clearly portrays yeast positively as a symbol of God's kingdom. Again, the number three (v 21; cf 11:5) has probably no significance beyond the parable, despite speculative attempts by some, for example body–soul–spirit and Jew–Samaritan–Gentile! The central point of the parables about God's kingdom is summed up in a more recent saying, "Big oaks from little acorns grow", an encouragement for the "little flock" of Jesus' disciples (12:32) and for the young Church of Luke's day.

Explain the main point of the two parables and how they illustrate it.

The narrow door (13:22–30)

Luke reminds us that Jesus is on a journey to Jerusalem (which started in 9:51ff), teaching as he goes. As often on this journey, and beyond, a question or comment by one of Jesus' hearers provides an opportunity for more teaching (eg 9:57; 10:25; 11:15,27,45; 12:13,41; 13:1). The unidentified inquirer introduces a favourite Lucan theme (salvation, being saved; see pp34–38) and is concerned about the apparently small number of those who are "being saved" (present tense, literally) – though he may have also been thinking about the final judgement. Indeed, Jesus had just spoken of the kingdom's small beginnings (v 18–21). While many Jews thought that only Israel would be saved, others, such as the sect that produced the Dead Sea Scrolls, limited salvation more narrowly to exclude unfaithful Jews. Around the end of the first century AD, the author of the Jewish apocalypse 2 Esdras wrote that while many have been created, "only a few shall be saved" (8:3), and that while God had made this world for many, the coming world was made "for the sake of only a few" (8:1). Jesus, as is often the case, does not directly answer the question, but says that "many" who will expect to get into God's future kingdom will instead find themselves excluded, while, unexpectedly, people from the four corners of the earth will be there.

Jesus responds with the brief parable of the "narrow door", the limited breadth of the door into 'God's kingdom' (cf v 28–29) implying that comparatively few will finally be saved (cf Mt 7:13–14). Using athletic language, Jesus urges his hearers to "strive" (Greek *agonizomai*) to enter the presently open door to the kingdom, and to do so urgently, because one day the door will be shut and all attempts at entrance will then be in vain (cf Mt 25:10–12). This closing of the door by "the owner of the house" (cf 12:39) pictures the future judgement (eg 10:12–15; 11:31–32) when the Son of Man will return (17:22ff). Jesus then is represented as the owner of the house, with whom those outside the door had eaten and drank (eg 11:37ff) and whose teaching they had heard. In this way, the parable combines Jesus' present ministry and future role as judge. At the final judgement, Jesus will not acknowledge the many who will try to get in (v 25; cf 12:9). Their association with Jesus during his ministry fell short of repentance (v 1–9), so their belated address of him as "Lord" is insincere (6:46ff) and they are dismissed as "evildoers" (v 27, echoing Ps 6:8; cf Mt 7:22–23).

When Jesus' hearers, called "the heirs of the kingdom" in Matthew's parallel passage (8:11–12), are excluded from the future "kingdom of God" (Lk 13:28; see pp80–81), they will weep and grind their teeth (a common expression in Matthew) in rage or despair (as in Acts 7:54; Ps 112:10). The patriarchs, or founding fathers, of Israel (cf 3:34; 20:37) will be there, as will "all the prophets" (a Lucan expression, not in Matthew's parallel passage), who foretold Jesus' coming (note "all the prophets" in 24:27; Acts 3:18,24; 10:43). Despite their racial descent from Abraham, they will not join him (cf 3:8). Instead, people from earth's four corners will be there at the feast of celebration in the future kingdom of God (cf Isa 25:6–8; Lk 6:21; 12:37; 14:15). That Luke has the four corners, and Matthew only two, reflects Luke's universalism (see p35). This shocking reversal of expectations in regard to the final membership of God's kingdom, with Gentiles on the inside and many Jews on the outside, is reinforced in the concluding saying about the first and the last (also in Mt 19:30; 20:16; Mk 10:31).

Tasks

a Explain how Jesus' answer relates to the question he was asked.

b Comment on the meaning of the parable (13:24–27).

c What is shocking about Jesus' concluding words in this passage (v 28–30)?

Herod's threat and Jesus' lament over Jerusalem (13:31–35)

While it is possible to consider Herod's threat to Jesus (v 31–33) and Jesus' lament over Jerusalem (v 34–35) as separate passages, the two are linked by Jerusalem's killing of the prophets (v 33–34) and by the theme of 'wanting' or 'desiring' (Greek *thelo*, v 31 and twice in v 34).

The interruption of Jesus by a comment or question (v 31), providing the opportunity for further teaching, is a common occurrence in Luke (eg v 1,23). While Pharisees are often characterised negatively (see comment on 11:37–44,53–12:1, pp99–102), some of them appear here to be concerned about Jesus' safety. However, their attempt to save him from death could be perceived as a misunderstanding of his mission, much like that of the disciples (9:44–45). They report a threat from Herod Antipas, the ruler of Galilee (3:1), in whose territory Jesus still apparently is. Herod's previous imprisonment and execution of John the Baptist (3:19–20; 9:9) is evidence enough that the threat is real. Jesus' disrespectful description of Herod as a fox may imply that he is viewed as an insignificant or deceitful or destructive person, since the metaphor was used in these various ways at the time. The latter of these three possibilities would appear to be the most likely in the present context and in the light of Herod's treatment of John the Baptist. Herod is thus characterised by Jesus as a verminous destroyer of God's messengers. Jesus' response to the Pharisees' advice continues the journey theme of the wider narrative – while they had told him to depart and "go" from Herod's threat (v 31, author's translation), he in turn told them to "go" to Herod (v 32) with a message that it was necessary for Jesus to "go" to Jerusalem (v 33, author's translation; Greek *poreuomai* in each case). Jesus would continue with his ministry, summed up here as exorcisms and healings (cf 4:40–41; 7:21; 9:1–2). The references to "today, tomorrow, and the third/next day" (v 32–33, author's translation) are not to be taken literally but probably refer to a short, indefinite period of time (cf 12:28), at the end of which Jesus will "finish" his mission (cf 12:50), or reach his goal, by suffering a prophet's fate in Jerusalem. Indeed, to continue to his destination and destiny is a "must" (a frequent word in Luke, eg 9:22; see p26). In the reference to "the third day" on which Jesus would "finish" (v 32), his disciples, and Christian readers of Luke, may have seen an allusion to his resurrection (cf 9:22; 18:33; 24:7,21,46).

The transition from Herod's threat to Jesus' lament is made by a double reference to Jerusalem as the place where prophets are killed (v 33b–34a). The rejection of the prophets, God's messengers, has been a recurring theme in Luke (4:24–27; 6:22–23; 11:47–51; cf Acts 7:52) and previously in the Old Testament (eg Neh 9:26; Jer 2:30; including in Jerusalem, eg Jer 26:20–23; 38:4–6). Jesus' lament over Jerusalem (also in Mt 23:37–39) may be seen as part of Luke's general emphasis on the city (see Geography, p28). It has been suggested that we have here a saying by 'Wisdom' (see comment on 11:49, p101), though others have argued that Jesus is speaking as wisdom's messenger (Sirach 24:7–12; Wisdom 7:27ff). The double use of Jerusalem (cf 10:41; 22:31) indicates the emotion or urgency with which the lament is made. 'Stoning' was used as a form of execution in the Old Testament, among other things, for blasphemy and apostasy (eg Lev 20:2; 24:14), so Jesus is saying that Jerusalem treated God's messengers as guilty of such capital offences. Jesus had "often" (which may imply other visits to Jerusalem, as in John) wanted to gather Jerusalem's "children" (ie her residents) as a hen (contrast "fox" in v 32!) gathers her chicks under her wings, a common Old Testament picture of God's protective care of his people (eg Deut 32:11–12; Ps 91:4). However, Jesus' will is contrasted with Jerusalem's (v 34) and Herod's (v 31). So, in a warning of impending judgement for her rejection of yet another of God's prophets, Jesus says that God will abandon her "house" (echoing Jer 12:7; 22:5), referring not to the Jerusalem temple (11:51; 19:46) but to the city collectively (cf Acts 2:36). Later, more specific warnings of judgement on Jerusalem will follow (19:41–44; 21:20–24; 23:28–31). Yet, from another angle, her people were no more guilty than others (v 4–5).

Jesus concludes by saying that Jerusalem will not see him again until they say, "Blessed is the one who comes in the name of the Lord", a quotation of Psalms 118:26, which seems to have been a priestly blessing on worshippers coming into the temple. In ancient Judaism, this psalm was apparently interpreted as referring to the Messiah, the expected coming king of Israel, and is applied again to Jesus later in Luke (19:38; 20:17). Indeed, the language of a 'coming one' seems to have become almost a technical term for the expected Messiah (3:15–16; 7:19). There is debate about when Jesus is referring to when he says that the people of Jerusalem would see him and speak approvingly of him. Certainly, these words from Psalm 118 were basically quoted when Jesus entered Jerusalem at the start of his last week (19:38), but that was by his followers and was rejected by the Jewish leadership. Therefore, some hold that the occasion envisaged is the future return of Jesus and that this is implied by Luke elsewhere (21:24; Acts 3:19–21).

Tasks

a Discuss the meaning of Jesus' reply to the Pharisees' advice.

b Comment on this passage's characterisation of Herod, Jerusalem and Jesus.

The healing of a man with dropsy on the Sabbath (14:1–6)

The setting of 14:1–24, a meal in the home of a prominent Pharisee on the Sabbath, recalls familiar Lucan themes – Jesus dining with others, especially Pharisees, as a teaching guest (5:27ff; 7:36ff; 10:38ff; 11:37ff), and conflict with religious leaders concerning the Sabbath (6:1–11; and see comment on 13:10–17, pp110–111). The opening scene (v 1–6), which shares several common features with the most recent Sabbath healing in Luke (13:10–17), introduces a man suffering from "dropsy" (also known as oedema), which involved swelling of the limbs due to accumulation in the body's tissues of fluid leaking from the circulatory system. He may have appeared on the way to the meal or 'gate-crashed' it (as in 7:37). Conscious of their close observation of him (cf 11:53–54), Jesus asks the host and his colleagues about the legitimacy of healing on the Sabbath (cf 6:9). Is it to be classed as 'work' and, therefore, a breach of the Sabbath command? Their silence may indicate division among them or a dilemma – to allow the healing would be unlawful in their view,

The Gospel of Luke

but to object might appear heartless. Alternatively, they may have wanted Jesus to continue with the healing and by so doing publicly to breach the Sabbath. After the healing, Jesus "sent him away", or 'released' him as the verb may be translated – referring rather to his actual healing (as in 13:12). As before (13:15), Jesus points to their own practice on the Sabbath as justification for the healing, noting that they would act "immediately" to rescue their children (some manuscripts have "donkey" instead of "son") or oxen from drowning. While later rabbis were divided over similar circumstances, the Jewish sect that produced the Dead Sea Scrolls, who were contemporary with Jesus, allowed a human but not an animal to be rescued in such circumstances. Again, the religious leaders are silent (compare their shame in 13:17), and Jesus' superiority as a teacher of Israel is demonstrated (cf 20:26), as is his concern to put human need before legalistic tradition.

Tasks

a **What Lucan themes are highlighted in 14:1?**

b **Explain the main point of this passage.**

A parable about guests at a wedding banquet (14:7–11)

Just as the Pharisees had been watching Jesus (v 1), he is observing them as fellow guests at the meal (v 7a). However, in contrast to their silence (v 4,6) he has something to say. Noticing that the dinner guests choose the "first seats" (v 7, literally), Jesus tells them a "parable" (possibly influenced by Prov 25:6–7), with the lesson coming in the concluding punch line (v 11). Understanding the parable requires an awareness of the cultural reality that seating arrangements at a meal indicated – they reinforced one's place in the social hierarchy. A meal was an opportunity to display and, if possible, enhance one's social status. Elsewhere in Luke, both the Pharisees and scribes are characterised as loving the "first seats" in the synagogues and, in the case of the scribes, also at banquets (11:43; 20:46). Here Jesus observes the same pursuit of social honour and position. We should note, however, that Jesus does not seem to have a problem with public recognition or social honour as such (v 10), but with the means by which a person attains it. It is not to be taken but received, not to be selfishly pursued but humbly accepted. Those who seek the "first seats" may ironically end up in the "last place" (v 9–10, literally), publicly shamed rather than honoured. Conversely, those who sit in the "last place" to begin with may be publicly honoured by having their social status enhanced by the host. Thus, Luke's theme of status reversal is continued (eg 1:52–53; 13:30). The parable's lesson on the need for humility is stressed in its concluding statement (v 11), which is also found elsewhere in different contexts (18:14; Mt 23:12).

a Explain the cultural background of this parable.
b What main lesson is Jesus teaching here?

Hospitality to the needy (14:12–14)

Having just addressed the guests, Jesus then speaks to the host, urging him not to invite friends, family and rich neighbours to meals, but rather the poor and disabled (the latter being a regular concern of Luke). A close comparison of this passage with the previous one shows that they share the same structure, the central feature being a negative followed by a positive instruction. The cultural expectation of reciprocation ensured that if people were hosts to their inner circle and the socially powerful, then they in turn would be their guests. This practice encouraged the pursuit of social status and also resulted in further social exclusion of the already marginalised poor and disabled. As in his previous instructions to the guests, Jesus is therefore calling for the abandonment of social conventions, in relation to meals, which ensured the continuation of the pursuit of prestige and the exclusion of the needy. However, Jesus' words should not be taken as a complete prohibition on inviting one's friends and family to a meal. We have here a Semitic idiom which puts the emphasis on the positive (v 13) rather than the negative (v 12). Thus, invitations should not be extended exclusively, nor even primarily, to one's own social circle (for the same idiom see, for example, 10:20; 23:28; Jn 6:27). Unlike the Pharisees' usual guests, the poor and disabled (v 13; the same list of four also occurs in v 21) would not have the means to reciprocate the host's invitation, but he would be blessed by being repaid by God at "the resurrection of the righteous" (part of the Pharisees' creed; 20:27,34–36; Acts 23:6ff; 24:15). The point is that hospitality and generosity should be shown to all without any expectation of repayment (see 6:32–36); yet just as those who do not seek recognition receive it (v 10), so those who do not seek repayment receive it (v 14).

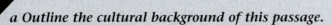

a Outline the cultural background of this passage.
b What main lesson is Jesus teaching here?
c In what way is Jesus' teaching socially subversive in this and the preceding passage?

The parable of the banquet (14:15–24)

A similar parable is found in Matthew (22:1–10), but there are enough differences to make it a matter of debate whether we have two distinct parables or two versions of the same parable. A similar story is also found in later Jewish literature (the Jerusalem Talmud, fifth century), involving a wealthy tax collector called Bar Ma'jan who invited city dignitaries to a banquet. Their refusal to come resulted in the poor being invited instead, lest the food go to waste. As often in Luke, an interruption of Jesus by one of his hearers provides an occasion for further teaching (see comment on 13:23, p112). Both the use of the word "blessed" (cf 11:27–28) and the reference to the future kingdom of God by the dinner guest (v 15) reflect Jesus' immediately preceding statement (v 14). The imagery of the end-time kingdom of God as a meal was a common Jewish symbol (see comment on 13:29, p113). On one level the parable may be read as an example of a host who puts into practice Jesus' immediately preceding instructions to his host (v 12–14). Indeed, the host in the parable is characterised much like Jesus' host, that is, a man of position and wealth (eg a "great" banquet, "many" guests) and, similarly, the social position of the initial invitees (v 18ff) probably corresponds to Jesus' fellow dinner guests.

On another level, triggered as it is by the guest's remarks, the parable probably relates to the eschatological (end times) feast of God's kingdom. The "master"/"owner of the house" then represents God, the banquet his kingdom, and the three groups of invitees have been understood to stand, in turn, for the Jewish leaders (whom Jesus is addressing), Jewish outcasts (v 21) and, finally, the Gentiles (v 23; outside the city, on the country lanes). In this view of the parable, the Jewish leaders have rejected God's invitation to his end-time kingdom in Jesus, and so the outcasts of Jewish society, and even the Gentiles, will be guests at God's table instead. In an ironic status-reversal, typical of Luke, those expected to be in God's kingdom will not, while the unexpected will. However, there is no indication in the parable or its context that the third group of invitees represents the Gentiles, even if this might be inferred from other passages (13:28–30; Isa 25:6–9). It may be that the second and third group of invitees are subdivisions of the same group – the outcasts and marginalised of Jewish society. The presence of the third group in the parable may be dictated simply by the narrative need of the master to fill his house, since he has prepared a "great" banquet. On the other hand, it could be argued that such a reading of the parable creates inconsistencies with Luke's wider theology, such as the idea that God is pictured as intending initially to invite only the Jewish leadership or the socially elite of Israel, and that the presence of outcasts and, possibly, Gentiles is but an afterthought. However, this problem may be due to overinterpretation of the narrative flow of the parable, since not every detail of the story may need to fit into a coherent set of correspondences.

Nevertheless, some comment on the details of the parable is necessary. The double invitation (v 16–17) was required in order for the host to have an idea of how many animals to kill in preparation for the feast and to allow guests time to make any necessary arrangements. The refusal of the guests to come after presumably accepting the initial invitation would have been perceived as a serious discourtesy, resulting in social dishonour for the host (hence his anger). The three sample excuses are similar to legitimate exemptions from military service in Deuteronomy due to the threat of death (20:5–7; 24:5). However, attendance at a meal presented no such threat and the excuses do not justify their snub to the host. The first two imply that the invitees are landowners, people of wealth and substance. While it might appear that the first excuse is unrealistic (who would buy something *before* inspecting it?), some transactions were subject to inspections after purchase. The second excuse is similar (a recent purchase) and the number of oxen suggests a wealthy farmer is in view (one or two yoke of oxen being sufficient for the average farm). The third excuse ("just been married") is abrupt and, unlike the others, is not accompanied by a request to be excused, or an apology. Also, it is not clear how it would prevent attendance at a meal and begs the question why his marriage was not mentioned at the initial invitation. The problem with all the excuses within the narrative is that they are not urgent enough to justify rejection of the host's invitation. In terms of the parable's application, the message is that possessions and people are not to be given priority over the call of God's kingdom, a theme underlined elsewhere in Luke (v 26,33; 8:14; 9:59–62; 12:33–34).

The decision to invite outcasts (v 21; the same list occurred in v 13) represents a departure from social convention since these people would not be able to reciprocate the hospitality. The contrast in social status and material prosperity between the host and the belated invitees is sharp. Indeed, while the initial group were "invited", the servant has to "bring in" and "compel" the others, such is their reluctance to break with convention and cross the social boundary to attend a banquet hosted by a stranger. Here we see, of course, Luke's special concern for the poor and needy (see The poor, pp36–37). A tragic example of misuse of a parable due to overinterpretation is found in the early Church bishop Augustine's justification of the forced conversions of heretics and schismatics on the basis of the words "compel them to come in" (author's translation). It is not clear if the concluding statement (v 24) is part of the parable or Jesus' challenge to his fellow guests. In favour of the former is the fact that it appears to be part of the master's statement to his slave (v 23–24), implying that the original invitees will not even receive the portion of food often sent to those unable to attend. However, the Greek word for 'you' in verse 24 is plural which suggests that Jesus is now addressing the religious leaders at the meal. Jesus' parables often end with a challenging punch line (eg v 11) and it may be that the parable here merges with its application, as Jesus makes its central character (representing God) speak directly and dramatically to the dinner guests. The refusal of the Jewish religious leaders to accept God's invitation to his kingdom, offered in Jesus, will be taken as final and Israel's outcasts (and possibly the Gentiles) will be at the feast instead (cf 13:22–30).

> **Tasks**
>
> a Discuss the interpretation and application of this parable.
> b Outline the message of the parable in a sentence.

Conditions of discipleship (14:25–35)

Both the audience and the setting now change as Jesus is no longer addressing Jewish religious leaders at a meal in a Pharisee's home (14:1–24), but is now teaching "large crowds" (cf 12:1,54) outdoors en route to Jerusalem. Indeed, Luke begins this section by reminding us of this journey that commenced in 9:51. As is often the case in Luke, Jesus "turned" to his hearers, indicating the importance of what follows (see comment on 9:55, p78). The theme of this section, and indeed of most of the remainder of the journey narrative, is discipleship. The word "disciple" occurs three times here (v 26,27,33) and is the usual translation of a Greek word (*mathetes*) meaning 'pupil', 'apprentice' or 'adherent'. The term was used for the students and followers of various religious, philosophical and political teachers and leaders in the ancient world. Jewish rabbis or teachers had their students to whom they taught and interpreted the Jewish Scriptures and Jesus was often addressed as "rabbi" in the other Gospels (eg Mt 9:5; Luke prefers "teacher", which was more understandable for his Gentile readers). In the Gospels the word is used of followers of the Pharisees, of John the Baptist (eg Lk 5:33) and of Moses (Jn 9:28), as well as of the followers of Jesus – including his followers generally (eg Lk 19:37) and the Twelve specifically (eg Mt 10:1). Luke uses the term for Jesus' followers generally and not of the Twelve specifically.

The three uses of the word "disciple" in our passage are found in parallel statements (in the Greek each contains a negative condition followed by "cannot be my disciple"), which set out the terms or conditions of discipleship. The universal application of these statements is seen in their opening words. The first statement (v 26) requires that Jesus be given priority over one's family (cf 8:19–21; 9:59–62; 12:51–53; 18:28–30 and the similar passage in Mt 10:37). The use of the word "hate" reflects an idiom meaning 'love less' (cf Mt 10:37), as in the case of Leah, where her being "hated" (Hebrew of Gen 29:31) is equivalent to Rachel being "loved ... more" than her (Gen 29:30). Clearly, the issue is priority of allegiance rather than an instruction to despise one's family, which would contradict Jesus' teaching elsewhere (eg 18:20b). After the mention of six family members who must not be given priority over Jesus, the list adds climactically that even one's own life must be secondary (cf 9:24; 17:33; Jn 12:25)[1]. The second statement (v 27; cf 9:23; Mt 10:38)

---

[1] The NRSV's "life *itself*" (v 26), while grammatically possible as a translation, is probably influenced by the desire for gender neutrality and gives the impression that Jesus is speaking about hatred of life generally rather than of one's own life. While the former is unknown in Jesus' teaching elsewhere, the latter is consistent with it (see references above). Further, the word translated "itself" is left untranslated by the NRSV both at the beginning of the verse and in the next verse, where it clearly refers to a person.

must be seen in the context of Jesus' journey to Jerusalem, where he will be crucified (9:22ff; 13:31ff). Those who follow him must metaphorically carry their crosses, that is, endure rejection and suffering (cf 12:4ff,11).

Then follow two brief, parallel parables, about a tower builder and a warring king (v 28–32). The basic point of each is the same, that a person should not begin what they can't finish – otherwise there will be tragic results (ridicule of the tower builder and defeat of the king). The occurrence of "first sit down" in both parables indicates the importance of not rushing thoughtlessly into something. The application of the parables, in a context where Jesus is spelling out the conditions of discipleship, would seem to be that before anyone begins to follow Jesus he or she should "first" consider the commitment that's required (cf 9:57–58), rather than end up in ridicule or failure (cf 8:13–14). If the third of the "cannot be my disciple" statements (v 33) is read as the concluding application of the two parables, then it appears to go way beyond their main point (hence, some regard it as a later addition). Alternatively, it may be highlighting the far greater commitment entailed in following Jesus than in construction or warfare (a lesser-to-greater argument). Alternatively, perhaps the statement should not be taken narrowly as a conclusion to the parables, but as a summing-up of this passage thus far, on the conditions of discipleship. Discipleship involves 'giving up' or 'saying farewell' (as in 9:61 where the same Greek word is used) to "all" one's possessions (cf 5:11,28; 6:24,30; 12:33; 18:22–24). However, it is clear elsewhere in Luke–Acts that some private ownership of goods is accepted as consistent with discipleship (4:38; 5:28–29!; 8:3; 19:8–9; Acts 5:1–4). Thus, it has been suggested that in verse 33 Jesus is addressing a select group of disciples such as the Twelve or that what is being demanded is the willingness to give up all rather than the act. The problem here is that neither view is supported by the text or context. At the very least, as with the previous sayings, Jesus is demanding an allegiance that has priority over everyone else and everything else.

The passage concludes with a parabolic saying about salt (v 34–35; cf Mt 5:13; Mk 9:49–50). At first sight it appears to be distinct from the preceding verses, yet it makes the same point as the two earlier parables – the need to finish what has been started. More specifically, just as salt may become useless as a flavouring for food and is then discarded, the implication is that those who begin to follow Jesus may end up not being "fit" (cf 9:62) for the task. However, while the general point of the saying is fairly clear, there are difficulties with the details. First, the text speaks of salt "becoming foolish" (v 34a, literally)! This may be explained as bringing the application into the parable itself, so that what may happen to disciples is attributed to the salt. Also, the underlying Aramaic word that Jesus used may well have had the additional meaning of 'saltlessness' (the Hebrew term certainly has both meanings), and indeed Mark's Greek favoured the latter (9:50). The second difficulty is with the idea of salt losing its saltiness, leading to the question, "... with what will it be seasoned?" (v 34b, literally). Salt cannot lose its

The Gospel of Luke

flavour, but the reference may be to salt contaminated with impurities, rendering it unfit for the seasoning of food. Alternatively, perhaps the saying reflects the practice of the collection of salt crystals from the Dead Sea after evaporation, when sometimes other, impure crystals were mistakenly gathered. The final difficulty concerns understanding the implied uses of salt in relation to the "soil/land" (author's translation) and the "manure heap" (v 35). It may have been used as a weedkiller and, possibly, as fertiliser, though the latter use is uncertain. Also, salt apparently may have been added to manure to slow fermentation until the time for its application. Whatever the contemporary functions and applications of salt and their specific relevance as metaphors for discipleship, the basic lesson is on the need for continuing commitment.

The passage finishes as it started, with an indication of its importance – the statement about the need to "listen" (cf 8:8) corresponding with how Jesus "turned" to address the crowds at the beginning (v 25).

Tasks

a Comment on the meaning of the three statements on discipleship in this passage (v 26,27,33).

b Explain the relevance to discipleship of the two parables (v 28–32).

c Discuss the meaning of the saying about salt and its connection with the preceding verses.

The parables of the lost sheep and the lost coin (15:1–10)

The context and key to the interpretation of these parables, as well as the one that follows them, are found in the opening verses of the chapter (v 1–2). The parables are a response to the complaint of the Pharisees and scribes (see comment on 11:37ff, p99ff) that Jesus was welcoming towards sinners, seen most clearly in his table fellowship with them (cf 5:29–32; ch 14; 19:7). Having concluded the previous section with Jesus' call to "listen" (14:35), Luke now notes that it is "all" the tax collectors (see comment on 3:12, p70) and sinners who are coming to "listen" to Jesus. This contrasts with the "grumbling" (cf 5:30; 19:7) of the religious leaders which recalls the complaints of the Israelites against God in Moses' day (eg Num 11:1; 14:27,29). Table fellowship was a sign of social acceptance and the leaders believed Jesus had crossed a boundary and compromised purity laws (see comment on 11:37ff, p99ff) in dining with such people.

The three parables which reply to the leaders' criticism, especially these first two, have similar structure and content, as well as sharing key words. The two short parables of the lost sheep and the lost coin both have a main character who searches for and finds something that is lost, resulting in joy with summoned friends and neighbours. The application of both parables is made to joy in heaven over repentant sinners. These parables provide an example of Luke's fondness for male–female pairing (see Women, p37). The much longer parable of the lost son continues these themes, and uses the vocabulary of losing, finding and rejoicing. It may also be noted that with each new parable the extent of the proportional loss increases (one out of one hundred, one out of ten, one out of two).

The first parable (v 4–7), as is often the case in the Old Testament (eg Ps 23), pictures God as a shepherd (on shepherds, see p38, footnote). In this context it may especially recall Ezekiel 34 (eg v 11ff), where Israel's leaders are characterised as bad shepherds while God himself seeks out his lost sheep. The attitude of the Pharisees and scribes to the lost sheep of Israel (v 1–2) is condemned and contrasted with that of God himself who has come seeking the lost in Jesus (19:7,10). Matthew has a similar parable about a straying sheep, in a context dealing with believers in Jesus (18:12–14). To speculate on debated details such as what the size of the flock implies about the wealth of the shepherd, who cared for the remaining 99, why the sheep is carried back (cf Isa 40:11; 49:22), and the apparently excessive joy of the shepherd, is to be diverted from the main focus of the parable – God's joy over the restoration of the lost sheep of Israel, a joy which contrasts sharply with the grumbling over Israel's contemporary religious shepherds. Both joy and repentance are, of course, favourite themes of Luke.

While this parable and the next focus on the personal search for a passive object (emphasising the initiative of God), the application highlights the active response (repentance) of the sinner, looking at salvation from both the divine and human angles. The "ninety-nine righteous people who need no repentance" (v 7) may be an ironic reference to the self-righteous religious leaders (v 1–2; 18:9ff) or may refer generally to those Jews who were not living as the tax collectors and sinners. The parable of the lost coin (Greek *drachma*, about a day's wage), unique to Luke, makes the same point (v 8–10). While it has been suggested that the coin may have been on a headdress as part of a wedding dowry, it is not clear that this is what is in view here. The woman's efforts to find the coin are stressed, which may point to the commitment of God to restore lost sinners, though, as with the previous parable, the accent falls on the sinner's repentance (v 10). This parable concludes by referring more specifically to joy among "God's angels" (author's translation; cf 12:8), rather than generally in "heaven" (cf v 7).

The Gospel of Luke

> **Tasks**
>
> a How does the context of these two parables provide the key to their interpretation?
>
> b What insight into the meaning of the parables is provided by their concluding applications?

The parable of the lost son (15:11–32)

Traditionally called the parable of the prodigal son, due to the younger son's lavish and wasteful behaviour (v 13), this well-known and uniquely Lucan story of Jesus belongs with the other two parables in this chapter, sharing with them a similar structure and common themes (see previous section). However, this parable develops these themes at greater length in a more detailed story, which heightens the sense of loss both in ratio (one out of two) and value (a son). As with the other two parables, the context and key to its interpretation are found in the opening verses of the chapter (v 1–2). In this light, the symbolism of the three main characters (v 11) is clear. The younger son represents the sinners (and tax collectors) with whom Jesus is dining and the older son stands for the Pharisees and scribes who are critical of Jesus for welcoming sinners. The father, then, symbolises God who both rejoices at the repentance of sinners (cf v 7,10) and urges the critical religious leaders to join in celebrating the return of the lost.

There is debate over where the focus of the parable lies, that is, over who should be viewed as the primary character. While traditional titles for the parable make the reader focus on the younger son (the prodigal/lost son), some feel that the main lesson of the parable is found in its climactic scene with the older son, since Jesus is primarily addressing the criticism of the religious leaders. Thus, it is argued that any title for the parable should reflect this (eg the reluctant/angry brother). On the other hand, it may be that the focus should fall on the father (and on the shepherd and the woman in the other parables?), as the unifying and central character of the parable, whose concern for both sons represents God's love for both sinners and the religious leaders. Again, the parable could be renamed to reflect this (eg the compassionate/patient father). Alternatively, perhaps equal importance should be attached to each character and its corresponding message (the parable of the father and his two sons). Indeed, it has been suggested that the parable should be read or heard three times, each time from the perspective of a different main character.

Structurally, the parable may be divided according to its three main characters, after their introduction in verse 11 – the younger son's departure and return (v 12–20a), the father's welcome (v 20b–24), and the older son's reaction (v 25–32). However, the parable can also be divided into two broadly parallel parts, each focusing on one of the sons – the younger son (v 11–24) and the older son (v 25–32). In each part we read of the particular son's return home (v 20,25) and of the reaction of the father (v 21ff, v 28ff). The two parts are paralleled also by common terms (eg field, slaves, fatted calf, celebration) and, importantly, each ends with the refrain concerning the younger son being dead then alive, lost then found.

The younger son's request for his share of his inheritance (cf 12:13) before his father's death, and his father's compliance with it, would probably have been unusual and reflected badly on the son (cf Sirach 33:19–23), even if the practice was not unheard of (cf Tobit 8:19–21). However, it is not clear if the request would have been seen as equivalent to the younger son wishing that his father were dead. Both sons receive their share of the inheritance, the older son receiving twice as much since he was the first-born (Deut 21:17). While the older son remains at home, the younger son's apparent rejection of his family is seen in his packing up "everything" (author's translation) and his quick departure from home to a "distant" country. Away from the demands and constraints of home, he becomes reckless – squandering his inheritance in self-indulgent living (his brother later mentions "prostitutes", v 30) which leaves him completely broke. The arrival of a severe famine makes his situation desperate, since now he has no resources left to see him through it. His descent is practically complete when he has to tend pigs, unclean to him as (presumably) a Jew (cf 8:32; Lev 11:7), and, indeed, yearns to eat their food. The "pods" (v 16) were the fruit of the carob or locust tree. A later saying from an early fourth-century rabbi states that the Israelites repent when they are reduced to carob pods (in *Leviticus Rabbah* 35.6), which was, of course, exactly the case with the younger son in our parable. Immediately before the repentance, we read of his lowest point in the words, "and no one gave him anything" (v 16) – no doubt due to the famine conditions.

The turning point in the younger son's situation is found in the expression "he came to himself" (v 17, ie to his senses), which marks the beginning of his repentance (cf v 7,10). He realises that even his father's temporary day labourers ("hired hands"; this position was more insecure than that of a household slave) are better off than he, since they are well fed while he is starving. The next step, after this realisation, is a plan of action (v 18–19). This involves a return to his father, and a rehearsal of a confession that he has sinned (cf v 1–2 – both against heaven (a reverent euphemism for 'God'; cf v 7) and before his father – and of an acknowledgement that he does not now deserve the status of son, (indeed, not even of one of his father's slaves, v 22), but can only hope for the position of a hired hand. It should be noted here that the observation that the father is distinct from God *within* the story (v 18) does not necessarily compromise the fact that he acts as a symbol for God *beyond* the story. The plan is then activated, the word "arising" (v 20a, author's translation; the same Greek verb is used at the start of v 18) referring literally to the beginning of his long journey from the distant country back to his father and metaphorically to his rising from death to life (v 24,32).

The focus of the parable then turns to the father's response to his returning and repentant son. The father's "compassion" for him (cf 7:13; 10:33), reflecting God's fatherly mercy (eg 6:36), is aroused by the sight of him in the distance even before he begins his confession. This, and the fact that he runs to meet him, embraces him and kisses him (cf Gen 33:4), all *before* the son's confession, probably points to God's initiative and eagerness in relation to the restoration of sinners. Before the son can get through his rehearsed speech, the father issues urgent orders to his slaves. The call for the best (literally "first") robe, ring and sandals probably reflects to some degree the son's destitute condition, but these items are primarily symbolic within the story of the restoration of his status and honour as son (v 24, "this son of mine"), and of his reinstatement within the family (compare symbols of honour in Esth 6:6–11). While some have seen the ring as a symbol of the father's authority (cf Gen 41:41–42; Esth 8:2), this is more than likely reading too much into its significance, not least because the older son as first-born had more authority (cf v 31). The killing of a fatted calf for the homecoming celebration implies a large banquet with many guests. The need to "celebrate" and "rejoice" (v 23,32) recalls the similar climax of the other parables (v 6,9), and symbolises God's joy over repentant sinners. This theme and its accompanying refrain ('dead but alive' and 'lost but found') will be repeated at the parable's climax. Since it is culturally unlikely that a snubbed, self-respecting Middle Eastern father would have so openly and lavishly welcomed a disgraced son back in these circumstances, it may be that these untypical details are intended to portray the extent of God's delight in welcoming sinners who come to him.

The final section of the parable (v 25–32) is taken up with the older son, who is symbolic of the Jewish religious leaders who grumbled at Jesus' welcoming attitude to sinners (v 1–2). The fact that he is "angry" (v 28) contrasts with the "compassion" (v 20) of his father. While the religious leaders are offended by Jesus' practice of eating with sinners, his actions are representative of God's love for such people. In the parable, then, Jesus is clearly presenting the leaders as contrary to God's will and himself as being in line with it. As with his actions towards the younger son, it is an act of grace that the father suffers the indignity of leaving the feast he is hosting to deal with the older son's disrespectful refusal to attend, especially since the older son was expected to play an active part on such occasions. In the father's "plead[ing]" with him (v 28) we can hear Jesus urging the leaders to join in the celebration for repentant sinners, rather than grumbling at a distance. The older son's response metaphorically characterises the Pharisees and scribes as those who feel they have served God for years and yet have not been rewarded in such a generous way as the sinners to whom Jesus offers the blessings of God's kingdom. Indeed, within the parable there does appear to be some point to the older son's sense of injustice, since apparently disgraceful recklessness is rewarded while loyal service is not. The older son adds to the earlier description of his brother's shameful selfishness by referring to "prostitutes", either because he wants to put him in as bad a light as possible or because he simply makes an assumption.

Ironically, while the older son seeks to present himself as loyal to his father, he also regards himself as a slave rather than a son (v 29). Added irony is apparent when we recall that this attitude is the exact reverse of that of the younger son (v 19). The slave may have said "your brother" and "your father" (v 27) when speaking to the older brother, but the latter reveals his sense of alienation from the family by referring to his brother as "this son of yours" (v 30; cf v 32) and failing to use the address "Father", unlike his brother (v 18,21). The father patiently and graciously reaffirms that he is still his son (v 31a; *teknon*: 'child', is an affectionate address; cf 2:48) and that "all" his father has is his. This clearly implies that God's kingdom is for the Pharisees and scribes as well, if they do not exclude themselves by refusing to go in (v 28). The celebration and joy over the younger son's return, expressive of God's joy at the repentance of sinners (v 7,10), was a must (v 32, using *dei*, a word common in Luke to indicate divine necessity), since the dead son was alive again, and the "lost" (translated "dying" by the NRSV in v 17) son, as with the sheep and the coin, had been found. The parable is left open-ended with no indication of what the older son's response to the father's plea was. Would he be persuaded to join the celebration or would he remain at a critical distance? The Pharisees and scribes, and any like-minded readers, are left to finish the story for themselves.

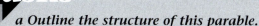

a **Outline the structure of this parable.**

b **How does the parable's context (v 1–2) help us interpret the symbolism of its main characters?**

c **What do you think would be the best title for the parable? Explain your answer.**

The parable of the shrewd manager (16:1–13)

The focus of Jesus' teaching now shifts from the Jewish religious leaders (15:2ff) to his disciples (16:1), though the former are still in view (16:14–15). The favourite Lucan theme of wealth runs through most of the chapter. This parable with which it opens has notable links with the immediately preceding parable (the lost son) such as, for example, their identical openings (literally "A certain man …") and the fact that possessions are "squandered" (15:13; 16:1; the same Greek word is used in both verses). There is difference of opinion over exactly where the parable originally ended, which affects its interpretation to some extent. It is generally agreed that verses 10–13 are not part of the parable but are rather developments of it, linked to the previous verses by various catchwords. However, some would end the parable proper in the middle of verse 8, viewing what comes after as its application. Others would find the parable's conclusion at the end of verse 8, with the application coming in verse 9.

Some locate the end of the parable even earlier, at the end of verse 7, by taking "the master/Lord" (v 8a, literally) as a reference to Jesus, rather than the master in the parable. However, if this is so, then there is an awkward grammatical change from third to first person in verse 9.

Whatever the limits of the original parable, its main difficulty is that the "dishonest manager" (v 8) is commended as an example for the disciples (v 8–9), even though he is apparently wasteful and falsifies his master's accounts. However, it should be noted that the manager is commended, not for his dishonesty, but "because he had acted shrewdly/prudently" (v 8, author's translation), and it is the greater shrewdness of "the sons of this age" (author's translation; cf 20:34–35) in comparison with "the sons of light" (author's translation; cf Jn 12:36) that is highlighted. Even though he loses money, the manager can not help being impressed at his manager's clever foresight in the face of his imminent dismissal. It has been suggested that the manager is in fact not acting dishonestly (even if he had done so earlier, v 1) in reducing the bills of his master's debtors, because he was simply removing the added interest, which should not have been charged in the first place (eg Lev 25:35ff). Such an action may have reflected well socially on his manager who would have appeared as a generous or merciful person. Alternatively, it may be that the master lost no money at all, because the manager was simply deducting his own commission, that is, the personal profit he made from the debtors. Some have even suggested that the manager reduced the bills, but made up the difference himself. However, these interpretations are not obvious in the text, even if realistic possibilities.

As for the parable's lesson, if it is seen as originally ending with verse 7, then its point may be a warning concerning dishonesty and the love of money. Beyond this, the first part of verse 8 may imply that the disciples will be commended by their master (cf 12:41ff) if they are wise stewards or managers of his gifts and resources, especially wealth. The second part of verse 8 understands the parable as a call to the disciples, as they live by God's light, to be as shrewd as people who live only for this world. The application of the parable in verse 9 is that just as the manager had used money prudently to ensure a future "welcome" (v 4) into the homes of those whose debts he had reduced, so the disciples should use "dishonest wealth" to gain friends in the present in order that "they" (ie the angels, v 22; or God, see comment on 12:20, p103; or those who receive alms, 11:41; 12:33; 18:22) may welcome them into "eternal homes/tents" (author's translation). The idea may be that as money (regarded as "dishonest" or, literally, 'unrighteous') is used to secure one's future in this world, the disciples should use it to ensure a welcome in the next by, for example, giving to the poor. Thus, various lessons and applications are drawn from the parable in these verses, whatever one considers its original conclusion and interpretation to be.

The following verses (v 10–14) are linked to the previous section, including the parable, by catchwords (dishonest wealth, master) and similar themes (responsibility for others' property, wealth). The opening verse of this little section makes the point that one's management of "very little" is a sure guide to how such a person would manage "much" (cf 19:17ff). This point is developed in the next two verses, which contain parallel rhetorical questions. Unfaithful stewardship (management) of money by the disciples in the present means that God will not in the future commit to them the "true" riches of heaven (12:33; 18:22; 19:20ff). The section concludes (v 13; cf Mt 6:24) with the observation that no one can *exclusively* serve two masters at once, since one will always have the servant's allegiance and the other his contempt. Therefore, the disciples cannot be mastered by both God and wealth.

Tasks

a Outline the different views on where this parable properly ends.

b What is the main difficulty with the parable for most readers?

c Discuss the possible lessons of the parable in its present context.

d Explain how verses 10–13 are connected with the previous verses and summarise their main points.

The hypocrisy of the Pharisees (16:14–15)

The Pharisees' mockery of Jesus because of his teaching about wealth was due, according to Luke, to their love of money. Clearly, they are being characterised as slaves of wealth, rather than of God (v 14). A contrast is drawn between their attempts to justify or vindicate themselves outwardly before people (cf 10:29; 18:9ff) and their true inward condition (cf 11:39–41; 12:1ff), the latter being known by God (cf Acts 15:8; 1 Sam 16:7). Human values and divine values are often starkly opposed to each other, since what people think highly of is detestable before God (cf Prov 16:5).

The Law and the kingdom (16:16–18)

For comment on verse 16, see page 75.

The last part of verse 16 has been both translated and interpreted in different ways. It could be translated "everyone acts forcefully/violently against it" (ie God's kingdom), referring to the general opposition to the kingdom. However, it was not rejected by all. On the other hand, it could be translated "everyone forces his way into it", which may refer negatively to Zealot-like attempts to bring in the kingdom violently (cf Mt 11:12–13), but not "everyone" was a political revolutionary. Alternatively, this particular translation may be viewed positively, as pointing to people's eagerness to enter the kingdom, although again the problem is that far from "everyone" was keen to do so. Finally, the translation "everyone is strongly urged to enter it" is possible (cf NRSV footnote), taking the verb in a passive sense (compare the translation of the related Greek verb in 24:29). Thus, the good news of the kingdom is being preached and "everyone" (another example of Luke's universalism) is strongly persuaded to come in (cf 14:23).

Jesus' statement that "the law and the prophets were until John" (v 16) seems to imply that they are no longer in force, now that God's kingdom has arrived. However, he immediately asserts the continuing validity and, in fact, permanence of the Law (v 17). It would be easier for creation to disappear than "for one horn of the law to fall" (literally), the "horn" referring to a small stroke of a pen which distinguished similar Hebrew letters (cf Mt 5:18). Jesus said a similar thing about his own teaching (21:33). How can these apparently contradictory statements about both the temporary (v 16) and permanent (v 17) nature of the Law be reconciled? It has been suggested that in verse 17 Jesus is sarcastically reflecting the view of the Jewish religious leaders, rather than presenting his own view. However, this does not fit Jesus' view of the Law elsewhere in Luke. On the one hand, the Law appears to be still in force (eg 2:22–24,27,39), even in Jesus' teaching (5:14; 10:25–28; 11:42; 16:29,31; 18:18–21), but on the other it is clear that Jesus has authority over the Law (6:1ff) and that his teaching, rather than the Law, is of central importance (6:46ff; 12:8–9). Further, the Law continues in that it reaches its fulfilment in Jesus (24:25–27,44; Acts 3:18,21,24), who nevertheless transcends and surpasses it. Indeed, in the very next verse (v 18) Jesus shows his authority over the Old Testament Law by stating that divorce and remarriage (the purpose of divorce in his culture) are in effect adultery against one's former spouse. Similarly, marriage of a divorced woman involves adultery against her former spouse. While the Law of Moses permitted divorce and remarriage (Deut 24:1–4), Jesus presents a stricter view of the matter than this (cf Mk 10:2–12). Matthew alone has an exception in Jesus' statement (5:31–32; 19:9). Thus, while the Law continues, the coming of God's kingdom with Jesus has resulted in its revision.

Tasks

a Comment on Jesus' challenge to the Pharisees as lovers of money (16:14–15).

b Did John the Baptist belong to the period of the Law and the Prophets or to the period of God's kingdom (16:16)?

c Can Jesus' statements about the Law in 16:16–17 be reconciled?

d How does Jesus' teaching about divorce and remarriage (16:18) differ from Old Testament Law?

The rich man and Lazarus (16:19–31)

With this story the chapter's general theme of wealth is continued, its message now being addressed particularly to the Pharisees (v 14ff). The passage is paralleled in similar ancient tales of the reversal in fortunes in the afterlife of a rich man and a poor man (eg a fourth-century BC Egyptian story and a fifth-century AD Jewish story about a wealthy tax collector called Bar Ma'jan). It is not called a parable and has features untypical of a parable of Jesus, such as the naming of characters and action in the afterlife. However, not all parables are specifically identified as such (eg 15:8ff,11ff; a fifth-century scribe used the term "parable" of our story). Also, its opening words (literally "A certain man") are typical of many of Jesus' parables (eg 12:16; 14:16; 15:11; 16:1). However, it appears to belong to that category of parable often known as an example story, since there is little if any metaphorical meaning in the story. The main point of the parable seems to be to illustrate something that Jesus has already taught his disciples in this Gospel:

> Blessed are you poor,
> for yours is the kingdom of God.
> Blessed are you who hunger now,
> for you will be filled …
> But woe to you rich,
> for you have received your comfort.
> Woe to you who are well fed now,
> for you will be hungry. (6:20–21,24–25, author's translation)

This reversal of fortunes is clearly seen in the afterlives of the poor man and the rich man in this parable (cf v 25) and is an important Lucan theme (eg 1:52–53).

The parable begins by sharply contrasting the conditions of the two men. The rich man, described first, is dressed in fine linen and clothing coloured with expensive purple dye, as a very visible sign of his wealth. His wealth is seen also in his daily, rather than occasional (cf 15:23), feasting and celebrating. The reference to "his gate" implies a residence of some note, possibly a mansion. At this gate the poor man "had been placed" (v 20, literally), implying that he was lame (cf Acts 3:2), which would account for his poverty. Undoubtedly, this was potentially a good location for a beggar who would hope to receive something from the rich man and his companions in their comings and goings. However, he does not even get as much as what falls from the rich man's table (which dogs could be sure of – Mt 15:27), though he longs for it (cf 15:16). In contrast to the rich man's fine apparel, the poor man is covered with ulcerating sores, which wild, scavenging dogs lick (cf 1 Kings 14:11), adding to his plight by making him ritually unclean. Indeed, in such a state many may have regarded him as being under God's curse or punishment (cf Deut 28:35; Jn 9:1–2), just as the rich man's wealth would have been viewed as a sign of God's favour (eg Prov 10:22). Finally, even in death their situation is contrasted since, while we read that the rich man has a proper burial, apparently no such dignity is given to the poor man. The one detail that points in the poor man's favour in this stark contrast is that while he is named, the rich man is anonymous. However, in a third-century manuscript the rich man is named as *Neues*, probably referring to the wealthy city of Nineveh which was judged by God (cf Nahum). Traditionally, he is called *Dives*, the Latin translation of 'rich man'. 'Lazarus' means 'God helps', which may be significant as a pointer to his dependence on God, though this is not mentioned in the parable. The name is a form of the common Hebrew name Eliezer, also borne by Abraham's servant (Gen 15:2). There is no reason to identify the Lazarus of our parable with the man of the same name in John's Gospel (chs 11,12).

The contrast between the two men continues into their postmortem conditions, but now their experiences are reversed. Lazarus is escorted by angels, God's heavenly messengers (cf 15:10), to "Abraham's bosom" (v 22–23, author's translation), that is, to the side of the founder of the Jewish race (cf 1:54–55,73; 3:8; 13:16). This may imply that he has left his hunger on earth for a banquet with the patriarch in heaven (cf 13:28–29). This contrasts with the rich man's experience in "Hades" (see comment on 10:15, p83), a "place of torment" where he is in "agony" in the "flames". Though it is possible that both men are in Hades – as the location of the dead generally – they are clearly separated (v 23,26) and in very different conditions. In Hades the unrighteous are punished, awaiting their final judgement in *Gehenna* (see comment on 12:5, p102). Some feel that this passage provides information about the 'intermediate state' between death and the last judgement, but others note the parabolic nature of the material and argue that the details should not be taken literally. While Lazarus remains silent throughout the parable, the rich man carries on a dialogue with Abraham, calling him "father", which is ineffective before God without repentance (cf 3:8; 19:9). His plea to Abraham for "mercy" is ironic, since he himself showed none to Lazarus (the words for 'mercy' and 'almsgiving' being related in Greek). He knows Lazarus by name, making his neglect of him clearly inexcusable, and seems still to adopt a superior attitude to him, viewing him as a servant to meet his need. On the other hand, perhaps he feels that Lazarus can influence Abraham to help him. The reversal of their fortunes is clearly evident in the rich man's inability to get even a drop of water from Lazarus, just as Lazarus was unable to get even a crumb from the rich man's table.

Abraham's negative response to the request for water is supported with two reasons. First, their postmortem experiences are a just and necessary reversal of their pre-mortem situations (cf 1:52–53 6:20–21,24–25). Within this parable the men's respective postmortem experiences are determined primarily by their pre-mortem economic conditions, but clearly the rich man's failure to "repent" for neglecting to help the poor, as required by Israel's Scriptures (v 29,31; cf Deut 15:7ff), is also implied. As for Lazarus, poverty and piety often went hand in hand in biblical culture, because of the inevitable dependence of the poor upon God. The second reason for Abraham's inability to help the rich man is that a "great chasm" (v 26; Greek *chasma mega*) has been "fixed" (ie by God), irreversibly sealing the postmortem destinies of the righteous and the wicked and preventing movement between the two. Just as the rich man's gate appeared to be an impenetrable barrier for Lazarus, so now access to Abraham's bosom for the rich man is out of the question. Realising that his own condition is beyond improvement, he requests that Lazarus be sent on a second errand, to warn (or "bear witness/testimony to", author's translation; eg Acts 2:40; 8:25) his brothers, which still indicates to some degree the rich man's continuing selfishness (cf 6:31ff; 14:12ff). Abraham insists that to "listen" to Moses and the Prophets (Israel's Scriptures; 24:27,44) is all the testimony they need to persuade them and effect their repentance (cf 15:7,10). This would not be bettered even by someone (such as Lazarus) rising from the dead, anticipating Jesus' resurrection (eg 18:33; 24:7). Thus, the common ancient idea of the dead visiting the living to communicate information about the afterlife is not encouraged.

Tasks

a Comment on parallel stories to this parable in ancient times.

b Discuss the classification of this story as a parable.

c What is the main point of the parable?

d Outline the contrasts between the two men in both their pre-mortem and postmortem conditions.

e Can this parable teach us anything about the afterlife and, if so, what?

Sin and forgiveness (17:1–4)

Jesus now turns from addressing the Pharisees (16:14–31) to speak particularly to his disciples. He deals first with the seriousness of causing someone to "stumble" (v 1, *skandalon*; v 2, *skandalizo*). Specifically, the reference is to causing "one of these little ones" to sin. In the parallel passages (Mt 18:6/ Mk 9:42) the "little ones" are children who believe in Jesus. In Luke's context the reference may also be to children, or to believers generally, regarded as insignificant by the wider society (cf 16:19ff). While causes for stumbling are regarded as inevitable, God's judgement would come on anyone responsible for such offences (cf 22:22). The "millstone" was a round, heavy upper-stone which was rotated on a lower stone to grind flour. Drowning in the sea with one of these round one's neck is regarded as preferable to facing God's judgement for leading others into sin or apostasy from the faith.

Jesus then moves from dealing with causing offence (v 1–2) to the issue of receiving offence (v 3–4). The offender must be challenged by the offended and, if there is repentance, forgiven (cf Mt 18:15ff). Furthermore, this forgiveness must be extended as long as there is repentance by the offender, no matter how many offences are received. Luke's 7 times daily and Matthew's 77 times or 70 times 7 (18:21–22) both refer to continual forgiveness. This demand for Jesus' followers to be forgiving is echoed elsewhere in this Gospel (6:36–37; 11:4).

Faith (17:5–6)

Characteristically, Luke himself twice calls Jesus "Lord" in this brief passage. From the larger group of "disciples" (v 1), the inner group of 12 known as the "apostles" (6:13ff; 9:1,10) speak to Jesus. The term 'apostle' (Greek *apostolos*) is related to a Greek word meaning 'send' (*apostello*, 9:2) and refers to an envoy or messenger. In the Gospels, the term is used of the Twelve as the specially commissioned representatives of Jesus. Here, in the light of Jesus' teaching about sin and forgiveness (v 1–4), they ask for greater faith. Jesus' reply is an example of hyperbole (rhetorical exaggeration) – a form of speech that he used for effect on various occasions (eg 18:25) – and so should not be taken literally. Sayings similar to this one are found elsewhere in the Gospels in different contexts (Mt 17:20; 21:21; Mk 11:22). In our text, Jesus contrasts the proverbially small mustard seed (cf 13:19) with, possibly, the deeply rooted fig-mulberry tree (there is uncertainty about precisely what tree is meant). While some think that the apostles may be asking for special, unusual, wonder-working faith, it may simply be a desire for stronger faith. Jesus then speaks graphically of the power of even a little faith. His reply seems to imply that the faith even of the apostles, let alone the wider group of disciples, is quite inadequate (cf 12:28).

Outline Jesus' teaching on sin, forgiveness and faith in this passage (17:1–6).

The parable of the unworthy slave (17:7–10)

Like other parables (eg 11:5–8), this one is in the form of a long question expecting a negative answer. Understanding the parable requires an appreciation of the first-century master–slave relationship as one in which no master would place himself under obligation to his slave (serving him, even expressing gratitude) and no slave could expect rewards or privileges for doing what was, in fact, his duty. While the parable focuses on the master, its application (v 10) highlights the slave. The disciples in general (v 1) and the apostles in particular (v 5) should not think that service of, and obedience to, their master (v 5–6, Jesus) is something deserving reward or special privilege. Doing God's will does not put God under obligation to them. Rather, they should regard this simply as a performance of their duty, and themselves as "worthless/useless" slaves (author's translation; cf Mt 25:30). Many prefer the translation "unworthy" in this context and note that the idea is of one to whom no favour or reward is due. Nonetheless, what is assumed to be culturally unacceptable in this parable is affirmed in another in this Gospel (12:35–38; cf 22:27), anticipating the reward of faithful disciples at the future return of the Son of Man.

Task

What main lesson is Jesus teaching in this parable?

The healing of ten lepers (17:11–19)

The passage opens with a reminder that Jesus is on a journey to Jerusalem. Indeed, as this journey now moves towards its completion, such references become more frequent (18:31,35; 19:11,28,41). Yet it is clear that little progress has been made since the start of the journey (9:51ff) – as then, Jesus now appears to be in a Samaritan village on the border between Galilee and Samaria.

The healing of the lepers, one of the few miracle stories in the journey narrative, recalls Jesus' healing of a leper early in this Gospel (5:12–14) and is similar in several ways to the healing of Naaman the leper (2 Kings 5; Lk 4:27). Healing of lepers was a sign that Jesus was the one who was to come (7:22). The words translated "leper" and "leprosy" in the Gospels, referred to a range of diseases affecting the skin and not necessarily to leprosy as identified in modern times. The account falls into two parallel parts – the healing of the ten (v 12–14) and the return of the one (v 15–19). In each part there is an approach, a calling out, a reply from Jesus and a statement that healing occurred.

That the lepers meet Jesus on the edge of the village "keeping their distance" is a reminder of the social and religious exclusion that such physical conditions entailed (Lev 13:45–46; Num 5:1–3). It is not known how they knew Jesus, but they address him as "Master". Here Luke uses a term (*epistates*) found only in his Gospel in the New Testament, and its six other uses are all by disciples (5:5; 8:24,45; 9:33,49). Their request for "mercy" may have been a desire for 'alms' (11:41; 12:33), the two words being related in the Greek. However, the word may have expressed something beyond this (cf 10:37) and their description of Jesus as "Master" may reflect an awareness of his miraculous power. In the light of the infancy narrative, the reader will see God's "mercy" being displayed in the lepers' restoration (1:50,54,58,72,78). Jesus' instruction to go and show themselves to the priests (cf 5:14) reflects the Old Testament requirement that priests inspect and declare such persons clean or unclean (Lev 13). While this did not involve the priests healing disease, their decision was necessary to determine whether the person could be restored socially to the community. In complying with Jesus' instructions, on the way to the priests they were "cleansed" (author's translation), which included the removal of both the physical and ritual impurity of their condition (Lev 13, eg v 3,6; 2 Kings 5:10,14). In this context (v 11,16) it is not clear whether the lepers would have gone to the Samaritan or Jerusalem temple for the priestly inspection.

We are told that the one leper who returns to Jesus does three things. First, he praises (literally 'glorified') God – a common response to miracles in Luke (5:25–26;

7:16; 13:13; 18:43) and an emphasis generally in his Gospel (see p39). Second, he falls face down at Jesus' feet (compare the earlier leper, 5:12), a physical sign of submission and respect (1 Sam 25:24,41; Lk 8:35,41; 10:39). Finally, he thanks Jesus, expressing gratitude for being healed. Luke then adds, "And he was a Samaritan" (v 16; emphasis on 'he' in the Greek), intentionally holding back his racial and religious identity until he has positively characterised him in the reader's mind. Thus, any reader with a prejudiced, preconceived dislike of Samaritans may have been unwittingly led into a trap by Luke's staging of the unfolding narrative. Out of the ten who are healed, it is the "foreigner" (v 18; as was Naaman) rather than "children of Abraham" (3:8, author's translation) who responds appropriately. The use of the term "foreigner" may be an indirect criticism of the exclusive nationalism of Jewish worship, since the same term was used on signs prohibiting non-Jews access to certain parts of the Jerusalem temple. This is of course the second time in Luke, and in the journey narrative in particular, that the 'hero' of a story is a Samaritan (10:30–37). Indeed, right at the beginning of the journey narrative we were introduced to Jesus' positive attitude to Samaritans, in contrast to his disciples (9:51–55; for details on the Samaritans see A Samaritan village, pp77–78). Consequently, this story is subversive in that it overturns traditional views concerning race and purity in relation to God's blessing. The point is underlined by Jesus' question concerning the ungrateful nine who did not return to glorify God (v 17–18). Jesus' final words to the Samaritan leper, "your faith has saved you" (literally; cf 7:50; 8:48; 18:42), reflect an important Lucan theme – namely salvation (see Salvation, p34ff) and its connection with faith. If these words refer to the man's cure from leprosy, it is unclear how this would not be true of the other nine, since the statement does appear to refer uniquely to this leper. Some, therefore, feel that the statement has been misplaced by Luke at this point in the story, or that the reference is to spiritual as well as physical salvation, which this leper alone experiences, demonstrated in his response to God and Jesus.

Tasks

a What other similar stories does this passage recall?

b Describe the structure of the passage.

c Discuss the nature and effects of "leprosy".

d Comment on the dialogue between the ten lepers and Jesus (v 13–14).

e Discuss the actions of the Samaritan leper and Jesus' response (v 15–19).

f Assess the view that the main point of this story is found in the words "And he was a Samaritan" (v 16).

The coming of the kingdom and of the Son of Man (17:20–37)

Jesus addresses the Pharisees about the coming of God's kingdom (v 20–22) and then the disciples about the revelation of the Son of Man (v 22–37). In fact, Jesus' instruction of his disciples on this theme continues to 18:8, where we read of the coming of the Son of Man. Jesus' words to the Pharisees and to the disciples here are on a related theme. Both sections are connected by the invitation to look "here" or "there" for the coming of the kingdom and the revelation of the Son of Man (v 21,23). Also, the entire passage is framed at one end by a question about the "coming" of the kingdom (17:20) and at the other by a question about the coming of the Son of Man (18:8).

The question of the Pharisees (see comment on 11:37, p99) represents the first of a number of occasions in Luke–Acts concerned specifically with the timing of future, climactic events (19:11ff; 21:7ff; Acts 1:6ff). Their question assumes, as with current Jewish belief generally, that God's kingdom (see comment on 9:60, pp79–81) is a wholly future reality, though Jesus had previously indicated to them that it was already present to some degree in his own ministry (11:20). Jesus' reply implies too that the Pharisees think of the kingdom in observable and localised or spatial terms. They are looking for a visible "sign" (11:16,29–32) concerning the future and yet can not read the significance of Jesus' ministry in the present (12:54–56). After rejecting ideas of the kingdom as visible or localised in nature, Jesus then states that the kingdom "is among" you (v 21). There is debate over both these words. Though the word "is" implies that the kingdom is present already, as elsewhere in this Gospel (again, see comment on 9:60, pp79–81), some take it in a future sense. This is because the word "coming" is used in a future sense in the previous verse, even though it is in the present tense. Also, the context, including 17:22ff, is all about the future. However, the change of verb (from "come" to "is") and the fact that "is" is in an emphatic position in the Greek sentence (the last word) suggest that Jesus is speaking of God's kingdom as already present. The word translated "among" (*entos*) is also disputed. It may mean 'inside/within' (as in Mt 23:26), but Jesus would hardly tell the Pharisees that God's kingdom is within them (cf 11:37ff), and this would be the only place in the New Testament where the kingdom is internalised. The word may also have the sense of 'within your grasp or power' – that is, a positive response to Jesus by the Pharisees would enable them to receive it. However, this meaning has been rejected by some on linguistic grounds. It has also been argued that it is not clear, from this view, how Jesus' answer would relate to the Pharisees' question. Finally, the word can mean 'among' when followed by a plural object, as in our text. Thus, in this view Jesus is telling the Pharisees, who are looking for signs of the coming kingdom, that it is already in their midst, even in the ministry of Jesus (cf 11:20).

The Gospel of Luke

Task

Discuss what the Pharisees' question and Jesus' reply tell us about their different understandings of God's kingdom.

Jesus turns from the Pharisees to his disciples (v 22). While he had spoken to the Pharisees about the kingdom of God as a present reality, he now speaks to his disciples about the future consummation and climax of the kingdom "on the day that the Son of Man is revealed" (v 30). Luke also has related material later in his Gospel (21:5–36) and seems to have divided into two (17:20–37 and 21:5–36) what Matthew and Mark have in one place (Mt 24/ Mk 13; in Jerusalem). This has resulted in various theories about what sources Luke had and how he made use of them, theories beyond the scope of our present study.

In the present passage, Jesus deals broadly with what the coming of the "Son of Man" (see comment on 9:58, p79) will be like (v 22–30), how people should respond (v 31–33), and the division that it will bring (v 34–37). In the future the disciples will long for one of the days associated with his coming (perhaps because of persecution, 12:11; 21:12ff), but will not see it (v 22). Some have seen this uniquely Lucan saying as part of a broader concern to deal with a perceived delay in Jesus' coming by Luke's time (see Theological, pp22–23). The disciples should not be tempted or fooled by claims that the longed-for coming has occurred in certain places (v 23; cf v 21), since it will be as universal and unmistakable as lightning flashing across the breadth of the heavens (v 24). Also, before that event there is the "must" (an important Lucan theme) of the Son of Man's suffering and rejection (cf 9:22) by "this generation" (v 25; cf 11:29ff). Jesus then draws a parallel between "the days" of Noah and Lot and "the days" of the Son of Man, and also between "the day" of judgement in the times of Noah and Lot and "the day" when the Son of Man is revealed (v 26–30). The implication appears to be that as people in the days of Noah (Gen 6:1ff) and Lot (Gen 18:16ff) carried on their daily, earthly pursuits right up to the day of their judgement by God, so it will be with people leading up to the day when the Son of Man comes in judgement. While Genesis emphasises the sinfulness of the days both of Noah and Lot, Jesus here focuses rather on their preoccupation with everyday concerns, which was suddenly interrupted by God's judgement. The picture is of people so immersed in the concerns of this life that they are not concerned with the will of God (cf 8:14; 12:15–21,29–30; 14:18–20). Thus, God's judgement takes them by surprise.

The proper response on the day that the Son of Man is "revealed" is urgent detachment from earthly possessions and concerns (v 31–33). Anyone on the flat roof of a typical home must not go down and indoors to collect possessions, and any worker in the field must not "turn back", like Lot's wife who was judged for such attachment to Sodom (Gen 19:26). Such 'looking back' has already been described as

...compatible with commitment to the kingdom of God (9:61–62). Ironically, attempts to save one's life will result in its loss and vice versa (cf 9:24). "On that day" (v 31) is followed by "on that night" (v 34), when there will be a division or separation, as in the days of Noah and Lot, with some "taken" (to safety) and others "left" (for judgement). This division by Jesus had been prophesied by Simeon in the infancy narrative (2:34–35) and by John the Baptist (3:17), had been spoken of by Jesus himself (12:51–53; 14:26), and now would be finalised at his return. Again, normal earthly routines are interrupted and the starkness of the separation is heightened by the different fates of paired individuals. There may be a typically Lucan gender balance here, in that two men may be in view in verse 34 ("one" and "other" are both masculine in the Greek), as well as the two women in verse 35. Later manuscripts have a third pair (two in the field; cf Mt 24:40) in verse 36, which is usually placed in a footnote. As this entire section began with the Pharisees asking *When?* (v 20), it now concludes with the disciples asking *Where?* (v 37). While this might appear to be an example of the disciples' lack of comprehension (cf v 23–24 and Mt 24:27–28), they might be inquiring about the location of the judgement of those left behind. Jesus' graphic reply, then, would mean that the location will be as obvious as that of a "body" (literally) from the presence of circling vultures.

Tasks

a Comment on the different setting of this teaching in Matthew and Mark.

b Outline what this passage says about the coming of the Son of Man in relation to:

   (i) what it will be like (v 22–30)

   (ii) what response should be made (v 31–33)

   (iii) the division it will bring (v 34–37)

The parable of the widow and the judge (18:1–8)

This parable and the one that immediately follows it – both unique to Luke – are linked by the very Lucan theme of prayer. In the present parable (v 2–5) a lesson appears to be drawn in the context from each of its two characters. The widow's persistence (v 3,5) represents the need for continuing prayerful faith by God's "chosen ones" in the interim before the coming of the Son of Man (v 1,7b,8b; cf 11:5ff), the latter being the general theme since 17:20. The judge's granting of justice to the widow (v 5) represents God's granting of justice to his chosen ones (v 6–8a). However, there is also a point of contrast between the judge and God, since the judge acts reluctantly and slowly on behalf of the widow (v 4–5), while God will act quickly on behalf of his people (v 7b–8a). As elsewhere in Jesus' teaching (eg 11:13), the argument moves from lesser (the judge) to greater (God).

There is a sharp contrast between the parable's two characters, specifically with regard to their gender and social position. The judge is characterised negatively as one who is not concerned with God or people. That God is distinct from the judge *within* the parable does not prevent the latter representing God *beyond* the parable (see comment on 15:18, p125). Widows consitute a special concern in Luke (see Women, p37) and in the Old Testament (eg Deut 10:18; Isa 1:17). Apparently with no male relative to represent her legally, she has to take matters into her own hands, and her frequent appeals to the judge may imply that poverty prevents her from ensuring a speedy resolution by means of a bribe. The parable stresses her persistence which (in his view) threatens to "wear out" the judge (v 5, if the Greek verb is used in a weakened sense) or even to leave him with a bruised face (if the verb is used in its normal sense)!

Characteristically, Luke introduces Jesus' apparent application of the parable by referring to him as "the Lord". The description of the judge as "unjust" (v 6; cf Greek of 16:8) contrasts with the widow's quest for "justice" (v 3,5) and God's granting of "justice" to his own people (v 7–8). Their calls to him "day and night", appropriately in this context, reflect the piety of widows in particular (2:37; 1 Tim 5:5). As in the Old Testament (cf Deut 7:6–7), God's people are described as his "chosen ones", stressing the initiative of God in his relationship with them. The delay of the judge is also contrasted with the speed of God, whose speedy vindication of his people is linked to the coming of the Son of Man (v 8; cf 17:22–37). Although Luke is often regarded as having downplayed the imminence of Jesus' return, here we have an example of the opposite. The challenging question the hearer and reader are left with is whether Jesus will find on earth the kind of persistent faith he has been speaking of.

Tasks

a **Contrast the parable's portrayal of its two characters.**

b **What lessons are drawn from the parable's two characters in the text?**

The parable of the Pharisee and the tax collector (18:9–14)

This parable is linked to the immediately preceding one by their common themes of prayer and justice, and, as with the previous parable, an introduction by Luke guides the reader in its interpretation. The parable is directed towards the self-righteous who are contemptuous of others. In the parable itself, it is the Pharisee (see comment on 11:37, p99) who represents this attitude (cf 10:29; 11:37–44; 14:1–14; 15:1–2; 16:14–15), but the mind-set was not exclusive to members of this sect (eg 9:46–50). The stark contrast between the parable's two characters recalls similar parables, as does the reversal of expectations created by the identity of the parable's hero' (eg the previous parable, the good Samaritan, and the rich man and Lazarus). The contrast includes the social position and roles of the two men (Pharisee and tax collector; for the latter, see comment on 3:12, p70), their postures (v 11a,13a) and prayers (v 11b –12,13b). Pharisees and tax collectors are contrasted elsewhere in Luke (eg 7:29–30; 15:1–2). The conclusion (v 14) summarises the contrasting attitudes and identifies the "justified" person.

The action of the parable takes place in the Jerusalem temple, a Lucan theme (see comment on 1:8ff, p52), which was a place of public prayer as well as sacrifice (cf 1:9; 19:45–46; 24:53; Acts 3:1). That the Pharisee is described as "standing by himself" (v 11) may reflect the separatism of the sect and contrasts with the posture of the tax collector. However, Luke's Greek may indicate the focus of his prayer ("to/about himself", author's translation) rather than his isolation. While his prayer begins in form as a thanksgiving to God (cf Ps 138), it continues in a self-centred way with no reference to God. This is apparent in the frequency of its self-references (five times), despite its brevity. The Pharisee begins negatively by stating what (or who) he is not like; then, positively, indicates what he does. His self-righteous 'holier-than-thou' attitude is evident in the contemptuous comparison he makes between himself and "others" (v 11, author's translation; cf v 9), particularly "this" tax collector in his vicinity. The irony for the reader of Luke is that the Pharisees are characterised in this Gospel as being guilty of the very sins that this Pharisee self-righteously attributes to others (cf 11:39,42; 16:14–15)!

Fasting (abstinence from food in dedication to God) and tithing were practised by the Pharisees (cf 5:33; 11:42) in a meticulous way that went beyond Old Testament requirements. Fasting was only compulsory on the annual Day of Atonement (Lev 16:29–31), but voluntary fasting was normally observed by Jews on Mondays and Thursdays (v 12, "twice a week"). The early Christian writing known as the *Didache* instructs Christians not to fast on these two days, thus avoiding the fasts of "the hypocrites", but rather to fast on Wednesdays and Fridays (8.1). The Pharisee in this parable also gives a tenth of "all" he obtains, even though some of this may already be tithed (eg harvested produce). From one angle, the character and conduct of the Pharisee as outlined in the prayer may be viewed as commendable. The problem appears to be that underlying the prayer is a self-righteous confidence in his own meritorious goodness, coupled with an arrogant contempt for others (v 9,14).

The tax collector's posture and prayer are very different. He too is "standing", a normal Jewish posture for prayer (eg 1 Kings 8:22ff; Mt 6:5), but "far off", maybe reflecting his sense of unworthiness. While "look[ing] up to heaven" often accompanied prayer (eg Mk 6:41), the tax collector is apparently too ashamed to do this (cf Ezra 9:6), his shame and remorse evident also in the beating of his breast (cf 23:48). His actions and his prayer clearly imply repentance before God on his part. Absent from his prayer is the air of self-confidence and self-righteousness found in the Pharisee's prayer. Rather, he characterises himself simply as "the sinner" (v 13, literally) and asks that God be "merciful" to him. The Greek verb translated "merciful"

The Gospel of Luke

here includes the ideas of atonement and reconciliation (cf Heb 2:17, where it is or translated 'to make atonement'). The tax collector's presence in the temple suggests that such ideas are not far from his mind. The conclusion is that the tax collector rather than the Pharisee "went down" (cf v 10) to his home "justified" (ie vindicated; cf 7:29,35; 10:29; 16:15). This use of the verb 'justify' is similar to Paul's in relation to being accepted as right before God (eg Rom 5:1; cf Acts 13:38–39). Finally, the contrasting attitudes of the parable's two characters (pride and humility) and their reversal of fortunes is underlined in a statement which has already formed the conclusion of an earlier parable (14:11).

Tasks

a **Explain how Luke's introduction (v 9) influences the readers' interpretation of this parable.**

b **Discuss the contrast of the parable's two characters in relation to their social position, posture and prayer.**

c **Comment on the conclusion to the parable (v 14).**

Little children and the kingdom of God (18:15–17)

For the first time since before the beginning of his long journey narrative, Luke shares substantial material with the other synoptics and in the same context (cf Mt 19:13–15/ Mk 10:13–16). With the introduction of "infants" (only in Luke's account) and "little children" Luke now, for the third passage in a row, shows Jesus' concern for the socially unimportant and marginalised (cf v 1ff, the widow; v 9ff, the tax collector). The desire for Jesus to "touch" their infants may indicate the parents' hope for God's blessing or, possibly, healing through physical contact (cf 5:13; 6:19; 7:14; 8:44ff). The disciples' "rebuke" of the parents (author's translation; cf 9:21,42,55) reflects the low value that contemporary society and culture generally attached to children. Jesus' attitude to the little children stands in sharp contrast to that of his disciples. In a characteristic reversal of social values, he calls for the children and demands that they be given access to him. The reason given by Jesus is "of such as these is the kingdom of God" (v 16, author's translation). He appears to be saying the little children should be allowed to come to him because it is precisely this kind of people to whom God's kingdom belongs or of whom God's kingdom consists. Indeed, successful entrance to the (future?) kingdom requires that the kingdom is received (ie accepted, welcomed) "as a little child" (v 17), which probably means 'as though one were a little child'. While the present passage does not specify exactly what it is about a little child that is exemplary in terms of receiving the kingdom, it may be that humility or lowliness is in mind (cf v 14; 9:46–48; Mt 18:4) or simply childlike receptivity. Finally, while some have suggested that the occurrence of a Greek word variously translated 'stop', 'hinder' or 'forbid' (v 16) implies the early Church's use the passage in relation to infant baptism (compare baptismal use of the term in 3:14; Acts 8:36; 10:47; 11:17), this speculation lies beyond the range of Jesus' words in their present context.

> **Tasks**
>
> a Contrast the attitudes of Jesus and his disciples to little children in this passage.
>
> b Comment on the meaning of Jesus' two statements about the kingdom (v 16–17).

The rich ruler (18:18–30)

This passage (paralleled in Mt 19:16–29/ Mk 10:17–30) contrasts with the one immediately before, in terms of social status (little children and a rich ruler). Typically of Luke (cf 1:52–53), this status is reversed as the children are presented as model recipients of God's kingdom (v 16–17), while the ruler apparently rejects it (v 23–25). The negative picture of the rich ruler in relation to the kingdom is consistent with Luke's usual portrayal of people with power (eg 1:51; 13:14) and wealth (eg 1:53; 6:24; 12:16ff; 16:19ff). That he knows the commandments and has kept them since his youth may imply that he is a religious leader, possibly a synagogue ruler. His address and question to Jesus recall the practically identical words of the religious lawyer (see detailed discussion of 10:25, p86). The reference to "eternal life" not only introduces (v 18) but also concludes (v 30) the passage, acting as its literary frame. The one difference between the lawyer's address to Jesus and the ruler's is that the latter calls him a "good" teacher. Jesus' apparently negative response to this (v 19) has been variously interpreted. It has been taken as an admission by Jesus that he is a sinner and that, morally, God alone is absolutely good. However, this conflicts with the early view that Jesus was sinless (eg 2 Cor 5:21; Heb 4:15). Conversely, Jesus' words have also been understood as an indirect claim that he is God, as if he were saying, 'Do you not see that by calling me "good" you are (correctly) calling me "God"?' However, this appears to be an unnatural way to read Jesus' words and does not cohere with the wider Lucan, and indeed synoptic, presentation of Jesus. It has also been suggested that Jesus is rejecting the ruler's empty flattery – especially if it is given in the expectation of a return compliment – and/or his careless use of terms that belong, in an absolute sense, uniquely to God (cf eg Ps 25:8). The immediate context supports the view that Jesus' reply indicates his concern to direct the ruler to focus on God and what he requires (v 20), with no necessary implications for Jesus' own identity. Matthew's version of this passage lessens the perceived difficulty (19:16–17).

Jesus' direction of the ruler to the commandments as the means of obtaining eternal life is consistent with his earlier teaching (10:25–28) and the Old Testament (eg Deut 30:15–20). The five commandments that Jesus quotes are from the latter half of the Ten Commandments (Deut 5:16–20), though not in their order (nor in that found in the parallel passages in Matthew and Mark). The exclusive focus on commands relating to people, with no mention of the commands relating to God (Deut 5:7–15), may be due to their particular relevance to the wealthy and powerful, who often selfishly disregarded others. While there is no need to be sceptical of the ruler's claim to have kept all the quoted commandments since his youth (cf 1:6; Phil 3:6), Jesus identifies one thing that he lacks. The call to sell all and give to the poor recalls demands of discipleship made earlier in this Gospel (12:32–34; 14:33; see comment on the latter reference, p121). It also continues the Lucan theme of Jesus' concern for the poor (see The poor, pp36–37). Reminiscent of earlier sayings too is the reference to "treasure in heaven" (12:21,33) and the call "follow me" (5:27; 9:59). The unwillingness of the very wealthy ruler to meet Jesus' radical demand provides for Jesus the opportunity to make a general point about how difficult an obstacle wealth is to entering God's kingdom. Jesus' comparison of this with a camel (largest animal in Palestine) going through the eye of a needle (smallest opening) is but one example of his use of rhetorical and humorous exaggeration as a teaching aid (cf 6:41; 17:2,6). A similar saying about the impossibility of an elephant going through the eye of a needle is attributed to a later rabbi. In an attempt to make Jesus' saying less shocking some later manuscripts have "rope" (*kamilos*) instead of "camel" (*kamelos*) and it has also been suggested that the "eye of a needle" was the name for a small door cut in a much larger door in Middle Eastern villages.

Jesus' words provoke a question about the possibility of anyone being "saved" (a favourite Lucan theme; see Salvation, p34ff), possibly because wealth, far from being an obstacle to God, was often regarded as a sign of his blessing and favour (eg Deut 8:1–10). Jesus responds to the question by stating that what lies beyond human possibility is possible for God (cf 1:34,37). Indeed, very soon Luke will provide his readers with an example of this human impossibility – the salvation of a rich man (19:1–10). We note here the variety of terms now used in this passage for the same basic reality – inheriting eternal life (v 18), entering God's kingdom (v 24–25) and being saved (v 26). Peter, typically the spokesman of the disciples (eg 9:20,33), reminds Jesus (v 28) that they had done precisely what the ruler had failed to do (5:11,28). Jesus replies that anyone who abandons home and family for the kingdom (cf 9:57–62; 12:51–53; 14:25–26) will receive "many times more" (author's translation) in this "time" (author's translation; *kairos*) and "eternal (*aionios*) life" in the coming "age" (*aion*). Here we have later Judaism's common distinction between two ages, present and future (cf 20:34–35). Mark's version of Jesus' words here spells out what Luke implies – disciples will receive in this age much more of what they left – that is, houses and family (Mk 10:30; cf Job 42:12ff). This seems ironic in light of Luke's emphasis on the reverse, but in Luke the disciples' new family are those who obey God's word (8:19–21). The mention of "eternal life" (v 30) brings the passage full circle (v 18).

Tasks

a Comment on the meaning of Jesus' response to the ruler in verse 19.
b Discuss Jesus' teaching on wealth and the kingdom in this passage.
c Comment on Jesus' teaching about the two ages (v 29–30).

Prediction of the passion and resurrection (18:31–34)

For the third time (cf 9:22,44) Jesus predicts his forthcoming suffering. This will happen in "Jerusalem", the imminent destination of the journey narrative and the place of destiny for Jesus (9:31,51,53; 13:33ff). There, all that "the prophets" have written (cf 22:37; 24:25,27,44) about the "Son of Man" (see comment on 9:58, p79) will be "accomplished/fulfilled" (author's translation). Such language indicates that these events are the realisation of God's purpose of old and in line with Israel's Scriptures. His 'handing over' or 'betrayal' (v 32; 9:22; same Greek verb in both verses) to the Gentiles (ie the Romans) is later recounted (23:1ff), as are the mockery and insults also predicted here (23:11,35–36,39). The pre-execution 'flogging' also figures later in the narrative (23:16,22). The vocabulary of suffering in our passage recalls the abuse of the suffering Servant of Isaiah (50:6) and represents the public humiliation and disgrace to which crucifixion victims were subjected. However, the rejection is followed by vindication on the third day. Luke emphasises (three times in v 34) the disciples' inability to understand what Jesus is saying (cf 9:45). They probably cannot see how the death of the Son of Man is part of God's plan, contained in the Prophets. The wording implies that God is preventing them from understanding Jesus' words (the passive voice, also in 9:45). Not until after Jesus' resurrection are they enabled to understand (24:21–22,25–27,44ff).

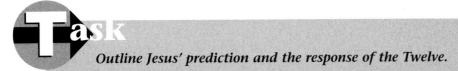

Outline Jesus' prediction and the response of the Twelve.

The healing of a blind man near Jericho (18:35–43)

With the reference to "going up to Jerusalem" in the previous passage (v 31), the language of journey comes to the fore again (v 35ff). The mention of Jericho, about 20 kilometres from Jerusalem, alerts the informed reader that this long journey narrative will soon be drawing to a close. The story is paralleled in Mark (10:46–52; where the blind man is named as Bartimaeus) and Matthew (20:29–34; where there are two blind men), though in both Jesus is leaving rather than approaching Jericho. The man whom Jesus heals is blind and, because of this disability, a beggar. The blind and the poor are precisely the kind of people to whom the good news of the kingdom relates (see 4:18–19). Jesus' ministry to them identifies him as the one who was to come (7:19,21–23), and signals that the long-expected age of salvation has dawned at last (Isa 35, especially v 5).

The blind man has apparently heard something of "Jesus of Nazareth", now a long way from home; he addresses him twice as "Son of David", reminding the reader of the infancy narrative's references to Jesus' Davidic ancestry (1:27,69; 2:4,11; 3:31) and its promise that God would give to him "the throne of his father David" (1:32, author's translation; see comment on this, pp53–54). The plea for "mercy" (cf 17:13) may have been just a request for alms (11:41; 12:33), but the title "Son of David" may express a desire for healing (with which the title is regularly associated in Matthew). Certainly, the blind man hopes for this (v 41). The identity of those "in front" who sternly order him to stop shouting is not revealed (Mt 20:31 attributes this to "the crowd"). Possibly they include Jesus' own disciples who had acted similarly only recently (v 15) or simply people at the head of the crowd. The irony here is that the blind man has apparently more insight than others in the passage who can see. However, the blind man's persistence (cf v 1ff; 5:19ff; 19:3ff) is rewarded. His second title for Jesus ("Lord") may indicate expectation of blessing and is appropriate in the light of Jesus' authority over disability. Jesus' question (v 41) may appear unnecessary but could have been an encouragement for the blind man to express his need to Jesus. The recovery of the man's sight points to Jesus' mission as the Spirit-anointed bringer of God's kingdom (4:18ff; 7:19ff), and the healing is an example of God's salvation ("saved") – the connection between this and "faith" (v 42) having been already noted in Luke (see comment on 17:19, p136). Luke characteristically states that the healing happens "immediately" (cf 1:64; 4:39; 5:25; 8:44,47,55; 13:13) and that God is glorified and praised (omitted in the other synoptic accounts). The theme of discipleship is implied when Luke notes that the man "followed him".

Tasks

a *How does this passage illustrate the mission of Jesus outlined earlier in Luke?*

b *Comment on the titles for Jesus used by the blind man in this passage.*

c *What actions of the blind man may be regarded as exemplary for the reader of Luke?*

Zacchaeus (19:1–10)

The journey continues as Jesus now enters the city that he was approaching in the previous passage. In a story unique to Luke, we are introduced to a man bearing the Jewish name Zacchaeus (2 Macc 10:19; compare its Hebrew form *Zaccai* in, for

...[example,] Ezra 2:9). He is also identified as a "chief tax-collector", a group despised (cf v 7) for their collaboration with the occupying Gentile Romans and for their self-enrichment through overcharging (cf v 2b,8; 3:12–13). However, Luke's special concern for them has already been evident (eg 18:9–14; see pp37–38). Thus, we have here another example from a number in the recent context of Jesus' concern for the socially unimportant or despised (ch 18 – widows, tax collectors, children, disabled). Zacchaeus is also described as "rich", due to his occupation. The recent narrative of Luke (18:18–25; the rich ruler), and indeed Luke's negative characterisation of the wealthy in general (see pp36–37), may lead us to expect a negative outcome in this passage. On the contrary, Zacchaeus is an example of Jesus' recent teaching about the possibility of the salvation of the rich (18:24–27).

In one of a number of references to vision (contrast the previous passage) in this story (v 2,3–5,7–8; not always noted in English translations), we are told that Zacchaeus is trying "to see" who Jesus is. As in previous passages, people prove to be an obstacle to the quest for Jesus (eg 5:19; 18:15,39). Zacchaeus' particular problem has often been considered to be his short size (v 3). However, the ambiguous Greek may mean that it is Jesus rather than Zacchaeus who is short (though nowhere else is there a hint that Jesus' height was unusual). The word translated "stature" (v 3, *helikia*) may refer to age rather than height (see also in 2:52; 12:25). Like others before him, Zacchaeus is not deterred by human obstacles to Jesus, but finds an imaginative solution to the problem (cf 5:19). Like the blind man on the outskirts of town before him, he knows that Jesus is "passing" (18:37; 19:1,4) and is not going to miss his opportunity. He climbs a "sycomore tree" (similar to an oak tree), not worrying about the possible social indignity of what may have been perceived as a childish act. While Zacchaeus had hoped to "see" Jesus (v 3), it is Jesus who "looked up" (v 5) and took note of him. There is a note of urgency in both Jesus' call and Zacchaeus' response ("hurry" in v 5 and v 6) explained by Jesus' words, "… for today I must stay at your house" (v 5, author's translation). These words contain three important Lucan themes – the importance of "today" (see p40), the "must" of God's purpose (see p26), and hospitality as the symbol of acceptance (see p29). The joy (v 6) with which Zacchaeus welcomes Jesus recalls another favourite theme of Luke (see Joy, p39). Zacchaeus' delight contrasts with the grumbling (see comment on 15:2, p122) of "all" who see Jesus go to be the guest of a "sinner". Tax collectors, because of their association with the Gentile Romans and their dishonesty, were not regarded by the Jewish leaders as suitable table companions (cf 5:27–32). Jesus' action indicates that he takes a different view concerning the boundaries of God's kingdom.

Both Luke (typically) and Zacchaeus refer to Jesus as "Lord" (v 8; cf 18:41). Zacchaeus' statement (v 8) raises a number of issues. He speaks in the present tense (in the Greek) as if the impact of Jesus upon him is taking immediate effect (cf NIV: "Here and now I give …"). However, it may be that the tense simply indicates his present determination to change from this point (cf NRSV) or that, far from changing,

The Gospel of Luke

Zacchaeus is claiming that this has been his usual practice – although the context does not appear to favour this latter view. His concern for "the poor" reflects a Lucan theme (see The poor, pp36–37), but it is not clear why "salvation" (v 9–10) for him involves the sharing of "half" of his possessions with the poor, while for the rich ruler it requires the giving of "all" he has to the poor (18:2; see comment on 14:33, p121). The fourfold restitution for defrauding others (cf 3:12–13) goes beyond normal Old Testament requirements (eg Num 5:5–7; but see Ex 22:1; 2 Sam 12:6) and reflects the reality of Zacchaeus' repentance. Jesus' response to Zacchaeus' statement (v 9–10) contains several Lucan themes: the apparent repentance indicates that Zacchaeus is a true "son of Abraham" (cf 3:8; 13:16), and it also demonstrates that "salvation" (see Salvation, p34ff) has come to this "house" (compare 'household salvation' in Acts, eg 11:14; 16:31) "today" (see comment on v 5, p147). A comparison of verses 5 and 9 practically equates Jesus with salvation, as Simeon had done (2:28–30). Jesus comes as a guest to the house of this "lost" person (compare the three parables of ch 15) because it is just such people that he, the "Son of Man" (see comment on 9:58, p79), has come "to seek and to save" (author's translation; cf 5:30–32). The latter words recall the parable of the lost sheep (15:3–7), and Ezekiel's condemnation of Israel's leaders for failing to care for God's flock along with the promise that God himself would seek for his lost sheep (Ezek 34:2,4,16,22–23). Zacchaeus finds that the one he was seeking to see (v 3) has come seeking him (v 10; same Greek verb in both verses).

a Comment on Luke's introduction of Zacchaeus (v 2).

b Discuss Zacchaeus' problem and solution (v 3–4).

c Explain the significance of Jesus' words in verse 5.

d Contrast the responses of Zacchaeus and the onlookers to Jesus (v 6–7).

e Discuss the meaning of Zacchaeus' statement in verse 8.

f Comment on Jesus' concluding words (v 9–10).

The parable of the pounds (19:11–27)

This last parable of Luke's journey narrative is both similar to and different from Matthew's parable of the talents (25:14–30), and the relationship between the two has been debated. Some view the two as versions of the same parable, which has been altered by the evangelists (mostly by Luke) or their sources. Others think that Luke has combined two different parables – the parable of the talents and a parable about a claimant to a throne who is rejected (Lk 19:12,14,15,27). Finally, some hold that the parables in Matthew and Luke were originally separate, though similar, parables taught on distinct occasions.

Luke provides a context for his parable as the key to its interpretation (v 11). Nearing the end of Jesus' journey, there appears to have been a mounting expectation that God's kingdom was about to appear in Jerusalem (cf 13:31ff). The parable is then seen as a corrective to imminent expectations of God's kingdom, and as a justification – especially relevant at the time of Luke's writing – of the apparent delay of the *parousia* (Second Coming) of Jesus (for this as a general concern of Luke, see Eschatology, pp39–40). The main characters of the parable (the nobleman, the slaves, and the citizens) appear to have symbolic significance. The nobleman who goes to a distant country to get royal power appears to represent Jesus, whose ascension to God's right hand marked his enthronement in Lucan thought (cf Acts 2:30–32; 17:7; also Lk 19:38; 22:29). The word "distant" implies the passage of some time before the nobleman's "return" and, therefore, before Jesus' return (cf 17:22ff; 21:27; 23:42). Although making this character represent Jesus appears to put the latter in a bad light (v 21–22), we recall that other parables also have unlikely characters representing Jesus or God (eg 12:39–40; 18:1ff). The nobleman's slaves appear to represent Jesus' followers, and the "pounds" (a *mina* was about three months' wages) would stand for any gifts or abilities which they are expected to use wisely in the interim. They will then give account of this to Jesus at his return, his "good" (v 17) servants being rewarded in accordance with their faithfulness and his "wicked" (v 22) servants being punished in accordance with their lack of service. Finally, the nobleman's citizens who hate him, and reject him as their king, symbolise within Luke the Jewish leaders who reject Jesus (eg 13:33–34; 20:9–19, especially v 17–19; 22:2,52–54; 23:1–2). The nobleman's vengeance on the citizens upon his return would then represent Jesus' judgement on his return of those who rejected him as king. The parable appears to reflect historical events connected with Herod the Great's son, Archelaus (cf Mt 2:22), who travelled to Rome in 4 BC to obtain confirmation that he would succeed his father as king. A Jewish delegation also went to Rome to oppose the appointment of Archelaus, who took vengeance on them when he returned with royal authority (*Ant* 17.299–323; *Jewish War* 2.80–100).

As with all the parables, it is possible to overinterpret the details when, in fact, they may have a purely narrative function. No particular significance should probably be attached to, for example, the amount of money given to the slaves, their proportionate rewards, and the reference to bank interest. We may note too that while there are ten slaves, only three give account, as in Matthew's related parable (25:14ff). Indeed, in Luke the third slave is referred to as "the other" (v 20), as if there were none left; although the words could be used in the sense of 'the next' (as in Mt 10:23). On another matter of interpretation, we may note that the statement in verse 25 can be taken as coming from Jesus' hearers or as from people within the parable itself. Either way, there is a sense of shock that one already well-rewarded should receive a further bonus (with the additional "pound" may have gone a corresponding city, as in v 17). Finally, the mysterious proverb in verse 26 (also in 8:18) may assume the word 'earned' ('have earned' and 'earned nothing'), tying it closely to the events in the parable. Alternatively, the last phrase of the verse may refer to people who think they have something when actually they have nothing – even their supposed something will be taken from them (cf v 24).

Tasks

a Discuss the relationship between this parable and the parable of the talents.

b Comment on Luke's context for this parable.

c Discuss the possible symbolism of the parable.

d What historical event may lie behind some of this parable?

e Comment on the mysterious proverb in verse 26.

Jesus enters Jerusalem (19:28–40)

At the journey's beginning (9:51,53) and throughout its course (13:22,33; 17:11; 18:31; 19:11), Jerusalem has been identified as its destination. Now that the city is within reach Luke builds up the suspense and tension with literary skill, by slowing down the pace of the final stage of the journey and increasing the geographical references to the city and its vicinity (v 29–30,37,41). Jesus now comes to the heart of the Jewish establishment and faces the destiny he has spoken of more than once en route (eg 13:31–35; 18:31–34). The events of the present passage, traditionally referred to as Jesus' 'triumphal entry' and celebrated annually on Palm Sunday, are recounted variously in all four Gospels (Mt 21:1–9/ Mk 11:1–10/ Jn 12:12–16). The passage concerns the obtaining of a colt (v 29–34) and Jesus' entry to Jerusalem upon it (v 35–40). The Mount of Olives was about 1,100 metres (about three-quarters of a mile) east of Jerusalem, from which direction Jesus approaches the city as he travels from Jericho (v 1). According to the prophet Zechariah, here the Lord would one day stand and fight against the nations, and be king over all the earth (Zech 14:3–4,9). From here too would Jesus ascend to heaven (Acts 1:9–12). The details about the obtaining of the colt (a young male horse) serve to show Jesus' initiative and control concerning the events at the start of his fateful visit to Jerusalem. The detailed knowledge also gives the strong impression of prophetic awareness of what lies ahead on the part of Jesus. The repeated references to the fact that the colt is tied may reflect Genesis 49:11, where the coming ruler of Judah similarly ties his colt. Further, the colt has "never been ridden" (compare the tomb in 23:53) and this may reflect the Greek version of Zechariah 9:9, where Jerusalem's king comes to the city riding on a "new colt" (author's translation; both Matthew and John quote Zech 9:9 in their accounts). Again, Jesus' authority in the acquisition of the colt is expressed in the words "The Lord needs it", representing royal rights (cf 1 Sam 8:10–18) and an ancient custom (called *angaria*) which allowed important persons to commandeer property. Thus, the various Old Testament echoes in this early part of our passage imply the royalty of Jesus, even before this is made explicit later in the entry to Jerusalem itself (cf also 1:32-33).

Until this point in the journey Jesus has travelled on foot, but now in this its climactic stage he significantly and symbolically chooses to ride into Jerusalem on a colt. This is a deliberate fulfilment of Zechariah 9:9 (made clear in Matthew and John), so that by this act Jesus is claiming to be the King of Israel. The royal associations of the mode of transport and the use of the cloaks (as a makeshift saddle and red carpet) are clear in the Old Testament (eg 1 Kings 1:32–40; 2 Kings 9:12–13). With a second reference to the Mount of Olives (v 37) Luke again stresses the imminence of the journey's end. Only Luke mentions "the whole multitude of the disciples" and that it is they who "praise" God "joyfully" (both Lucan themes). The praise of God is for all the "powerful deeds" (author's translation) they have seen, a regular reaction to Jesus' miracles in Luke (eg 7:16; 17:15; 18:43). The praise begins with a quotation from Psalm 118 (v 26), used earlier in Luke by Jesus (see comment on 13:35, p115). The addition of the words "the king" to this quotation (v 38; unique to Luke among the evangelists) may reflect the Psalm's ancient use in the annual re-enthronement ceremony, or may be due to the influence of Zechariah 9:9 and/or 2 Kings 9:13. The quotation's reference to "the coming" one (author's translation) recalls messianic language earlier in the Gospel (3:15–17; 7:19–20). The declaration of praise ends with words (v 38b) which echo the praise of the heavenly host at Jesus' birth (2:14), although there the peace was "on earth" rather than "in heaven". These words continue the Lucan theme of peace, while "glory" replaces the Jewish "hosanna" of the other Gospel accounts, making the praise more understandable to Luke's Gentile readers. The negative attitude of some Pharisees (v 39) contrasts with the immediately preceding praise by disciples of Jesus. Their demand that Jesus "rebuke" (author's translation) his disciples repeats the mistake of others in the recent context (18:15,39; the same Greek verb is used in these verses). It may also reflect the political nervousness of the Jewish establishment about the reaction of the Roman authorities to messianic fervour at Passover time (22:1). Certainly, as the events of the passion narrative will confirm, it is clear that the Jewish leadership does not share the belief of Jesus' disciples that he is the Messiah, the King of Israel (cf also v 14,44). Jesus' reply about the stones crying out (v 40) recalls similar imagery used by John the Baptist (3:8), and underlines the futility of the Pharisees' attempt to silence the declaration of Jesus' Messiahship.

Tasks

a Explain how the royalty of Jesus is implied in verses 29 to 36.

b Comment on the Lucan themes found in verse 37.

c Discuss the declaration of the disciples (v 38)

d Comment on the demand of the Pharisees and Jesus' reply (v 39–40).

Jesus predicts the destruction of Jerusalem (19:41–44)

In this last section of the journey narrative (see p76 for debate over end point) we have a prophetic lament such as is found in the Old Testament (eg Jer 9:1ff; 13:17ff; Am 5:1ff), as Jesus weeps over the city he now enters. Jesus addresses the city (note the repeated use of the pronoun "you"), charging it with a failure to "recognise" two things – "the things that make for peace" (v 42) and "the time of your visitation" (v 44). The words "on this day" (v 42) indicate that the arrival of Jesus in Jerusalem as its king is the event that brings her "peace" (v 38). However, she failed to recognise this (cf v 14,39) and it is "now" hidden from her eyes. The "visitation" (cf 1:68,78; 7:16; where the related Greek verb is used) here refers to God coming in salvation to his people. Because of this spiritual ignorance and blindness (cf Acts 3:17; 13:27), Jesus prophesies judgement upon the city (cf 13:34–35; 21:20–24; 23:28–31). The detail here in Luke's unique description of the Roman destruction of Jerusalem in AD 70 (v 43–44) has led most to conclude that this was written after the event. However, others argue that the language reflects standard Old Testament language for the destruction of cities (eg Jer 6:3,6; 52:4ff; see p10). Jesus' entry into Jerusalem and subsequent events (eg v 45ff) mark the beginning of his final conflict with Jerusalem's leadership. The stage is set for the passion narrative.

Tasks

a *Comment on the Old Testament background to this passage.*

b *Discuss the reasons for Jerusalem's judgement as presented here.*

c *Comment on the description of the forthcoming judgement.*

Practice essay titles

1 (a) Outline your knowledge and understanding of the main events of Luke's journey narrative. (30)

(b) Explore the claim that Jerusalem has a special importance in Luke's Gospel. Justify your answer. (15)

2 (a) Outline your knowledge and understanding of Luke's account of either the mission of the Seventy or Zacchaeus. (30)

(b) Explore the claim that 'journey narrative' is a misleading name for the central section of Luke's Gospel. Justify your answer. (15)

PASSION NARRATIVE (chs 22–23)

The passion narrative in the Gospels is the account of Jesus' suffering and death, beginning with the conspiracy of the Jewish leaders and Judas Iscariot against Jesus and ending with the burial of Jesus. In the synoptic Gospels this constitutes the last two chapters but one in each case (Mt 26–27/ Mk 14–15/ Lk 22–23) and the amount of detail provided indicates the central importance of the suffering and death of Jesus to early Christianity. While Luke's passion narrative is similar to Mark's and probably dependent upon it, there are notable differences in both order and content, as well as similarities with John's passion narratives. This has led some to hold that Luke had access to additional source material, that he reshaped Mark's account, that he created material, or some combination of these views. We shall note various emphases in Luke's passion narrative, some of which exist throughout his Gospel, such as the innocence, compassion, prayerfulness and divinely-planned destiny of Jesus, and Satan's role in the events of the passion. One notable characteristic, in comparison with the other synoptics, is Luke's more positive, less tragic, portrayal of the passion. For example, we do not read of Jesus' abandonment by all his disciples, Peter's restoration is prayed for and assumed, there are no false witnesses or outraged high priest at his Jewish trial, the women of Jerusalem are urged not to weep for Jesus, there is no mock coronation by Pilate's soldiers or mockery from passers-by and, on the cross, instead of a cry of derelction ("My God, my God, why have you forsaken me?") there is a prayer of committal ("Father, into your hands I commend my spirit"; only in Luke does Jesus address God as "Father" on the cross).

The conspiracy against Jesus (22:1–6)

The passion narrative begins by setting its events in the context of the annual Jewish festival of Unleavened Bread/Passover, which fell in the spring. Passover celebrated Israel's liberation under Moses from slavery in Egypt (the Exodus), when the Israelites ate unleavened bread (bread without yeast) because of their quick exit from Egypt (Ex 12). The festival lasted seven days (Lev 23:4–8) and hundreds of thousands of pilgrims were in Jerusalem for its celebration. With so many Jews in the holy city celebrating national liberation from a Gentile power, Passover was a politically volatile time, during which the Romans were ever watchful for any new would-be Moses attempting to liberate the Jews from their current Gentile overlords. The Passover also provides the religious context in which to understand the significance of the events about to be recounted – Jesus' suffering and death.

The "chief priests" were the leaders of the temple and the "scribes" were experts in and teachers of the Jewish Law. Jesus had predicted their involvement in his passion (9:22) and particularly since Jesus' recent action in the temple (19:45–47) the Jewish leadership had sought to get rid of him (20:1,19–20,26). However, their fear of the people, with whom Jesus was popular, was frustrating their intention (v 2; cf 19:48; 20:19; 21:38). The leaders' dilemma is solved by "Judas called Iscariot, one of the twelve" (cf 6:12–16). The meaning of the term "Iscariot" is uncertain and various suggestions have been made – a place in Judea (Josh 15:25), from the Aramaic meaning 'false one', from the Latin *sicarius* meaning 'dagger man, assassin', or it may mean 'dyer' indicating his occupation. Luke, as well as John (13:2,27), attributes Judas' betrayal of Jesus to Satan, the enemy of God (see comment on 10:18, pp84–85). The temple police, necessary because the Gentile Romans were not normally permitted in the temple, are also part of the conspiracy. That the leaders "rejoiced" (v 5, literally) at satanically inspired treachery contrasts with the acts of God which normally produce this response in Luke (eg 19:37). Not only Satan, but also love of money is behind Judas' betrayal, a danger highlighted regularly in Luke (eg 16:13–14). The devil had withdrawn from Jesus until "an opportune time" (4:13) and it is such a time that the satanically driven Judas now looks for (v 4) to betray Jesus. In line with the leaders' desire, it must be when no crowd is present.

> **Tasks**
> a Comment on the significance of the timing of the passion events.
> b Discuss the motives of the various conspirators, including Satan.

Preparation for the Passover (22:7–13)

There are similarities between this passage and the preparation for Jesus' entry to Jerusalem (cf 19:28–34), most notably the apparent prophetic foresight of Jesus, which is underlined in both accounts with a reference to the disciples finding things just as they have been told. Thus, while the beginning of the passion narrative may give the impression that others are in charge of events, we see now that Jesus is in control of what lies ahead. Luke's unique reference to the necessity of the sacrifice of the Passover lamb (v 7, "had") reflects its scriptural requirement (Deut 16:1ff), but also recalls Luke's regular theme of divine necessity (eg 9:22; 13:33). Preparations for the meal would have included the sacrificing of the lamb in the temple (in the afternoon), the roasting of the lamb, and preparation of other foodstuff and wine. The man carrying the jar of water is probably a servant of "the owner of the house" (v 11). The large upstairs room, already furnished (undoubtedly with couches to recline on), is sufficient for Jesus and the twelve disciples. Since the Passover was normally celebrated in family groups (Ex 12:3–4), the implication is that a new family has been formed around Jesus as its head (cf 8:19–21). While Judas is serving Satan and money, two other members of the Twelve are serving Jesus by preparing for the Passover.

> **Tasks**
> a Comment on the similarities between this passage and 19:28–34.
> b Contrast this passage with the one preceding it.

Passover meal/ the Last Supper (22:14–38)

This important passage begins with the meal itself (v 14–20), followed by Jesus' prophecy of his betrayal (v 21–23), a dispute among the apostles about which of them is the greatest (v 24–30), Jesus' prophecy of Peter's denial (v 31–34), and closing instructions about the hostility that lies ahead (v 35–38).

We have already noted the importance of meals in Luke, especially as occasions when Jesus teaches his table companions. Since this is Jesus' last meal before his death it has particular significance. It shares similarities with a widespread ancient literary form, that of a 'farewell discourse' – when a leader imparts parting reflections, teachings and prophecies to his family and/or followers before his impending death (eg Gen 49; Acts 20:17–38). Also of significance for understanding Jesus' teaching and imminent death is the Passover context of the meal, with its themes of sacrifice, liberation and hope. Jesus' eagerness to have this Passover meal with the Twelve is explained by the fact that he will not do this again until it is "fulfilled" in God's kingdom (v 16,18). Here Jesus thinks of the kingdom in its future consummation, the eschatological banquet (see comment on 13:28–29, p113; 14:15).

Task

Discuss the significance of the following for our understanding of this passage:

a) farewell discourses   b) the Passover setting   c) the kingdom of God

The institution of the Lord's Supper (as it is often called) comes in verses 17 to 20. While the other synoptics have the bread followed by the cup, Luke has a cup-bread-cup sequence, the two cups reflecting the fact that there was more than one cup in the Passover meal (in fact, there were four). The situation is complicated further by the omission of Luke's second cup in some manuscripts. However, the manuscript evidence for the originality of verses 19b to 20 is very strong. The first cup (v 17) may be the second of the Passover meal, since words of explanation were spoken then, as Jesus does here (v 18). His description of wine as "the fruit of the vine" may reflect the wording of the Passover grace, "Blessed are you, Lord our God, King of the universe, who has created the fruit of the vine."

Jesus' four actions with the bread (v 19; taking, thanking, breaking, giving) repeat what he did in the feeding of the five thousand (9:16; which has "blessed" rather than "thanks"). While Jesus does not refer to any symbolic significance in relation to the Passover lamb (cf 1 Cor 5:7), he does so concerning the bread and the (second) cup. Jesus interprets the bread metaphorically as representing his body. Such appears to be the meaning of "is" (v 19; cf 8:11), which has no equivalent in Jesus' Aramaic, but is clearly implied. That his body is "given for" the apostles indicates that his imminent death will be on their behalf; both these words were used in connection with sacrifice (eg Ex 30:14; Lev 5:7,10), which is consistent with what is said concerning the cup (v 20; cf Acts 20:28). The command to the apostles to repeat what Jesus had done with the bread in order to remember him is only found in Luke's and Paul's (1 Cor 11:23–25) accounts of the Last Supper, and in Luke only in connection with the bread. Remembrance of God's deliverance of his people was, of course, an important part of the Passover celebration from the start (Ex 12:14; Deut 16:3). While it has been argued that the words "for my remembrance" (literally) are concerned with God being reminded of Jesus through the apostles' repetition of the meal, it is more likely that the apostles are being urged to remember Jesus' death on their behalf (cf I Cor 11:23ff).

The second cup in Luke comes "after supper", being probably the third cup of the Passover, which followed the main meal. The cup (ie its contents) represents the "new covenant" that Jeremiah wrote of (Jer 31:31–34) – the new binding relationship that God would make with his people as a replacement for the former covenant he had with them. This new covenant, says Jesus, is "in my blood", recalling the sacrificial means by which God entered into covenant with the people of Israel in Moses' day (Ex 24:8; cf Mt 26:28/ Mk 14:24). This blood (or the cup) is "poured out", indicating death by violence or sacrifice (eg Gen 9:6), which may reflect words concerning the suffering Servant in Isaiah (53:12, "he poured out himself to death"). It is poured out "for you", that is, the apostles, who represent Israel as its new leaders (v 28–30).

Comment on:

a) the cup-bread-cup sequence

b) the background and meaning of Jesus' comments about the bread and second cup

Jesus then declares what the reader, but not the apostles, already knows – that his betrayer is present at the Last Supper (v 21–23). In the immediate context, Judas' self-serving treachery stands in sharp contrast to Jesus' self-sacrifice for his people. That a table companion of Jesus is also his enemy recalls the lament of the righteous sufferer (Ps 41:9; cf Jn 13:18) and Jesus' earlier teaching concerning the inadequacy of such companionship on Judgement Day (13:26ff). Jesus' awareness of Judas' treachery underlines his prophetic knowledge of events to which he is no mere passive victim. His statement about his death in verse 22 couples divine predeterminism and human responsibility in an uneasy tension, as elsewhere in Luke's writing (cf Acts 2:23; 4:27–28; 13:46,48). Thus, though both Satan (v 3) and God (v 22a) are behind the events leading to Jesus' death, Judas bears responsibility for his act of betrayal (v 22b;

Selected narratives

'woe' see comment on 11:42ff, pp99–101). A leading emphasis of the passion narrative surfaces here in the indication that God's plan is being worked out despite, indeed through, satanic and human malice.

> **Task**
>
> Discuss what Jesus' sayings about his betrayal tell us concerning:
> a) Jesus   b) the causes of Jesus' death

After asking "which one of them" could be the traitor (v 23), the apostles then debate "which one of them" should be considered the greatest (v 24). Concern about the identity of the traitor apparently leads them to reflect on their comparative importance as individuals and, possibly, on the need for a successor to Jesus as leader of the group. Such an attitude itself is, in fact, a betrayal by all of them of Jesus' previous teaching on this very issue (9:46–48). Their presence at a meal would have probably brought issues of relative status and honour into focus, since seating arrangements on such occasions were determined by and reflected one's social importance (see comment on 14:7–11, p116; cf 20:46; Jn 13:23–25). In response to their debate Jesus implies that their attitude reflects Gentile politics (cf 12:30–31). Such rulers called themselves "benefactors", since as wealthy patrons they were in a position where they could gain power over and expect loyalty from dependent clients (cities and individuals) who benefited from their wealth. Thus, economic privilege and political power were closely linked. Jesus' words "But not so with you" can be read as a criticism of the apostles for failing to be benefactors, as the Gentile rulers were. Alternatively, more likely in the context, Jesus is telling the apostles that their leadership of the new or renewed Israel should be unlike that of Gentile rulers. Rather than being concerned with status, power and expecting something in return, the reverse should be the case (an important theme in Luke). The "greatest" should become as the youngest (of little or no status) and the leader as one who serves. Clearly the one being served ("at the table") is greater than the one serving (cf 17:7–10), yet Jesus himself has taken the inferior role of a servant (cf 12:35–38) and the implication is that it is he, rather than Gentile rulers, whom the apostles should imitate.

> **Tasks**
>
> a Comment on the reasons for the apostles' concern with individual greatness.
> b Discuss the meaning of Jesus' response to this concern.

The Gospel of Luke

However, despite their egotistic denial of Jesus' teaching, he commends them for their loyalty to him in his "trials/temptations" (author's translation; cf 4:13, where the same Greek word is found). Indeed, he had taught them about the need for such endurance in these very circumstances (8:13,15; again, Luke uses the same word in v 13). Just as his Father (see comment on 2:49, pp67–68) had conferred a kingdom on him (1:32–33; 19:12,14,27), so now Jesus rewards the apostles' loyalty by doing the same for them (cf 19:17,19). This concern with the appointment of successors by a parting leader was a feature of ancient farewell discourses. While this royal authority was apparently a present gift (eg the apostles' leadership of the early Church in Acts), it would be fully realised only in the end-time banquet of God's future kingdom (v 30a; cf v 16,18; 12:35–38; 13:29; 14:15). God's kingdom had been assigned to Jesus, who can therefore refer to it as "my kingdom". Then the twelve apostles, as the new leaders of the renewed Israel, will exercise their royal authority as they sit on thrones (cf Ps 122:4–5; Dan 7:9) judging its twelve tribes. This has been taken as a reference to national Israel, judged for its rejection of Jesus and his disciples (cf 10:12–16), or to the new multi-national people of God (cf Acts 10,11). Judas, of course, would be replaced as one of the Twelve (Acts 1: 15–26).

Comment on Jesus' words in verses 29 to 30.

In a passage unique to Luke, in part (v 31–32), Jesus then turns his attention to Peter, addressing him both by his proper name, "Simon" (cf 4:38; on its double use here, see comment on 10:41, p89) and by the name he had given him, "Peter" (6:14). With the extraordinary awareness typical of Jesus in the passion narrative thus far (v 10–13,21), he informs Peter of the request (or demand) of Satan (see comment on 10:18, pp84–85) to sift all the apostles as wheat. Thus, the one who inspired Judas' treachery (v 3) also seeks the destruction of the faith (cf v 32) of the other apostles. Satan's role here, including the seeking of divine permission to assault God's people, recalls the opening two chapters of Job (cf also 2 Cor 12:7). Various suggestions have been made about the precise meaning of Jesus' agricultural metaphor – to separate the wheat from the chaff (distinguishing between true and false faith), to collect the refuse while letting the grain fall through (Satan collecting evidence with which to accuse the apostles? cf Sirach 27:3; Rev 12:9–10), or to shake the disciples to test their faith. Peter's faith will survive Satan's sifting of the apostles because of Jesus' prayer (a Lucan emphasis) for him. Then, when Peter has "turned back" (ie repented of his denial of Jesus: v 34) from Satan's power (cf Acts 26:18) he must strengthen his brothers, including his fellow apostles. As the story continues into Acts we indeed find Peter as the leader of the early Church in Jerusalem (especially chs 1–12). Jesus' talk about Peter's imminent temporary failure brings from Peter a protest that, far from failing, he is prepared to go with Jesus to prison (cf 21:12; Acts 4:1ff; 5:17ff; 12:3ff) and death (cf Acts 5:33). The Jewish day had begun at sunset and in the matter of hours between the evening Passover meal and cock crow Peter would deny that he knows Jesus. Here we have another example of Jesus' prophetic knowledge in the passion narrative. The serious implications of such denial of Jesus have already been spelled out in this Gospel (12:9). In light of the prediction, Jesus' use of the name "Peter" (meaning 'rock') is as ironic as Peter's use of the title "Lord".

Tasks

a Discuss the meaning of the metaphor in verse 31.

b Comment on Jesus' prayer and prophecy concerning Peter (v 32–34).

Finally at the Passover table, and only in Luke, Jesus warns the apostles that they cannot now count on the hospitality they previously enjoyed as missionaries (cf v 35 with 9:3–4; 10:4ff). "Now" they will need to be self-sufficient and, indeed, to prepare for hostility by purchasing swords (v 36). While it is possible to take the latter instruction literally, to do so contradicts Jesus' instruction later that very evening, (v 49–51) as well as his earlier teaching (6:27–31). Rather, it is possible to take Jesus' reference to swords metaphorically (cf 12:51/ Mt 10:34; Lk 2:34–35) as a symbol of the hostility and violence that the apostles will face in the events of the passion. The apostles' response (v 38) is therefore to be read as a literalistic misunderstanding of Jesus, which in return is rebuked by him ("It is enough"; cf eg Gen 45:28). Jesus sees the hostility he faces as a fulfilment of a passage concerning Isaiah's suffering Servant (53:12). If we take our passage's references to swords literally, then it is possible that the "lawless" among whom Jesus is counted by others are his own apostles. However, it may be that the "criminals" with whom Jesus was crucified (23:32–33) are in view here.

Tasks

a What is the significance of "But now …" in verse 36?

b Discuss this passage's references to swords.

c Comment on the fulfilment of the Scripture quoted in this passage.

Jesus prays on the Mount of Olives (22:39–46)

We are introduced to a change of scene as Jesus leaves the Passover meal indoors and goes outdoors to the Mount of Olives (cf 19:29), as was his custom (cf 21:37). The passage is framed by the opening and closing command of Jesus to his disciples to pray that they will not "enter into temptation/trial" (author's translation; v 40,46). He has already taught them to pray for this very thing (see comment on 11:4, pp92–93;

cf 21:36) and revisits a theme he has just raised indoors (v 28). Though Satan is not specifically mentioned in the passage, the use of the term "temptation/trial" (author's translation; cf 4:13; 8:12–13) and recent references to him (v 3,31) may imply that his activity is now in view. Sandwiched between the two commands to the disciples to pray is the focus upon Jesus himself at prayer (a favourite theme of Luke). As in Luke generally, prayer is something that Jesus practises as well as preaches. The main point of the passage appears to be that the disciples should follow Jesus' example (cf v 39b) in overcoming temptation/trial through prayer.

Jesus' relative solitude ("about a stone's throw") and submissive posture ("knelt down"; cf Acts 7:60; 9:40; 20:36; 21:5) are both noted by Luke. Jesus addresses God as "Father", recalling his special relationship as God's Son (see comment on 2:49, pp67–68; 10:21–22; 22:29) and how his disciples too should address and perceive God in prayer (11:2,11–13). The brief prayer focuses on God's "will/purpose" (author's translation; a key theme in Luke), with which it begins and ends. The struggle that Jesus now faces with the approaching events of the passion is the relationship of his will to his Father's. The prayer indicates that the two wills are distinct ("my will … yours") and even different ("*not* my will *but* yours"). Jesus prays that "this cup" (a symbol of suffering and God's judgement, eg Isa 51:17,22) be taken from him. He nevertheless acknowledges that such avoidance of suffering and death is conditional upon God's will, to which he yields his own. As with the temptation he faced at the beginning of his ministry (4:1–13), so now at its end he puts God's will first. The reference to the angel and the agony (v 43–44) may not be original (eg it is absent from the oldest surviving manuscript of Luke), but if it is, Luke is indicating the physical and emotional intensity that Jesus experiences as he submits himself to God's will. Now Jesus experiences the angelic assistance promised in the Jewish Scriptures to God's people (Ps 91:11–12), a Scripture which the devil had misused in Jesus' earlier temptation (4:9–12). This heaven-sent angel ("from heaven") gives Jesus the strength to pray "more earnestly"; later, Luke will describe the prayer of the early Christians in the same way (Acts 12:5). The word translated "anguish" (v 43, *agonia*) is related to the term for athletic contest and struggle (cf Heb 12:1, "race" = *agon*), an idea associated with prayer elsewhere in the New Testament (Col 4:12, *agonizomai;* this verb is also found in Luke 13:24). The physical symptoms of Jesus' emotional anguish are apparent in his sweat dripping on the ground. The comparison with "drops of blood" is another of Luke's similes (cf "like/as" – author's translation – 3:22; 10:18; 11:44; 22:31) and should not, therefore, be read as a literal sweating of blood. The sleep of the disciples contrasts with Jesus' earlier command (v 40; hence its repetition in v 46) and Jesus' own prayerfulness. However, it is noted that their sleep is due to grief (over Jesus' imminent death). As the passage began so it ends, on the note of the necessity of prayer in the midst of temptation/trial.

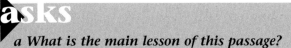

Tasks

a **What is the main lesson of this passage?**

b **Discuss the relationship between Jesus' will and the Father's will, as portrayed here.**

c **Comment on the authenticity and meaning of verses 43 to 44.**

The betrayal and arrest of Jesus (22:47–53)

Jesus' instruction of his disciples about the need for prayer in the midst of trial is interrupted by the approach of a crowd led by Judas. Since Jesus has just resigned himself to God's will in prayer, he faces this trial with composure. However, the disciples have been in a prayerless sleep and react to the trial with anxiety and violence. Indeed, Jesus' control of and compassion in this situation contrast with the treachery of Judas, the violence of a disciple, and the malice of the Jewish leaders.

The kiss is the prearranged signal of Jesus' identification (cf Mt 26:48/ Mk 14:44), possibly to avoid any confusion or mistake in the dark of night. In Luke alone, Judas' attempt to kiss Jesus is interrupted by Jesus' question. The irony and hypocrisy of a sign of affection and friendship (cf 7:38,45; 15:20) being used as a means of betrayal (cf Joab, 2 Sam 20:8–10) is highlighted by Jesus (cf similarly v 21; 21:16). In this way, far from being a passive victim of circumstance Jesus takes the initiative by exposing Judas' treachery. Jesus' control of events is confirmed by the observation that he had predicted what is now taking place (v 21–23). The irony of Judas' kiss of death is matched by the disciples' address of Jesus as "Lord" (characteristic of Luke) while in the same breath advocating violence (despite 6:27–36!). Their reference to the sword recalls Jesus' earlier discussion with them (v 35–38), and their attempt to resist the arrest of Jesus reveals their failure to understand that in these events God's purpose is being fulfilled (cf 9:44–45). The slave of the Jewish high priest – one of the temple entourage who has arrived (v 52; cf v 2–3) – is present, indicating in the narrative that the conspiracy against Jesus goes all the way to the top of the Jewish establishment. While a disciple (Peter, according to John 18:10) cuts off this slave's ear (both Luke and John say it is his "right" ear), Jesus reverses this act of violence by an act of healing (only in Luke among the four evangelists). By word ("No more of this!") and deed (healing by touch; cf 4:40; 7:14) he demonstrates his opposition to the act of violence and thus, in this last healing of his ministry, continues its theme of restoration rather than destruction (cf 9:54–55).

As Jesus had used a question to confront and expose the duplicity of Judas' actions, so he does with the high priest's posse (v 52–53). After Judas' kiss and the disciples' address of Jesus as "Lord" comes a third irony in the story. The temple authorities treat the unarmed, clearly pacifist Jesus as if he were a "bandit", while they themselves are, bandit-like, armed to the teeth (cf 19:46)! Not in daylight when Jesus is teaching daily and publicly in the temple precincts do they arrest him for fear of the crowds (cf 19:47–48; 20:1,19,26; 21:37–38), but rather under the cover of the darkness of night. This is their "hour" (cf 20:19) and the darkness of the night symbolises "the power of darkness" which, like Judas (v 3–6; cf Acts 26:18), they are now serving. The arrest itself (v 54) forms the bridge to the next passage.

> **Tasks**
>
> a Comment on the relationship of this passage to the one immediately before it.
>
> b Discuss the ironies of the account.

Peter's denial (22:54–62)

The temple authorities who arrested Jesus now bring him from the Mount of Olives to the high priest's house in the city. Luke's description of Peter's physical location is also a metaphor for the state of his discipleship at this point, for he is now closer to Jesus' enemies ("sat among them") than he is to Jesus himself ("following at a distance"). The three denials by Peter that Jesus had earlier predicted (v 31–34) are reported in quick succession, yet Luke notes that some time elapses after both the first two denials (v 58–59), during which Peter would have had the opportunity to recall Jesus' recent prophecy of his failure. To consider whether Peter, with his knowledge of Jesus' prophecy, has any choice to repent before his third denial (and render Jesus a false prophet in the process) raises the wider dilemma of the relationship between divine foreknowledge and human responsibility. The dilemma is particularly sharp here because the moral agent (Peter) shares in the divine foreknowledge. The social and gender identity of the first person to challenge Peter ("a servant-girl") adds in that culture to the cowardice of his first denial, while his response mirrors the terms of Jesus' prophecy (v 57; cf v 34). While in his first denial he disowns Jesus, in his second he disowns his fellow disciples, and in his third his Galilean origins too (possibly apparent from his accent; cf Mt 26:73).

Unlike the first two denials, there is no time delay after the third, for "immediately" (author's translation; *parachrema*; a favourite word of Luke's), indeed "while he was still speaking" (v 60; cf v 47) the cock crowed. Only Luke says, characteristically, that "The Lord turned" and looked at Peter, indicating his proximity in the courtyard of the high priest's house and highlighting Peter's guilt (cf 9:55). It is Jesus' look in particular, rather than the crowing of the cock, that reminds Peter of Jesus' prophecy. Luke also underlines Jesus' role as a prophet by describing his prophecy as "the word of the Lord" (cf 3:2; Hos 1:1; Joel 1:1). The expression reflects Luke's fondness for calling Jesus "the Lord" (twice in v 61), but also implies that Jesus speaks in the place of God himself, since while the prophets were distinct from the Lord whose word they brought, here Jesus is the Lord whose word Peter remembers. Satan is now sifting Peter (cf v 31), but Jesus' prayer for him has ensured that a complete loss of faith is avoided (v 32). Peter's bitter weeping (v 62; cf 6:21; 7:38) is the beginning of the turning back that Jesus also foresaw (v 32). Although being ashamed of Jesus and denying him before others have serious consequences (9:26; 12:9), forgiveness and restoration are also possible (12:10). Replacing Peter's cowardice before a servant-girl, Luke will recount his courage before the temple leaders themselves (Acts 4:13).

Tasks

a Comment on the pacing and wording of the three denials.
b Discuss whether Peter was a free moral agent during his denials.
c Consider Jesus' role as a prophet in this passage.
d What does Peter's bitter weeping signify?

Jesus is mocked and beaten (22:63–65)

In the other synoptics, this passage comes at the end of Jesus' trial before the Jewish council (Mt 26:65–68/ Mk 14:65). The "men ... holding Jesus" are those who arrested him – the temple leaders and guards (v 52). Ironically, by mocking Jesus' role as a prophet they are in fact confirming it (18:32)! The rejection of God's prophets (cf Isa 50:4–6) has been a recurring theme in Luke (eg 6:22–23; 11:47–51; 13:33–35) and reaches its climax in the rejection of Jesus. As in the previous passage, Jesus is presented, albeit indirectly, as a prophet. The scepticism of Jesus' prophetic ability, which recalls an earlier passage in Luke (7:39), manifests itself in the ridicule of a game of blind man's buff. While the word translated "insults" (v 65, *blasphemeo*) can refer to general slander, its more specific sense of blaspheming against God may be implied here as Jesus' role as God's messenger is mocked.

Task

Comment on this passage's ironic portrayal of Jesus as a prophet.

The trial before the Jewish council (22:66–71)

The trial of Jesus in Luke (22:66–23:25) begins with the Jewish council (22:66–71), followed by Pilate (23:1–5), then Herod (23:6–12), and ends with Pilate again for the verdict and sentencing (23:13–25). In each of these four scenes the Jewish leaders are present as Jesus' accusers.

There are notable differences between Luke's account and the other synoptic accounts (Mt 26:57–66/ Mk 14:55–64) of the trial before the Jewish council. In

Matthew and Mark, Jesus' trial is during the night, followed by a morning meeting of the council to finalise charges before going to Pilate (Mt 27:1–2/ Mk 15:1). However, in Luke the trial is in the morning (22:66), Jesus having been detained throughout the previous night, as would be the case with the apostles in the sequel to Luke (cf Acts 4:1–5; 5:17–21). Since Luke's morning trial is very similar to the other synoptics' night trial, it has been argued that one or the other has got the timing wrong. However, it has been suggested that the night-time investigation of Jesus lasted until morning and that Luke has simplified matters by telescoping the details. Other differences include Luke's omission of any reference to the high priest (but implied from v 54? cf Acts 5:27; 23:1–5), witnesses (but implied in v 71?), the temple, blasphemy, a verdict (but again implied in v 71?), and abuse of Jesus (found earlier, in v 63–65).

We are told that the "assembly of the elders of the people" consists of both chief priests and scribes/lawyers (v 66), recalling Jesus' first prediction of his passion (9:22) and, particularly, the recent hostile intent of the Jewish leaders since Jesus' arrival in Jerusalem (19:47; 20:1,19–20; 22:1ff,52). They bring Jesus to their "council" (Greek *sunedrion*), which may refer to a place rather than the group of leaders (the Sanhedrin). Later Jewish Law (the *Mishnah*, c. AD 200), which probably contains first-century traditions, states that trials should not be held during festivals (such as Passover) and that verdicts in capital cases must not be passed on the trial's first day. However, it also notes exceptions to this, as in the case of a false prophet leading Israel astray – the very thing which later Jewish writings attribute Jesus' execution to.

The brief account of the trial consists of two questions, two replies and the council's conclusion. The first question is really a demand that Jesus confess if he considers himself to be the Messiah/Christ (see Messiah/Christ, p31). While Jesus himself has not openly claimed to be the Messiah before now in Luke, the reader has been encouraged to view him as such (2:11,26; 4:41; 9:20; 20:41ff). Jesus does not provide a direct answer to their question (cf Mk 14:62), but states that they would not believe him if he did answer their question, nor would they answer any question he might put to them (cf 20:1–8,41–44). The implication appears to be that the Jewish leadership is not interested in the truth about Jesus' identity, but only about whether he is making claims that they already consider to be false. Jesus continues his reply by characteristically preferring his favourite and self-chosen title "Son of Man" (see p79 for details) to that of Messiah (cf 9:20–22). The words "from now on" in Luke frequently indicate a new turning point and imply that Jesus' enthronement and exaltation to God's right hand is imminent (cf 1:48; 20:41–44; Acts 2:33–36; Ps 110:1). Thus, the implication is that Jesus will very soon be honoured and vindicated by God, despite the indignity and dishonour he is presently experiencing at the hands of the Jewish leadership. Jesus' use of a reverent euphemism as a substitute for the name of God ("power", as in Mt 26:64/ Mk 14:62) has been expanded in Luke to include God's name (v 69), possibly to clarify the expression for his Gentile readers. Also, Luke does not have the reference to seeing the Son of Man coming on/with the clouds of heaven, found in the other synoptics, which is often interpreted as part of Luke's perceived downplaying of Jesus' Second Coming (see Eschatology, pp39–40).

Jesus' answer to the first question provokes a second, which draws out the logic of the answer he has just given (v 70). Jesus' claim to be at God's "right hand" is understood, on the basis of Psalms 110:1, as a claim to be Israel's king, who was also known as son of God (eg 1:32–33; Ps 2:2,6–7; 2 Sam 7:13–14) – hence the council's reply, "Are you, *then*, the Son of God?" This question is in fact just a repeat of their first question, since Jewish kings were not only called sons of God, but also God's Messiahs/anointed ones (eg 23:2; Ps 2:2,6). Indeed, Messiah/Christ is closely associated with Son of God elsewhere in Luke–Acts (4:41; Acts 9:20–22; cf Mt 16:16). We may note here that while the questions about Jesus' Messiahship and divine sonship are separate in Luke, they are combined in the other synoptics, implying their virtual equivalence (Mt 26:63/ Mk 14:61). So, as far as the council is concerned, while the first part of Jesus' reply (v 67–68) does not answer their question about his Messiahship, the second part does (v 69), and indeed answers in the affirmative. Jesus' reply to their second question (v 70, "You say that I am"; cf 23:2) may be an ironic affirmative – "Yes, and you yourselves have said it, despite your unbelief!" Alternatively, it may be a reluctant admission, or Jesus' way of noting that this is the council's inference. Whatever the case may be, the Jewish leaders now achieve what they have long hoped for – they catch Jesus by his own words (v 71; cf 11:53–54; 20:19–20,26).

Tasks

a Comment on the differences between the accounts of Jesus' trial before the Jewish council in Luke and the other synoptics.

b Discuss the background and meaning of the council's questions and Jesus' replies.

The trial before Pilate (23:1–5)

While Luke does not explain why the Jewish leaders brought Jesus before Pontius Pilate, the Roman Governor of Judea (AD 26–36; cf 3:1), it appears that their plan to have Jesus killed (19:47) requires Roman authority (cf Jn 18:31). Luke stresses the collective responsibility of the council (v 1) in bringing Jesus to Pilate. They make three charges against Jesus (v 2; although the second and third may simply be elaborations of the first). The charge that Jesus was perverting or leading astray the nation of Israel reflects the Jewish leadership's view that Jesus' teachings and practices are not in line with their traditions and interpretations of Scripture. In effect, they are calling him a false prophet. Pilate, however, may understand the charge to mean that Jesus is a subversive. The second accusation, that Jesus was forbidding payment of taxes to the Roman emperor, reflects a recent dialogue between Jesus and the Jewish leaders on this very issue, the pretext of which was to get Jesus before

Pilate (20:20–26). Jesus' carefully chosen answer then is now being misrepresented as political treason. Finally, Jesus is charged with claiming to be the Messiah (cf 22:67ff), and the Jewish leaders underline the royal associations of this Jewish term for the Gentile governor's benefit ("a king"). The political ramifications of such a claim are spelt out in Luke's sequel (Acts 17:7–8). The view that the 'religious' charges of the Jewish trial have been transformed into 'political' charges before Pilate in order to secure a conviction seems to be influenced by modern distinctions between religion and politics which were unknown in the ancient world, where the two were inextricably linked. Nonetheless, the wording of the charges before Pilate does appear to highlight imperial implications.

Pilate gives the accused an opportunity to respond to the charges made against him, in line with Roman legal procedure (cf Acts 25:16). The governor's question (v 3) focuses on the last of the three charges, and Jesus replies in practically the same way as he did to the question of the Jewish council (see 22:70). Pilate's innocent verdict (cf also v 14,22) indicates that he does not view Jesus as a serious threat to Rome. The leaders may have "found" Jesus to be a criminal (v 2), but the governor "find[s]" differently (v 4; also v 14,22). However, the chief priests (the temple authorities) and "the crowds" are insistent. The mention of "the crowds" is unexpected here, since in Jerusalem they have been on the side of Jesus rather than the Jewish leaders (cf 19:47–48; 20:1,19; 22:6). Unlike Matthew (27:20) and Mark (15:11), Luke does not attribute the change to the influence of the Jewish leaders in his passion narrative. It is just possible, however, that by "the crowds" Luke is referring to the Jewish leadership and its entourage (23:1, literally "all the multitude of them"; cf 22:47,52,66). They repeat their first charge with similarly emotive language ("stirs up"; cf v 2). This time they stress the geographical scope of his allegedly subversive teaching – "throughout all Judea", understood in the broad sense of 'the land of the Jews' (cf 4:44; 7:17), and beginning from "Galilee" (cf 4:14ff; Acts 10:37). His teaching has now reached "this place" (v 5), that is, Jerusalem (cf chs 20–21) – the home of Israel's leaders and temple.

Tasks

a **Why did the Jewish leaders bring Jesus to Pilate?**

b **Discuss the charges they made against Jesus.**

c **Comment on Pilate's question and Jesus' reply.**

The trial before Herod (23:6–12)

The Jewish leaders' reference to Jesus' Galilean origins (v 5) leads Pilate to send Jesus to Galilee's ruler, Herod Antipas (3:1) – an episode found only in Luke. This manoeuvre by Pilate is probably motivated by a desire to avoid a confrontation with the Jewish leaders by making Jesus someone else's problem, rather than by political courtesy (cf v 12). Also, it may be that the Gentile governor feels a Jewish ruler could better deal with this case. Herod's presence in Jerusalem is possibly due to the Passover (cf Acts 12:4,19). His delight at seeing Jesus is attributed to a long-held desire for such a meeting, which in turn is attributed to reports about Jesus (cf 9:9) and a hope that he might see Jesus perform a "sign". This latter hope has already been generally condemned by Jesus in this Gospel (11:16,29–30). Other teaching of Jesus is also recalled by this ruler's unfulfilled desire (10:24).

Herod's many questions are contrasted with Jesus' total lack of response, recalling, as Luke's passion narrative often does, Isaiah's suffering Servant of the Lord (Isa 53:7–8; cf Acts 8:32–33). Jesus' refusal to reply contrasts with his response to the Jewish council (22:67–70) and Pilate (23:3). It may be that Jesus now feels, even more than earlier (22:67–68), that response is useless. As in each stage of the trial of Jesus, Luke notes the presence of the Jewish leadership as Jesus' accusers (cf 9:22; 22:66), this time highlighting the vehemence of their opposition (v 10; the Greek adverb is also used by Luke in Acts 18:28, where the NRSV translates it as "powerfully").

While Luke does not have the mock dressing-up of Jesus by Pilate's soldiers found in Matthew (27:27–31), Mark (15:16–20) and John (19:1–3), he reports similar acts by Herod's soldiers here. The 'mocking' recalls the third passion prediction (18:32) and is a regular theme of the passion narrative (22:63; 23:36). Herod joins in the ridicule, his opposition to Jesus (13:31) and his forerunner (3:18–20; 9:7–9) having already been noted in Luke. The "elegant/brilliant robe" (author's translation) which Herod puts on Jesus is probably part of the mockery, ridiculing claims that Jesus is King of the Jews (v 2–3,37–38), rather than Herod's attempt to symbolise Jesus' innocence for Pilate (v 13–15). Previous hostility between Herod and Pilate (cf 13:1) is removed by their united hostility against Jesus. Luke wants to highlight that otherwise divided individuals and groups are united by their opposition to Jesus (compare Herod and Pilate, etc in Acts 4:26–27).

Discuss Luke's characterisation of the following in this passage:

a) Pilate   *b) Herod and his soldiers*

c) Jesus   *d) the Jewish leaders*

Pilate sentences Jesus (23:13–25)

Two sets of contrasts dominate this passage, one between Pilate and the Jews and the other between Jesus and Barabbas. Three times Pilate tries to release Jesus and three times the Jews and their leaders loudly protest. There is therefore a clash between what 'Pilate willed' (v 20, author's translation) and 'their will' (v 25, author's translation), and the latter prevails. The other contrast is between Jesus who is declared innocent of all charges (whose "release" Pilate wants), and Barabbas who has been convicted of serious crimes (whose "release" the Jews want).

Pilate summons the Jews, both leaders (of whom the chief priests are singled out for special mention) and people (v 13; cf v 4). He repeats their key accusation against Jesus (cf v 2) and informs them that upon examination he has found Jesus innocent of all their charges. In support of his verdict Pilate notes that Herod is apparently of the same opinion, for he has sent Jesus back to the Roman authorities. Jesus is not guilty of the capital crimes laid against him, therefore he will not face the capital punishment that such crimes deserve. However, Pilate's decision is that Jesus will undergo corporal punishment (flogging/whipping), probably because he regards him as a public nuisance and hopes that this will be enough to satisfy Jesus' hostile opponents. Unlike the other Gospels, we do not read in Luke of Jesus actually being flogged; nor in the others does Pilate offer this as a compromise to avoid Jesus' execution. Pilate reviews the case and his findings in accordance with the typical stages of a Roman trial (v 14–16) – arrest ("You brought …"), charges ("perverting the people"), investigation ("I have examined him"), verdict ("not … guilty"), and acquittal ("nothing to deserve death").

Luke underlines the unanimous opposition of the Jewish people and leaders in Jerusalem to Pilate's intention to release Jesus (v 18; cf v 13). Their cry is for Jesus to be taken away (cf Acts 21:36; 22:22) and for the release of a certain Barabbas, who has not been mentioned in the narrative before and whom Luke immediately identifies as a murdering rebel against Rome. Unlike the other Gospels, Luke does not explain why the crowd could expect Pilate to release a prisoner for them (the so-called 'Passover privilege'), though later scribes sought to make up for Luke's omission (v 17; or after v 19). No other evidence of such a Passover custom has yet been found, though Roman law did take into consideration the acclamation of the people (*acclamatio populi*) and there are examples of Roman magistrates who followed public opinion. The irony is that while the people are calling for the execution of Jesus who has been cleared of all charges, they are also demanding the release of a man who has been convicted of similar charges. Luke will highlight the injustice of this as he brings this passage to a close, by repeating Barabbas' crimes (v 25) and, indeed, it will resurface in his sequel (Acts 3:14). Pilate attempts a second (v 20) and a third time (v 22) to get the people to agree to Jesus' release (cf Acts 3:13), but now their more general demand (v 18, "Away with this man", author's translation) is replaced by the specific cry for his crucifixion (v 21,23). Luke's words "and their voices prevailed" (v 23) explains to some extent why Pilate reverses the verdict – the people are becoming increasingly vocal (v 18,21,23; cf Mt 27:24). Avoiding a riot by many is apparently more important than securing justice for one. Pilate has already angered the Emperor Tiberius (cf 3:1) by causing Jewish protests over insensitivity to their religious beliefs (in Philo's *Embassy to Gaius* 38.299–305) and would want to avoid the political embarrassment of more unrest in his province. The passage concludes by noting that the people's two demands are granted by Pilate – he releases Barabbas and hands Jesus over (v 25).

The four stages of the trial of Jesus in Luke are now complete and together they have stressed that the Romans, along with their subordinate Herod Antipas, have

Selected narratives

Jesus to be innocent, but that this verdict was reversed at the unanimous insistence of the Jewish residents of Jerusalem and, especially, of their leaders. If Theophilus, to whom Luke is writing, is a Roman official, then clearly this explanation of Jesus' execution by the Roman authorities is of apologetic value for him and Luke's wider readership (see Political, pp23–24)[1].

Tasks

a **Outline the two sets of contrasts in this passage.**

b **Comment on the people's demand for Barabbas' release.**

c **Discuss the reasons for Pilate's change of verdict.**

On the way to the crucifixion (23:26–32)

This passage is concerned with the journey from the place where Pilate's final verdict was given to the site of Jesus' crucifixion, a journey during which Luke provides more details than the other Gospels. In turn, it introduces the characters Simon of Cyrene, the women of Jerusalem and two criminals. Luke does not specify exactly who it is that is leading Jesus to crucifixion. His ambiguous "they" (v 26) may be a way of highlighting the collective responsibility of both Jews and Romans for the death of Jesus (cf Acts 4:27). Since the Roman soldiers will not bear the shame of carrying the cross (probably the horizontal crossbeam), they commandeer a certain Simon from Cyrene in North Africa (in modern Libya). Later, Luke will refer to Jews from here (Acts 2:10; 6:9) and it may be that Simon himself is Jewish. That he is "coming from the country" into Jerusalem (possibly for Passover) indicates that he is not among those demanding Jesus' crucifixion (v 13–25). Luke does not mention why Jesus does not carry his own cross, which he does in John (19:17), though it may be because he is weakened by the Roman flogging which, according to the other Gospels, he endures. In carrying the cross behind Jesus, Simon is doing literally what disciples of Jesus have been called upon to do metaphorically (cf 9:23; 14:27).

The heart of the passage concerns a large number of people who follow Jesus (probably curious to see his fate), among whom are women mourning for him. Only Luke has this story, an example of his characteristic concern for women. Their actions may recall a passage in Zechariah about people in Jerusalem mourning for the one they have pierced (Zech 12:10–14), in anticipation of Jesus' crucifixion. Jesus "turned" to them, as often in Luke before rebuke or warning (cf 22:61), and told them that the focus of their mourning was misplaced. Rather than weeping over his fate, they should be weeping over their own and that of their children, for "days are surely coming" (an expression anticipating tragedy and judgement, eg 17:22; 19:43; 21:6; Am 4:2) when there will be a reversal in what is to be regarded as a divine blessing (v 29; cf 1:24–25).

---

[1] On the issue of whether Luke in general, and his passion narrative in particular, is anti-Jewish, see pp269–276, especially pp269–271.

Then the people of Jerusalem, whom the women represent, will take words from Hosea (10:8) about relief from God's judgement on Israel, and long for a speedy death (v 30). Jesus' words to the women are about the forthcoming destruction of Jerusalem in AD 70, about which he has already spoken in this Gospel (13:33–35; 19:41–44; 21:5–6,20–24). On the way to his crucifixion, Jesus knows that Jerusalem's rejection of her Messiah is now almost complete and prophesies again its coming judgement by God. He had wept over Jerusalem (19:41) and now he urges its women to do the same. Finally, Jesus speaks a proverb to the women (v 31), using lesser-to-greater logic (cf 11:13) – which basically means "If this is what they do to a living tree, what will happen to a dead one?" Thus, the calamity that has befallen Jesus will be even greater on others. Some think Jesus is saying that if this is how the Romans treat an innocent person (Jesus), then how much worse will they treat Jewish rebels in the forthcoming revolt? Alternatively, the meaning may be that if God ("they"; see comment on 12:20, p103) did not spare Jesus, how much more will unrepentant Jerusalem not be spared in its coming judgement? Again, there may be a veiled contrast between Jesus' cross ("moist/green" – author's translation – wood not burned up) and Jerusalem's wood ("dry" wood burned up by the Romans in AD 70). Luke adds that two criminals, who will feature significantly a little later in the narrative, are also led away to be crucified with Jesus (cf 22:37).

Tasks

a Who led Jesus to his crucifixion?

b Comment on the role of Simon of Cyrene in this passage.

c Discuss the significance of Jesus' words to the women (v 28–31).

The crucifixion (23:33–43)

Like the other Gospels, Luke does not give any details about the crucifixion itself (all four Gospels simply say 'they crucified him'), but rather focuses on events surrounding it. Three separate instances of mockery of Jesus are recounted, in apparently descending order of the offenders' status – the Jewish leaders, the Roman soldiers, and a crucified criminal. The common theme of their mockery is whether Jesus can "save" himself and the implications of this for his allegedly messianic identity. Contrasted with these negative responses to Jesus, specifically with that of the criminal, is the positive stance of the other criminal, whose words have important functions within the narrative. Neither negative nor positive is the seemingly neutral characterisation of "the people", who are merely spectators (though see v 13,18ff). In the midst of all this is the central character, Jesus, who responds to these various attitudes to himself with a prayer for forgiveness and a promise of paradise.

As in the other Gospels, the site of the crucifixion is a place known as "The Skull", though only Luke avoids using its foreign (Aramaic) name (*Golgotha*), probably to

Selected narratives

Gentile readership (compare his avoidance of 'Gethsemane' in 22:39ff). The name may reflect the physical shape of the crucifixion site, which was probably located outside the city walls (cf Jn 19:20). Jesus is crucified between the two criminals, reflecting the final verdict against him. Crucifixion was used throughout the ancient world by various nations and empires as a cruel method of punishment and execution. It was employed by the Romans mostly for people of low status such as slaves and criminals, particularly for rebels against its political authority, thus acting as a deterrent against revolution. Victims, along with the crossbeam which they carried, would have been nailed or tied to an upright stake, arms raised and extended, the instrument of execution being in what we know as the traditional cross shape or a 'T' shape.

Jesus' prayer to God for the forgiveness of his executioners (v 34a) appears, on the basis of the manuscript evidence, not to be original to Luke (as indicated by the NRSV's double brackets). However, some scholars argue for its authenticity because of, for example, the presence of Lucan themes and the greater ease with which its omission, rather than its addition, can be explained. On the latter point, scribes may have omitted it because they perceived it to be a contradiction of Jesus' earlier teaching about the coming judgement on Jerusalem (see comment on v 28–31, pp169–170). Only, Luke of the four Gospels, has Jesus address God as "Father" on the cross (v 46) and, if original, this prayer would be a second instance. It would also recall similar, earlier indications of Jesus' filial relationship with God (2:49; 10:21–22; 22:42). Thus, even on the cross his sense of God as his Father is secure. The theme of forgiveness is Lucan too (eg 1:77; 7:47–50; 24:47; Acts 2:38; 5:31) and, as Jesus' dying prayer for his executioners, this request is the model for Stephen in Luke's sequel (Acts 7:60). Again, the prayer's reference to the ignorance of those who are crucifying Jesus (given as the basis of the appeal for forgiveness) becomes a theme in Acts, especially in relation to Jewish involvement in Jesus' death (3:17; 13:27; 17:30; see comment on Lk 12:47–48, p107; 19:42,44). Jesus' action here is also an instance of him practising what he preached (6:27–28, "pray for those who abuse you"). The prayer may also reflect Isaiah's suffering and dying Servant of the Lord, who "made intercession for the transgressors" (53:12). Victims of crucifixion were often stripped naked to add to their shame and humiliation and, as in the Gospel accounts, there is evidence that their executioners could take their final possessions, such as clothing (v 34b). Jesus' clothes are gambled for by the casting of "lots" (possibly pebbles here; cf 1:9; Acts 1:26) The wording reflects the suffering of the righteous man in Psalm 22 (v 18).

Crucifixions were often sited in public places, such as near main roads, to maximise their deterrent value and to invite the abuse of passers-by. While "the people" (cf v 13,27) merely spectate (v 35a), Jesus is mocked in turn by the Jewish leaders, the Roman soldiers and one of the crucified criminals – ridicule of Jesus being a theme of the passion narrative (cf v 11; 22:63). The Jewish leaders (cf v 13) "scoffed" at him, as the Pharisees had done before (16:14), recalling again the suffering of the righteous man in Psalm 22 (v 7; the same Greek verb is used in these three passages). "He saved others", they say, probably referring to his miracles (eg 6:9ff, where the Greek verb is used), so he should now be able miraculously to "save himself" from his crucifixion, "if", of course, he is what he claims to be. This sceptical "if" recalls the attitude of the devil (4:3,9) and the Jewish council (22:67), and will be repeated by the Roman soldiers (v 37). The leaders use the same title as they used in their trial of Jesus ("Messiah/Christ") and another, only used of Jesus by Luke among the four Gospels ("chosen"; cf 9:35). This latter term describes Isaiah's suffering Servant (42:1) and was used of the Messiah in the first century (eg 1 Enoch 39:6–8; 48:6–10). The Gentile soldiers also mock Jesus (as predicted in 18:32), ridiculing his apparent claim to be the "King of the Jews" (the Gentile form of the Jewish term 'Messiah'; cf 22:67; 23:35 with 23:2–3,38). Their offer to Jesus of cheap, sour wine (recalling Ps 69:21, where the same Greek word for the wine is used), rather than superior, sweet wine fit for a king, is part of the mockery. Again, as with the leaders before them, they demand that Jesus save himself to verify the messianic claims. Placards containing details about the condemned criminal and his crime(s) served the purposes of public shame and deterrence. While all four Gospels have different accounts of the wording of the inscription, they all include the charge "King of the Jews". For the Romans, this was political rebellion, treason against the emperor, and a capital crime requiring capital punishment. For the Christian reader, it was and is an ironic inscription, for the Roman charge is also the Christian confession.

In a passage unique to Luke (v 39–43), we read that one of the criminals who are being "hanged" there (cf Acts 5:30; 10:39) is also "deriding" Jesus. Luke used the same word (*blasphemeo*) to describe the actions of those who arrested Jesus (22:65), which may also contain the idea of blaspheming against God. Like the leaders and soldiers, the criminal demands that Jesus prove the claims to Messiahship/royalty by saving himself and, he adds, "us". The verb 'to save' has now been used four times of Jesus by his opponents at the cross, and in connection with his alleged identity as Messiah/King of the Jews, ironically highlighting one of Luke's major themes. The other criminal, who in the other synoptics also insults Jesus (Mt 27:44/ Mk 15:32), rebukes this derision of Jesus. Firstly, the mocking criminal should view his execution (and that of the other criminal) as the just judgement of God and "fear God" (cf 1:50; 12:5; 18:2). Secondly, while justice is being served in the execution of the two criminals, it is not in the case of Jesus, for he is innocent. So now, along with Pilate and Herod, we have another apologetically useful witness to the innocence of Jesus in Luke's passion narrative.

The second criminal then speaks to Jesus (v 42), the only person in the Gospels to address him simply by his name (though some manuscripts add "Lord"). The request that Jesus "remember" him (ie for good; cf Ps 106:4–5) is similar to inscriptions found on gravestones at the time. It is debatable "when" the criminal wants this remembering to occur, depending on what preposition should be read before "your kingdom" (the manuscripts differ). If we read 'into', then the request may refer in Lucan thought to Jesus' ascension and exaltation to God's right hand (cf 19:12;

s 2:29–36; 5:30–31). However, if we read 'in', and understand "kingdom" (βασιλεία) in its more usual dynamic, non-spatial sense ('reign'), then the request may refer to Jesus' future coming as king (cf 17:20,24,30; 18:8; 21:27–28), accompanied by the resurrection of the dead and judgement (cf Acts 17:31; 24:15). The irony, found elsewhere in this Gospel, is that while the leaders and the powerful mockingly reject Jesus' royal identity (v 35–38), an outcast perceives and embraces it (cf 1:52–53). Jesus' solemn reply ("Truly I tell you ..."; cf eg 4:24; 21:32), assures the criminal of more than he has asked for – present paradise, rather than just future remembrance. The "today" is a favourite Lucan term, highlighting the present character of salvation (eg 2:11; 4:21; 19:9) and implying here the existence with Jesus of a consciously blessed intermediate state between death and the final resurrection, for believers in him (cf 16:22ff; Acts 7:55,59). The Greek for 'paradise' here (*paradeisos*) came from the Persian for 'garden, park' and was used of the Garden of Eden in the Greek Old Testament (LXX; Gen 2:8). It became a term for the future blessedness of God's people (Isa 51:3) and in Judaism for the abode of the righteous before the final resurrection (eg 1 Enoch 17–19). Elsewhere in the New Testament the word is associated with heaven (2 Cor 12:2,4; Rev 2:7; cf 22:2). The passage concludes, then, by showing that Jesus is still able to save others (v 35), even while on the cross (cf also v 34).

Tasks

a What is the significance of the name of the crucifixion site?

b Outline the nature and function of crucifixion in the Roman world.

c Comment on the authenticity and significance of Jesus' prayer.

d Discuss the mockery of Jesus by the leaders, the soldiers and a criminal.

e What criticisms did the second criminal make of the first?

f Comment on the meaning of the second criminal's request and Jesus' reply.

The death of Jesus (23:44–49)

Jesus' death (v 46b) is preceded by two signs and a prayer (v 44–46a), and is followed by three responses (v 47–49). The significance of the two signs that Luke (and the other synoptics) associates with the death of Jesus is not explained in the text and has been variously interpreted. In ancient literature the deaths of significant individuals were sometimes accompanied by extraordinary phenomena, such as an eclipse of the sun when Julius Caesar was killed (Pliny the Elder, *Natural History* 2.30.97–98). The untimely darkness which covered the entire land (or earth) in connection with Jesus' death could be read in the context of the passion narrative as a symbol of evil or Satan (22:3,31,51; cf 1:78–79 and Acts 26:18). Alternatively,

the darkness may symbolise the judgement of God (cf Ex 10:21–23), as d...
has apocalyptic and eschatological connotations in the Old Testament (Z...pi...
Joel 2:30–31 which is applied to the "last days" in Acts 2:17–21). Particularly re... nt
to our passage is God's promise of judgement upon Israel in Amos – "I will make
the sun go down at noon, and darken the earth in broad daylight" (Am 8:9). The
darkness can therefore be read in connection with Jesus' prophecies of judgement
upon Jerusalem and Israel for rejecting the Messiah (see comment on v 28–31,
pp169–170). It may be viewed as an act of God, displaying his displeasure at the
human wickedness which conspired to kill his Son. Unlike the other synoptics, Luke
adds as an explanatory note that "the sun failed" (author's translation). Some have
understood Luke to be erroneously referring to an eclipse of the sun (v 45, *eklipontos*),
which would not have been possible at Passover time's full moon (and was thus
corrected by later scribes: "the sun was darkened"). However, the phrase may simply
mean that the sun failed to shine. If this darkening of the sun was due to a local
sirocco wind, then the timing of the darkness is the extraordinary element of the
event.

While the first sign relates to "the whole land", the second is focused on "the
temple" in Jerusalem. In the other synoptics the second sign comes later, immediately
following Jesus' death, while Luke keeps the two signs together. The temple "curtain"
may be the one at the entrance to the "most holy place" (the "Holy of Holies",
Heb 9:3), separating it from "the holy place" (cf Ex 26:31–34). On the other hand, it
may be the outer curtain or screen at the entrance to "the holy place" (cf Ex 26:36–37;
Heb 9:1–8). It has been argued that the reference is more likely to be to the outer
curtain since its tearing in two appears to have been a public act. As with the
darkness, so there are different views about the symbolism here. It can be seen as
the beginning of God's judgement upon the temple, as predicted by Jesus (19:45–46;
21:5ff). Like the darkness then, it may be viewed as an apocalyptic portent of God's
end-time judgement. Another related interpretation is that it may be a sign of God's
abandonment of the temple as the means by which access to and fellowship with
him is mediated (cf Acts 7:44–50), although the early Christians continue to make
some use of it for a while in Luke's sequel (eg Acts 2:46; 3:1). Since the curtain,
especially the inner curtain, was a barrier to God's presence, the symbolism may
be that through Jesus' death there is now access to God and paradise (v 43) for all.
While Luke does not anywhere explain Jesus' death in these terms, it was certainly
an early Christian understanding of it, also using the imagery of the temple curtain
(Heb 6:19–20; 10:19–22).

The final act before Jesus' death is his loud prayer. While all the synoptics say
that Jesus cried out with a loud voice before he died, only Luke tells what he said.
Characteristically addressing God as "Father" (see comment on v 34, p171), he
commits his "spirit" (ie life; cf Eccl 12:6–7) to God, using the words of the suffering
righteous man of Psalm 31 (v 5), words that would be used in later Judaism as an
evening prayer before retiring for the night. In Luke's sequel, dying Stephen will

prayer to Jesus himself (Acts 7:59). Jesus' prayer in Luke expresses his ... in God even in the midst of rejection and execution and, in the light of h... previous predictions (9:22; 18:33), his assurance that God will soon vindicate him (cf Mt 27:46/ Mk 15:34). His final breath (v 46; literally "he breathed out/expired") appears to come suddenly. According to Mark (15:25,34ff), he was crucified at 9 am (but cf Jn 19:14) and died some time after 3 pm; he had therefore survived at least six hours on the cross. Indeed, crucifixion was intentionally a slow, painful death that could last several days (cf Jn 19:31–33).

Immediately following Jesus' death we have three different responses (v 47–49). The first two are parallel in form, while all three are presented as witnesses of Jesus' death (note verbs of sight throughout these verses). Firstly, the Roman centurion overseeing the crucifixion "glorified" God (author's translation; a common Lucan theme, absent from the parallel passages) and declares as a certainty that Jesus is "righteous/innocent" (author's translation). No doubt the unusual darkness and possibly Jesus' prayers on the cross have had an impact upon him. Roman centurions are presented elsewhere in Luke in a similarly favourable light (7:1–10; Acts 10:1–4). While the other synoptics have the centurion referring to Jesus rather as "the/a son of God", Luke provides yet another witness (along with Pilate, Herod, and a criminal) in his passion narrative to the innocence of Jesus, despite his condemnation. The apologetic value of this repeated and varied testimony to Jesus' innocence for Luke's Roman readership, in particular, is obvious. This theme will continue into Luke's sequel (Acts 3:14; 7:52; 13:28; 22:14). The already noted irony of a criminal responding positively to Jesus, while the Jewish leaders mockingly reject him, is now compounded by this Gentile response. The word "righteous" (author's translation) also reinforces the existing links between the passion narrative and Psalms concerning the righteous sufferer (22,31), as well as Isaiah's suffering Servant (53:11). The second response is by "all the crowds" who have gathered for the "spectacle" (as crucifixions often were). Their reaction as they leave is one of mournful regret, physically expressed in the usual way (cf 18:13), which contrasts with their apparently initial support for Jesus' crucifixion (v 13,18ff). Possibly, as with the centurion, subsequent events have resulted in a change of heart. Thus, as there were mourners on the way to the crucifixion (v 27–28), so there are returning from it, and both are unique to Luke. The final response concerns "all those who knew him" (author's translation), which must include his apostles, of whom we have not heard since his arrest. Among Jesus' acquaintances specific mention is made of the women who accompanied him from Galilee (cf v 55; 8:1–3). Despite being described in more intimate terms in relation to Jesus than the other witnesses of the cross, this final group are ironically the most disengaged with the crucifixion. Instead of praise and confession (v 47) or mourning (v 48), like Peter (22:54) they are physically remote, merely observing (cf v 35). Their response provides yet another echo of the righteous sufferer of the Psalms (38:11).

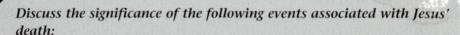

Task

Discuss the significance of the following events associated with Jesus' death:

a) the two signs   b) Jesus' prayer   c) the responses to his death

The burial of Jesus (23:50–56)

The final passage of the passion narrative introduces us to a man who asks Pilate's permission to take Jesus' body and then places it in a tomb, the latter act being witnessed by women disciples who make preparations to anoint Jesus' corpse. The account echoes the Jewish emphasis of Luke's infancy narrative by noting the piety of both Joseph and the women. The passage is transitional, as Jesus' burial is a confirmation of his death and also a preparation for his resurrection.

First in the list of details (in Luke's Greek) about Joseph is that he is a member of the Jewish council – the council that had collectively brought Jesus to Pilate and made charges against him (22:66–23:5; cf 22:1ff), and that had demanded his crucifixion (23:13,18ff). However, Luke is quick to add that he is a "good and righteous" man, recalling the characterisation of individuals in the infancy narrative (1:6; 2:25) and the centurion's recent description of Jesus (v 47; Luke uses the same word of Joseph). Most importantly, Luke further notes that while Joseph is a "councillor" (author's translation; *bouleutes*), he had not agreed to their "counsel, plan" (author's translation; *boule*) or action (v 50–51), despite the apparent unanimity of the council. As Simeon had prophesied at the other end of Jesus' life, a division in Israel has been caused by the coming of the Messiah (2:34). Luke also stresses Joseph's Jewishness by indicating, alone among the four evangelists, that his home town of Arimathea (location uncertain) is "Jewish". Reminding us again of characters in the infancy narrative, we are told that Joseph is "looking forward/waiting expectantly" (v 51, author's translation; cf 2:25,38; the same Greek verb is used in all these verses). The focus of his expectation is the "kingdom of God" (see comment on 9:60, pp79–81). While Matthew (27:57) and John (19:38) state that Joseph is a disciple of Jesus, Luke focuses rather on his role as a Jewish leader in these events (cf Acts 13:27–29).

Joseph's "good and righteous" character (v 50) is evident in his decision not to leave Jesus' corpse to the birds (as was often the case with victims of crucifixion), but instead to ensure its burial, as required by Jewish Law (Deut 21:22–23; cf Jn 19:31). This needs Pilate's permission, as the governor who had sanctioned Jesus' execution. Since Joseph is a member of the Jewish council, Pilate probably sees no danger of possible exploitation of the corpse of an apparent rebel to create political unrest. Having probably first washed the body, Joseph clothes it in a linen shroud and lays it in a tomb which has been cut into the side of a rock face. We are told that no one has ever been laid in this tomb (Mt 27:60 says it is Joseph's own "new" tomb), reminding us of the colt that had "never been ridden" (19:30), on which Jesus entered Jerusalem.

of a proper burial in a new tomb accorded to Jesus as a dishonoured person was unusual (cf 1 Kings 13:21–22; Jer 26:23).

The last section of the burial account is framed by two references to the Jewish Sabbath (what we call Saturday; v 54,56b). The day before the Sabbath was known as the Day of Preparation, since on this day all the work had to be completed which enabled rest on the Sabbath to be observed. The Sabbath is now beginning or "dawning" (author's translation), which may be a reference to the first star of the evening, when the Sabbath began. The women who had come with Jesus from Galilee (cf v 49) follow Joseph and see the tomb and how Jesus' body is laid in it. As they were eyewitnesses of his crucifixion (v 49), so now they are of his burial, as they will be too of the empty tomb (24:1–3). Their observation of the tomb that Jesus is placed in enables them to return to the right place after the Sabbath (24:1ff). They prepare "spices" (*aromata*) and "ointments/perfumes" (author's translation; *myra*), which would be used to reduce the stench of rapid decomposition in a warm climate. However, the anointing of the body would have to wait, since the commandment (Ex 20:8–11; Deut 5:12–15) requires that they rest on the Sabbath, which is now beginning (v 54). Thus, as in the infancy narrative, Jewish piety is in evidence as the commandments are observed (1:6) and the Law is fulfilled (2:22–24,39).

Tasks

a Comment on Luke's characterisation of Joseph of Arimathea.

b Discuss the roles of Joseph and the women in the burial of Jesus.

Practice essay title

1 (a) Outline your knowledge and understanding of Luke's account of either the Last Supper or the arrest of Jesus. (30)

(b) Explore the claim that betrayal is an important theme in Luke's passion narrative. Justify your answer. (15)

RESURRECTION NARRATIVE (ch 24)

The concluding chapter of each synoptic Gospel and the last two chapters in John concern Jesus' rising from the dead[1]. Luke's resurrection narrative has four parts – the empty tomb (v 1–12), Jesus' appearance to two of his followers on the road to Emmaus (v 13–35), Jesus' appearance to the disciples (v 36–49), and Jesus' ascension

---

[1] On the debate over the historicity of Jesus' resurrection, see The resurrection and history, pp191–192.

to heaven (v 50–53). Luke's opening empty tomb account shares some simi Mark (16:1–8), which most scholars think Luke has edited and rewritten. Howev there are many differences which may imply that Luke had access to another sour sources here, as appears to be the case for the rest of the chapter which consists almost entirely of unique material. Characteristically Lucan themes in the narrative include the focus on Jerusalem and its environs (v 13,18,33,47,52), where all the resurrection appearances of Jesus occur (in the other synoptics they occur in Galilee); the fact that the Hebrew Scriptures/Prophets are "fulfilled" in the consequently "necessary" death and resurrection of the Messiah (v 7,25–27,44ff); Jesus' table fellowship with others (v 29–30); the journey motif (v 13–17,28,32–35,50–52); concern with individuals (v 18); peace (v 36); joy (v 41,52); repentance (v 47); forgiveness of sins (v 47); universalism (v 47), the Spirit (v 49, indirectly); worship (v 52–53); and the temple (v 53).

Thus, in this concluding chapter, Luke brings closure to his Gospel by recalling and reinforcing many of the distinctive themes that he has highlighted throughout the book. In particular, in this closing section (resurrection narrative) of his Gospel he recalls and reflects its opening section (infancy narrative) by various links and parallels between the two. As the Gospel began so it ends, with worship in the temple (1:8–10/ 24:53). In both narratives an angelic message brings unexpected news, which is met with male unbelief and eventual joy at its confirmation (1:11–20,58/ 24:4–11,41,52). There is also a parallel emphasis on Jesus as "Messiah" (2:11,26/ 24:26,46). We may note too the shared hope for the redemption of Jerusalem/Israel (2:38/ 24:21) and the common blessing of the "Gentiles/nations" (author's translation; Greek *ethnos* in both 2:32/ 24:47) through Jesus. We shall later consider several notable parallels between two particular stories from these opening and closing narratives of Luke's Gospel – the 12-year-old Jesus at the temple (2:41–52) and Jesus' appearance to two of his followers on the road to Emmaus (24:13–35).

However, this resurrection narrative not only recalls the Gospel. It also anticipates Acts – Luke's sequel to his Gospel. While Luke 24 may be seen, from one angle, as the conclusion of the Gospel, it may also be viewed as the beginnings of an introduction to Acts, a transitional narrative linking the two books as one continuing story. We find that Luke 24 and Acts 1, in particular, are joined by several common elements – a resurrection appearance of Jesus to his apostles, the instruction to wait in Jerusalem for what the Father has promised, the reference to the apostles as "witnesses", the universal scope of their witness to Jesus, the ascension of Jesus, the presence of women, and the fulfilment of Scripture.

Task

To what extent is Luke's resurrection narrative both a review of the Gospel and a preview of Acts?

Selected narratives

The empty tomb (24:1–12)

As in the other Gospels, Luke begins his resurrection narrative with the discovery that Jesus' tomb is empty. The passage is linked to and proceeds from the immediately preceding account of Jesus' burial. The women had had to rest on the Sabbath (the seventh day), but now, very early on "the first day of the week" (what we call 'Sunday'), they come to the tomb with the spices they had previously prepared (see 23:56 and comment, p177). Unlike the other synoptics, Luke delays naming the women (v 10) at this point, apparently wanting to report their discovery as quickly as possible. With two uses of the verb 'to find' (v 2–3), Luke tells us that they find something they did not expect to find (the stone rolled away) and that they do not find something they did expect to find (Jesus' body; cf 23:55)! The entrance to the tomb would have been closed by a large stone in the shape of a disc, possibly placed in a channel cut into the rock below it. Its purpose was to secure the tomb, protecting the corpse from wild animals and grave robbers. The corpse would probably have been placed on a bench-like inset, cut in a side wall of the chamber. That the corpse is described as the body "of the Lord Jesus" (v 3, in the best manuscripts) reflects Luke's preference for referring to Jesus as "the Lord", and indeed hints at Jesus' resurrection (cf v 34; Acts 2:32–36; for other examples of Luke's use of "Lord Jesus" see Acts 1:21; 4:33; 8:16).

The women's perplexity at their discovery turns to terror when they suddenly see what is later called "a vision of angels" (v 23). Here the angels are described as "two men in dazzling clothes" standing beside the women, anticipating Luke's other sudden appearance of "two men in white clothes" (author's translation) standing beside the apostles at Jesus' ascension (Acts 1:10; cf 10:30). The brightness of the clothing conveys the glory and splendour of God and of heaven from where they've come (cf 2:9,13–15; 9:29,32). John also refers to two angels in the tomb ("in white", 20:12), which may reflect the Jewish need for at least two witnesses to confirm a testimony (Deut 19:15; cf Mt 18:16; 2 Cor 13:1). The women's response (v 5; fear and reverence) is typical of reactions to angelophanies (appearances of angels) in biblical literature (cf 1:11–12; Dan 8:15–18; 10:5–12,15–19). As later with the two messengers in Acts 1, so here the two men preface their remarks with a question which contains an implied rebuke. As they go on to say, the women should have remembered Jesus' teaching in Galilee about the necessity (a Lucan emphasis; cf v 26,44) of the Son of Man's forthcoming betrayal, crucifixion and resurrection on the third day (cf 9:22,44). The implication is that these women were present with the apostles when Jesus predicted his resurrection (cf 8:1–3; 23:49,55). Two new elements in the angelic summary of Jesus' Galilean predictions are the more specific description of his killing as a crucifixion and the characterisation of his killers as "sinners", representing their crucifixion of Jesus as an offence against God. Unlike the other synoptics, the women are not told to tell the apostles that Jesus is going ahead of them to Galilee and that they will see him there, since all of Luke's resurrection appearances are in and around Jerusalem. Thus, in his angelic statement "Galilee" is not the place where they will see

Jesus in the future, but rather the place where he taught them in the past. The core of the angelic message is the announcement "He is not here, but has risen" (absent from some manuscripts), of which the empty tomb is a visible symbol.

The women's first response to the angels' words is one of obedience, for they have now "remembered", as they have just been told to, Jesus' predictive words – just as Peter had before this (22:61). It had taken a look by Jesus to jog Peter's memory and it has now taken angelic words to jog the women's. The remembrance in each case is more than just a mental recollection; it also triggers understanding of the significance of what has just occurred. Although they have not been told to do so, they spontaneously report "all" that has happened to the apostles and "all" the rest (cf Acts 4:20). Luke now belatedly (compared with the other synoptics) names some of the women who have been to the tomb. Like all the other Gospels, Luke first mentions Mary Magdalene (from Magdala in Galilee), who in John's Gospel is the only woman at the tomb and the first person to see the risen Jesus (Jn 20). Mary Magdalene is earlier named as one of the women who provided practical support for Jesus and his disciples and from whom seven demons had been expelled (8:1–3)[1]. Then Luke mentions Joanna as being at the tomb. She is also second in the earlier list, where we are told that she too had been cured and that she was the wife of the manager of Herod Antipas' household (8:3; she is not mentioned outside Luke). The third woman, mentioned only here in Luke, is identified as "Mary the (mother) of James", the word "mother" being assumed from Mark 15:40 and 16:1. Just as the eleven apostles are distinguished from "all the rest" (v 9), so these three are from "the rest" (v 10, author's translation; same Greek in both verses) of the women. This distinction and naming may imply that these were prominent females in the early Christian community.

The women's failure to remember Jesus' predictions of his resurrection is paralleled by the men's unbelieving rejection of their report as "an idle tale" (v 11; cf v 41). The Greek word that Luke uses for the latter is not found elsewhere in the New Testament and was properly a medical term for delirium; it was also employed in popular use, as in our passage. Since the men apparently heard "all" that the angels had said (v 9) and should therefore, like the women, accept that Jesus has possibly been raised (v 5–7), it appears that their scathing unbelief reflects the general cultural perception of women as unreliable witnesses, which may well account also for Paul's omission of women from his list of witnesses of the risen Jesus (1 Cor 15:3–8). For instance, the first-century Jewish historian Josephus stated that evidence should not be accepted from women, because of the "levity and rashness" of their sex (*Ant* 4.219). However, despite the apparent unanimous dismissal of the women's news by the apostles, Luke adds that Peter runs to the tomb and sees the abandoned grave clothes (cf 23:53), which along with the vacant tomb appear as a tangible symbol of the resurrection. This detail about Peter, accepted by most as original to Luke despite its absence from some manuscripts, is found also in John (20:3–9). Thus, as earlier in the Gospel and later in Acts, Peter is singled out for special mention (eg 22:31–34, 54ff; Acts 1:15ff; 2:14ff). Nevertheless,

---

[1] There is no evidence in the New Testament for the later belief that she was a prostitute.

...ment at what has happened (cf eg 2:18; 8:25; 20:26), like the response of the women, is not characterised as faith, even if both reactions are more positive than that of the others (v 11).

Consequently, the opening passage of Luke's resurrection narrative concludes in an open-ended manner, with a variety of responses to the significance of the empty tomb, none of which is characterised as faith in the reality of Jesus' resurrection.

Tasks

a Comment on the roles and characterisation of the women, the two angels and Peter in Luke's account of the empty tomb.

b Discuss in detail what the angels said to the women.

Jesus appears on the road to Emmaus (24:13–35)

This, the central and longest passage in the resurrection narrative, is a dramatic and vivid example of Luke's skill as a storyteller (cf eg 4:16–30). Unique to Luke (although see Mk 16:12–13), such a detailed account is likely to have come originally from one or both of the travellers, although some hold that it is an unhistorical creation by Luke for theological purposes. As mentioned earlier, several parallels have been noted between this story and that of the 12-year-old Jesus in the temple, at the other end of this Gospel (2:41–52). Both have a Passover setting; a pair journeying from Jerusalem; Jesus being absent for three days; a sudden, unplanned return visit to Jerusalem; and a rebuke of the pair by Jesus, in the form of a question relating to the necessity of his actions. There is contrast too, for in the journeys from Jerusalem one pair is unaware of Jesus' absence while the other is unaware of his presence!

While these correspondences appear impressive, it is uncertain whether they are a matter of conscious parallelism on the part of Luke. If the story looks back, it also looks forward to yet another of Luke's stories, for parallels have been drawn also with the passage about Philip and the Ethiopian eunuch (Acts 8:26–40). There too, on a journey from Jerusalem, the relevance of Old Testament Scripture to Jesus is explained by a stranger who suddenly vanishes from sight. Links with the rest of Luke are apparent also in the characteristic themes present in the Emmaus story, especially its frequent 'journey' vocabulary, the necessary fulfilment of Israel's Scriptures in Jesus, Jesus having a meal/table fellowship with others, and interest in ordinary individuals (see p29).

Tasks

a Discuss the parallels between this story and Luke's accounts of Jesus as a 12-year-old in the temple and Philip and the Ethiopian eunuch.

b What Lucan characteristics are apparent in this story?

Structurally, the story appears to have been arranged in the form of a chiasm – a concentric or inverse parallelism (see below). The first section of the story (A) paraliels the last (A'), and the second section (B) parallels the second from last (B'), and so on, until the significant point or message of the story is reached in the centre (H).

The chiastic structure of Luke 24:13–35

- A   Journey *from* Jerusalem (v 13)
- B   Dialogue (v 14–15a)
- C   Appearance of Jesus (v 15b)
- D   Visual non-recognition of Jesus (v 16)
- E   Interruption of journey (v 17)
- F   Review of "the things" concerning Jesus (v 18–24), including:
- G   Empty tomb and visual experience (v 22–23a)

- H   Jesus alive (v 23b)

- G'   Empty tomb and no visual experience (v 24)
- F'   Interpretation of "the things" concerning Jesus (v 25–27)
- E'   Interruption of journey (v 28–29)
- D'   Visual recognition of Jesus (v 30–31a)
- C'   Disappearance of Jesus (v 31b)
- B'   Dialogue (v 32)
- A'   Journey *to* Jerusalem (v 33–35)

A broader, purely linear outline of the passage divides the story into four parts: the meeting of Jesus and the two travellers (v 13–16), the conversation concerning recent events (v 17–27), the meal revealing Jesus' identity (v 28–32), and the report to the apostles and the others (v 33–35).

The opening words of the passage relate it closely to the one immediately before it. Thus, the story is set on the "same day" as the discovery of the empty tomb, on "the first day of the week" (v 1; cf v 21,33). Also, the words "of them" (v 13) indicate that the two travellers were among those who had just rejected the women's claims as "an idle tale" (v 11). In addition, the topic of their conversation is described as all "these" things that have happened (v 14). Their leaving Jerusalem may be an expression of their disillusionment (cf v 17,21) and Emmaus may be their home village, to which they now return. Luke locates Emmaus about seven miles (or 11 km) from Jerusalem (although some manuscripts give the distance as equivalent to about 18½ m/ 30 km). Its actual location is uncertain and three possibilities have been suggested. Traditionally, it has been identified as the Ammaous of Maccabean times (eg 1 Macc 3:40), later known as Nicopolis and as 'Amwas today, some 20 miles from Jerusalem. While some argue that Luke's distance is, therefore, an error (though it would approximate to the alternative manuscript reading), it may be that the traditional location is wrong (could the two pedestrians have covered a 40-mile round trip in one day?). The medieval crusaders identified Emmaus with el-Qubeibeh, which is about the same distance from Jerusalem as Luke's Emmaus. However, it cannot be shown that this site existed in the first century. Finally, Emmaus has been identified with an Ammaous mentioned by Josephus (*Jewish War* 7.217), which he locates half as far from Jerusalem as Luke's Emmaus, though Luke might have given the round-trip figure.

In what is the first resurrection appearance in Luke, "Jesus himself" joins the two travellers. However, their eyes "were kept" from recognising him. When no subject of the verb is given, the passive voice often indicates an act of God (see also 9:44–45; 18:34), although some have suggested that the cause of their failure to recognise Jesus lies in their own unbelief (v 11,41) or in Satan. The non-recognition of the risen Jesus is also a theme of John's resurrection narrative (20:14–15; 21:4). Certainly, within our present passage it has the effect on the reader of creating dramatic suspense.

Tasks

a Comment on the structure of the passage.

b Evaluate the various suggestions concerning the identity of Emmaus.

c Discuss the travellers' non-recognition of Jesus.

Jesus' question (v 17) implies an ignorance which shocks the travellers to a standstill, their gloomy expressions revealing their view of recent events. The one who replies is named as Cleopas, unknown elsewhere in the New Testament, although it has been suggested that he is the Clopas of John 19:25 (unlikely on linguistic grounds alone). The anonymity of Cleopas' companion has invited speculative suggestions, such as Peter (but v 34) or Cleopas' wife (providing another of Luke's male–female pairings). Cleopas' question (v 18) implies that the recent crucifixion of Jesus is a matter of public knowledge, which even this "stranger" (non-Jerusalemite pilgrim or resident) should "know". Since the omniscient narrator has already informed us of the identity of the stranger, the reader can now appreciate the irony of Cleopas rebuking Jesus for his ignorance, while he himself is ignorant of the fact that he is talking to Jesus! The irony continues as the two travellers 'inform' Jesus of what has happened to him. By the end of the journey, they will realise that this apparently ignorant stranger is, in fact, the "only" person (v 18) who does know what has happened (v 25–27).

The travellers' reference to "the things" (v 18–19; Greek *ta* in both verses) concerning Jesus begins a discussion which will end with Jesus likewise referring to "the things" (v 27; Greek *ta*; also found in the last verse of the whole passage, v 35) concerning himself. The term acts as an *inclusio*, framing this section (v 18–27) and indicating its main theme, which recurs within it in similar language (v 19, "What things?"; v 21, "these things" – author's translation – twice; v 26, "these things";

cf v 14, "these things"). It is clear from the discussion that we have two very views of "the things" that happened to Jesus – that of the travellers (v 19–24) and that of Jesus himself (v 25–27). The travellers call him "Jesus of Nazareth" (cf 18:37), an expression used by Luke in connection with Jesus' miracles (eg 4:34ff; 18:37ff; Acts 2:22; 3:6) and, therefore, appropriate in the light of their immediately following description of Jesus as "a prophet powerful in deed and word before God and all the people" (author's translation). This characterisation of Jesus, as well as reinforcing Luke's general portrayal of Jesus as a prophet (see Prophet, p31), also uses language which implies that Jesus is the expected prophet-like-Moses (Deut 18:15,18–19/ Acts 3:22; cf Lk 9:35). Moses will be described in the same terms in Luke's sequel (Acts 7:22; cf Deut 34:10–12). The irony is that even though the travellers acknowledge Jesus as a prophet they have apparently forgotten his prophecies, within Luke's narrative, concerning his suffering, death and resurrection (cf v 5–8; yet v 21). At the very least, they should not be surprised that a prophet has met a prophet's end (cf 11:47ff; 13:33ff). The reference to both Jesus' deeds and words recalls his miracles and parables in particular, and will be repeated by Luke as a convenient summary of Jesus' ministry (Acts 1:1). The "power" evident in Jesus' ministry is often attributed by Luke to the Holy Spirit (4:14,18–19,36; 5:17; 6:19; 8:46; Acts 10:37–38). Jesus' ministry is presented, too, as having met with both divine and human favour (cf 2:52).

"The things" concerning Jesus which have just happened in Jerusalem, and which the travellers have been discussing, are now identified by them as his crucifixion (v 20) and alleged resurrection (v 21–24). Despite the fact that Jesus was a mighty prophet who had the approval of God and all the Jewish people, the Jewish leadership (cf 19:47–48; 22:2; 23:35) handed him over to condemnation and crucified him. Luke knows, of course, that it was actually the Romans who crucified Jesus (23:24ff) and, indeed, that "the people" had a part to play in Jesus' condemnation (23:13ff); but here (v 20) the language is compressed to stress that the main responsibility for Jesus' death lies with the Jewish leaders. The travellers' disappointment and failure to understand Jesus' mission are captured in their statement of despair, "But we had hoped that he was the one who was going to redeem Israel" (v 21, author's translation; cf Acts 7:35 for Moses as Israel's "redeemer/liberator", author's translation). That this was a legitimate hope is clear from the other end of this Gospel (2:25,38; cf 1:54–55,68ff; 2:32,34; Acts 1:6–7), but, with yet more irony, they cannot see how a crucified Jesus could set Israel free. Thinking in terms of political liberation from their Gentile overlords (cf 1:67–75), Jesus' destruction by the Romans was the very opposite of what they expected. Because of most recent events (v 1–12), the travellers then go into greater detail about Jesus' alleged resurrection (v 21b–24). Their mention of the "third day" may be related to a Jewish belief about the soul leaving the body by the fourth day (Jn 11:39) or may be a vague recollection of something Jesus said, which, like the women, they appear to have forgotten (v 6–8). Again, it may be just yet another ironic statement by the travellers, who are simply noting how long it has been since Jesus' death without realising the significance of "the third day" (v 7; 9:22; 13:32; 18:33). They give a more positive account of their response to the women's report (cf v 22

Selected narratives

...) and mention that more than just one man (cf v 12; Jn 20:3–10) went to the ...verify the women's story. The women's angelic "vision" of this last chapter (23) matches Zechariah's angelic "vision" of the first (1:22). The travellers' sceptical point is that although both the women and the men found the tomb empty, neither saw Jesus (v 22–24). The reader is aware of yet more irony here, since they now see Jesus – and yet don't (v 16)!

Tasks

a Comment on the identity of the two travellers.

b Discuss the literary function of the expression "the things" in this passage.

c Outline your understanding of the travellers' reply to Jesus in verses 19 to 24.

d Note examples of irony in the story.

Jesus' response (v 25–27) to the travellers' perspective of "the things" that have happened reveals his very different view of recent events. With some exasperation (v 25, "Oh ..."; cf 9:41; in the Greek of both verses), he rebukes their lack of understanding and deep-seated reluctance to believe all that the prophets have spoken. While Jesus himself may be included as one of these prophets whom they have been slow to believe (v 6–8,19), the immediate context points to the Hebrew Scriptures (v 27; cf v 44ff). Jesus' words parallel the earlier angelic message to the women (v 5–7), as both refer to the necessity of Jesus' suffering and resurrection (a Lucan theme). Instead of the usual reference to resurrection, though, we read of his "glory" (v 26) – the divine splendour he will know at God's right hand (cf 22:69 with Acts 7:55), which was anticipated at his transfiguration (9:31–32) and which will be revealed at his return (9:26; 21:27). Until now in Luke repeated mention has been made of the necessary suffering of the "Son of Man" (9:22,44; 17:25; 18:31ff; 22:22), but here for the first time we have explicit reference to the suffering of the "Messiah/Christ", a change that will continue into Acts (v 46; Acts 3:18; 17:3; 26:23). This idea of a suffering Messiah appears to be a new development, unknown in first-century Judaism. However, Jesus sees it as something that was anticipated in the Hebrew Scriptures/Old Testament (v 25,27,44–46), when properly "interpreted" (v 27,45). While Jesus refers to the whole of the Jewish Bible ("all the scriptures"; cf v 32,45), we are told that he begins from "Moses and all the prophets" (cf 16:31; Acts 26:22; 28:23), probably reflecting the first two of the three main divisions of the Hebrew Bible. "Moses" is shorthand for the first five books of the Bible, sometimes simply called the Law (Hebrew *torah*) or the Law of Moses (cf 2:22–24,27,39). The Prophets include the books of Joshua, Judges, Samuel, and Kings (the Former Prophets), as well as Isaiah, Jeremiah, Ezekiel and the 12 minor Prophets (the Latter Prophets). The third main

The Gospel of Luke

division is known as the Writings and may be referred to later in the resurrection narrative (see comment on v 44, pp188–189). While no specific examples are given here of apparently 'messianic' Old Testament texts, there are some later in Luke's sequel (from 'Moses', eg Acts 3:21–23,25–26; from 'the Prophets', eg Acts 8:32–33; 13:34).

Tasks

a According to Jesus, what accounted for the travellers' despair (v 25–26)?

b What new elements appear in Jesus' words in verse 26?

c Discuss the meaning of verse 27.

The scene changes as the travellers near their destination (v 28). Jesus appears to be parting company with them and this creates some narrative tension for the reader who, on the first reading, will wonder if his true identity is to remain hidden from the others. However, he is persuaded to lodge with them for the night, which now creates narrative suspense – they may yet discover who the stranger is. As so often in Luke, we find Jesus as a table guest, receiving hospitality from others in a setting which becomes an occasion for teaching or revelation (5:29ff; 10:38ff; 14:1ff; 19:1ff). Here, Jesus acts as the host even though he is the guest (v 30), possibly reflecting the hosts' growing respect for this impressive stranger (cf v 32). His four actions at the table are those appropriate for the beginning of any Jewish meal (cf Acts 27:35) and recall the feeding of the thousands (9:16) and the Passover meal with his apostles (22:19; which has "had given thanks" as the equivalent of "blessed"). The result of Jesus' actions is the reversal of their previous non-recognition of him (cf v 16 with v 31), and, as unexpectedly as he appeared, he now disappears. Their eyes have been "opened" by Jesus' breaking of the bread, just as Jesus had been "opening" the Scriptures on the road (v 32), and just as the minds of the others will soon be "opened" by Jesus that they might understand the Scriptures (v 45). Now that they realise who this stranger was, they reflect on how their "slow hearts" (v 25, author's translation) have become burning "hearts" (cf Ps 39:2–3) through Jesus' messianic interpretation of the Jewish Scriptures (v 32; cf v 25–27). Clearly, through Jesus' opening of the Scriptures and breaking of the bread, their initial view of the recent "things" concerning Jesus has been transformed – sadness (v 17) and despair (v 21) have given way to emotional excitement (v 32) and visual confirmation of Jesus' resurrection (v 31; cf v 23).

In their excitement, despite the late hour they return to Jerusalem "That same hour" on this all-important "third day" (cf v 1,7,21). As with the women at the other end of this day (v 9–10), they have the spontaneous desire to tell the news to the eleven and those with them. In contrast to the response to the women (v 11), they find a positive reaction. In fact, the apostles and the others already know that "The

" (cf v 3) has risen "indeed/truly" (author's translation; emphatically first in the Greek), and report that he has appeared to Simon (ie Peter), who is of course one of these eleven. This appearance (cf 1 Cor 15:5) has not been mentioned by Luke before this (cf v 12) and may be his way of recalling Jesus' words about Peter's restoration after the denials (22:31–33) and of anticipating his apostolic credentials as a witness of Jesus' resurrection (Acts 1:22). The two travellers report both what happened on the road and at the table, thus highlighting the importance of both the interpretation of the Scriptures and the fellowship meal as the contexts in which to encounter and experience the risen Lord. Jesus was made known to them in "the breaking of the bread", an expression which anticipates the fellowship meals of the early Christians in Acts (2:42,46; 20:7), and which possibly was a term for what was later called the Eucharist or Communion.

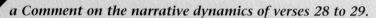

a Comment on the narrative dynamics of verses 28 to 29.

b Discuss the importance and impact of Jesus' role at the table.

c What two factors account for the transformation of the travellers' experience?

Jesus appears to the disciples (24:36–49)

In this passage Jesus appears to the whole company of disciples (v 36), assuring them of the physical reality of his resurrection (v 37–43), showing them the messianic and missionary significance of the Jewish Scriptures (v 44–48), and telling them to wait in Jerusalem for the power of God (v 49). While the two who have returned from Emmaus are talking with the eleven and the others about resurrection appearances earlier that day (v 33ff), "Jesus himself" appears among them. Thus, we have another example of the general pattern of appearances to individuals being followed by an appearance to a group (cf Jn 20:11–18,19–23; 1 Cor 15:5–11). In a Gospel where 'peace' is an important theme (cf p35), often associated with salvation, the words of the risen Lord (v 36) have a richer significance than the customary Jewish greeting (*shalom*). The group's reaction (v 37), particularly their perception of Jesus as a "spirit" (author's translation; Greek *pneuma*), implies an initial failure to recognise him or an expectation that any appearance would be non-physical.

As with the two on the road to Emmaus, Jesus has questions for them – questions which imply that there are no grounds for the fear or "doubts/thoughts in their hearts" (author's translation; the same Greek expression occurs in 2:35; 3:15; 5:22; 9:47). He then provides two proofs that, far from being a ghost or spirit, he is physically alive again. First, he urges them to use two of their physical senses (sight and touch) to confirm that he has undergone a bodily resurrection (v 39–40; cf Jn 20:25ff). Jesus is both visible and tangible. The reference to his "hands" and "feet" probably relates to the wounds of his crucifixion, indicating the continuity of identity between the pre- and post-resurrection Jesus (cf v 39, "it is I myself"). This is no disembodied spirit, but a "flesh and bones" appearance of Jesus (v 39). Later, Luke will note that Jesus' body has not been dead long enough for the decay of decomposition to set in (Acts 2:27–29; 13:35,37). The second piece of conclusive evidence that Jesus provides for the physicality of his resurrection is his eating of cooked fish "in their presence" (v 41–43; cf Jn 21:9). As well as his hands, feet, flesh and bones, his digestive system too is apparently still intact! Later, such evidence for the reality of Jesus' resurrection will be appealed to in Acts (10:41; cf 1:3–4). Indeed, absence of digestion would have been consistent with the appearance being but a 'vision' rather than an actual event (as in Tobit 12:19). We have met before the reactions of disbelief and wonder (v 11–12), but this time the disbelief is "from joy" (v 41, literally). In other words, they are delighted that Jesus is alive again but can hardly believe their eyes – it is almost too good to be true. This "joy" (a Lucan theme) will soon become "great joy" (v 52) as the reality of Jesus' resurrection sinks in. Consequently, we have here two of the "many convincing proofs" which Luke says Jesus presented to his disciples to confirm that he was alive again (Acts 1:3). While many assume that Luke's (and John's) emphasis on the physical nature of Jesus' resurrection reflects the growing threat of Docetism (denial that Jesus had a real body) in the later first century (cf 2 Jn 7), it is unlikely on this view that he would also have included in his resurrection narrative an unrecognised Jesus who suddenly appears and disappears.

After providing evidence to confirm that he is physically alive again, the risen Lord then teaches the disciples that he is the subject both of past prophecies and the future mission of the disciples (v 44ff). Since these are Jesus' last words (cf v 50–51) – his farewell discourse (cf Jacob's in Gen 49 and Moses' in Deut 33) – what he says is of particular importance. Recalling earlier parts of the chapter, Jesus refers to his own previous teaching (cf v 6–8) and to the necessity of the fulfilment (cf 4:21) of all that was written about him in Israel's Scriptures (cf v 25–27). In addition to his earlier reference to Moses and the Prophets, which he now repeats, Jesus mentions the "psalms". This may be shorthand for the third main division of the Hebrew Bible (see comment on v 27, pp185–186), the Writings, since the Psalms constituted its first and longest book. The threefold division of the Hebrew Bible appears to have existed before the time of Jesus, apparently reflected in the prologue to Sirach and in the epilogue of a Dead Sea Scroll (4QMMT). Within Luke's writings the Psalms often have messianic significance (cf 13:35; 20:17,41–44; Acts 2:25–36; 4:25–27; 13:32–33). Reflecting another earlier theme of this narrative is the reference to Jesus' opening of the disciples' minds to understand the Scriptures (cf v 27,32).

According to Jesus here, three things have already been "written" down in Israel's Scriptures concerning the Messiah – that he is "to suffer", that he is "to rise" from the dead on the third day, and that repentance for forgiveness of sins is "to be proclaimed in his name to all nations, beginning from Jerusalem" (v 46–47). We have met the two before in this chapter (see comment on v 6–7, pp179–180, and on v 25–27, pp185–186) and the third now introduces, in anticipation of Acts, the commission and mission of the disciples. The claim that this universal mission was anticipated in the Scriptures may reflect Isaiah (49:6), where we read of the Servant of the Lord being made a light for the Gentiles and bringing God's salvation to the ends of the earth. This text seems to provide the background for the mission of Jesus and the early Church in Luke–Acts (Lk 2:30–32; Acts 13:46–47). The terms of the mission abound with Lucan themes – "repentance" (eg Lk 3:3; 5:32; 10:13; 15:7; Acts 2:38; 3:19), "forgiveness of sins" (eg Lk 1:77; 3:3; 5:20–21; 7:47–49; Acts 2:38; 5:31; 10:43), "proclaimed/preached" (author's translation; eg Lk 4:18–19,44; 8:1; Acts 8:5; 9:20; 10:42), "in his name" (eg Lk 9:48–49; 21:8; and especially in Acts, eg 2:38; 3:6; 4:12), "all nations" (Luke's universalism, eg Lk 2:32; 3:6; Acts 1:8; 10:34–35), and "Jerusalem" (eg one of five mentions in this chapter alone). Indeed, Jerusalem will be the starting point of the disciples' universal mission (cf Acts 1:8). The direction of the Gospel of Luke is thereby reversed in Acts, as the end point of Jesus' journey now becomes the starting point of his disciples'. It is also a reversal of the Old Testament theme of all the nations coming *to* Jerusalem (eg Isa 2:1–4), a centrifugal rather than a centripetal movement. The disciples are "witnesses" of the events Jesus has been speaking of (v 44–46), a role which will be repeatedly underlined in Acts to verify the reality of the events the disciples testify to (cf 1:8,22; 2:32; 3:15; 5:32; 10:39,41; 13:31; 22:15,20; 26:16). As Jesus had given power to his disciples for an earlier mission (9:1–2), so now he tells them to wait in Jerusalem to be clothed with power "from on high" (cf 1:78), which he himself will send (cf 3:16; Acts 1:5; 2:32–33). This power of the Holy Spirit will enable them to be his "witnesses" to all nations (v 48; Acts 1:8); "my Father" (cf eg 2:49), says Jesus, has promised this (cf 11:13; Acts 1:4–5; 2:16–17,33).

Tasks

a Comment on the two proofs that Jesus provides for the physical nature of his resurrection (v 37–43).

b Discuss Jesus' description of the Hebrew Scriptures (v 44–45).

c According to Jesus, what three things were written in these Scriptures concerning the Messiah (v 46–47)?

d Identify the characteristically Lucan themes in verses 47 to 48.

e Comment on the promise of power for the disciples' mission (v 49).

The ascension of Jesus (24:50–53)

This is the final and climactic passage in Luke's resurrection narrative and, indeed, his Gospel. It recalls other farewell and departure passages which also include the blessing of others by the one departing (eg Gen 49; Deut 33). Jesus' leadership of the disciples is reflected in the opening words of the passage as he leads them out to Bethany, about three kilometres from the city, on the Mount of Olives – from where he had made his significant entrance to the city (19:29ff). Jesus' action in "lifting up his hands" and blessing the disciples recalls not only the farewell passages mentioned above, but also, and more specifically, priestly passages (Lev 9:22; Sirach 50:20–22). If this is intentional, then Luke ends his Gospel as he began it, with a priest (1:5ff). However, while Zechariah's priestly activity was within Jerusalem and the temple, that of Jesus is outside both (v 50–53). On the other hand, since Luke nowhere else presents Jesus as a priest it may be that we can read too much into this parting benediction, which may instead simply reflect the farewell passages already noted (cf also 2:34). The double mention of his blessing of the disciples underlines the message that they part with his, and his Father's, approval and favour.

The ascension of Jesus into heaven, anticipated earlier in the Gospel (9:31,51), is recounted by Luke in more detail in Acts 1:2,9–11. The timing of the ascension in both accounts appears to be different, since in the Gospel it seems to happen on the same day as Jesus' resurrection, while in Acts it occurs "forty days" later (1:3). However, Luke does not actually say in his Gospel that Jesus ascended on the day of his resurrection. He has probably telescoped details as he concludes the Gospel, but repeats the event in more detail at the start of Acts to provide continuity between his two books. To the resurrection is now added the ascension as evidence of God's vindication of Jesus, seen as the divine reversal of Jewish rejection of their Messiah. The ascension "into heaven" is a necessary prelude to his being seated at the right hand of God (20:41–44; 22:69), from which exalted position he will send upon the disciples what his Father has promised – the Holy Spirit (v 49; Acts 2:30–36). Furthermore, in Luke Jesus' heavenly reign is the prelude to his future return in glory to restore all things (9:26; 19:12; Acts 3:21).

The disciples respond by worshipping Jesus (v 52; in the best manuscripts). This is the only place in Luke's writings where we read of Jesus being "worshipped" and this is particularly significant in the light of 4:8, where worship is to be given to God alone (cf Acts 10:25–26). Now that Jesus is in heaven at God's right hand, worship is an especially appropriate response. The disciples' return to Jerusalem appears to be a conscious recollection of Jesus' instruction to wait in the city for "power from on high" to enable them to fulfil their mission (v 49). This return is with "great joy", recalling the words of the angelic annunciation of Jesus' birth (2:10) and, indeed, a general Lucan theme. The Gospel then ends as it began, with the "blessing" of God in the temple (v 53; cf 1:8–10; 2:27–28), the temple which will be the setting of much of the action in the opening chapters of Luke's sequel (eg Acts 2:46; 3:1; 5:42). The constancy of the disciples' praise in the temple is reminiscent of Anna (2:37). Jesus had just "blessed" the disciples and now they are "blessing" God, as well as worshipping Jesus. The last line of Luke's Gospel, then, gathers up several of its key themes in quick succession – Jerusalem, joy, the temple, and praise (v 52–53).

Tasks

a What previous farewell/departure biblical passages are recalled here?
b Discuss the claim that Luke presents Jesus as a priest in this passage.
c Comment on the meaning of Jesus' ascension for Luke.
d Discuss the responses of the disciples to Jesus' ascension.

The resurrection and history

The debate over whether the bodily resurrection of Jesus from the dead is a historical fact cannot be dealt with in detail here. The diverse views of New Testament scholars on this issue range from outright denial[1], through historical agnosticism[2], to confident affirmation[3]. The dominant understanding of Jesus' resurrection, which is broadly accepted by New Testament scholars and also by many mainstream churches, has been recently summarised by NT Wright[4] in several points which may be paraphrased as follows:

1 The Jewish background indicates that 'resurrection' had various meanings.
2 Paul, the earliest Christian author, understood resurrection in a more spiritual rather than a bodily sense.
3 The first Christians used the term 'resurrection' (and its related forms) to refer to Jesus' exaltation and glorification in heaven, and only later did they come to use it in connection with an empty tomb and apparent sightings of Jesus.
4 The resurrection narratives in the Gospels (the empty tomb and appearances of Jesus) were invented to support the later understanding of the resurrection, namely that Jesus was bodily alive again.
5 The apparent 'sightings' of Jesus were internal, subjective experiences (similar to Paul's religious conversion on the Damascus Road), fantasies or hallucinations, rather than external, objective realities.
6 Jesus' body was not resuscitated, and was definitely not raised from the dead, in the way the Gospels seem to declare.

---

[1] eg Ludemann, Gerd, *The Resurrection of Jesus: History, Experience, Theology,* London: SCM, 1994. Ludemann suggests that belief in Jesus' resurrection originated with completely subjective and psychologically explicable visions experienced by Peter and Paul.
[2] eg Wedderburn, AJM, *Beyond Resurrection,* London: SCM, 1999. Wedderburn proposes that Jesus' resurrection cannot be historically verified and is, therefore, an open question.
[3] eg Wright, NT, *The Resurrection of the Son of God,* London: SPCK, 2003. Wright asserts that the empty tomb and the appearances of Jesus are historically secure facts, for which the best historical explanation is the bodily resurrection of Jesus.
[4] Wright, *The Resurrection of the Son of God* (op cit), p7, also pp588–589

Wright himself presents historical arguments against each of these points and for the bodily resurrection of Jesus from the dead.

As for the Gospel resurrection narratives themselves, Wright rejects the widely held view that they are apologetically motivated inventions, reflecting the 'later' understanding of Jesus' resurrection as his bodily return from death. He notes four characteristics of these narratives which, he argues, point to their being early accounts rather than late inventions[1]. First, there is practically a complete lack of quotation from or allusion to Israel's Bible (the Old Testament), despite the fact that this is a marked feature of the preceding narratives, and the passion narrative in particular. Wright's point is that if the resurrection narratives are late creations then this is very strange, for we would expect the authors to make much of the 'argument from prophecy', as early Christian preaching on Jesus' resurrection apparently did (eg Acts 2:24–32; 13:32–37). Second, the absence of any reference to Jesus' resurrection as the basis for the Christian's own resurrection and hope of life beyond death is strange if these narratives are late developments, since this understanding of Jesus' resurrection was an important early Christian theme (eg I Thess 4:13ff). Third, Jesus himself is not portrayed in these narratives as a heavenly person, shining in supernatural radiance, as, for instance, is characteristic of the resurrected in the book of Daniel (12:2–3). Later narrative creations would surely, Wright argues, have wanted to present the risen Jesus as a divine, heavenly, exalted being, yet he is presented still in very human terms. Fourth, legendary narratives designed to convince people that Jesus had really risen from the dead would not have women as the ones to find the empty tomb and as the first witnesses of the resurrection. This is because in antiquity women were generally not regarded as acceptable or reliable witnesses (see comment on Lk 24:10–11, p180). Taken together, argues Wright, these points imply that the resurrection narratives of the Gospels have preserved very early oral tradition with little sign of later development. Further, the apparent inconsistencies between the narratives also argue for their early character and against the collusion or harmonisation that would probably characterise later accounts.

---

[1] Wright, *The Resurrection of the Son of God* (op cit), pp599–608

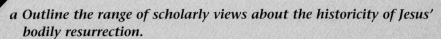

Tasks

a Outline the range of scholarly views about the historicity of Jesus' bodily resurrection.

b What is the dominant academic understanding of Jesus' resurrection?

c Summarise NT Wright's view of the resurrection narratives in the Gospels.

Practice essay title

1 (a) Outline your knowledge and understanding of Luke's account of Jesus' appearance on the road to Emmaus. (30)

(b) Explore the claim that this event helped Jesus' followers to believe in his resurrection. Justify your answer. (15)

The words and deeds of Jesus

PARABLES

TEACHERS OFTEN REFLECT NOT only on *what* they teach (content), but also on *how* they teach (method). When we think of the parables of Jesus we come to his characteristic method of instruction, parables accounting for about a third of his recorded teaching. However, due to academic disagreement over the definition of the term 'parable' and, therefore, over what should be classed as a parable in Jesus' teaching, there is difference of opinion concerning the number of parables found in the Gospels.

Definition

The word 'parable' comes from the Greek *parabole*, meaning 'comparison'[1]. At the most basic level, a parable may be defined as a figurative saying or story, in which comparison or correspondence is implied between its literal form on the one hand and religious/moral teaching on the other. The literal world of the parable is thus a metaphor for the religious/moral teaching which it symbolises. While the English word 'parable' is often used to refer to a short story told by Jesus with some religious and/or moral lesson or lessons ('an earthly story with a heavenly meaning'), it is clear

---

[1] In the New Testament *parabole* is found outside the synoptic Gospels only in Hebrews 9:9 and 11:19, where it is translated in the NRSV as "symbol" and "figuratively" respectively.

that *parabole* has a wider range of meaning in the synoptic Gospels – from a brief "proverb" of three words (Lk 4:23) to a detailed allegory with numerous symbolic features (Lk 8:4–15, the parable of the sower)[1]. The common idea that unites its various uses is the metaphorical or figurative element.

Origin

Figurative sayings and stories existed throughout the ancient world before the time of Jesus. Comparisons have been made between Aesop's fables (sixth century BC) and Jesus' parables, but none of Jesus' recorded parables is a fable in which personified animals and plants speak and act as humans (but see Judg 9:7–15; 2 Kings 14:9). The origins of Jesus' parabolic method of teaching are found, rather, in the Jewish world to which he himself belonged. Indeed, before Jesus we have several parables in the Hebrew Bible/Old Testament – the poor man's lamb (2 Sam 12:1–4, the clearest OT parallel to Jesus' parables), the two brothers (2 Sam 14:5–7), the escaped prisoner (1 Kings 20:39–40), the song of the vineyard (Isa 5:1–7); the eagles and the vine (Ezek 17:2–10)[2]; the lioness and her cubs (Ezek 19:2–9), and the vine (Ezek 19:10–14). We see here that short, figurative stories were used by Israel's prophets before the time of Jesus and that his use of such stories is but one indication that he was part of that Jewish prophetic tradition (cf eg Lk 4:24; 24:19). More specifically, it has been argued that the nearest parallel and background to Jesus' parables is found in the symbolic stories of Jewish 'apocalyptic' literature[3] (eg Dan 7, the four beasts). About 200 years before Jesus, another Jesus characterises Jewish wisdom teachers as those able to deal with "the subtleties of parables" and "the obscurities of parables" (Sirach 39:2–3), though here the reference is probably to puzzling sayings rather than symbolic stories (of which none is found in Sirach).

The Jewish context for Jesus' parables has often been linked to the parables of the rabbis, of which over 1,500 survive. However, only 324 of this collection can be dated before AD 200, and just three can be placed before Jesus' time (from Rabbi Hillel, a generation before Jesus). Because of this, some scholars hold that Jesus was one of the first, if not the first, to use parables in the sense of short, symbolic stories. However, the existence of so many rabbinic parables from the centuries after Jesus may imply that he was part of a wider tradition of Jewish parabolic teachers. That practically no other first-century Jewish parables have survived is not surprising in light of the general scarcity of first-century Jewish literary remains. Certainly, despite some notable differences, there are striking similarities between the parables of Jesus and other rabbis, which may imply that both were using a common mode and form of Jewish

---

[1] There are 18 occurrences of *parabole* in Luke's Gospel: 4:23; 5:36; 6:39; 8:4,9,10,11; 12:16,41; 13:6; 14:7; 15:3; 18:1,9; 19:11; 20:9,19; 21:29.

[2] In Ezekiel 17:2 the NRSV translates the Hebrew *mashal* as "allegory", while the Greek version has *parabole*.

[3] Wright, NT, *Jesus and the Victory of God*, London: SPCK, 1996, pp177,181

religious instruction. CL Blomberg has compared and contrasted the two collections of parables[1]. He includes as similarities:

- *Introductory formulae* – rabbinic parables often begin with "... to what may it be compared? It is like ..." (cf Lk 7:31–32) or occasionally with "A certain man ..." (cf Lk 10:30).
- *Logic* – rabbinic parables sometimes use 'from the lesser to the greater' logic (cf Lk 11:13).
- *Length and structure* – both sets of parables are often brief with only two or three characters who are regularly contrasted (cf Lk 6:47–49).
- *Topics and imagery* – shared topics and images include, for example, kings, banquets, farmers, landlords and merchants (cf Lk 19:11ff).
- *Allegorical interpretation* – rabbis often interpreted their parables as allegories (ie various details had symbolic meaning) and it is arguable that Jesus' parables were similarly allegorical (cf Lk 8:1–15; 15:1–2,11–32).
- *Purposes* – the parables of the rabbis and of Jesus are designed both to reveal and to conceal (cf Lk 8:1–15).

However, Blomberg also notes differences between Jesus' parables and those of the rabbis:

- *Conventional and scriptural* – most rabbinic parables reinforce traditional Jewish wisdom and interpret Scripture, while Jesus' parables are often subversive and rarely deal with Scripture.
- *Kingdom of God* – the distinctive theme and context of Jesus' parables is God's kingdom.
- *Explicit interpretation* – a far higher proportion of rabbinic parables have specific interpretations and applications than is the case with Jesus' parables.

As an illustration of the similarity between the rabbinic parables and Jesus' parables we may note just one example – the parable of the two trees by Rabbi Eleazar ben Azariah (about AD 50–120), which is comparable to Jesus' parable of the two builders (Mt 7:24–27/ Lk 6:47–49):

> "He whose wisdom is in excess of his works, to what is he like? To a tree whose branches are many and whose roots are few; and the wind comes and uproots it and overturns it. But he whose works are in excess of his wisdom, to what is he like? To a tree whose branches are few and whose roots are many; though all the winds come against it, they cannot stir it from its place."[2]

---

[1] Blomberg, CL, *Interpreting the Parables,* Leicester: Apollos/IVP, 1990, pp58–68

[2] Cited, for example, in Blomberg, *Interpreting the Parables* (op cit), p61; and AM Hunter, *Interpreting the Parables,* London: SCM, 1960, p113

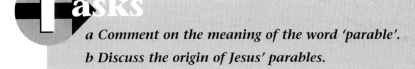

Tasks

a Comment on the meaning of the word 'parable'.
b Discuss the origin of Jesus' parables.

Types

We have noted above that the Greek word *parabole* has a wider range of meaning in the synoptic Gospels than what is usually understood by the word 'parable' in English. We have also referred to the disagreement among biblical scholars about what a parable is and, therefore, about what parts of the teaching of Jesus may be properly classed as parables. We should therefore understand that attempts to classify and categorise the parables of Jesus are secondary analyses of the teaching of Jesus, on which there is no unanimous agreement. Precise, formal classification of the parables is not possible. However, the parables of Jesus are often categorised in one of two main ways – according to their perceived literary form or topical content.

Literary categories

Modern academic study of Jesus' parables began with the German scholar Adolf Julicher in the late nineteenth century[1]. Julicher distinguished four literary categories for the study of parables that are still made use of today: similitudes, parables, example stories and allegories[2].

Similitudes

While a simile makes a simple, explicit comparison using the word 'as' or 'like' (eg Lk 3:22, "like a dove"), a *similitude* is an expanded simile, extended or developed into a more detailed picture, which refers to a common, recurring event, often in the present tense. For example, compare Jesus' use of a grain of mustard seed both as a simile (Lk 17:6) and a similitude (Lk 13:18–19); in the latter the image is developed into a picture. Other examples of similitudes in Luke include the guests of the bridegroom (5:33–35), the new garment and the new wine (5:36–39), the lamp (8:16–17), the father and the child (11:11–13), the strong man (11:21–23), the yeast (13:20–21), the lost sheep (15:3–7), the lost coin (15:8–10), the worthless slaves (17:7–10), and the fig tree (21:29–31). It will be noticed that some of these examples begin with a general introduction (such as "Which one of you ..."), reflecting the typical nature of the events depicted in similitudes.

---

[1] Julicher, Adolf, *Die Gleichnisreden Jesu*, 2 vols, Freiburg: Mohr, 1888/98; which has not been translated into English

[2] So Snodgrass, Klyne in *The Face of New Testament Studies* (op cit), p179. Snodgrass notes that debate remains whether allegory and example story are proper categories.

Parables

While a metaphor is a simple, implicit comparison without the word 'as' or 'like' (eg Lk 13:32 – "tell that fox", ie Herod), a *parable* is usually considered to be an expanded metaphor (or simile), extended or developed into a story, which refers to a particular event or events in the past. Examples of these narrative parables in Luke include the banquet (14:15–24), the lost son (15:11–32), the shrewd manager (16:1–9), and the widow and the judge (18:1–8). Unlike similitudes, the story parables have a specific rather than a general introduction (such as "A certain man had two sons ...").

Example stories

While similitudes and parables are analogies containing comparative imagery, example stories contain real, non-metaphorical illustrations of behaviour which is to be imitated (or avoided). Example story parables are found only in Luke: the good Samaritan (10:29–37), the rich fool (12:16–21), the rich man and Lazarus (16:19–31), and the Pharisee and the tax collector (18:9–14). The exemplary nature of the parable of the good Samaritan is highlighted in the concluding "Go and do likewise" (10:37).

Allegories

Allegories are narratives with multiple symbolic details and metaphorical elements. For example, the parable of the sower as we find it in the synoptic Gospels is interpreted as having several allegorical details (Lk 8:4–8,11–15). CL Blomberg[1] has argued that while some of Jesus' parables are "one-point" parables (eg the tower builder and the warring king, Lk 14:28–32; the mustard seed and the yeast, Lk 13:18–21), others are "two-point" (eg the Pharisee and the tax collector, Lk 18:9–14; the two builders, Lk 6:47–49; the unworthy servant, Lk 17:7–10; the rich fool, 12:16–21; the barren fig tree, 13:6–9; the widow and the judge, Lk 18:1–8; the friend at midnight, Lk 11:5–8; the householder and the thief, Lk 12:39–40), and yet others are 'three-point' parables (eg the lost sheep, coin and son, Lk 15; the two debtors, Lk 7:41–43; the rich man and Lazarus, Lk 16:19–31; the pounds, Lk 19:11–27; the good Samaritan, Lk 10:29–37; the banquet, Lk 14:15–24; the shrewd manager, Lk 16:1–13). Basically, the number of symbolic points is often determined by the number of main characters or groups of characters. For example, in the parable of the lost son, within the context of Luke 15 the father represents God, the younger son the tax collectors and sinners, and the older son the Pharisees and scribes (Lk 15:1–2,11–32). Indeed, within Jewish literature, including the rabbinic parables, there are a number of standard metaphors and fixed images with commonly accepted symbolism, for example kings for God, sons or vineyards for Israel, and servants for prophets.

---

[1] Blomberg, *Interpreting the Parables* (op cit)

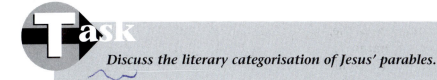

Task

Discuss the literary categorisation of Jesus' parables.

Topical categories

Rather than classifying Jesus' parables into literary categories, it is possible to arrange them by topic or theme according to their perceived content and teaching. For example, they are sometimes grouped into four topical categories – parables of God's mercy, of the kingdom, and of crisis and of discipleship.

The parables of the kingdom (eg Lk 13:18–19), of crisis (eg Lk 12:42–46) and of discipleship (eg Lk 14:28–33) will be studied later (p301ff), but in this present chapter we will make special reference to the first of the four categories – the parables of God's mercy. This is one of nine thematic categories into which Joachim Jeremias groups the parables in his famous and influential book *The Parables of Jesus*[1]. Jeremias includes in this group parables which we have studied before: the lost sheep, coin and son (Lk 15, see pp122–127), the Pharisee and the tax collector (Lk 18:9–14, pp140–141), and the father and the child (Lk 11:11–13, pp93–94). Also included is Jesus' saying about the "sick" rather than the "healthy" (author's translation) needing a doctor, paralleled with his saying that he had come to call "sinners" rather than the "righteous" to repentance (Lk 5:31–32). The preceding context for this saying relates how the Pharisees and scribes complained that Jesus' disciples were eating and drinking with tax collectors and sinners (5:29–30). Clearly, Jesus' analogy portrays the sinners as morally and spiritually ill and himself as the doctor (cf 4:23), whose prescription is "repentance" (a common Lucan theme, absent from the parallel passages in Mt 9:13 and Mk 2:17). The Jewish leaders, however, regard themselves as "righteous" and in no need of Jesus' prescription. In this group of parables Jeremias also refers to the parable of the two debtors (Lk 7:41–43). The two debts are significantly different (a denarius was a day's wage for a labourer), and are "cancelled" (the Greek word is found only in Luke among the Gospels) by the creditor. The parable's closing question about which debtor will love/be grateful to the creditor more is related to the context of the parable – the anointing of Jesus by a woman who is a sinner, in the home of a Pharisee (7:36–50). Jesus contrasts the Pharisee's minimal hospitality with the extravagant devotion of the woman, the latter being an expression of her love/ gratitude to Jesus for forgiving the "debt" of her sin (7:44–50; cf 11:4). The parable in its context implies that both the Pharisee and the sinful woman are forgiven, but the latter more, as evidenced by her greater gratitude.

---

[1] Jeremias, Joachim, *The Parables of Jesus,* revised edition, London: SCM, pp124–146 ('God's Mercy for Sinners')

In his topical categorisation of the parables, Jeremias arranges them into the following nine groups according to their perceived message:

> Now is the day of salvation (eg Lk 5:36–38; 8:16)
> God's mercy for sinners (see p199)
> The great assurance (eg Lk 13:18–21; 18:1–8)
> The imminence of catastrophe (eg Lk 12:16–21,54–56)
> It may be too late (eg Lk 13:6–9; 14:15–24)
> The challenge of the hour (eg Lk 16:1–8,19–31)
> Realised discipleship (eg Lk 10:25–37; 12:24–30)
> The Via Dolorosa and exaltation of the Son of Man (eg Lk 9:58; 17:24)
> The consummation (eg Lk 14:11; 17:26–30)

RF Capon has the parables of Jesus in three topical categories corresponding to the consecutive periods of the ministry of Jesus[1]:

> kingdom (eg Lk 8:4ff)
> grace (eg Lk 15)
> judgement (eg Lk 20:9ff)

A topical classification of Luke's parables by DL Bock organises them into six distinct, yet at times overlapping, categories[2]:

> kingdom (eg 5:33–39; 8:5–8)
> spiritual life (eg 6:47–49; 7:41–44)
> jewish leadership (eg 7:31–35; 13:6–9)
> judgement (eg 12:13–21; 13:6–9)
> future (eg 12:39–40,41–46)
> evangelism (eg ch 15)

It is possible too to regard all the parables as concerned with the one main theme of the kingdom of God, the central topic of Jesus' teaching, and group the parables into subdivisions of this. AM Hunter has categorised the parables into four different aspects of the kingdom[3]:

> the coming of the kingdom (eg Lk 8:5–8; 13:18–21)
> the grace of the kingdom (ie God's love to the undeserving, parables of God's mercy, eg Lk 14:7–11,16–24)
> the men of the kingdom (ie citizens of the kingdom, discipleship, eg Lk 10:30–37; 14:28–32)
> the crisis of the kingdom (eg Lk 12:42–46; 13:6–9)

---

1 Capon, RF, *The Parables of the Kingdom*, Grand Rapids, Michigan: Zondervan, 1985; *The Parables of God's Grace*, Grand Rapids, Michigan: Eerdmans, 1988; *The Parables of Judgment*, Grand Rapids, Michigan: Eerdmans, 1989
2 Bock, *Luke 1:1–9:50* (op cit), pp948–949
3 Hunter, *Interpreting the Parables* (op cit)

JD Crossan classified parables into three groups relating to different "modes of the kingdom's temporality"[1]:

parables of advent (eg Lk 13:18–21; the kingdom as God's gift)
parables of reversal (eg Lk 10:30ff; the reversal brought by the kingdom)
parables of action (eg Lk 20:9ff; the kingdom requires decisive action)

Blomberg has also used the kingdom as the theme by which to organise the teaching of the parables[2]:

the king of the kingdom (God; eg Lk 11:5–8; ch 15)
the subjects/citizens of the kingdom (God's people; eg Lk 10:25–37; 14:28–32)
those who are not subjects/citizens of the kingdom (not God's people; eg Lk 7:31ff; 13:6–9)

However, as with the literary categories, we must note that the topical categories vary according to the particular analyses of individual scholars and their understanding of the meaning of separate parables.

Other methods of classifying Jesus' parables into various types are, of course, possible. For example, Blomberg has also categorised the parables as follows[3]:

nature parables (eg Lk 13:6–9)
discovery parables (eg Mt 13:44–50)
a fortiori parables (ie 'lesser to greater' logic, eg Lk 11:5–8,11–13)
contrast parables (eg 15:11–32; 18:9–14)

Tasks

a **Discuss the topical categorisation of Jesus' parables.**

b **Outline your knowledge and understanding of the parables of God's mercy.**

Purpose

Why did Jesus use parables in his teaching? An answer to this question must begin with a passage in the synoptics which presents Jesus' own explanation for his use of parables (Mt 13:10–15/ Mk 4:10–12/ Lk 8:9–10). Here a distinction is made between the disciples and others. The others ("outsiders", author's translation) are given the message of God's kingdom in the cryptic, enigmatic, coded language of parables to prevent them understanding it, but the "secrets" (Greek *mysteria*) of God's kingdom are revealed to the disciples (cf Dan 2, especially v 18–19,27–30,47). Indeed, the public parables are privately explained to the disciples as Jesus decodes them when

---

[1] Crossan, JD, *In Parables: The Challenge of the Historical Jesus*, New York and London: Harper & Row, 1973 – as quoted in Snodgrass, *The Face of New Testament Studies* (op cit), p183

[2] Blomberg, *Interpreting the Parables* (op cit), pp293–296

[3] Blomberg, *Interpreting the Parables* (op cit), p292, footnote 9

they are alone (Mk 4:33–34). However, the authenticity of this passage (Mk 4:10–12 and parallels) is rejected by many scholars, who regard it as the creation of the Church, put into the mouth of Jesus, to explain Jewish rejection of Jesus as Messiah. Not all scholars are persuaded and believe that the words go back to Jesus himself. Attempts have been made to soften the passage, such as the claim that the Greek word translated "so that" (Mk 4:12/ Lk 8:10) is a mistranslation of an Aramaic word which could have meant 'who'. In this case, the purpose of parables is not, then, to prevent understanding of the kingdom. Again, it has been argued that "so that" is an abbreviation for 'so that it might be fulfilled', referring to the fulfilment of Isaiah 6 which is immediately quoted.

However, if the apparent meaning of the passage is allowed to stand, it is possible to interpret it in the wider context of the ministry of Jesus. Clearly, those who are not disciples of Jesus can understand his parables to some degree (Mk 4:33; Lk 20:19). It appears though that they cannot understand the nature of the kingdom or its presence in the ministry of Jesus (eg Lk 4:14–30; 11:14ff; 12:54–56). While the forms of the passage in Mark (4:10–12) and Luke (8:9–10) use Isaiah 6 to stress God's purpose in Jesus' use of parables, the parallel passage in Matthew focuses on the human responsibility of Jesus' hearers (Mt 13:10–15; as does Jn 12:37–41 and Acts 28:24–28 in their use of Isaiah 6). Isaiah's ministry appears to have been a confirmation of God's judgement on Israel for its rejection of God's ways (Isa 1–5) and, by analogy, so is Jesus' ministry in his use of parables. It is nevertheless clear from elsewhere in Jesus' ministry that his parables have other purposes, even for those apparently outside the kingdom. For instance, by the parable of the good Samaritan a Jewish lawyer is instructed to act as the Samaritan had (Lk 10:25–37), and the parables of the tower builder and the warring king are used to teach the crowds about the demands of discipleship (Lk 14:28–32). Similarly, the parable of the Pharisee and the tax collector is directed to the self righteous (Lk 18:9–14). Unless we hold that the synoptic contexts of the parables (their introductions and conclusions) are creations of the evangelists, it is apparent that they are sometimes specifically applied by Jesus even to those who are not yet his disciples. Of course, Jesus also uses parables to teach his own disciples many lessons which, as we have seen, may be grouped in various ways into separate topics (see Types, p197ff, for topics and corresponding parables).

Generally, the parabolic method sharpens the focus of Jesus' teaching by turning abstract religious concepts into concrete examples (eg God's joy over repentant sinners in the parable of the lost son) and general moral principles into specific instances (eg 'Love your neighbour' in the parable of the good Samaritan). Parables challenge people to think (What "do you think …?", eg Mt 8:12; Lk 10:36; or "Which of you …?", author's translation, eg Lk 11:5,11) and help them visualise ("It is like …", eg Lk 13:18–21). By likening God's kingdom to everyday things and events, often in his rural Galilean environment, Jesus vividly illustrates his message in ways his hearers can relate to. Of course, his parables often make shocking and even subversive points, which challenge convention and tradition and require a radical reversal of attitudes and actions on the part of his hearers (eg stories about a neighbourly Samaritan and a justified tax collector). The undeniable logic of a parable's narrative is designed to draw the listener to the inescapable truth of the message that it symbolises (eg Lk 11:11–13).

> **Tasks**
>
> a Discuss the passages in the synoptics in which Jesus explains the purpose of his use of parables.
>
> b Comment on the purposes and functions of his parables in his wider ministry.

A brief historical survey of how Jesus' parables have been interpreted, demonstrates that various approaches have been taken concerning their purpose and function. During the early and medieval periods of Church history the parables were treated as allegories in which nearly every narrative detail was interpreted as having some spiritual, theological or moral meaning. Mostly, ideas not found in either the literary context of the parables or the historical context of Jesus' ministry were read into them from later in the New Testament or Church history. A classic example of this is the allegorisation of the parable of the good Samaritan (Lk 10:29–37) by, among others, Augustine (AD 354–430) who was Bishop of Hippo in North Africa. For him the parable coherently symbolised in its various details the story of humanity's fall into sin and its restoration in Christ and the Church:

> The man on a journey = Adam
> Jerusalem from which he went down = the city of heavenly peace
> Jericho to which he went = the moon, waxing and waning, representing human mortality (exploiting the similarity between the Hebrew words for Jericho and moon)
> Robbers = the devil and his angels
> Stripped = taking his immortality
> Beaten = persuading him to sin
> Half-dead = dead due to sin yet alive in his knowledge of God
> Priest = ineffective priesthood of the Old Testament
> Levite = ineffective ministry of the Old Testament
> Good Samaritan = Christ
> Bandaged wounds = restraint of sin
> Oil = comfort of hope
> Wine = encouragement to fervent work
> Animal = body of Christ/incarnation
> Inn = Church
> Two denarii = two commandments of love
> Innkeeper = Apostle Paul
> Return of the Samaritan = resurrection of Christ[1]

---

1 Augustine, *Questiones Evangeliorum* ii.19

In the sixteenth-century Reformation there was a reaction against such allegorisation by Martin Luther and John Calvin. However, this continued to be the main way of treating the parables until the late nineteenth century, when Adolf Julicher argued that parables were only interpreted as allegories at a later stage than Jesus' ministry[1]. Julicher argued that Jesus himself only made one point of comparison with his parables, but very soon his followers found more and read them back into Jesus' teaching (so Mt 13:18–23,36–43). However, while Julicher's main thesis was largely (though not entirely) accepted, his reduction of the parables to timeless moral lessons was criticised. In the 1930s CH Dodd argued that the message of the parables must be interpreted in the historical context of Jesus' own ministry and message, which centred on the arrival of God's kingdom[2]. In the next decade Joachim Jeremias developed Dodd's work and tied the parables more closely to Jesus' Palestinian culture. More recent work has viewed the parables as dynamic 'speech-events' or 'performance utterances' which actually effect their message, rather than merely expressing it[3]. The metaphor itself is powerful and does not need interpreted. In it Jesus confronts and changes his hearers. Thus, we have here an almost sacramental rather than merely symbolic view of the parables, in which they are dynamic rather than descriptive discourses. Another approach argues for the 'polyvalence' or multiple meanings of parables, depending on variables brought to the text by any given reader[4]. Also, a recent trend, while rejecting the anachronistic allegorising that dominated earlier Church history, holds that the parables of Jesus are best seen as intentional allegories. Indeed, the rabbinic parables were allegories and provide the best historical context against which to understand Jesus' parables[5]. In summary, a whole range of theological, moral, historical, literary and other approaches have been applied to the parables of Jesus with varying results.

Task

Briefly outline some of the main approaches to understanding the purpose and function of the parables in the history of their interpretation.

To conclude our study of the purpose of Jesus' parables we may note some principles of interpretation, which are based on the assumption that some historical and literary pointers do exist as guidelines for the modern reader.

First, to avoid the danger of anachronistic readings which reflect concerns and agendas later than the time of Jesus, we should interpret the parables *within*

---

[1] Julicher, *Die Gleichnisreden Jesu* (op cit)

[2] Dodd, CH, *The Parables of the Kingdom*, London: James Nisbet and Company, 1935

[3] eg Fuchs, Ernst, *Studies of the Historical Jesus*, trans A Scobie, Naperville, Illinois: Allenson, 1964

[4] eg Tolbert, Mary Ann, *Perspectives on the Parables: An Approach to Multiple Interpretations*, Philadelphia: Fortress, 1979

[5] Blomberg, *Interpreting the Parables* (op cit)

the ministry of Jesus, specifically in line with its focus on the present and future arrival of the kingdom of God (see pp80–81). Judged by this criterion, much of the allegorising of the parables in the history of the Church and of more recent polyvalent understandings of the parables, appears to be off the mark.

Second, along with the historical context of Jesus' ministry, attention should be paid to the literary context of the parables within the Gospels, particularly to their introductions and conclusions (eg Lk 15:1–2,7,10,32; 18:1,8,9,14). A problem arises here in that most scholars believe that the parables were passed on orally in mostly independent units, and that by the time they were incorporated into our written Gospels their original contexts and applications in the ministry of Jesus were unknown. For example, the evangelists sometimes provide different contexts and applications for the same parable – such as the lost sheep, which in Luke relates to unrepentant sinners but in Matthew to straying believers (cf Lk 15:1–7/ Mt 18:6,10–14). Again, a parable may be provided with several different applications in its final form in the Gospels (eg cf Lk 16:8–13, following the parable of the shrewd manager). Many scholars, therefore, believe that the literary context of the parables in the Gospels reflects the concerns and creativity of the later Church as it passed them on as oral tradition (see Form Criticism, p246ff) and/or of the evangelists as they composed their Gospels (see Redaction Criticism, p254ff), rather than telling us anything about the original purposes and functions of the parables in the 'life-setting' of the ministry of Jesus. However, some scholars have argued that it is possible to exaggerate the extent to which this has happened and that the Church and the evangelists have substantially preserved and faithfully transmitted the original meanings of the parables, noting that Jesus himself probably repeated parables while giving them new applications.

A third principle of interpretation requires us to pay attention to the literary features of the parable itself – such as structure, characters, plot, scenes, repetition and parallelism – which can often provide clues and hints to its meaning and application. For example, a parable's main characters often have symbolic significance, involving an authority figure as a standard Jewish image for God (eg king, father) and two contrasting subordinates or groups of subordinates representing positive and negative responses to God's kingdom (eg Lk 15:1–2,4–10,11–32). Other parables may have one (eg Lk 14:28–33) or two points (eg Lk 18:1–8,9–14), depending on the details of their narrative[1]. Again, within the parable narrative note should be made of untypical, improbable and unrealistic elements which intentionally signal some significant point (eg Mt 18:23–25, the colossal 10,000-talent debt serves to underline the generosity of God's forgiveness). Care must be taken not to read as significant or symbolic detail which may just provide narrative background or colour. Finally, it is important to be accurately informed, as far as is possible, about background factors which may illuminate the dynamics of the parable, such as current historical, political, religious, cultural, agricultural and social issues. Such understanding is crucial, for example, in appreciating the parables of Luke 14 and 15.

---

[1] Blomberg, *Interpreting the Parables* (op cit)

The Gospel of Luke

The issue of whether we have a Christology in the parables – that is, whether they teach anything about Jesus himself – is a debated point. Many scholars hold that the parables of Jesus are theocentric – that is, they focus on God, specifically on his kingdom. It is accepted though that the parables indirectly point to Jesus as a powerful teacher and prophet. Blomberg[1] notes that some see in Jesus' parables an explicit Christology (eg the shepherd looking for the lost sheep, the nobleman in the parable of the pounds, the son in the parable of the tenants), and others an implicit Christology (eg Jesus' association with sinners is paralleled in God's concern for them in the parable of the lost sheep; Jesus' pronouncing of God's forgiveness on others as in Lk 7:36–50). To some degree Jesus is implying something about his own identity and mission in the parables and expects his hearers to associate him with God in some way – as God's representative and agent who brings in his kingdom.

Tasks

a *Discuss principles for interpretation of the parables which would help readers to understand their purpose.*

b *Comment on whether the parables tell us anything about Jesus himself.*

MIRACLES

A miracle (from the Latin *miraculum*: 'amazement, wonder') may be defined as an extraordinary event, considered to have a supernatural cause. In common with the other New Testament Gospels, Luke presents Jesus as a worker of miracles and, indeed, as the object of miraculous activity. As examples of the latter in Luke we may note Jesus' virgin conception (1:26ff), baptism (3:21–22), transfiguration (9:28ff), resurrection (24:1ff), and ascension (24:51). Jesus also gives his apostles miraculous powers (9:1–2). Other events and activities which may be considered miraculous include angelophanies (1:11ff,26ff; 2:9ff), prophecies (eg 3:16ff; 21:20ff) and portents (23:44–45). In Luke Jesus performs some 20 specific miracles, which may be generally categorised as:

    healings (eleven: 4:38–39; 5:12–16,17–26; 6:6–11; 7:1–10; 8:43–48; 13:11–13;
        14:1–4; 17:11–19; 18:35–43; 22:50–51)
    exorcisms (four: 4:31–37; 8:26–39; 9:37–42; 11:14)
    nature miracles (three: 5:1–11; 8:22–25; 9:12–17)
    raisings from the dead (two: 7:11–17; 8:40–42,49–56)

These are general rather than precise categories since, for example, exorcisms may also include physical healing (cf 11:14), and raisings from the dead may be

---

[1] Blomberg, *Interpreting the Parables* (op cit), pp313–324

classified as nature miracles by some. Certainly, neither Luke nor the other evangelists categorised the miracles. Most of these miracle stories are found also in Mark, but two are shared with Matthew alone (Lk 7:1–10; 11:14) and six are unique to Luke (5:1–11; 7:11–17; 13:11–13; 14:1–4; 17:11–19; 22:50–51). Before concluding with some general observations about the function, purpose and characteristics of the miracles in Luke, we shall study the miracle stories individually, apart from those we have examined earlier (11:14, pp94–96; 13:11–13, pp109–111; 14:1–4, p115; 17:11–19, pp134–136; 18:35–43, pp145–146; 22:50–51, p161).

The demon-possessed man in the synagogue (4:31–37)

Jesus has just begun his ministry in nearby Nazareth (4:14–30) where, in another synagogue, he announced the nature of this ministry in terms of Isaiah's vision of release for the captive and the oppressed by a Spirit-anointed servant of God. Immediately following this, we now have an example of such ministry at work, as Jesus releases a man from demonic captivity and oppression (cf Acts 10:38). As in Nazareth, so now in Capernaum, Jesus is in a synagogue on the Sabbath (compare discussion of 13:10, p109). The passage begins and ends with reference to Jesus' "authority" and this *inclusio* or framing device identifies its key message – the authority of Jesus as a teacher and exorcist (on the latter and demons, see comment on 10:17ff, pp84–85). Ironically, the devil had recently offered Jesus "authority" (v 6), and now Jesus uses divine "authority" against him. The passage is also framed with reference to the astonishment of the people which, while falling short of positive commitment, indicates the extraordinary nature of Jesus' ministry.

Since this is Luke's first account of an exorcism, he uses an (unusual) expression which introduces his range of vocabulary for such a situation (v 33, "spirit of an unclean demon"). This spirit is described in very different terms than the "Holy" Spirit with which Jesus has been anointed and in whose power he now carries out his ministry (3:22; 4:1,14,18). The word "us" may reflect the man's total possession by the demon so that the destruction of one would entail the destruction of the other. Alternatively, the destruction of this one demon may be seen as an assault against demonic forces in general, as a declaration of war by God's kingdom on Satan's kingdom (cf 11:14–22). The demon's recognition that "Jesus of Nazareth" is also the "Holy One of God" (cf 1:35; Acts 3:14; 4:27,30) contrasts with the people's lack of perception regarding Jesus' true identity (cf also v 41). The term "rebuked" (v 35) is often used of Jesus' conquest of demons, disease and even hostile natural forces (eg v 39,41; 8:24). The demon tries to control the situation (v 34a, "Let us alone!"), but Jesus demonstrates his authority over the demon by silencing it. This act of silencing may also reflect Jesus' concern that no one conclude from the demon's positive identification of him that Jesus himself is in fact on the side of Satan. Again, this 'messianic secret' motif (cf v 41) may be due to Jesus' desire to distance his own mission from popular misunderstandings of Messiahship. For him, this mission

The Gospel of Luke

involves suffering and death as well as healings and exorcisms and this must be made clear before his true identity is publicly announced. That the demon's expulsion has no harmful effects on its victim, points to the complete restoration that Jesus has brought.

Tasks

a *Comment on the relevance of 4:18–19 to 4:31–37.*
b *How does the structure of the story help us see its main point?*
c *Outline your knowledge and understanding of the narrative details.*

Simon Peter's mother-in-law (4:38–39)

The scene changes from a synagogue to a home – specifically the home of Simon Peter, who will later be introduced as Jesus' leading disciple (5:1ff; 6:12–16). That his mother-in-law resides with him implies that she is a widow without sons to support her. Unlike the other synoptics Luke says she has a "high" (literally 'great') fever, which is consistent with the usual medical terminology. However, the description may highlight the extent of the ailment in order to underline the extent of the miracle. While the other synoptics refer to physical contact (cf v 40), Luke says that Jesus "stood/bent over" (author's translation) the woman, reflecting his authority over the ailment. This posture and the use of the word "rebuked" imply that an exorcism is taking place (as in the immediately preceding passage), although this is not specifically stated. No physical illness is mentioned in the preceding exorcism and no demon possession is mentioned in the healing in our present passage (cf v 40–41). Nevertheless, the two are connected (cf 11:14; 13:10ff) and, in general in Luke, physical ailments are apparently viewed ultimately as the result of satanic oppression (Acts 10:38). As the demon left the man at Jesus' rebuke (v 35), so with the woman's fever. Thus, hard on the heels of Jesus' self-referential use of Isaiah (4:18–19), Luke provides a second example of its outworking in his ministry. Unlike the parallel accounts, Luke stresses the immediacy of Jesus' healing of the woman. That she then "serve[s]" them (cf 10:40) demonstrates the reality of the miracle, but also reflects more generally the language of discipleship (eg 8:1–3; 12:37; 22:26–27).

Tasks

a *Discuss the relation between demon possession and illness in Luke.*
b *Comment on the relevance of 4:18–19 to this passage.*
c *Outline your knowledge and understanding of the narrative details.*

The miraculous catch of fish (5:1–11)

This is the first of three nature miracles in Luke. The context of the present miracle finds Jesus teaching, not now indoors in a synagogue (4:16ff,31,44) but outdoors by the "lake of Gennesaret" (only Luke refers to this region this way; never, as the other evangelists do, the "Sea of Galilee"). The crowds want to hear "the word of God", a regular term in Luke–Acts (eg 8:11,21; 11:28; Acts 4:31; 6:2,7), which implies that Jesus is a prophet (cf 1 Sam 9:27). Here, it refers to "the good news of the kingdom of God" (4:43). The pressure of the crowd causes Jesus to commandeer one of two fishing boats by the lake, from which to teach. The boats are not in use since the fishermen are washing their nets, probably 'trammel' nets which were used at night when they were not visible to the fish and then washed in the morning.

The focus in the passage is on Simon Peter, as Jesus teaches from his boat and asks him to push it out a little. The miracle itself has several similarities with a post-resurrection miracle in John (21:1ff) and some think that Luke has relocated it to Jesus' pre-resurrection ministry. Others think that John is the one who has moved the story, while some, noting differences, hold that the two episodes are distinct. Peter, addressing Jesus as "Master" (Greek *epistates*; seven times in Luke and unique to this Gospel), states why he thinks Jesus' plan will be unsuccessful, but submits to Jesus' command instructing him and his companions to go fishing again (cf 1:34,38). Peter's statement that they have worked all night and caught nothing serves to highlight the extent of the miracle – under the weight of the catch the nets start to break and the two boats start to sink. The contrast is notable between toiling all night with no catch and one attempt resulting in a massive haul.

Peter's response to the miracle is one of humility and a sense of personal unworthiness, expressed physically in his posture (v 8a; cf 22:41; Acts 7:60; 9:40) and verbally in his confession (v 8b; cf 7:6–7; 18:13). Now he addresses Jesus as "Lord" which, in light of the miracle, is probably more than a mere courtesy. His request that Jesus depart contrasts with previous attempts of the crowds to prevent Jesus' departure (4:42). The reason for Peter's request is a sense of sinfulness, apparently caused by the obvious presence of divine activity in the miracle (v 9). While it has been suggested that Peter's reaction is but the superstition of a fisherman who has just witnessed unusual activity in the lake, it is more likely that this is another example of the effect of a divine revelation (cf Ex 3:5–6; Isa 6:5). Indeed, similarities have been noted between this section of our passage (v 4–10) and Isaiah 6:1–10; both include a divine revelation, a response of unworthiness, a word of reassurance and a concluding commission. Luke also mentions, as an effect of the miracle, the amazement of Peter along with the brothers James and John, his fishing "partners". Jesus turns the miracle into a metaphor with his pun about "catching people" (v 10). Thus, this miracle becomes an acted parable or a parabolic miracle, symbolising the Church's mission – its own missionary labours will prove ineffective (v 5a), but at the powerful word of Jesus (v 5b) the success of the mission is assured (v 6ff). "From now on" (v 10; representing a turning point in Luke, eg 1:48; 12:52) the nature of Peter's fishing will be very different – to 'catch alive' (as the Greek verb means) people for God's kingdom. In the Old Testament, fishing was often used as a metaphor for God's judgement (eg Jer 16:16; Am 4:2), but here rescue is in mind (cf 3:6; 4:18–19). This new task involves the others as well, for they all "left everything" (their boats, the huge catch, family) and "followed him" (the negative and positive sides of discipleship). In this way, Jesus enlists others in his mission of proclaiming the good news of God's kingdom (4:43).

Outline your knowledge and understanding of this passage, with particular reference to its parabolic function.

The man with leprosy (5:12–16)

Reference should be made to 17:11–19 and the accompanying notes (pp134–136) for much of the current passage, particularly the nature and effects of 'leprosy', Old Testament background and regulations, and the implications for Jesus' identity (cf 7:18–23). Lepers were normally excluded from urban centres, so the presence of this leper in such a place may indicate local flexibility in the application of the rules, or this individual's resolve to be cured. Of the synoptics, only Luke states that the man is "covered" (literally 'full') in leprosy, which highlights the extent of Jesus' miracle. The leper's approach, posture, plea and choice of words reflect his humility and helplessness on the one hand and Jesus' superiority and authority on the other. The passage's emphasis on "cleansing" points to the ritual impurity or defilement connected with this condition. Jesus' act in stretching out his hand and touching the leper presents Jesus as one who crosses boundaries and touches the 'untouchables'. He has come to release the oppressed and proclaim the time of God's favour (4:18–19) to those who are socially and religiously excluded. The rejected are now accepted; the excluded are now included. However, while seeming to disregard recklessly the Mosaic requirement for segregation of lepers (Lev 13:45–46), Jesus still demands compliance with the same Law in regard to consultation with the priest and the need for an offering (Lev 14). As previously (4:39), the healing is immediate. Jesus' demand for silence (v 14; see comment on 4:35, p207) does not prevent ever-increasing publicity. The passage concludes by noting that Jesus' ministry combines word and deed (v 15; cf 4:32,36) and is marked by private prayer (v 16).

a Comment on the nature and effects of this man's condition.
b Discuss what this incident tells us about Jesus and his ministry.
c Outline your knowledge and understanding of the narrative details.

The paralysed man (5:17–26)

With this passage Luke introduces for the first time the Pharisees and teachers of the Law (for details see comment on 11:37ff,45ff; pp99–101), Jewish religious leaders concerned primarily with the proper interpretation and implementation of the Law. That this delegation represents every community in the land, including Jerusalem itself, indicates its formal character. Their "sitting" (v 17) seems to be more than just the normal posture for teaching (eg 4:20); rather the unfolding narrative reveals that they are actually sitting in judgement on this rival teacher (v 17). Indeed, this is the first of five consecutive episodes of conflict between Jesus and Jewish religious leaders (see also 5:27–6:11). Luke alone of the synoptics mentions in our passage that "the power of the Lord" is there, enabling Jesus to heal, recalling that the effectiveness of his ministry is due to his anointing with God's Spirit (3:22; 4:1,14,18ff; Acts 10:38) and that his miracles are acts of God worked through him as a divine agent (cf also Acts 2:22). The man in need of Jesus' healing is paralysed and, as such, is dependent on others for his survival (cf Acts 3:2). Such people were excluded from the Jewish priesthood (Lev 21:16–23). Luke alone uses a term for this man's condition (v 18,24) that was also used in medical literature (also in Acts 8:7; 9:33; and elsewhere in the NT only in Heb 12:12). Elsewhere Luke uses a more general term for the lame (eg 14:13,21). The first obstacle to Jesus that the man's companions meet is "the crowd" (cf 19:3), but, undeterred, they imaginatively find a way round the obstacle, so determined are they to get to Jesus (cf 19:4). They let their friend down through the flat clay roof of the house, right in front of Jesus. Only Luke mentions roof "tiles" (v 19) and it is often argued that this is an inaccurate accommodation to his non-Palestinian readership. However, some hold that tiled roofs did exist in Palestine and that, regardless, the word Luke uses (*keramos*) can mean 'clay' (as in 2 Sam 17:28). In this view, the plural would refer to pieces of clay removed to gain access.

For the first time in Luke we have the word "faith" – a recurring theme in Jesus' ministry in general and in his miracles in particular (eg 7:9,47–50; 8:48; 17:19; 18:42). It is the faith of the man's friends, as well as that of (presumably) the man himself, that Jesus responds to. Jesus' reference to the man's "sins" brings a new element into the episode. While sickness, disability and tragedy are sometimes regarded as the result of personal sin (eg 1:20; Acts 13:8ff; I Cor 11:30; Jas 5:15–16; compare paralysis in 1 Macc 9:54–55), this linkage is not to be assumed (cf 13:1–5; Jn 9:2–3; Job). The thought may be more in terms of sin as the ultimate, general cause of imperfection in creation, although Jesus does refer to the sins of the paralysed man ("your sins"). Forgiveness of sins is of course a Lucan theme and an expected blessing of the new age of salvation (1:76–77; Acts 5:31). The word 'forgive' (v 20) is in the passive voice (indicating that the forgiveness is from God) and the perfect tense (in the Greek, "have been forgiven") which may imply God's previous forgiveness of the man's sins, which Jesus is authorised to declare.

The Jewish leaders represent the second obstacle to the man's restoration as they charge Jesus with "blasphemies" (see comment on 12:10, p102) for apparently taking to himself the uniquely divine privilege of pardon, although God's forgiveness could be communicated through human agents (cf 2 Sam 12:13; Isa 40:1–2). Jesus exposes the thoughts in their hearts (cf 2:35). He then demonstrates that the "Son of Man" (first occurrence in Luke; see comment on 9:58, p79) has "authority" (from God; Dan 7:13–14) "on earth" (cf 2:14) to forgive sins. The logic of the demonstration is that it is harder to do something that can be visually confirmed (heal paralysis) than to say something that cannot be visually confirmed (forgive sins). If Jesus can do the former then his opponents should accept that he can do the latter – his words are verified by his deeds. In Jesus' ministry there is from God both power to heal (v 17) and authority to forgive (v 24). The man has been both physically and spiritually restored. His instant healing is confirmed by his standing upright, gathering of his mat and journey home. This also verifies that his sins are forgiven by God. Thus, we have another instance of God's anointed one bringing release to the captives (4:18; in the Greek here, twice we have the noun form of the verb translated "forgive" in our present passage). Moreover, for Jesus, the lame walking is a sign that he is the one who was to come (7:20–22). The passage concludes by noting various typical responses to a miracle, including amazement, awe and glory to God (twice; unique to Luke is the healed man's glorifying of God). The climactic line of the account is the general statement that "unexpected things" (author's translation; Greek *paradoxa*) have been witnessed. Characteristically, only Luke has the word "today' in this statement (cf eg 2:11; 4:21) – the blessings of God's salvation are presently available and observable in the ministry of Jesus.

Task

Outline your knowledge and understanding of this passage, focusing on the role of its various characters: the Jewish leaders, the paralysed man and his companions, Jesus, and the crowd.

The man with the withered hand (6:6–11)

This passage is the last of five consecutive accounts of Jesus in conflict with Jewish religious leaders (5:17–6:11). It is closely linked with the one immediately before it (6:1–5), both focusing on the issue of what is "lawful" (v 2,9) on the Sabbath. Jesus had taught in a synagogue on the Sabbath before and had worked a miracle on one such occasion, without any controversy (see comment on 4:31–37, pp207–208). However, word of his ministry is spreading (4:37) and, crucially, the Jewish religious leadership is taking notice (5:17ff). The scribes and Pharisees (see comment on 11:37,45, pp99–101) are monitoring him to see if they can bring charges of violating the Sabbath against him. The possibility of such violation exists for them because of the presence of a man in need of healing. Only Luke of the synoptics mentions that it is the man's "right" hand that is shrivelled (cf 22:50, also unique among the synoptics). This heightens awareness of the man's need in that it probably had been his strongest hand. As far as the watching leaders are concerned any attempt by Jesus to heal this man, whose condition is not urgent, on the Sabbath would be an infringement of the Sabbath commandment (Ex 20:8-11/ Deut 5:12-15).

Knowing their thoughts (cf 2:35; 5:22), Jesus tells the man to stand in a prominent position. This makes him, and thus human need, the focus of the congregation and also an object lesson (cf 9:47). Luke alone slows down the narrative pace a little to build suspense, by describing how the man does exactly as he is told (v 8; cf 4:17,20). Then Jesus, unlike the immediately preceding Sabbath debate, takes the initiative in raising the matter. He confronts the leaders' prioritising of Sabbath regulations over human need with a question that focuses on the latter (cf 14:1-6). Jesus has come "to save" (cf 2:11; 19:10) and this is the 'today' of God's salvation (2:11; 4:21; 5:26), even (especially?) on the Sabbath. The passage began with the leaders watching Jesus (v 7), but now it is he who is looking round at them (v 10). The man stretches out his hand, perhaps in obedient faith, and it is restored. Thus, the liberating mission of God's anointed continues (4:18-19). In this episode Jesus confirms what he had just stated in the previous passage – "The Son of Man is lord of the sabbath" (v 5; cf 5:24). The concluding response is not, as in previous miracles, one of praise or wonder, but rather of fury and conspiracy against Jesus on the part of the leaders (cf 19:48). They are the legitimate teachers of Israel and this subversive newcomer must not be allowed to challenge their position.

Outline your knowledge and understanding of this passage, with particular reference to its contrasting views of the Sabbath.

The centurion's servant (7:1-10)

This story is also found in Matthew (8:5-13), in which there are no delegations and the centurion meets with Jesus face to face. A similar story, yet with substantial differences, is recorded in John (4:46-54). Here we see that God's salvation in the ministry of Jesus extends beyond Israel to the Gentiles (v 9; cf 2:29-32; 3:6). Indeed, there are notable similarities between this passage and the story of the healing of the Gentile soldier Naaman (2 Kings 5), already referred to in Luke (4:27) – Naaman was highly valued by his master, Jewish pleas were made for his healing, Naaman did not meet Elisha, and the healing occurred at a distance. Precedent from the Jewish Scriptures, then, is implied for Jesus' (and the Church's) concern for the Gentiles.

The Gentile centurion is a Roman commander in charge of around 100 soldiers. His terminally ill slave is highly valued by him, probably for more than just his service, but also as a trusted friend. Presumably having heard of Jesus' previous miracles in Capernaum (4:23,31ff), the centurion sends some of the local Jewish council to Jesus, possibly respecting Jewish sensibilities about contact with Gentiles, not least with one of the occupying forces. The Jewish elders characterise the centurion as a patron and benefactor of the local Jewish community. According to the social conventions of patronage, he has placed them, as his clients, in his debt and under obligation to him. Therefore, "He is worthy" of Jesus' help, since he loves the Jewish people and built their local synagogue (cf 4:31ff). He may be a 'God-fearer', one of the Gentile semi-converts to Judaism that Luke will often mention in Acts (eg chs 10–11, another centurion, Cornelius), but the language here does not demand this. There is literary evidence from the time of such Gentile generosity to Jews, not least an inscription concerning the Gentile erection of a Jewish place of prayer[1]. Indeed, the Emperor Augustus saw synagogues as useful for preserving social order and morals[2], so a political motivation for the centurion's generosity is also possible.

Although Jesus does not share the norms of the patron–client system within which the Jewish elders appear to operate (cf 6:27–38), he starts out with them for the centurion's house. This very act implies that neither did he share the traditional Jewish reluctance to enter a Gentile home (cf Acts 10:28; 11:3). The journey is interrupted by a second delegation from the centurion – this time his "friends", who may be expected to be more his equal than the client Jewish elders and who may more accurately represent the centurion's position. Indeed, there is a marked contrast between the elders' view ("He is worthy") and the centurion's own view ("I am not worthy") as conveyed by his friends. Luke told us that the centurion wanted Jesus to come to his home (v 3), so we must assume that he had a change of heart, for now he feels unworthy of this (cf 3:16; 15:19,21) and of even meeting Jesus (v 7; but compare Matthew's account). The centurion draws an analogy between his ability to issue effective orders and Jesus' effective word (cf 4:32,36,39; 5:5ff,23ff), even when spoken at a distance. As the centurion is "under authority", so "also" (v 8) Jesus serves and represents God – the centurion has Rome behind him, but Jesus acts on heaven's authority. Jesus is "amazed", which is normally the reaction of others when he performs a miracle (eg 4:36; 5:9,26). Indeed, this is one of only two occasions in the Gospels where we read of Jesus' amazement (cf Mk 6:6, for the opposite reason!). He turns, a term which in Luke often introduces an important statement or action (eg 7:44; 9:55), and addresses the crowd, whose presence is only mentioned now to add dramatic effect to the climactic announcement of this story. Ironically, a Gentile has a faith which is unrivalled even in Israel. The importance of faith in the miracle stories is highlighted again (see comment on 5:20, p211). A Gentile recognises Jesus' authority, whereas Israel's leaders do not (cf 5:21,24; 6:5,7,11; 20:1ff). Consequently, it is underlined once more that God's approval is not a matter of ethnic privilege (3:7–9; Acts 10:34–35). Finally, the centurion's faith is rewarded and Jesus' authority confirmed by the discovery that the servant has been restored to health.

---

[1] Fitzmyer, *The Gospel According to Luke I–IX* (op cit), p652
[2] So Josephus, *Antiquities* 16.6.2 162–165; 19.6.3 300–311

Task

Outline your knowledge and understanding of this passage, with particular reference to the perspectives of its main characters: the Jewish elders, the Roman centurion, and Jesus.

The widow's son (7:11–17)

This is the first of two raisings from the dead performed by Jesus in Luke (also 8:40–42,49–56), and is found only in this Gospel. Along with the immediately preceding passage, it is another example of Luke's gender balancing through the use of male–female pairings (eg 4:25–27; 15:3–10). However, the contrast is more than one of gender. The centurion is a man of rank and wealth (v 5) while the woman is a now childless widow and, therefore, destitute. He was losing a servant while she has lost her only son. Important Old Testament background for this story is the account of the prophet Elijah and his involvement in the raising of another widow's only son (1 Kings 17:8–24; compare also Elisha in 2 Kings 4:18–37). Other similarities here include Elijah's meeting of the widow at the town gate and the return of the raised son to his mother. The connection is strengthened by Jesus' previous reference to this story (4:24–26, again unique to Luke) and the acclamation of Jesus as "A great prophet" within the story itself (v 16). Thus, clearly Luke's prophet-Christology (cf 24:19; see also p31) is to the fore in this episode. However, there is an unequal parallelism with Elijah, seen in significant differences between the two passages. Luke refers to Jesus' "compassion" and his raising of the young man by the power of his word to the corpse rather than, as in Elijah's case, by pleading with God in prayer (cf Acts 9:40) and physical ritual (cf Acts 20:10). Indeed, while in the Elijah passage it is God who raises the dead, here it is Jesus who does so directly and is also called "the Lord" (v 13). Also important for understanding our passage is the immediately following passage, in which raising the dead is listed by Jesus as a sign that he is the one who was to come (v 20–22).

The town of Nain in Galilee lay about six miles south-east of Nazareth. Two large crowds meet at the town gate – those accompanying Jesus (including his disciples) and the mourners in the funeral procession. The dire extent of the woman's situation is underlined in two ways – she is "a widow" and she has just lost her "only" son (both being Lucan concerns; see Women and Children, p37). Later we are told that he was young. Without any male family member left, she has now become economically destitute and socially marginalised. However, it is specifically to "the poor" (another Lucan concern; see The poor, pp36–37) that Jesus has come with the "good news" (v 22; 4:18). Jesus' "compassion" for the visibly grieving widow is noted as a motive for the miracle and only here in Luke do we read this of Jesus. The reference to compassion is at the centre point of the story, as is also the case in

The Gospel of Luke

both the other places where the Greek word occurs in Luke (both parables: 10:33 and 15:20). Notable too is the fact that in all these three occurrences the compassion is the result of sight. Luke characteristically refers to Jesus as "the Lord" as he narrates (see p30), an appropriate term in light of what follows. The Lord tells the widow not to weep (cf 6:21) and brings the funeral procession to a halt by touching the wooden plank on which the corpse was being carried. This latter act would have compromised Jesus' ritual purity (cf Num 19:11–22), but Luke has already shown that he is more concerned with human need (5:12ff). Jesus' powerful word (compare discussion of v 7, p214) brings the corpse to life (cf 8:54–55), evidenced by the son's sitting upright and speaking (cf 8:55; Acts 9:40–41). Like Elijah before him (1 Kings 17:23) Jesus then returns the son to his mother, who herself can now live again.

Typically, this miracle account includes and concludes with responses (v 16–17), here made by the two large crowds which have converged at the town gate (v 11–12). Characteristically, there is fear or awe (cf 5:26), glory to God (cf 5:25–26) and publicity (cf 4:37; 5:15; we note in v 17 Luke's broad use of Judea, see Palestinian geography, p45). The people also interpret the significance of the miracle with two statements. First, Jesus is acclaimed as a "great prophet", the *adjective* recalling Gabriel's prophecy (1:32) and the *noun* the Elijah background of the event as well as Luke's general presentation of Jesus as God's prophet (see Prophet, p31). Second, the people proclaim that in this miracle God has "looked favourably on/visited" (author's translation) his people, recalling Zechariah's song (1:68,78, where the same Greek verb is used in both verses).

Task

Outline your knowledge and understanding of this passage, with particular reference to its Old Testament background, its presentation of Jesus, and its distinctive Lucan emphases.

Calming the storm (8:22–25)

This is the first of four consecutive miracles in Luke 8. The first two (the calming of the storm and the exorcism of the demoniac) parallel each other to some extent with, for example, detailed accounts of the problem Jesus encounters, the power of his word over hostile forces, the resulting calm and order that he brings, and the reaction of fear. This is Luke's second nature miracle, the first also occurring on this lake (5:1–11). Then too Jesus displayed his power over the sea (the miraculous catch of fish), was addressed as "Master", and brought fear and amazement to his disciples. The storm is described in vivid terms and appears to have been sudden and dramatic. Such a storm is explained by the topography of Lake Galilee, being about 700 feet (213 metres) below sea level and surrounded by hills. Cool air would have swept rapidly down the hills and collided with warm air at the lake, producing a sudden storm which was then contained by the surrounding hills. Even though some of the disciples are fishermen familiar with the conditions of the lake (cf 5:1ff), it appears to them that they are in a life-threatening situation (v 24). Their vocal panic contrasts with Jesus' quiet sleep. They address Jesus as "Master, Master", and here Luke uses a favourite word only found in his Gospel in the New Testament, always in miraculous contexts (seven times: twice here and 5:5; 8:45; 9:33,49; 17:13). The title reflects Jesus' leadership of the group and is also appropriate in light of what follows.

The terms used to describe Jesus' calming of the storm (v 24, rebuke; v 25, command) may imply that the storm is demonic and that its conquest is an exorcism (cf 4:35–36), reflecting similar Old Testament ideas concerning the demonic sea (cf Ps 74:12–14; 89:8–10). However, there is no explicit demonic vocabulary in the passage. Rather, the language (particularly "rebuked") recalls the God of Israel's power over the hostile sea (eg Ps 65:7; 104:7; 106:9; 107:23–32; Nah 1:4). Thus, in controlling the sea Jesus is acting as God did in Israel's past, not least in the Exodus under Moses (Ex 14:15–16), and in the entry to the Promised Land under Joshua (Josh 3:10–13; compare also Elijah in 2 Kings 2:8). Two Old Testament passages in particular share notable similarities with our passage – the story of Jonah (cf Jon 1:4–6,10–11,15–16) and the Lord's calming of a storm in Psalm 107 (cf v 23–32). Gentile readers of our passage may have recalled stories in their literature of the gods, emperors (eg Caligula), kings (eg Xerxes) and wise men (eg Apollonios of Tyana) exerting power over the sea, though no human appears to have used his own power directly.

Faced with their panic, Jesus challenges his disciples concerning the whereabouts of their "faith" (a regular theme in the miracle stories; compare discussion of 5:20, p211). Having already witnessed his power over the sea (5:1ff), they should have shown faith in the face of its hostility. Their faith was being tested, as Jesus had just taught them (v 13), and they appear to have failed the test (contrast Paul's faith in the midst of another Lucan storm, Acts 27:25). In a now familiar pattern in the miracle stories, they respond with fear and amazement and ask a question about the implications of this miracle for the identity of Jesus (v 25). The reader is left to ponder this question at the climactic conclusion of the story.

Outline your knowledge and understanding of this passage, with particular reference to its characterisation of Jesus and the disciples.

The Gerasene demoniac (8:26–39)

Having survived the storm, Jesus and his disciples arrive at the other side of the lake, "opposite Galilee". We have already noted that this and the previous miracle are linked by more than just being part of the same journey. There are manuscript variations concerning the name of the residents of the region in which this miracle occurs (v 26,37). Three options exist: *Gerasenes* (of the city of Gerasa, over 30 miles/ 48 kilometres south-east of the lake), *Gadarenes* (of the city of Gadara, over 5 miles/ 8 kilometres south-east of the lake) and *Gergesenes* (of the city of Gergesa, on the shore of the lake). Despite the distance of Gerasa from the lake, the best manuscripts read *Gerasenes* in Luke (and Mk 5:1), while in Matthew (8:28) the best reading is *Gadarenes* (there is evidence that the region extended to the lake). While some hold that the textual confusion points to a lack of local geographical/political knowledge on the part of the synoptic evangelists, it has been suggested that the reading in Luke and Mark reflects a regional use of Gerasa that extended to the lake or another Gerasa unknown to us. Matthew's reading has been viewed as an alternative designation for the region. What is clear is that, for the first and only time in Luke, Jesus has entered Gentile territory. Apart from the geographical information, this is evident in the mention of pig farming and the apparent indifference about ritual impurity from living among the tombs. Earlier parts of this Gospel have shown us that the Gentiles were not to be excluded from God's salvation (2:29–32; 3:6; 7:1ff).

The man Jesus meets is repeatedly and variously described throughout the account as demon-possessed (see pp84–85), the terms "demon" (both singular and plural) and "unclean spirit" being used. The personal and social effects of his demon-possession are outlined. Even though he is from the city, he is not socially fit to live in the community, having for a long time rejected the social decency that clothing provides. His home is therefore in the tombs, among death and decay, and for Jews a place with the potential for ritual impurity (Num 19:11ff). He has frequently experienced demonic seizures, and human attempts to contain him have proved futile. The demon has driven him to "deserted places" (v 29, author's translation), the favoured haunt of such spirits (cf 11:24).

At the sight of Jesus the man falls down before him, out of reverence or in submission, or possibly defensively in light of the exorcism. As in the previous exorcism (4:34), the demon inquires defensively through his victim what Jesus has to do with it and recognises something of his true identity. It calls him "Son of the Most High God", as Gabriel had prophesied (see comment on 1:32, pp53–54; "Most High" or literally "Highest" is a favourite Lucan term, and a term for Jesus' followers too – 6:35). The devil himself has already addressed Jesus as God's Son in Luke (4:3,9), and now his agent does the same. Similar language will also be used by another demoniac in Luke's sequel, referring to Paul and his companions as "slaves of the Most High God" (Acts 16:17). The demon here realises that in Jesus it has met superior power, since he is no less than the agent of the "Most High" God, who now authoritatively evicts the unclean spirit. For the demon, this is torment (v 28). The demon's sense of inferiority is seen also in the frequent references to its begging and pleading (v 28,31,32) with Jesus. Jesus' power over the demon is further seen in his ability to secure its name. Legion (Latin *legio*) was a military term for a unit of about 6,000 Roman troops, although the number varied (see 8:2 and 11:24–26 for concern with numbers of demons). The military language heightens the sense that a battle is being waged against Satan's kingdom (cf 11:17–23). Some have seen in the name for the demon and its transference to the pigs an insult to the occupying Romans, although this would not sit easily with Luke's apologetic concern for the Romans (see Political, pp23–24).

The demon, realising that it has met more than its match, seeks to negotiate a concession. It wants to avoid confinement in the "abyss" (v 31; Greek *abyssos*), the underworld and abode of the dead (cf Rev 9:1ff; 20:1ff). It is therefore given permission to enter a large herd (Mk 5:13 says it was about 2,000 strong) of pigs – "unclean" (v 29) demons entering "unclean" animals (15:15; Lev 11:7). Demon-possession proves destructive for the animals as for the man. However, unlike its former victim who only lived among the dead, it goes to death itself – the abyss that it has tried to avoid. It may be that the watery lake is not a place where the spirit can survive (see 11:24). The behaviour of the pigs serves as a confirmation that the exorcism has truly occurred. Josephus reports similar confirmation of an exorcism he witnessed, performed by a certain Eleazar who commanded the expelled demon to overturn a container of water placed nearby (*Ant* 8.46–48).

Those tending the pigs spread the word and a large number of witnesses gather to see a point-for-point reversal in the man's condition (v 34–35). Once untameable (v 29), he is now seated at Jesus' feet like a disciple learning from his teacher (cf 10:39; Acts 22:3). Once naked (v 27), he is now clothed. Once deranged (v 28), he is now in his right mind. He has been "healed" or, as the word is normally translated, "saved" (cf v 12). God's salvation has come, as had been prophesied (3:6). The Saviour (2:11) has come to save (19:10) and this is an example of his liberation of the captives for which he has been anointed (4:18–19; Acts 10:38). This exorcism demonstrates that the kingdom of God has arrived (11:20). However, the locals are gripped with great fear (v 35,37), but not, it seems, in awe of the miraculous and the divine (cf 5:8,26). They reject Jesus, asking him to leave their region. Luke does not say what motivates their fear and rejection of Jesus, though some have speculated that it has to do with economic loss (the pigs; cf Acts 16:16,19; 19:23ff) or the disturbing manifestation of supernatural power. Jesus does not stay where he is not welcome and returns to Galilee. While the locals ask Jesus to leave, the exorcised man begs that he might be with him, as part of the company of followers that travel with Jesus (cf 8:1–3; including others who have been exorcised). However, Jesus instructs the formerly homeless man to return home where, restored to community life, he is to bear witness to his divine deliverance. While Jesus' instruction is theocentric ("how much *God* has done"), the man's testimony is Christocentric ("how much *Jesus* had done"). Clearly there is a close association, though not identification, between God and his anointed agent, the bearer of his kingdom (4:18–19; 11:20). The man is instructed to do what Luke himself is now doing (v 39: "declare" and 1:1: "account" are related in the Greek). Indeed, the word that is used of the man's activity (v 39, "proclaim(ing)") is also used of Jesus and his apostles (cf v 1; 9:2).

The Gospel of Luke

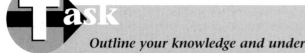

Task

Outline your knowledge and understanding of this passage, with particular reference to the nature of the exorcism, the transformation in the demoniac's condition, and the responses to Jesus.

A dead girl and a sick woman (8:40–56)

These last two miracles in the series of four in Luke 8 are climactic in that, while we began with Jesus rebuking the disciples for their lack of faith (v 25), we end with Jesus commending and rewarding faith (v 48,50,54ff). The two stories may be considered separately, but they are intertwined in our passage, not only as matter of historical reality (the woman is healed en route to the girl's home), but also at a literary level. That is, they are further linked by several common terms and themes – falling down before Jesus, daughter, 12 years, extreme need, purity issues, contact, fear, saving faith and instant healing. In addition, we appear to have here another example of Luke's male–female pairing (see comment on 7:11ff, pp215–216). The delay in Jesus' journey to tend to the dying girl also creates some dramatic tension and suspense for first-time readers of the story. Why is Jesus holding things up? Should the dying girl not be the priority? Will he get to her in time? In fact, as the narrative progresses it appears that he has not and that the delay has been unwise; that is, until the climax of the story reveals otherwise! We may note too that this is the second of Luke's two accounts of Jesus raising the dead (also 7:11–17; see The widow's son, pp215–216). Indeed, there are several links between the two passages – an only child, similarities with the corresponding Elijah passage (1 Kings 17:8–24), and Jesus' instruction not to weep.

The beginning of the passage contrasts notably with the conclusion of the previous one. On the other side of the lake the people had urged Jesus to leave, but here there is a welcome waiting for him from the crowd. There he was in Gentile territory unconcerned about Jewish purity laws (tombs, pigs); here it is obvious that we are in Jewish territory once again, as Jesus is immediately faced with a synagogue leader who would be concerned with the observance of Jewish Law (see comment on 13:14, pp110–111). Not for the first time in this chapter do we read of someone falling before Jesus (v 47; cf v 28; 5:8,12) and pleading with him (cf v 28,31–32,38), as Jairus approaches Jesus with humility and desperate urgency. His "only" daughter (see comment on 7:12, p215) is dying and she is only about 12 years old, approaching marriageable age in Jewish culture.

Without a word, Jesus makes for Jairus' home. The welcoming crowd (v 40) has now become "crowds" that exert an unwelcome pressure on Jesus upon his journey (v 42, "pressed" = "choked" in v 14 in the Greek). En route, someone among the crowds experiences Jesus' miraculous power. No doubt Luke is happy to record that this person is a woman, in light of his special concern for them (see Women, p37) in a culture where they were accorded low status. As long as Jairus' daughter has lived, this woman has suffered what is probably uterine bleeding. This physical condition has social consequences in that it has left her in a constant state of ritual impurity (Lev 15:19–31). It has also left her in a state of poverty, since she has spent all she has seeking an effective treatment from various doctors. Some of these may have been opportunistic frauds, but even genuine physicians could have proved very expensive. In view of the manuscript evidence, it may be that the reference to doctors here is not original to Luke. Even if it is, it does not paint as negative a picture of physicians as Mark's account does (5:26). It has been inferred, on the assumption that Luke wrote our Gospel, that "the beloved physician" (Col 4:14) had a more sympathetic view of his profession! The bottom line is that the woman is apparently incurable (v 43; cf v 29). She feels that Jesus can solve her problem, and decides to access his power covertly, approaching him from behind and using the pressing crowds as cover. The reason for such secrecy is that her very presence here represents a threat to those around her, in light of her contagious ritual impurity. Her anonymity therefore prevents public hostility, not least that of the synagogue leader. She touches the edge of Jesus' cloak, which may refer to the tassels that hung on the corners of the garment as a reminder of God's commandments (Num 15:37ff; Mt 23:5). As is typical in the miracle stories, the cure is immediate (v 44; repeated in v 47).

However, Jesus does not allow the woman to blend in with the crowd. His question as to who touched him brings from Peter a title that he used for Jesus in a previous miracle story, where he similarly drew attention to the apparent absurdity of what Jesus said (see comment on 5:5, p209). While various people in the thronging crowds may have been bumping into him, the physical contact of this one woman is consciously different because, motivated by faith, it draws "power" from Jesus (cf 5:17; 6:19). This has been viewed as a magical understanding of Jesus (cf Acts 5:15; 19:11–12), who has been likened here to a charged battery – his energy flow is triggered by faith. However, the context for Jesus' "power" in Luke is his anointing with God's Spirit (cf 3:22; 4:1,14,18; Acts 1:8; 10:38). By insisting that the woman reveal her identity, Jesus not only provides a public testimony to the instantly effective power of God's salvation in his ministry, in response to faith, but also restores the woman to normal community relations, since it is now clear that the reason for her social isolation (ritual impurity) is gone. Indeed, Jesus' address of her as "Daughter" may point to her full restoration to the community of God's people (cf 13:16; 19:9). Her falling before Jesus in humility echoes similar postures earlier in the chapter, especially that of Jairus (v 41; cf v 28). The importance of "faith" in the miracle stories is highlighted, and the words "saved" (in the Greek) and "peace" recall Lucan themes (v 48; cf 7:50).

The delay in Jesus' journey to Jairus' house, caused by the incident with the woman who touches him, means that the girl who was initially "dying" (v 42) is now "dead" (v 49). A messenger from Jairus' home bears the news and says that Jesus should not be "trouble[d]" (cf 7:6) any longer. His description of Jesus as "the teacher" is a courtesy title often used of Jesus by those who are not his disciples (cf 7:40; 10:25). The messenger clearly believes that the limits of Jesus' power have now been reached with the girl's death. Jesus urges that fear be replaced by faith and once again links faith and salvation (v 50; cf v 48). At the house Jesus allows only his three closest disciples (cf 9:28; Mk 14:33) and the girl's parents to enter. This seems to be part of the secrecy element of the narrative (cf v 56; see comment on 5:14, p210). While the demoniac in the immediately preceding passage had been told to publicise the miracle in Gentile territory, secrecy is required in a Jewish context where there are messianic expectations with which Jesus would not identify. The demand for secrecy contrasts with the insistence on openness concerning the woman who has just been healed.

Although we expect to be with the select few in the house, Luke has Jesus addressing the mourners; as previously, he has arranged the narrative for dramatic reasons (compare Mark's more logical ordering here, 5:37–40; see also Luke 8:28ff and 3:20–22 with parallels in Mark for similar reorganisation). The command not to weep recalls Jesus' raising of the widow's son (7:13) and is followed by his figurative use of 'sleep' for 'death'. She is dead, but not irreversibly, since Jesus' miracle will reveal her death to be as temporary as sleep, from which he will presently waken her. While no pastoral, post-Easter use is made of this in the passage, Christian readers will have (and will yet) read the resurrection hope in this incident. Jesus did promise that those who weep would laugh (6:21), but here the people's laughter is ridicule. Jesus' raising of the girl involves deed (physical contact) and word ("Child, arise", author's translation), the physical contact with the corpse compromising Jesus' ritual purity (see comment on 7:14, p216). Once again in this passage, the immediacy of Jesus' miraculous power is highlighted. The return of the girl's life ("spirit"; cf 23:46; Acts 7:59; I Kings 17:21) animates her, and her sitting upright and eating are tangible signs of her return from the dead (cf 24:41–43). The astonishment of her parents is another example of the amazement that Jesus' miracles generally cause (eg v 25). Elsewhere in Luke, Jesus points to his raising of the dead as a sign that he is the one who was to come (7:18–23).

Task

Outline your knowledge and understanding of this passage, with particular reference to the links that connect its two miracle stories, and the presence of Lucan themes.

The feeding of the five thousand (9:12–17)

This is the third and final nature miracle in Luke (also 5:1–11; 8:22–25), although it is not a typical miracle story in that, for example, no request is made for help and no response is made by those who witness it. From one angle, the suggestion of the twelve disciples (v 12) makes good sense. However, from the perspective of the passage's wider context it appears to reveal a lack of faith. When Jesus sent them out he told them to take no bread (v 3), apparently training them to trust in God for material provision (cf 12:22ff); yet now their request indicates a lack of thought for such divine providence. Further, some of them have already witnessed Jesus' miraculous ability to provide abundant food in the most unlikely of circumstances (5:1–11), yet they do not turn to him and ask for his provision now. Again, knowledge of Israel's Scriptures should make them aware of God's miraculous provision of food in the past. In particular, two incidents seem to provide the background for the present miracle. First, through the prophet Elisha, 100 men were fed with 20 loaves, with some left over (2 Kings 4:42–44). We have already noticed parallels between Elisha and Jesus in Luke (4:24,27). Thus, our passage may serve to underline Luke's prophet-Christology (see p31; at the end of John's account of this miracle, the people speak of Jesus as the expected prophet, 6:14). Second, our miracle recalls God's provision of manna in the desert for Israel at the time of Moses (Ex 16). This connection is strengthened by the detail that the five thousand are in a "deserted place" (v 12), and by the transfiguration story in the near context (v 28–36) with its reference to Moses and echoes of Sinai. There may be implicit Christology in our story here too, with Jesus being the new Moses, the new leader of God's people through whom God supplies their needs. Certainly, both before and after our passage there is a concern with the identity of Jesus (v 7–9,18–20). In light of all this then, the disciples' suggestion to Jesus does not seem to reflect well on them. Jesus puts the ball back into their court, so to speak (v 13), but again they focus on their own lack of adequate resources and even speak of purchasing food, despite Jesus' earlier instruction to take no money with them (v 3). It seems that Jesus is using this situation to test their faith (cf 8:13), and that they are not doing well.

Jesus then involves the Twelve in meeting the people's needs (cf v 1ff), as they arrange the large crowd into groups of about 50 each (so about 100 groups) and set the food before them, acting as good stewards or managers of their master's provision (cf 12:42–48). Jesus' four actions with the five loaves and two fish (taking, blessing, breaking and giving) will be repeated again at the Last Supper (22:19–20) and at Emmaus (24:30), for these were the usual actions performed at any Jewish meal – an acknowledgement of and thankfulness for God's provision of food (cf 11:3; 12:24). Thus, while some see Eucharistic significance in this miracle, there is nothing in the text that demands this interpretation. Meals in general, of course, are important in Luke and no less here (see p29). Without any apparent concern about rituals or conventions relating to meals as occasions of social exclusion (cf 5:30) and status indication (cf 14:7ff), Jesus provides for all of the huge gathering. Here we have an echo of Mary's song at the news of Jesus' coming birth, celebrating God's mercy as he "filled the hungry with good things" (1:53; cf v 17 of our passage). This is the kingdom of God in action, as "the hungry" are "filled" (cf 6:20–21; and references to the kingdom near our passage, v 2,11). Indeed, meals are symbolic of the future

The Gospel of Luke

kingdom of God in its fullness (cf 14:15ff). This miracle, then, is an acted parable (cf 5:1–11). No explanation is given of how such a small amount of food could have "filled" the five thousand, with leftovers remaining – the text presents the event as a miracle. That there are "twelve" baskets of leftovers is regarded by some as having no symbolic significance (as with the number of loaves and fish). However, repeated reference to the Twelve in the near context (v 1,10,12) seems to suggest otherwise. The passage thus begins and ends with reference to "twelve". The story that began with the apostles lacking faith in Jesus now ends with them experiencing his provision.

> **Task**
>
> *Outline your knowledge and understanding of this passage, with particular reference to its characterisation of Jesus and the Twelve, and its possible relevance for Christian readers.*

The demon-possessed boy (9:37–42)

The introduction to this passage links it to the account of Jesus' transfiguration, which it immediately follows. The day before, some of the Twelve had experienced an epiphany of Jesus' glory on the mountain, but here their descent from the mountain (v 37) is almost a metaphor for the harsh reality of earthly existence to which they now return. A man from among the great crowd that meets Jesus addresses him as "Teacher" (see comment on 8:49, p222) and pleads with him concerning the man's "only" son. We have already noted Luke's concern for the 'only' child (7:12; 8:42). Neither Mark (9:14–29) nor Matthew (17:14–21) mention in their parallel accounts that this is an only child (and the same holds in the story of Jairus' daughter). The man's plight is therefore heightened by the fact that the only heir to continue the family line is in a very vulnerable condition. This condition is graphically described, to indicate that it is a severe case. All the synoptic accounts present it as a case of demon possession (see comment on 10:17ff, pp84–85), but Matthew also refers to it as epilepsy (17:15) and the symptoms are consistent with this. The father is now begging Jesus to do something because he has already begged Jesus' disciples to exorcise the spirit, "but they could not". This is despite the fact that at the beginning of this chapter we read of how Jesus had given them power and authority over "all" demons, which must include the one that they are now incapable of expelling. They are now in the same category as the doctors who could not cure the sick woman in the previous chapter (8:43), yet soon they will try to hinder the work of effective exorcists (v 49–50)!

Jesus' response expresses a sense of frustration (v 41, "how much longer …?") at the unbelief and perversity of his generation (cf 11:29). The language echoes that of Moses concerning the children of Israel (Deut 32:4–5) and thus continues the new Moses/new Exodus theme of this chapter (see comment on v 12ff, pp222–223; also v 28ff). Jesus is apparently referring to his contemporaries in general, but also specifically to his disciples, whose failure to exorcise has just been raised by the boy's father. It is not that they have not been given the power and authority to exorcise (v 1), rather it is their lack of faith (v 41, "faithless"; cf 8:25) that accounts for their ineffectiveness. Jesus orders that the boy be brought to him and, as in previous exorcisms, the very presence of Jesus disturbs the demon (cf 4:33ff; 8:28ff). Also typical of such exorcisms is Jesus' effective rebuke of the demon (see comment on 4:35, p207). Jesus' successful exorcism of the demon and healing of the boy stands in contrast with the disciples' failure. His authority over demons is a sign that he is God's anointed who is bringing release to the oppressed (4:18–19; Acts 10:38), that he is the one who was to come (7:18–23), and that the kingdom of God has arrived in their midst (11:20). Jesus returns the boy to his father (cf 7:15) and the response of the crowd underlines, typically in Luke, the theocentric nature of the miracle – that is, "all" are astounded at *God's* "greatness/majesty" (author's translation; the same Greek word is used by Luke in Acts 19:27). Then in the next line we read that "all" are similarly amazed at "all" Jesus is doing (in the Greek). As we have noticed before, there is a close association between God and his anointed agent through whom the kingdom is coming (cf 8:39).

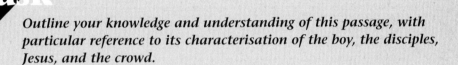

Outline your knowledge and understanding of this passage, with particular reference to its characterisation of the boy, the disciples, Jesus, and the crowd.

Having studied Luke's presentation of the miracles of Jesus we may make some general observations about their function, purpose and characteristics. First, we note that the synoptic miracle stories in general have a similar, almost stereotypical structure or pattern, though the common features and their arrangement may occasionally vary. We often read of:

- A plea made by a troubled person or his representatives, accompanied by falling to the knees
- The presence of hostile opponents
- Words of assurance and command by Jesus, sometimes accompanied by physical contact
- Instruction given to the persons benefiting from the miracle and/or their relatives
- Return of the person to their family or community
- Responses of wonder, praise, acclamation and publicity or, occasionally, of criticism and rejection

Usually the movement is from desperation through resolution to celebration.

In Luke the ministry of Jesus, including his miracles, is consciously set within the context of Isaiah's vision of a prophetic figure proclaiming "the year of the Lord's favour", the time of God's salvation (Lk 4:18–19, quoting Isa 61:1–2; 58:6). The background appears to be the "year of jubilee" when the people were liberated from slavery and debts every 50 years (Lev 25:8–17), which is now a metaphor for the prophet's announcement of God's deliverance of his needy people. Only in Luke does Jesus quote these words from Isaiah in the synagogue at Nazareth, where he had been brought up. The location of this event is significant in Luke, coming right at the beginning of Jesus' ministry as an outline of its program and significance. Luke expects his readers to understand the ministry of Jesus which immediately follows, including his miracles, in the light of Isaiah's words. Jesus comes as God's anointed prophet (cf 4:18,24) to proclaim good news to the poor, release for the captives, sight for the blind, and freedom for the oppressed – in short, to proclaim that the time of God's favour has arrived (cf "Today", author's translation, 2:10–14; 4:21). Certainly, in the miracles that follow we see the outworking of Isaiah's vision, as occasions when God favourably visits his people (cf 7:16). This sense of the 'today' of God's salvation is highlighted by the use of this favourite term of Luke's in connection with Jesus' miracles (5:26, absent in the synoptic parallel passages; see also 13:31–33). Thus, Luke's view of salvation history is apparent in this emphasis on the present deliverance of God's people. The ancient prophecies concerning God's coming salvation and vindication of his people are now being fulfilled in Jesus' ministry (see also Isa 29:18–19; 35:4–6; cf Lk 7:22).

This era of salvation is also known in the synoptic Gospels as the kingdom or reign of God (cf Lk 18:24–27), the main theme of Jesus' ministry (cf Lk 4:43; 8:1). Jesus' miracles, as well as the miraculous powers with which he gifts his apostles and others, are viewed as demonstrations of this royal power of God (see 6:18–21; 9:1–2,11; 10:9,11). This is particularly the case in regard to Jesus' exorcisms which are interpreted by him as the overthrow of Satan's kingdom and the establishment of God's kingdom in its place (see 11:14–23, especially v 20). Indeed, Jesus' healings in general are regarded as the conquest of God's reign over Satan's (cf 13:16; Acts 10:38). However, since God's kingdom would come fully and finally only in the future (eg 11:2), the miracles of Jesus are anticipations of the worldwide renewal which the future kingdom would usher in. In connection with the miracles as demonstrations of the presence of God's kingdom, we note the theocentric (God-centred) rather than Christocentric character of Luke's miracle stories. Thus, Jesus' miracles are the result of the "power" of his anointing with God's Spirit, received at the beginning of his ministry, working in and through him (see 3:22; 4:1,14,18ff; 5:17; 6:19; 8:46; Acts 2:22; 10:38). Consequently, God is praised and acknowledged in Luke's miracle stories more than in the other synoptics (see 5:25–26; 7:16; 8:39; 9:43; 13:13; 17:15,18; 18:43; 19:37). Related also to the theocentric character of Luke's miracle stories are his references to Jesus at prayer in connection with the miracles (5:16ff; 6:12–19). The implication is therefore that the miracles of Jesus flow from his prayerful dependence on God.

However, while Luke's miracle stories are clearly *theo*logical, they are also *Christo*logical, in that they also say something about Jesus himself. Indeed, one miracle at least causes the disciples to reflect on his identity (8:25). In this way, Luke's prophet-Christology (see p31) is reinforced in Jesus' miracles (4:16–30; 7:11–16; 24:19). We note too that when John the Baptist wants to know if Jesus is "the one who is to come", Jesus affirms that he is by listing a variety of his miraculous deeds (7:18–23; cf 3:15–17; see p72). While there is no clear pre-Christian evidence that Jews expected a miracle-working Messiah, it appears that some did regard Moses, the miracle-working deliverer of God's people, as a prototype of the Messiah (see also on 9:12–17, p223; Mk 13:21–22). The identity of Jesus is also of particular significance in his exorcisms (see comment on 4:34–35,41, pp207–208; and on 8:28, p218; Holy One of God; Son of God; Messiah/ Christ). Again, we note that Luke alone uses a term for Jesus (*epistates*: 'Master') that it is mostly found appropriately in his miracles (5:5; 8:24–25; 17:13; see also 9:33,49), and that in some miracles we find other favourite Lucan titles for Jesus ("the Lord", 7:13 and 13:15; "teacher", 8:49 and 9:38). We have noted too the compassion of Jesus the miracle worker (7:13), particularly in his concern for women (4:38–39; 8:43–48; 13:10–17), widows (7:11–17), the only child (7:12; 8:42; 9:38), Gentiles (7:1–10), Samaritans (17:11–19) and outcasts (5:12–16; 17:11–19; 8:26–39; 18:35–43). Here, of course, we see general concerns of Luke found throughout his Gospel.

Other characteristic Lucan themes and terms in the miracle stories include salvation (6:9; 8:36,48,50; 17:19; 18:42; all these verses have the Greek verb normally translated "save"), joy (13:17; 19:37), forgiveness (5:20,24) and peace (8:48). Of particular note in the miracle stories is the role of faith; the sick woman (8:48), the Samaritan leper (17:19) and the blind beggar (18:42) are all told by Jesus, "Your faith has saved you" in the Greek). Faith features in other Lucan miracle stories as well (5:20; 7:9; 8:25,50). Here, faith is consistently presented as the precondition and effective cause of the miraculous benefit. However, the miracles of Jesus also serve to encourage faith, providing divine authentication and approval of Jesus and his ministry[1] (cf 10:13; Acts 2:22). We note also Luke's emphasis on the immediacy of Jesus' miracles (4:39; 5:13,25; 8:44,47,55; 13:13; 18:43; where he mostly uses *parachrema*, which is used elsewhere in the Gospels only in Mt 21:19–20). Finally, Luke clearly has a preference for a particular Greek term for Jesus' healing activity in comparison with the other Gospels (Greek *iaomai*: 'to cure/heal, 5:17; 6:18–19; 7:7; 8:47; 9:2,11,42; 14:4; 17:15; 22:51; the verb is found four times in Matthew, once in Mark and three times in John).

> **Task**
>
> *Outline your knowledge and understanding of the characteristics and functions of Jesus' miracles in Luke.*

---

[1] Achtemeier, PJ, *The Lukan Perspective on the Miracles of Jesus,* Journal of Biblical Literature 94, 1975, pp547–562; reprinted in *Perspectives on Luke–Acts,* ed CH Talbert, Danville, Virginia: Association of Baptist Professors of Religion/ Edinburgh: T&T Clark, 1978, pp152–167

Practice essay titles

1. (a) Outline your knowledge and understanding of the origin and types of the parables of Jesus in Luke. (30)

   (b) Assess the claim that Jesus taught in parables to conceal the message of God's kingdom. (15)

2. (a) Outline your knowledge and understanding of **either** the parable of the lost son **or** the parable of the Pharisee and the tax collector. (30)

   (b) Explore the claim that each parable of Jesus makes only one main point. (15)

3. (a) Outline your knowledge and understanding of the characteristics of Jesus' miracles in Luke. (30)

   (b) Assess the claim that Luke's miracle stories serve several purposes. (15)

4. (a) Outline your knowledge and understanding of **either** the healing of the centurion's servant **or** the calming of the storm. (30)

   (b) Explore the claim that faith is essential in Luke's miracle stories. (15)

Christianity according to Luke[1]

SALVATION HISTORY

THE TERM 'SALVATION HISTORY' refers to the idea that human history is ordered by a divine plan according to which God acts in history in order to save people. This religious, as opposed to secular, interpretation of history is apparent throughout the Bible. The emphasis in the Old Testament falls on God acting in history to save the nation of Israel and in the New Testament on God acting in history to save all people through Jesus Christ. We have already seen the importance for Luke of both salvation (see Salvation, p34ff; review especially Luke's concept of Jesus as Saviour) and history (see History, pp27–28). We have also noted that Luke's religious view of history is apparent, in general, in his references to supernatural beings, forces and experiences – such as God, Satan, angels, demons, visions, prophecy and miracles (see p42). Particularly relevant to Luke's presentation of salvation history has been our consideration of the theocentric character of Luke, particularly its stress on God's purpose (see Theology, pp26–27). Also pertinent to our present topic has been our observation that, for Luke, history is not the mere chronicling of events; rather, he lets us know right at the start of his Gospel that he is concerned with "the events that have been *fulfilled* among us" (1:1). He presents his story of Jesus and the early Church as part of the flow of biblical history – that is, salvation history – connected with, and indeed the climax of, Israel's history and Scriptures, in accordance with the saving purpose of Israel's God (see Theological, pp22–23).

JA Fitzmyer identifies five elements in Luke's writings which indicate his view of salvation history[2]. First, there are references to God's plan or purpose, which is behind John's baptism, the crucifixion of Jesus and the message of the early Church, as it had been behind David's life many centuries before (Greek *boule*; see Lk 7:30; Acts 2:23; 4:28; 5:38–39; 13:36; 20:27). It is found also in Jesus' prayer on the eve of his crucifixion: "Father, if you are willing [Greek *boulei*], take this cup

---

[1] This is the title used in the CCEA Specification.
[2] Fitzmyer, *The Gospel According to Luke I–IX* (op cit), pp179–181

from me; nevertheless, not my will [Greek *thelema*] but yours be done" (22:42, author's translation; cf Acts 21:14). Second, Luke writes of certain things having been determined or ordained by God, such as the crucifixion of Jesus, his appointment as judge and Paul's missionary calling (see Lk 22:22; Acts 1:7; 10:42; 17:31; 22:14; 26:16). Third, there is regular reference to the necessity of certain things happening in relation to Jesus. This is evident in Luke's frequent use the Greek verb *dei* ('it is necessary/must'), of which about 40 per cent of the New Testament occurrences are found in Luke–Acts (see eg Lk 2:49; 4:43; 9:22; 17:25; 22:37; 24:7,25–27,44). Fourth, the idea of a divine plan of salvation is seen in the common theme of fulfilment or accomplishment, not only in relation to the Old Testament (cf Lk 4:21; 18:31; 22:37; 24:44), but also to events in the life of Jesus which are viewed as the completion of God's plan (cf Lk 1:1; 9:31; 12:50). Certainly, the Gospel's opening infancy narrative and its closing resurrection narrative locate the story of Jesus within the larger story of Israel, as the fulfilment of its hopes and history (eg 1:68–75; 2:29–32; 24:25–27,44–47). This sense of historical continuity and climax is reinforced in the preaching of, for example, Stephen and Paul in Acts (ch 7; 13:16–41). Fifth, in addition to the previous points which all suggest divine determinism in Jesus' life and ministry, there is a notable emphasis in Luke on salvation. This is apparent in his use of the title 'Saviour' for Jesus (2:11; unique among the synoptics) and his frequent use of the words 'save' and 'salvation' (eg 2:30; 3:6; 7:50; 19:9–10). Thus, the term 'salvation history' is particularly appropriate for Luke.

Some have exaggerated the importance of Luke in relation to the idea of salvation history by claiming that he, in fact, created or invented the concept (eg S Schulz). However, the notion is found elsewhere in the New Testament, such as in Matthew (eg 1:18–23; 4:12–17), John (eg 12:12–15,37–38) and Paul (eg Rom 10:4; 13:11–14)[1].

Tasks

a What is meant by the term 'salvation history'?

b Outline the evidence for such a concept in Luke.

One name that is particularly associated with salvation history in Luke is that of the German scholar Hans Conzelmann (1915–1989). As we have seen earlier (see Theological, pp22–23), Conzelmann argues that Luke's scheme of salvation history (German *heilsgeschichte*) was an attempt to deal with a crisis in the late first-century Church[2]. Initially, the Church expected an imminent return of Jesus, but as time progressed the delay of the *parousia* (ie of the 'coming' of Jesus) became a disillusioning embarrassment for the Church. Luke's solution, according to Conzelmann, was to revise his sources (eg Mark) by removing this early expectation of an imminent return of Jesus and replacing it with an ongoing salvation history,

---

[1] Fitzmyer, *The Gospel According to Luke I–IX* (op cit), pp19–20

[2] Conzelmann, *The Theology of St. Luke* (op cit)

which would conclude in the distant future where Luke had now pushed Jesus' Second Coming. Indeed, for Luke the coming of the Spirit is a substitute for the Second Coming of Jesus. While the earliest Christian belief was that the arrival of Jesus (his first coming followed almost immediately by his Second Coming) was, in fact, the end of time, Luke has placed Jesus in the 'middle of time'[1] by writing a sequel to his Gospel about the ongoing history of the Church. Thus, what was originally an eschatological (end time) event has been 'de-eschatologised' and historicised by Luke.

Conzelmann represents Luke's history of salvation as having three periods or phases:

- the period of Israel (from creation to John the Baptist's imprisonment; the time of prophecy and promise)
- the period of Jesus (the ministry of Jesus, from his baptism to his ascension; the time of fulfilment and salvation)
- the period of the Church (from Jesus' ascension to his *parousia*/coming, which Luke has now pushed into the distant future; the time of stress for the Church)

Conzelmann characterises the period of Jesus (the 'middle of time') as a Satan-free period, between the times Satan left him after his temptation (4:13) and returned to inspire Judas to betray him (22:3,53). Fitzmyer notes that three main passages in Luke were seen as supporting this scheme[2]:

- Luke 16:16, where we read that the Law and the Prophets (ie the Old Testament) were "until John" and "from then" (literally) the good news of God's kingdom is being proclaimed. Conzelmann takes "until" in an inclusive sense with the result that John is placed in the period of Israel (see notes on this verse, p75).
- Luke 22:35–37, in which Jesus tells the apostles that "now" each of them must acquire a purse, a bag and a sword, even though he had forbidden them to have such things in an earlier mission (10:4). Thus, the period of Jesus is "now" giving way to the period of the Church under stress, which would continue after Jesus' ascension (see notes on this passage, p159).
- Luke 4:21, where at the beginning of his ministry Jesus says of Isaiah 61:1–2, "*Today* this scripture is fulfilled in your hearing" (author's italics and translation). Thus, the period of Israel is concluded as its prophecies are coming to fulfilment with the commencement of the ministry of Jesus. Conzelmann notes Luke's emphasis on the beginning of Jesus' ministry and argues that this marked a definite and new stage in the history of salvation (see Lk 3:23; 23:5; Acts 1:1,22; 10:37; 13:23–25).

As Luke writes his Gospel and Acts towards the end of the first century, he is conscious that he is in the period of the Church, looking back to the period of Jesus, the period of salvation – the middle of time.

---

[1] This refers to the title of Conzelmann's book in the original German: *Die Mitte der Zeit*.
[2] Fitzmyer, *The Gospel According to Luke I–IX* (op cit), p182

Task

Outline Hans Conzelmann's understanding of salvation history in Luke.

Conzelmann's interpretation of salvation history in Luke has been both endorsed and criticised. Firstly, it is true that there does not seem to be the emphasis on the imminence of Jesus' return that we find in the other synoptics, that Luke's stress is on the present (see Eschatology, pp39–40), and that Luke wrote a history of the Church beyond Jesus' ascension. However, there is still evidence that Luke did expect an imminent return of Jesus, although there is also an awareness of an interval of time preceding this return. Unless it is held that these 'interval' passages are inventions of the early Church and the evangelists, it can be argued that talk of a crisis caused by a delay of the *parousia* misrepresents and exaggerates the situation in early Christianity. Indeed, Luke may have been seeking to correct two extremes concerning the *parousia* – an over-emphasis on either the delay or the imminence of Jesus' return. Alternatively, while conscious of the delay, Luke may have regarded the imminent return of Jesus as a possibility in his own day (on both these points, see Theological, pp22–23). Thus, eschatology and salvation history should not be regarded as mutually exclusive categories, with Luke substituting the latter for the former. The end time began with Jesus' first coming and continues in the interval between his ascension and *parousia*, in the history of the Church (cf Acts 2:16–17). Further, on this first main point, Conzelmann's idea of the coming of the Spirit as a substitute for the Second Coming of Jesus does not fit the evidence in Luke, since the Spirit is active in all three of the proposed periods of salvation history.

Difficulty has been found, secondly, with Conzelmann's division of Luke's salvation history into three distinct periods. It has been argued that this threefold periodisation does not arise naturally from Luke's own presentation of salvation history. While the crucial text of Luke 16:16 does indicate separate periods, mention is made of two rather than three. Nor is it clear from this text that John the Baptist belongs in the period of the Law and the Prophets, that is, Conzelmann's period of Israel. Indeed, a good case can be made for Luke having *two periods* in his scheme of salvation history – the period of prophecy/promise (the Old Testament/Israel) and the period of fulfilment and salvation (Jesus and the Church – all of Luke–Acts; for discussion of these issues in relation to Lk 16:16, see p75). Controversial too is Conzelmann's rejection of the infancy narratives (Lk 1–2) as Lucan, which allows him to exclude John the Baptist and the earlier life of Jesus from the time of fulfilment and salvation. Such exclusion is unacceptable when these narratives are regarded as relevant to Luke's presentation of salvation history. Also problematic is Conzelmann's characterisation of the period of Jesus as a Satan-free period. As with Luke 16:16, so 4:13 and 22:3,53 appear to be overinterpreted by being made to bear a significance that they do not demand. Indeed, on closer inspection this period turns out not to be free from satanic activity (cf 8:12; 10:17–18; 11:14–22; 13:11–17; 22:28). It has been noted too that the boundary line between Conzelmann's second and third periods is not clear (Satan's 'return' at Judas' betrayal? Jesus' ascension?). Again, the first verse of Acts may imply that the period of the Church is a continuation of the period of Jesus, since the latter is characterised as the beginning of his ministry – a ministry that he continues by his Spirit in the period of the Church (cf Acts 16:7). This too is the period of Jesus and his salvation (cf Acts 3:16; 4:12). However, even if Luke–Acts as a whole is viewed as one and the same period in Luke's understanding, his double mention of the ascension of Jesus (at the end of Luke and the start of Acts) does seem to imply a subdivision within this period. Certainly, the ascension of Jesus is of crucial Christological and salvation–historical significance for Luke (Acts 2:32–36).

Evaluate Hans Conzelmann's understanding of salvation history in Luke.

BIBLICAL CRITICISM

In the term 'biblical criticism' the word 'criticism' is not used in its popular sense of negative fault-finding. Rather, it is used in a formal, technical sense to refer to the process of the investigation and analysis of the biblical writings and all related matters in order to make intelligent decisions or judgements about them (compare Latin *criticus*: 'critic'; from Greek *krites*: 'judge'; Heb 4:12, *kritikos*: "able to judge"). The same idea is in view when we speak of the 'criticism' practised by various 'critics' in connection with literature, art, music and film.

In the past it was common in biblical studies to distinguish between 'lower' criticism, which was concerned with the reconstruction of the original text of the Bible (ie textual criticism), and 'higher' criticism, which related to matters such as date, authorship, sources, composition and purposes of the biblical writings (ie what are often termed introductory and background issues). The terms 'lower' and 'higher' here reflect an architectural metaphor – when the foundation of an accurate biblical text is first laid, then investigation of the other matters builds upon it. However, these terms are rarely used in biblical scholarship today. Rather, a variety of critical methods or interpretative techniques have developed as distinct strategies or tools with which to approach the biblical writings. The following criticisms have been applied to the Gospels:

- *Textual criticism* seeks to reconstruct the original text of the biblical writings (which no longer exists) by a study of the many diverse Greek manuscripts and other evidence that has survived.

- *Historical criticism* investigates the original historical context and meaning of the texts and thus overlaps with some of the criticisms listed here.

- *Tradition criticism* or tradition history is concerned with the historical development of traditions about Jesus during the oral period before the Gospels were written. It overlaps with form criticism (see below).
- *Source criticism* tries to identify the sources, oral and written, that the authors made use of in the composition of the Gospels (see p236ff).
- *Form criticism* categorises the various sayings and stories of the Gospels according to their form (eg prophetic sayings, parable stories) in order to discern their use and development in the Church during the period of oral tradition before the Gospels were written (see p246ff).
- *Redaction criticism* seeks to discover how the authors of the Gospels have redacted (ie edited) their sources to convey their own theological emphases (see p254ff).
- *Narrative criticism* analyses the Gospels as stories with narrative features such as structure, setting, plot, characters, audience and themes (see p260ff).
- *Rhetorical criticism* is related to narrative criticism and is concerned with the persuasive literary techniques (eg arrangement of content, figures of speech, key words) used by an author to make their work effective.
- *Canonical criticism* examines the Gospels in the context of their place in the Bible and relationship to its other books (ie the complete biblical canon).
- *Reader-response criticism* focuses on the act of reading and how it affects the interpretation of texts under the influence of the reader (eg background and biases).
- *Advocacy criticism* is a term sometimes used of approaches to the texts which advocate or promote a particular ideology or agenda, such as Liberation and feminist critics who are concerned respectively with injustices against the poor and women.
- *Social-scientific criticism* applies the insights of the social sciences (eg sociology, anthropology) to the texts, which are seen as both reflecting and addressing the social divisions and dynamics of their times.
- *Structuralism* is a very technical and complex form of literary criticism which investigates the deep (rather than surface) structures of the text (eg opposites such as good/bad, life/death) as the key to its meaning.
- *Post-structuralism* (sometimes called *deconstructionism*) approaches the Gospels with the view that all language and texts are unstable and have no inherent meaning.

Quite often these criticisms are categorised according to where their focus lies in relation to the text itself. Some are concerned with what lies *behind the text*, which is seen as a 'window' through which to look at its pre-history (eg historical, tradition, source and form criticisms); some work *within the text* itself, which is viewed as a 'portrait' to be looked at for itself (eg narrative and rhetorical criticisms); and some relate to what goes on *in front of the text*, which becomes a 'mirror' that reflects the readers' own concerns (eg reader-response criticism). However, this is only a general classification, since some criticisms cannot be confined within the boundaries of one category. Traditional biblical criticism has been concerned mostly with what lies *behind the texts* and is often referred to as the *historical-critical method*.

While many have generally welcomed biblical criticism, particularly in its more positive and constructive forms, others have argued that it is incompatible with, and even destructive of, historic Christianity's belief in the divine inspiration and reliability of the Bible. For example, in Germany Gerhard Maier has argued that the historical-critical method is incompatible with divine inspiration and revelation, and replaces them with human reason and experience[1]. Also in Germany, E Linnemann, a former practitioner of the historical-critical method, has stated that its secular presuppositions are inconsistent with a Christian view of the Bible and that its apparent advantages are as nothing compared with its dangers[2]. She argues that many of its so-called assured results are, on closer investigation, unproven hypotheses. Again, others have presented a case against historical criticism of the Gospels, viewing it as a denial of their historical reliability[3]. However, other scholars have seen no necessary incompatibility between responsible use of biblical criticism and traditional Christian belief in the divine inspiration of the Bible. Indeed, they argue that the human, historical and literary dimensions of the Bible require a proper use of biblical criticism[4].

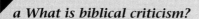

Tasks

*a **What is biblical criticism?***

*b **Comment on the distinction between 'lower' and 'higher' criticism.***

*c **In your own words, outline and explain the main types of Gospel criticism.***

*d **Discuss different attitudes to the appropriateness of biblical criticism.***

---

[1] Maier, Gerhard, *The End of the Historical-Critical Method,* trans EW Leverenz and RF Norden, St Louis: Concordia, 1977; German edition, 1974

[2] Linnemann, E, *Historical Criticism of the Bible: Methodology or Ideology?,* Grand Rapids, Michigan: Baker, 1990; *Biblical Criticism on Trial: How Scientific is 'Scientific Theology'?,* Grand Rapids, Michigan: Kregel, 2001; both translated by Robert Yarbrough

[3] Thomas, R, and D Farnell (eds), *The Jesus Crisis: The Inroads of Historical Criticism into Evangelical Scholarship*, Grand Rapids, Michigan: Kregel, 1998

[4] eg Ladd, GE, *The New Testament and Criticism,* Grand Rapids, Michigan: Eerdmans, 1967; Black, DA, and DS Dockery (eds), *Interpreting the New Testament: Essays on Method and Issues*, Grand Rapids, Michigan: Zondervan, 2001; Stein, *Studying the Synoptic Gospels* (op cit)

The Gospel of Luke

In this section we shall study source (including the Proto-Luke theory), form, redaction and narrative criticisms, focusing particularly on their relevance to the Gospel of Luke.

Source criticism

The problem

As noted on page 234, Gospel source critics seek to identify the sources used by the authors of the Gospels. It has long been observed that the synoptic Gospels in particular are both similar to, and different from, each other. This can be seen clearly and conveniently in a Gospel synopsis in which the contents of the Gospels are presented in parallel columns (see p15). Comparisons can also be made with a copy of the New Testament, preferably using one of the more literal or direct translations (eg NRSV). The attempt by source critics to account for both the similarities and the differences has been called the 'Synoptic Problem'.

Similarities

The synoptics are similar in the following ways:

- *Content* – they all present the ministry, death and resurrection of Jesus generally in a very similar way.

- *Wording* – there is often close verbal similarity in the authors' Greek and occasionally the wording is identical. This is apparent even in English translation. For example, compare the following parallel passages: Matthew 8:1–4, Mark 1:40–45 and Luke 5:12–16 (the healing of a leper). This includes even editorial comments (cf Mt 9:6/ Mk 2:10/ Lk 5:24 and Mk 5:8/ Lk 8:29) and quotations from the Old Testament in an unusual form (cf Mt 3:3/ Mk 1:2/ Lk 3:4).

- *Order* – the sequence of the stories is often the same or very similar (clearly visible in the index of a synopsis; cf Mt 12:46–13:58/ Mk 3:31–6:6/ Lk 8:19–56).

Differences

However, there are differences in these three areas too:

- *Content* – Matthew and Luke, in particular, have unique material (cf Mt 13:36–52; Lk 18:1–14).

- *Wording* – the wording of similar accounts differs in places (cf Mt 8:23–27/ Mk 4:35–41/ Lk 8:22–25).

- *Order* – the sequence of stories is not always the same. For example, the account of Jesus' rejection at Nazareth is at the start of Jesus' ministry in Luke (4:16–30), but is placed later by Matthew (13:53–58) and Mark (6:1–6).

Task
What factors give rise to the synoptic problem?

The solutions

Some have tried to explain the similarities and differences between the synoptics by arguing that the authors made *independent* use of a common oral or written source or sources, rather than there being any literary dependence among the synoptics themselves (ie they didn't make use of each other's Gospels). For example, in the eighteenth century JG Herder held that common oral tradition lay behind the synoptics, while GE Lessing thought that they depended on a common written source (an original Gospel). Thus, the similarities are explained by the common source material, while the differences are due to the synoptics' independent use of the material and/or variant forms of the material. However, while a few still argue for the literary independence of the synoptics[1], the vast majority of scholars argue for synoptic literary dependence. This is due to their substantial similarity in the three areas noted on page 236.

Three main solutions concerning the literary *interdependence* of the synoptics have been proposed:

The Augustinian hypothesis

The early Church Father Augustine (AD 354–430) held that the synoptics were composed in the order we have them in our New Testament, with each author making use of his predecessor(s) (Matthew > Mark > Luke). In modern times this view has been defended by BC Butler[2].

The Griesbach/two-Gospel hypothesis

In the late eighteenth century the German scholar JJ Griesbach reversed the order of Mark and Luke in the Augustinian hypothesis, arguing that Luke used Matthew, and that Mark made use of both of them (Matthew > Luke > Mark). It came to be known as the 'two-Gospel' hypothesis in distinction from the 'two-source' hypothesis (see below). In modern times this view has been defended especially by WR Farmer[3].

The two-source hypothesis

This view has been held by the majority of scholars since the early twentieth century and argues that Matthew and Luke independently used two sources – Mark and a

---

[1] eg Linnemann, E, *Is There a Synoptic Problem? Rethinking the Literary Dependence of the First Three Gospels,* Grand Rapids, Michigan: Baker, 1992; German original, 1992

[2] Butler, BC, *The Originality of St. Matthew: A Critique of the Two-Document Hypothesis,* Cambridge: CUP, 1951

[3] Farmer, *The Synoptic Problem: A Critical Analysis* (op cit)

hypothetical source which has been labelled Q (probably from the German word for source: *quelle*). Q refers to material which is common to Matthew and Luke, but not found in Mark. Thus, Mark is regarded as the first of the synoptics to be written (Marcan priority). In Germany, Karl Lachmann argued for Marcan priority in the 1830s and HJ Holtzmann developed the two-source hypothesis in the 1860s. In what has become a classic and fundamental work in Gospel source criticism, BH Streeter added two more sources to account for the unique material in Matthew (called M) and Luke (called L)[1]. This development of the two-source hypothesis is sometimes known as the four-source hypothesis. On Luke's use of sources based on this hypothesis, reference should be made to our earlier study (see Sources, pp15–21)[2].

Outline the main proposed solutions to the synoptic problem.

Marcan priority

The two-source hypothesis, which is generally accepted by scholars today, argues that Mark was the first Gospel to be written and that Matthew and Luke were dependent upon it. The main arguments for Marcan priority are:

Length

Mark is the shortest Gospel (661 verses), compared with Matthew (1,068 verses) and Luke (1,149 verses). It appears more plausible that Matthew and Luke added material to Mark than that Mark omitted so much of them (eg the birth of Jesus, the Sermon on the Mount/Plain). While it has been argued that Mark produced an abridged version of one or both of the other synoptics, the fact is that the stories he shares with them are actually usually longer (eg Mt 19:23–30/ Mk 10:23–31/ Lk 18:24–30).

Language

Mark's Greek is not as good as the others. For example, he uses a slang word for 'bed' where the others have more formal words (Mk 2:4, *krabatton*; Mt 9:2, *klines*; Lk 5:19, *klinidion*). Also, Mark has Aramaic words which the others are more likely to have omitted than he to have added (eg 3:17; 5:41). Further, Mark has over 200 grammatically redundant expressions which, again, are more likely to have been omitted by the others than added by Mark (eg compare the start of Mk 1:32 with Mt 8:16/ Lk 4:40).

---

[1] Streeter, BH, *The Four Gospels: A Study of Origins,* London: Macmillan, 1924

[2] Another possibility is to argue for the priority of Luke (Luke > Mark > Matthew), which is the position of a group of scholars based in Jerusalem (the 'Jerusalem school') led by Robert Lindsey and David Flusser. However, very few have been persuaded that the most Gentile of the synoptics is the earliest.

Development

Mark's presentation of both Jesus and the apostles appears to be less developed. Thus, while he has the title 'Lord' for Jesus only six times, the others use it of Jesus frequently. Again, Mark makes much more reference to the human emotions of Jesus (see p16). Also, by comparison with the other synoptics, Mark appears to limit Jesus' power more (eg cf Mk 1:34/ Mt 8:16/ Lk 4:40 and Mk 6:5/ Mt 13:58). On this point, it is significant that the others omit Mark's story about Jesus' gradual (rather than immediate) healing of a blind man (Mk 8:22–26). We may note too Matthew's apparent modification of a Marcan passage which could be read as a denial of the sinlessness and deity of Jesus (cf Mk 10:17–18/ Mt 19:16–17 in a modern version), although Luke (18:18–19) is the same as Mark here. Mark also seems to have a less developed characterisation of the apostles (see p16 for details). It is unlikely that Mark would have produced a more primitive picture of Jesus and the apostles on the basis of the more developed presentation in the other synoptics, but more understandable if the reverse were true.

Agreements

Matthew and Luke practically never agree against Mark about the sequence of stories and events in the overall synoptic narrative, even though Mark agrees with Matthew against Luke and with Luke against Matthew in this matter. A similar situation holds in regard to actual wording. This is best explained by Marcan priority than by the alternative theories.

However, there are several arguments against Marcan priority:

- There is a significant number of agreements of Matthew and Luke against Mark, implying that there was dependence between Matthew and Luke (eg compare Peter's weeping in Mk 14:72/ Mt 26:75/ Lk 22:62 and the guards' question in Mk 14:65/ Mt 26:67–68/ Lk 22:63–64). These are sometimes explained as being due to Mark overlapping with Q or overlapping oral traditions or scribal changes in the process of copying the Gospels.

- Luke's 'Great Omission' of Mark 6:45–8:26 is hard to explain if he was dependent on Mark. However, he may have wanted to leave space for his unique material or have been motivated by geographical reasons (see Geography, p28).

- The synoptic agreements and disagreements over order of contents can be explained without Marcan priority, for example by the Griesbach hypothesis. Those who hold Marcan priority are often guilty of what has been called the 'Lachmann Fallacy' – assuming Marcan priority in discussions about narrative order in the synoptics.

- The Marcan 'redundancies' (see Language, pp238–239) may be explained to some degree by Mark's desire to include the wording of both Matthew and

Luke, just as New Testament scribes often harmonised variant readings in the manuscripts (eg cf Mk 1:32/ Mt 8:16/ Lk 4:40 and Mk 4:21/ Mt 5:14/ Lk 8:16).

- Early Church evidence is unanimous that Matthew was the first Gospel to be written, even if this is assumed rather than demonstrated.

Evaluate the claim that Mark is the earliest of the synoptic Gospels.

Q

As noted on page 238, Q is the name for a hypothetical source, or sources, believed to be behind the non-Marcan material common to Matthew and Luke, of which they both made independent use. This material consists mostly of sayings of Jesus and amounts to around 240 verses shared by Matthew and Luke (for details, see pp17–18). The similarity in the wording of the material varies – from exact correspondence (eg Mt 7:7–8/ Lk 11:9–10), through minor differences (eg Mt 7:11/ Lk 11:13), to significant divergence (eg Mt 6:9–13/ Lk 11:2–4). This had led to speculation over whether Q consisted of oral or written material or both. For the many uncertainties concerning this hypothetical source material, its character, its apparent use in Luke and reconstructions of its development, reference should be made to our earlier study of Luke's sources (see Q, pp16–18).

Arguments for the existence of Q, particularly as a written source (a document or documents), include:

- the close and at times almost exact similarity between its versions in Matthew and Luke

- a similar sequence of the material in Matthew and Luke, despite some differences (see pp17–18)

- Matthew and Luke have 'doublets' – that is, two versions of the same stories or sayings. In these cases, one version apparently comes from Mark, while the other implies the existence of a separate source, namely Q (eg Mt 13:12/ Lk 8:18 from Mk 4:25 and Mt 25:29/ Lk 19:26 from Q).

Some have sought to dispense with the need for the Q hypothesis by arguing for a literary dependence between Matthew and Luke, and mostly for a dependence of Luke upon Matthew[1]. Indeed, the agreements between Matthew and Luke against Mark, that we noted above, would lend weight to this view. However, most scholars are unconvinced of such a dependence because:

---

[1] See footnote 1, p16. See also MS Goodacre, *The Case Against Q*, Harrisburg, Pennsylvania: Trinity Press International, 2002

- Matthew and Luke do not have each other's unique material (by definition) and this is improbable if one was dependent on the other.
- In material common to all the synoptics, Matthew's additions to Mark's material are not found in Luke (eg Mk 1:32–34/ Mt 8:16–17/ Lk 4:40–41; Matthew's addition is 8:17) and vice versa (eg Mk 2:1/ Mt 9:1/ Lk 5:17). The absence of such additions to Mark's material is unlikely in the event of a Matthew–Luke dependence.
- Either way, the rarity of instances of agreement in wording and order between Matthew and Luke against Mark favours the independence of Matthew and Luke.
- The improbability of Luke's dependence upon Matthew, in particular, is apparent in his far less structured arrangement of Q material, which Matthew arranges tidily into five blocks of teaching. It is unlikely that an author who describes his work as an "orderly" account (1:3) would replace Matthew's careful arrangement of this material with his own haphazard presentation of it.
- Luke's use of Mark argues against his use of Matthew, since he followed Mark's order closely and yet not so with Matthew.

Evaluate the claim that Q is an unnecessary hypothesis.

Proto-Luke

The Proto-Luke theory holds that the first draft of Luke's Gospel originally consisted of Q and L (the latter being Luke's unique material; see L, pp18–20), into which Marcan material was inserted at a later stage. Although forms of this theory existed earlier, its first main exponents were BH Streeter[1], followed by Vincent Taylor[2]. It is conjectured that after obtaining Q, Luke collected additional material (L) during the time of Paul's imprisonment in Caesarea (Acts 23:33–26:32). Here he wrote Proto-Luke, which began at 3:1, by combining Q and L. Later, while in Rome with Paul (Acts 27–28), he came across Mark's Gospel (traditionally linked with Rome) and expanded his Proto-Luke by adding Marcan material to it and possibly also, at this stage, his infancy narratives (chs 1–2).

The main arguments for the Proto-Luke theory are as follows:

Arrangement of Marcan material

Luke has grouped his Marcan source material into five separate blocks (see p15), which alternate with non-Marcan sections. This arrangement is consistent with

---

[1] Streeter, *The Four Gospels: A Study of Origins* (op cit)
[2] Taylor, Vincent, *Behind the Third Gospel,* London: Macmillan, 1926

Mark being a secondary source, from which material was later inserted into an already existing Proto-Luke.

Fusion of Q and L

Luke's Q and L material is combined, the former being expanded by the latter. This apparent fusion of these two sources is distinct from the Marcan material.

Continuity of Proto-Luke

When the Marcan material is removed from Luke, there is a relative continuity about the remaining material, pointing to its previous existence as a self-contained, broadly coherent work – Proto-Luke.

Beginning and end

The infancy narratives with which Luke begins and the passion and resurrection narratives with which it ends are distinct non-Marcan sections. Indeed, our present Luke appears to have two beginnings, with chapter 3 (note v 1–2 and the genealogy of Jesus in v 23ff) being the commencement of the earlier Proto-Luke. The non-Marcan character of the passion and resurrection narratives is clear, although it may be that the passion narrative was later edited with Marcan material. When the latter is removed, the passion narrative is a continuous narrative. Thus, Mark was not a base source for these narratives, even if some Marcan modification of them occurred later.

Omission of Marcan material

Luke omits almost 50 per cent of Mark (although estimates vary). The Marcan material accounts for about one-third of Luke, preference and priority being given to his earlier Proto-Luke. Constraints on length due to the size of a papyrus scroll would also have restricted the amount of supplementary Marcan material that Luke could have added to Proto-Luke[1].

Composition method

The use of Mark assumed by the Proto-Luke method is consistent with Luke's use of sources in the composition of his writings, as indicated by the preface of Luke and the 'we' sections in Acts.

Linguistic variation

Luke uses different words for the Jewish legal experts in his Marcan (*grammateus*) and Q (*nomikos*) sections, which supports the two-stage development of the Gospel envisaged by the Proto-Luke theory. Similarly, Luke calls Jesus 'the Lord' at least 14 times, but never in his Marcan material (see p30).

---

[1] According to Bruce Metzger (*The Text of the New Testament,* 3rd edition, New York: OUP, 1992, pp5–6) the usual Greek literary scroll rarely exceeded 35 feet and Luke, the longest book in the New Testament, would have filled an ordinary scroll of 31–32 feet.

However, the theory is not without its problems:

Marcan material in Proto-Luke

CM Tuckett sees the presence of Marcan influence in some of the QL material[1] (eg 4:23; 12:10; 17:31). Some of the phrases in parts of Luke 3 and 4 assigned to Q and L are, in fact, identical to Mark. Indeed, it has been estimated that about half of Luke 3:1–9:50 is Marcan. Also, Mark's passion narrative may have been known to Luke, who modified its content, wording and narrative sequence with his unique material.

Discontinuity of Proto-Luke

Not all are convinced that Proto-Luke has continuity and, in fact, it is viewed by some as an unstructured collection of material. Donald Guthrie refers to the "awkward gap" that remains in 8:3–9:51 when Mark's material is removed and to Proto-Luke's lopsided focus on Jesus' later ministry, particularly on his journey to Jerusalem[2].

Priority of Marcan material in doublets

JA Fitzmyer notes that when doublets occur (see p240) Mark's version is given before Q's and argues that this favours Mark as the primary source for Luke[3].

Original Marcan structure

Tuckett points out that Luke's arrangement of Marcan material into blocks may have come before he added his QL material, rather than the reverse[4].

Unnecessary hypothesis

While the Proto-Luke hypothesis may explain some features of Luke, it is not demanded by the evidence noted on pages 241 to 242, which is explicable in other ways.

Different views exist concerning the value of the Proto-Luke theory. Donald Guthrie mentions four main advantages that are attributed to the theory[5]:

- an early authority comparable to Mark
- confirmation of traditions in the Gospel of John (eg Samaritan ministry, Jerusalem resurrection appearances)
- a basis for some of Paul's ideas (eg 'justified' tax collector, command to repeat Last Supper)
- confirmation of early character of Luke's portrait of Jesus

---

1 Tuckett, *Luke: New Testament Guides* (op cit), p24
2 Guthrie, Donald, *New Testament Introduction,* 4th edition, Leicester: IVP, 1990, pp205–206
3 Fitzmyer, *The Gospel According to Luke I–IX* (op cit), pp90–91
4 Tuckett, *Luke: New Testament Guides* (op cit) p24
5 Guthrie, *New Testament Introduction,* (op cit), p207

The Gospel of Luke

However, Guthrie himself feels that too much is claimed for the theory here, especially if a shorter interval of time exists than is usually envisaged between the supposed Proto-Luke and the composition of Luke's Gospel. Tuckett is even more sceptical of the value of the theory, wondering what is gained by suggesting an earlier form of Luke which combined material from diverse sources[1]. For him, the Proto-Luke theory is unverifiable and ultimately of little use.

Tasks

a **Outline the Proto-Luke theory.**

b **Assess the evidence for the existence of Proto-Luke.**

c **Comment on the claim that the theory is of little value.**

Value of source criticism

A negative view of source criticism of the Gospels would characterise it as a highly speculative attempt to reconstruct hypothetical sources based on various dissections of the Gospels as finished literary products. We have noted the lack of complete agreement about the solution of the synoptic problem, evident in the debate over the order of synoptic literary dependence and the existence of Q. The uncertainty of the Proto-Luke theory is another example of the hypothetical and speculative nature of some source-critical study of the Gospels. Again, some people's faith in the Gospels as directly and divinely inspired, completely consistent records of the life and ministry of Jesus, is challenged by source criticism's focus on synoptic differences and literary dependence.

However, source criticism of the Gospels has been widely regarded as valuable for the following main reasons:

Historical criticism

Source criticism can assist in identifying the earliest source or sources behind our Gospels. It is held that, in theory, these should be the most historically accurate and objective sources, since they should have been least affected by the developing theology and worship of the early Church in general and the evangelists in particular. Thus, Mark and Q are often valued as among the earliest source material for any attempt to reconstruct the life and ministry of the 'historical Jesus' (if one accepts the general view of synoptic origins). The identification of separate sources behind the Gospels is also viewed as assisting in establishing the historicity or otherwise of the contents of the Gospels, since if a saying, story or idea is supported by several independent sources ('multiple attestation') then it is regarded as more likely to be historically accurate. For example, that the historical Jesus taught about the kingdom of God is confirmed

---

[1] Tuckett, *Luke: New Testament Guides* (op cit), p24

by the presence of this theme in Mark, Q, M, L and John. Further, when a Gospel author includes material which seems to go against his own distinctive emphases, then its historical accuracy is confirmed. For example, Matthew's emphasis on the continuing validity of the Law (eg 5:17–20; 23:23) does not prevent him including teaching of Jesus that seems to suggest otherwise (11:13).

Redaction criticism

If the order of literary dependence among the Gospels can be established then it is possible to identify an author's theological emphases and distinctive message by noting the ways in which he has redacted (edited) his source material. For example, we can see Luke's special emphasis on prayer in his redaction of Mark (cf Lk 9:28–29/ Mk 9:2–3) and on the Holy Spirit in his redaction of Q (eg Lk 11:13/ Mt 7:11).

Form criticism

In their attempt to trace the development of traditions about Jesus, form critics are assisted by source criticism, as they work backwards from later sources (Matthew and Luke) via earlier ones (Mark and Q) to the earliest form of a saying or story.

Textual criticism

Textual critics too are influenced by the conclusions of Gospel source critics, as they seek to identify original readings among differing Gospel manuscripts. For instance, belief in the priority of Mark assists textual critics in spotting scribal harmonisation of the different Gospels.

Nature of the Gospels

A comparison of the Gospels and the apparent use they make of their sources informs us about the nature and character of these writings. Thus, it is clear that they do not always have the precision in chronological sequence (eg cf Mk 10:46/ Lk 18:35; 19:1) or verbal reporting of Jesus' words (eg cf Mk 6:8/ Lk 9:3) that is often claimed for or expected of them. Rather, the comparative textual evidence reveals a certain amount of freedom and flexibility on the part of the evangelists in their accounts of Jesus' life and ministry, a reality that must be taken into account in any view of the divine inspiration of the Gospels[1].

Task

Discuss the claim that source criticism is more a hindrance than a help to our understanding of the Gospels.

---

[1] RH Stein ('Synoptic Problem' in *Dictionary of Jesus and the Gospels*, eds JB Green, S McKnight, and IH Marshall, Downers Grove, Illinois/ Leicester, England: IVP, 1992 p792) includes hermeneutical benefits in his excellent survey of the value of Gospel source criticism – such as how Matthew 10:37–38 throws light on the meaning of Luke 14:26 – but it seems to me that this is more a benefit of redaction criticism.

Form criticism

As noted on page 234, Gospel form criticism categorises the various sayings and stories of the Gospels according to their form or shape (eg prophetic sayings, parable stories) in order to discern their use and development in the Church during the period of oral tradition. This is when the sayings and stories of Jesus were passed on by word of mouth, before the Gospels were written. Therefore, while source criticism is concerned primarily with the *written* sources behind the Gospels, form criticism is interested in the earlier *pre-literary* stage, in what happened between the time of Jesus' ministry and the writing of the Gospels.

While form criticism had been used earlier by Old Testament scholars, Gospel form criticism began in the years immediately following the First World War, with the pioneering work of three German scholars – Karl Schmidt (1919)[1], Martin Dibelius (1919)[2] and Rudolf Bultmann (1921)[3]. The work of these scholars was introduced to English speakers by the more conservative British form critic Vincent Taylor[4]. Among other reasons, form criticism arose because source criticism seemed to have gone as far as it could go in presenting Mark and Q as the earliest sources behind the Gospels. Form critics sought to go back earlier, into the period of oral tradition – right back to Jesus himself.

Task

Explain the meaning and origins of Gospel form criticism.

Principles

Form critics work with a number of assumptions which should be noted as the basic principles of form criticism.

Oral period

The writing of the Gospels was preceded by a period of at least about 30 years when the stories and sayings of Jesus were passed on by word of mouth (cf Lk 1:2; 2 Thess 2:15). Indeed, this process of oral tradition continued even after the Gospels were written down. Papias, Bishop of Hierapolis (about AD 130), wrote of how he preferred the "living voice" to what could be learned from "books", when it came to finding out what the Lord's disciples had said[5].

---

[1] Schmidt, Karl, *Der Rahmen der Geschichte Jesu* ('The Framework of the Story of Jesus'), Berlin: Trowitzsch & Sohn; no English translation

[2] Dibelius, Martin, *From Tradition to Gospel,* trans BW Woolf (from the second edition, 1933), London: Ivor Nicholson and Watson, 1934; German original, 1919. The title of the German work translates as 'The Form-history of the Gospels'.

[3] Bultmann, Rudolf, *The History of the Synoptic Tradition,* trans John Marsh (from the third edition, 1957), Oxford: Basil Blackwell, 1963

[4] Taylor, Vincent, *The Formation of the Gospel Tradition,* London: Macmillan, 1933

[5] Eusebius, *Ecclesiastical History,* 3.39.4

Independent units

The stories and sayings of Jesus were circulated in the oral period, not in the connected form in which we find them in the Gospels, but as independent, isolated units of tradition. These units have been compared to individual pearls which Mark, as the earliest of our evangelists, joined together on a string – the latter being the narrative framework of his Gospel. Therefore, the Gospel writers are sometimes characterised not as authors but as 'scissors and paste' compilers of otherwise unconnected units of tradition. The evidence for this is seen in the vague 'seams' with which Mark joins his individual stories together, which often contain little or no information about their original temporal or geographical context (eg 2:18; 4:1,21; 7:1; 8:1; cf Lk 5:1,12,17; 6:12; 11:1 and Acts 20:35; 1 Cor 7:10). We may note too how the evangelists place the same stories in different contexts, for theological and literary reasons, as an indication that their original context in the ministry of Jesus was unknown (eg Mk 6:1–6/ Lk 4:14–30). Also, some material seems to be grouped together topically, rather than because of any original temporal order in Jesus' ministry (eg the controversy stories in Mk 2:1–3:6 and the miracle stories in Mk 4:35–5:43). There is also the fact that in the oral period it was easier to remember shorter units of tradition than longer collections of narrative in their original chronological sequence or geographical contexts. However, exceptions to this include the passion narrative, which appears to be a continuous, interdependent collection with connecting detail.

Distinct forms

The stories and sayings in the Gospels can be categorised according to various stereotypical forms, which they acquired during their use in the period of oral tradition. For example, Vincent Taylor classified the Gospel material into the following four main forms[1]:

Pronouncement stories

Dibelius called these 'paradigms' (examples) and Bultmann referred to them as 'apophthegms'. These are stories which end with a significant statement or pronouncement of Jesus as a punch line (eg see Lk 10:38–42; 18:15–17; 20:20–25). Bultmann subdivided this group into controversy (eg Lk 20:20–25), scholastic/didactic (eg Lk 18:18–30) and biographical stories (eg Lk 10:38–42).

Miracle stories

Dibelius called these 'novellen' (tales). Unlike the previous category there is little or no teaching of Jesus, but the story of Jesus' miraculous power. They usually have a stereotypical pattern involving the description of a problem, followed by a statement of Jesus' miraculous solution, and climaxing with

---

[1] Taylor, *The Formation of the Gospel Tradition* (op cit)

the effects of the miracle. Again, Bultmann has subdivisions such as:

> healings (eg Lk 5:12–16)
> exorcisms (eg Lk 4:31–37)
> nature miracles (eg Lk 8:22–25)
> raisings from the dead (eg Lk 7:11–17)

A more recent and much more detailed categorisation of the miracle stories has been provided by Gerd Theissen, who finds six themes (exorcisms, healings, epiphanies/appearances, rescue, gift, and rule miracles) and 33 motifs[1].

Sayings and parables

This category covers all the teaching of Jesus apart from the pronouncement stories. Dibelius calls this 'paraenesis' (exhortation) and has six subdivisions:

> maxim/proverb (eg end of Lk 6:45)
> metaphor (eg Lk 8:16)
> parable (eg Lk 15:1–7)
> prophetic call (eg Lk 6:20–26)
> short command (eg Mt 18:10)
> extended command (eg Lk 6:27–49)

Bultmann names this category 'sayings' and has five subdivisions:

> logia/wisdom sayings (eg Lk 11:17–18)
> prophetic or apocalyptic sayings (eg Lk 6:24–26; 21:7ff)
> legal sayings (eg Lk 12:10)
> 'I' sayings (eg Lk 5:32)
> parables (eg Lk 18:1–8)

Stories about Jesus

Dibelius refers to 'legends' (stories about holy people, not just Jesus, eg Lk 2:41–51; 3:1–20; 19:1–10) and 'myths' (stories about divine intervention, Lk 3:21–22; 4:1–13; 9:28–36), while Bultmann refers to 'historical stories and legends' for this general category. The terms used by Dibelius and Bultmann here are no indication in themselves of their view of the historicity of these stories.

Finally, we may note that form critics distinguish sometimes between 'pure' and 'mixed' forms, the latter having the characteristics of more than one of the categories listed above (eg see Lk 5:17–26).

Church influence

The Gospel material was preserved because of its usefulness to the Church in various situations and contexts such as worship (eg Lk 22:17–20;

---

[1] Theissen, Gerd, *The Miracle Stories of the Early Christian Tradition*, trans F McDonagh, Philadelphia: Fortress, 1983; German original, 1974

cf 1 Cor 11:23–25), teaching (eg Lk 6:17–49; 10:1ff), mission (eg Lk 19:1–10), apologetics (eg Lk 4:31–37) and church discipline (eg Lk 12:10). Indeed, the particular forms that the stories developed were due to the specific uses and functions that the Christian community made of them during the oral period. For instance, Dibelius believed that the form of the pronouncement stories was shaped by their use as illustrations in the preaching of early Christian missionaries. Form critics hold that the form of the material is a clue to its 'life-setting' (German *Sitz im Leben*) in the Church during the oral period and try to reconstruct its original life-setting in the ministry of Jesus (the two are often distinguished). Thus, the Church has modified and adapted the material, giving it new applications. Some form critics argue that the Church also created some of the Gospel material and read it back into the ministry of Jesus. It is claimed that this material may have come from Christian prophets, inspired by the risen Jesus (cf Rev 3:20; 16:15; Acts 11:27–30), and was then attributed to the historical Jesus.

Tradition's tendencies

Early form critics, in particular, believed that oral tradition developed certain tendencies over time as stories were passed on by word of mouth. These 'laws' of tradition could be identified in 'folk' literature containing popular stories such as Greek writings, rabbinic literature, apocryphal Gospels and the folklore of contemporary societies. Such tendencies of oral transmission include the following: stories were usually expanded with more details, reported speech became direct speech, cultural idioms were clarified and variant accounts were harmonised or conflated (eg cf Mk 3:1/ Lk 6:6; Mk 9:17/ Lk 9:38; Mk 14:13/ Lk 22:8; Mt 10:37/ Lk 14:26). By identifying these later additions, form critics seek to trace the evolution of a story or saying back to its original form in the ministry of Jesus.

Authenticity criteria

Form critics often use criteria (standards by which judgements are made) to enable them to decide which sayings and stories attributed to Jesus in the Gospels are historically authentic (ie genuine) and which are inauthentic (created by the early Christians). These 'criteria of authenticity' include:

- the criterion of *dissimilarity/discontinuity* – any sayings or deeds of Jesus that are unlike what we find in Judaism or the early Church may be treated as authentic (eg his distinctive use of parables focusing on God's kingdom).

- the criterion of *multiple attestation* – sayings and deeds of Jesus that are found in several independent sources (Mk, Q, M, L, Jn) or forms are more likely to be authentic (eg miracles).

- the criterion of *Jewish/Palestinian context* – sayings and deeds of Jesus that reflect his Jewish/Palestinian language, culture and environment, rather than the Gentile world into which the early Church developed, are probably authentic (eg Sabbath controversies).

The Gospel of Luke

- the criterion of *embarrassment* – sayings and deeds of Jesus which are likely to have caused embarrassment for the early Church are probably authentic (eg Lk 18:19).
- the criterion of *coherence* – sayings and deeds of Jesus that cohere, or are consistent with those established as authentic by the other criteria, are probably authentic too.

Briefly outline, with examples, the key principles and presuppositions of form criticism.

Evaluation

Gospel form criticism has been viewed both positively and negatively. The following are regarded as among its positive contributions.

Historical criticism

Form criticism sheds light on the earliest period of the Church – the oral period before the Gospels were written. The stories and sayings of Jesus in the Gospels were selected and preserved because of their relevance and usefulness to the early Church and, therefore, give us some insight into the concerns and controversies, as well as the preaching and worship, of the early Christian communities. However, the inferential nature of form criticism at this point should be noted. We might *infer* from the Sabbath controversy stories in the Gospels that the presence of Gentiles in the early churches led to tensions over Sabbath observance, but without other corroborating evidence it remains an inference. Form criticism is also regarded as having historical value by those involved in the 'quest for the historical Jesus', who seek to identify where the early Christians modified, and even created, sayings and stories of Jesus, in order to get back to Jesus himself.

Interpretation

By classifying the Gospel material into different forms or types, form criticism has provided important insights into the meaning of the material. This is because the key to the interpretation of a passage is often provided by its form or genre. Thus, the structure of a pronouncement story guides us to its climactic statement as the key to its meaning. For example, the meaning of Luke 8:19–21 is not Jesus' seeming indifference to his family, but rather the nature of his true family as those who hear and heed God's word. Again, the interpretative focus of the story about Jesus calming the sea is not on the miracle itself, but on the identity of the miracle worker (Lk 8:25). Interpretation of other material should also be sensitive to, and guided by, its specific forms (eg parables, proverbs).

The nature of the Gospels

Form criticism teaches us to view the Gospels not as biographies of Jesus, at least not in the sense of modern biographies which provide comprehensive and chronological details of a person's life. Rather, the Gospels are mostly anthologies of sayings and stories of Jesus which the early Church found to be useful in contexts such as preaching and worship. Thus, we note also that they are the preserve and possession of the whole Church and not individual products of personal interpretation. We learn too that the authors of the Gospels or their sources have often structured and organised the units of tradition topically and *form*ally rather than chronologically. For example, note the grouping together of controversy-pronouncement stories (Lk 5:17–6:11), miracle stories (Lk 8:22–56) and parables (Lk 14:7–16:31).

The use of the Gospels

While some form-critical suggestions about the uses of the various forms of tradition in the oral period have been speculative and contradictory, others seem plausible. For example, the use in a worship setting of the account of the Last Supper (Lk 22:17–20) seems to be confirmed by Paul's reference to it in correspondence with the Corinthian church (1 Cor 11:23–25). Such insights about how the early Christians might have used the Gospel material may provide help on how the Church today can make use of it in its various forms.

In what ways has form criticism proved to be valuable?

On the negative side, criticisms of form criticism include the following:

Oral period

Form critics have often operated with the assumption that the so-called oral period was exclusively oral. However, just as the disciples of the rabbis made some written notes of their mentors' teachings, the disciples of Jesus may have done similarly, not least for the missions of the Twelve and the Seventy (Lk 9:1–6; 10:1–17). Certainly, there was no practical difficulty in doing so (cf Lk 1:63). Also, unless we take his words as pure rhetoric or mere convention, Luke indicates at the beginning of his Gospel that "many" apparently written accounts of Jesus had preceded his, which would imply more than the two written sources normally envisaged (Mark and Q).

Independent units

Many form critics hold that most of the Gospel material (apart from the passion narrative) was passed on in brief, independent, unconnected units. However, there is some evidence that there may have been, during the oral period, larger collections of tradition and even an outline of the ministry of Jesus. Some of the topically and formally united groupings of material in Mark (eg the controversy stories of 2:1–3:6 and the parables of 4:1–34) may imply that this material existed as collections of tradition in the oral period. In addition to these larger complexes of material, CH Dodd argued in an important article that a traditional outline of the ministry of Jesus also existed in the oral period and that Mark structured his Gospel on the basis of it, adding independent units and larger collections of tradition to the framework[1]. Dodd found the evidence for such an outline in early Christian preaching, especially Acts 10:34–43 – which corresponds to the structure of Mark's Gospel.

Distinct forms

Form-critical categories are not as neat and distinct as many assume. Some stories, in fact, have been called 'form-less' (eg the confession of Peter, the entry to Jerusalem) and others have been characterised as 'mixed' or 'impure' forms (eg Lk 5:17–26 – miracle/pronouncement story). Again, quite often a story is not categorised by its form, shape or structure at all, but simply by its perceived content. For example, Dibelius classifies the story of Jesus' temptation as a 'myth', even though it has the formal features of a controversy story. It could be argued that the only 'pure' forms are pronouncement stories, miracle stories, parable stories and 'I' sayings, and even the last two are debatable. The variety of categorisations given by scholars to the same passage indicates how imprecise and subjective formal classification can be. For example, Luke 5:1–11 has been variously labelled by scholars as legend, miracle story, nature miracle, gift miracle, pronouncement story, commission account, epiphany-call and mandate account[2]! Furthermore, too rigid classification of forms can influence historical criticism of a passage; since Luke 5:33–34 is regarded as a pure pronouncement story, verse 35 is often viewed as a secondary addition by the Church, corrupting the original form.

Church influence

The idea that the *form* of traditions can tell us something about their *function* in the oral period and, therefore, about the Church's influence on the material, is plausible. However, not only is there disagreement concerning forms, but it is also acknowledged that a particular form could have served several different functions. Thus, attempts to identify a specific life-setting in the early Church for each form are speculative. Further, it is unwarranted to reason that because a tradition is viewed as useful in a certain Church life-setting, then it must have been created by that life-setting and, therefore, have come from the early Church and not Jesus. This is a circular argument. It is just as possible, and

---

[1] Dodd, CH, 'The Framework of the Gospel Narrative' in *Expository Times* 43, 1932

[2] Black, DA, and DS Dockery (eds), *New Testament Criticism and Interpretation*, Grand Rapids, Michigan: Zondervan, 1991, pp188–192

many would argue more probable, that the traditions from Jesus' ministry were preserved precisely because of their relevance to the developing Church. Again, the idea that the early Christians made no distinction between sayings of the earthly Jesus and those of the risen Jesus given through Christian prophets does not fit the first-century evidence (eg 1 Cor 7:10/ Mk 10:11 and 1 Cor 7:12,25). The fact that the early Church did not feel free to read later concerns back into the earthly ministry of Jesus is clear from the notable absence of post-Easter issues from the Gospels (eg Jewish–Gentile controversy over circumcision). We may note too, for example, how the Lord's Prayer (Lk 11:2–4) lacks signs of post-Easter modification. Finally, during what was a relatively brief oral period the original apostles and eyewitnesses (eg Lk 1:2; Acts 2:42), including opponents, would have acted as a safeguard against the wholesale creation of new material and the substantial revision of the old.

Tradition's tendencies

The so-called 'laws' of tradition have been examined by EP Sanders, who concluded that there are no hard laws and that in all the supposed tendencies the tradition actually developed in opposite directions[1]. Stories can become less detailed – for example, when Mark's reference to "green grass" (6:39) is omitted in later accounts (eg Lk 9:14). Two Swedish scholars, H Riesenfeld and B Gerhardsson, have also argued that Jesus' disciples would have carefully memorised and accurately transmitted his main teachings and certain narratives in line with the practice of the disciples of other Jewish rabbis[2] (cf 1 Cor 11:23ff; 15:3ff). However, some scholars have argued that this comparison is not valid since, for example, the rabbinic evidence is later than Jesus' time and clear differences do exist between the Gospels. In defence of accurate preservation of traditions about Jesus, R Riesner has appealed to educational methodology practised by Israel and surrounding nations[3]. Among other things, Riesner points to the memorable nature of the various forms of Jesus' teaching and evidence of Jesus instructing his disciples to learn and pass on his teaching (eg Lk 10:1–17; 11:1). However, on the basis of studies of oral traditions in pre-literate societies and other considerations, many favour a model of informal, flexible transmission of oral tradition which has nevertheless some controls and limits[4]. Again, it has been questioned how much *written* texts can tell us about *oral* tradition.

---

1 Sanders, EP, *The Tendencies of the Synoptic Tradition*, Cambridge: CUP, 1969

2 Riesenfeld, H, *The Gospel Tradition*, trans EM Rowley and RA Kraft, Philadelphia: Fortress, 1970 (see pp1–29 which contains the relevant original 1959 article); Gerhardsson, B, *Memory and Manuscript: Oral Tradition and Written Transmission in Rabbinic Judaism and Early Christianity with Tradition and Transmission in Early Christianity*, trans EJ Sharpe, Grand Rapids, Michigan: Eerdmans, 1998 (combined edition of two original works published in 1961 and 1964). See also Gerhardsson's *The Origins of the Gospel Tradition* (London: SCM, 1979; original, 1977) for a brief and popular outline of this position.

3 Riesner, R, *Jesus als Lehrer*, Tubingen: Mohr, 1981

4 eg Bailey, KE, 'Informal Controlled Oral Tradition and the Synoptic Gospels' in *Themelios* 20, 1995

Authenticity criteria

It can be argued that these criteria are of limited historical value. They can authenticate only a limited amount of Gospel material since, for example, Jesus *will* have said and done things that are similar to Judaism and the early Church, that may well be attested in only one source and that reflect Gentile culture to some degree (Galilee, in particular, was subject to Gentile influence). Indeed, when the criteria are used negatively – that is, with the assumption that what they cannot verify is historically inauthentic – then they are going beyond their proper application. Many would argue that the historical status of the Gospel material should be considered innocent until proven guilty, rather than the reverse.

Outline the main weaknesses of form criticism.

Redaction criticism

Redaction criticism tries to identify how the authors of the Gospels have redacted (ie edited, changed) their sources in order to convey their own theological emphases. On the basis of this, redaction critics then seek to reconstruct the particular Church settings which the authors represent and/or address. Thus, while form criticism is concerned with what the Church did with the traditions about Jesus during the oral period before the Gospels were written, redaction criticism examines what the Gospel authors did with their sources. It investigates the interaction between tradition (sources) and redaction (interpretation). Redaction criticism, then, is a further and distinct stage in the development of the early traditions about Jesus, which nevertheless builds on the conclusions of form and source criticism.

As with the beginnings of form criticism, the origins of redaction criticism are often linked with three German scholars who, in this case, wrote significant works after the Second World War (rather than after the First, as in the case of form criticism). G Bornkamm's 1948 article on 'The Stilling of the Storm in Matthew' marks the beginning of the discipline[1]. In it he argued that Matthew edited and interpreted Mark's story of the stilling of the storm to make it convey lessons on discipleship (cf Mk 4:35–41/ Mt 8:23–27). Matthew places the story in a new context, with two short discipleship narratives immediately preceding it (8:18–22). Further, Matthew continues the theme of the preceding verses by uniquely beginning the story of the storm with a reference to the disciples 'following' Jesus. We note too that only in Matthew's account do the disciples address Jesus as "Lord". For such reasons, among others, Bornkamm held that Matthew was not only the first to hand on

---

[1] See Bornkamm, G, G Barth, and HJ Held, *Tradition and Interpretation in Matthew,* London: SCM, 1963, pp52–57

Mark's story, but was also its first interpreter. The next significant redaction critic was Hans Conzelmann, whose 1953 work on Luke's Gospel, with its claim that Luke had replaced Mark's imminent *parousia* with a salvation history scheme, we have already considered (see Salvation history, pp229–233). Finally, redactional work on the remaining synoptic Gospel was pioneered by Willi Marxsen in 1956, who argued that Mark's Gospel was written to prepare believers for Jesus' imminent *parousia* in Galilee[1]. Marxsen himself was the first to use the term *Redaktionsgeschichte* ('redaction-history', referred to in English as 'redaction criticism'). And he also made the important distinction between three life-settings of the developing traditions about Jesus – those of Jesus' ministry, the early Church and the evangelists. While form criticism had focused on the second of these, it had neglected the third and final *Sitz im Leben* – that of the Gospel authors. This would become the concern of redaction criticism.

Explain the meaning and origins of Gospel redaction criticism.

Method

GR Osborne regards the process of redaction criticism as involving two stages – the study of individual passages within a Gospel ('individual analysis') and the study of the Gospel as a whole ('holistic analysis')[2]. Thus, redaction criticism operates at both micro- and macro- levels. Redactional analysis of individual passages may also be termed 'horizontal' reading, since it involves looking across the page in a Gospel synopsis to compare the parallel passages in the other Gospels. And redactional analysis of a whole Gospel may also be referred to as 'vertical' reading, since it involves looking down a column in a Gospel synopsis to see the contents and arrangement of an entire Gospel[3].

Individual passages

S McKnight lists seven types of editorial activity which a Gospel author may apply to his sources[4]. These are summarised below with reference to individual passages and on the assumption that Luke was dependent on Mark.

Conservation

This is where an author conserves unchanged what his source says. For example, Luke (and Matthew) retains even Mark's editorial comment on occasion (Mk 2:10/ Lk 5:24).

---

[1] Marxsen, Willi, *Mark the Evangelist: Studies on the Redaction History of the Gospel,* New York and Nashville: Abingdon, 1969; German original, 1956

[2] Osborne, GR, 'Redaction Criticism' (op cit), p665

[3] For these terms see Blomberg, *Jesus and the Gospels* (op cit), pp93–94.

[4] McKnight, S, *Interpreting the Synoptic Gospels,* Grand Rapids, Michigan: Baker, 1998, pp85–87

Conflation

Here the author conflates or combines two of his sources. Luke (and Matthew) appears to combine material from Mark and Q in the story of Jesus' temptation (Mk 1:12–13/ Lk 4:1–13; cf Mt 4:1–11).

Expansion

The author may add material to his source, such as Luke's references to prayer in his use of Mark's account of Jesus' transfiguration (Mk 9:2–3/ Lk 9:28–29).

Transposition

This occurs when the author changes the position of the material in his source by giving it a new setting and context. For instance, we note that Luke has transposed (and expanded) the account of Jesus' rejection at Nazareth from its placement in Mark to the start of Jesus' ministry (Mk 6:1–6/ Lk 4:14–30).

Omission

For various reasons, an author may omit material in his source. Luke leaves out some of Mark's wording, apparently to avoid redundancy (see the start of Mk 1:32 and Lk 4:40).

Explanation

Explanatory information may be added, such as Luke's reference to Satan in the account of Judas' decision to betray Jesus (Mk 14:10/ Lk 22:3–4).

Alteration

While nearly all editorial activity involves altering sources in various ways, here the alteration is to avoid possible misunderstanding. For example, it has been suggested that Luke's reference to "tiles" in the roof of a Palestinian house was an alteration of Mark in order to make the story more understandable to those outside Palestine (Mk 2:4/ Lk 5:19).

Whole Gospels

In addition to comparative analysis of individual passages, redaction critics study an entire Gospel in itself to identify the distinctive theology of its author. GR Osborne notes that attention should be paid to the following[1]:

Seams

These are the transitional links between individual passages and episodes in the Gospel, such as introductions and conclusions. Seams provide insight into an author's theological interests as they often contain his distinctive language and personal interpretation of a passage, as well as his rationale for including the material in his Gospel. For example, Luke introduces the

---

[1] Osborne, 'Redaction Criticism' (op cit), pp665–666

parable of the widow and the judge with a statement of its purpose, which reflects Luke's general emphasis on prayer (18:1).

Summaries

An author's summary of material or activity often points to his theological concerns. We see, for instance, in one of Luke's summaries an example of his concern to show Jesus as a man of prayer (5:16).

Asides and insertions

These editorial additions can also tell us something about the author's perspective. For example, Luke mentions that "the power of the Lord" was present to enable Jesus to heal the sick (5:17), recalling his emphasis on the divine power behind Jesus' ministry (cf 4:14; Acts 10:38).

Favourite terms

Repeated use of words and phrases reflect the author's special interests. For example, the fact that Luke has about 40 per cent of the New Testament occurrences of the Greek word *dei* ('it is necessary/must') underlines his general concern to emphasise God's purpose.

Themes

Related to the previous point is the presence of recurring ideas and topics, as an indication of the special interests of an author. For instance, we have already considered the importance of salvation for Luke (see Salvation, p34ff).

This analysis of a whole Gospel, along with literary features such as structure, plot and setting, is sometimes referred to as 'composition criticism', since it is concerned with how the author has composed his entire work. While some scholars regard this as part of the discipline of redaction criticism, others feel that it belongs more properly within narrative criticism (see p260ff).

Finally, on the basis of the theological patterns and tendencies that redactional analysis uncovers, inferences are made about the author's church or community (his *Sitz im Leben*). For example, we have seen that Luke's particular eschatology has led to the suggestion that he was trying to correct two extremes in his church – fanatical expectation of Jesus' imminent return on the one hand, and a loss of eschatological hope on the other (see Theological, pp22–23). Again, Luke's concern for the poor and criticism of the rich may reflect a largely affluent church that was neglecting social justice. It might also be inferred, from the emphasis in Luke's passion narrative on Jesus as a righteous sufferer, that the Gospel was written to a church that was suffering persecution.

Outline, with examples, the methodology of redaction criticism.

often regarded as his theological creations and literary inventions, with no basis in historical fact (eg only Luke has Jesus praying at his baptism). However, such redactional changes may be legitimate interpretations of source material or the result of access to additional source information. Again, it is not safe to assume that because something is expressed in an author's characteristic style or vocabulary that it is pure invention – how else would an author present traditional material?

Rejection of harmonisation

Related to our previous point is the general suspicion and rejection of even plausible attempts to harmonise diverse material in the Gospels. Rather, the emphasis is on differences and their possible significance. Thus, Luke's parable of the pounds (19:11–27) and Matthew's parable of the talents (25:14–30) can be viewed not as different forms of one original parable, but as different forms of similar parables used by Jesus on more than one occasion in his itinerant preaching.

Outline the main weaknesses of redaction criticism.

Narrative criticism

Narrative criticism views the evangelists as storytellers and the Gospels as stories (narratives). While traditional criticism focused on reconstructing the history behind the text (oral forms and written sources), narrative criticism is concerned with the text itself. Thus, it is in some ways the child of redaction or composition criticism, taking further its interest in the text in its final form. Narrative criticism, then, is text-centred rather than author- or reader-centred in its focus. Each Gospel has its own narrative world, features and devices which require literary analysis. Narrative critics are especially interested in the 'poetics' or 'aesthetics' of the Gospels – evidences of the literary skill and narrative artistry of their authors. The text, in effect, becomes autonomous – independent of its authorship and readership – although narrative critics are interested in how the text has been constructed in order to affect its readers. In this respect, this approach begins to merge with rhetorical criticism and some types of reader-response criticism.

Gospel narrative criticism reflects developments in secular literary criticism. In the early twentieth century there was a move away from traditional literary concerns with the world behind texts, with authors and their circumstances, to a concern with the texts themselves and their own literary integrity. This new approach was known as practical criticism, then as new criticism or formalism, concerned as it was with the formal features of the text. However, it was not until the 1980s that narrative criticism was applied to the Gospels in earnest. The first important application of narrative-critical principles to the Gospels was the ground-breaking American study *Mark as Story: An Introduction to the Narrative of a Gospel* by David Rhoads (an NT historian) and Donald Michie (an English teacher)[1]. Similar work soon followed in the US on the other Gospels, including R Alan Culpepper on John[2], JD Kingsbury on Matthew[3] and, of particular relevance for us, Robert C Tannehill's pioneering narrative-critical study of Luke[4]. However, some time before Tannehill's specifically narrative-critical study, CH Talbert had urged a literary-critical approach to Luke[5].

Explain the meaning and origins of narrative criticism.

Method

In practice, narrative critics are concerned with the following:

Authors and readers

Narrative critics often distinguish between the *real* and *implied* authors of a text. The real author is the actual person who wrote the text, whose identity may or may not be known. The implied author is what the text alone tells us about the author, what it reveals about his perspectives and values. The implied author, then, is the text's 'point of view' and this is what the narrative critic is interested in. Thus, whether the historical Luke actually wrote the Gospel of Luke is of no concern; rather, what matters is the picture of the author that we get in the text itself.

Parallel to this is the distinction between the *real* and the *implied* readers. Again, the real or authorial readers are those to whom the text is actually addressed, while the implied or ideal readers are those who meet the expectations of the implied author, as they are revealed in the text. Again, it is the text alone that provides the crucial information. So, while Luke is formally addressed to Theophilus, narrative critics are concerned with the picture of the ideal audience painted by the text as a whole. Some critics also distinguish between

---

[1] Rhoads, David, and Donald Michie, *Mark as Story: An Introduction to the Narrative of a Gospel,* Philadelphia: Fortress, 1982; 2nd edition with J Dewey, 1999

[2] Culpepper, R Alan, *Anatomy of the Fourth Gospel: A Study in Literary Design,* Philadelphia: Fortress, 1983

[3] Kingsbury, JD, *Matthew as Story,* Philadelphia: Fortress, 1986; 2nd edition, 1988

[4] Tannehill, Robert C, *The Narrative Unity of Luke–Acts: A Literary Interpretation, Vol 1: The Gospel According to Luke,* Philadelphia: Fortress, 1986

[5] Talbert, CH, *Literary Patterns, Theological Themes, and the Genre of Luke–Acts,* Missoula: Scholars Press, 1974; *Reading Luke: A Literary and Theological Commentary on the Third Gospel,* New York: Crossroad, 1982. Talbert viewed 1974 as a turning point in Lucan studies, moving from historical concerns with sources and the study of individual passages to literary analysis of the complete text (so IH Marshall in *Themelios* Vol 14 No 2, Jan/Feb 1989, p53).

the narrator (who tells the story within the text) and the narratees (those who receive the story, as implied by the text). However, these terms mostly correspond in practice to the implied author and the implied readers. Within the text the narrator is often omniscient (knowing, for instance, the motives of characters), intrusive (interpreting and evaluating characters and events) and authoritative (a reliable commentator)[1].

Settings

The setting of a story may be temporal (eg Lk 1:5; 2:1; 3:1–2), physical/spatial (eg 4:1; 9:28) and social/cultural (eg 2:22; 10:38ff). These contexts may have a significant, even symbolic, function in the narrative.

Characters

Individuals and groups of people can be presented by the storyteller in a flat, one-dimensional way (eg the Jewish leaders are regularly opponents of Jesus) or in a round, complex way (eg the disciples are portrayed both positively and negatively; cf 8:10; 9:44–45). The main character or 'hero' of the story is called the *protagonist* (eg Jesus in the Gospels), while his opponents are the *antagonists* (eg the religious leaders in the Gospels). *Characterisation* refers to how characters are portrayed in the narrative and this is achieved through the author's own description (eg 1:6), the reactions and comments of others (eg 1:22) and self-characterisation (eg 5:8). The characterisation is designed to influence the reader's response, evoking sympathy for some characters and antipathy for others.

Plot

This is the story line or 'action', an arranged sequence of related events with a beginning, middle and end (for Luke's plot, see Structure, pp48–49). Often the plot involves and is propelled by a conflict or series of conflicts, which eventually come to a happy or tragic resolution in the climax of the story. In the Gospels, the growing conflict between Jesus and the Jewish leaders is resolved in his crucifixion (tragedy), which is followed by his resurrection as the climax of the narrative. Within the overall plot of the book, there are often smaller mini-plots or stories, such as the miracles and parables in the Gospels. The order in which an author has arranged events is often significant. For example, Luke's placement of Jesus' rejection at Nazareth at the beginning of his ministry, rather than later as in the other synoptics, provides an interpretative introduction to that ministry (4:16ff). Again, the amount of narrative space and time given to an event within the plot can indicate its importance. For instance, while a number of years can be summarised in one line (eg 2:52), the events of a single day can be recounted at length (eg ch 24). The slowing down of the pace of the narrative by the inclusion of incidental detail may be an attempt to create

---

[1] Kingsbury, JD, *Conflict in Luke: Jesus, Authorities, Disciples*, Minneapolis, Minnesota: Fortress, 1991, p10

suspense (eg 4:20–21). Further, repeated references to an event can serve to underline its importance for the plot (eg 9:22,44; 18:31–34; 24:7).

Themes

The themes or motifs of a narrative are its leading or recurring ideas. In our study of Luke's characteristics we have seen, for instance, the importance of the themes of salvation and prayer. Literary analysis of Lucan themes include JD Kingsbury's study of conflict[1].

In addition to these areas storytellers employ various other literary devices, narrative techniques and rhetorical strategies in their stories, with an eye to influencing their readers. For example, irony (eg 18:9–14), symbolic figures of speech (eg 9:23), hyperbole or rhetorical exaggeration (eg 6:41ff) and foils (eg 4:1ff; the contrast between Satan and Jesus serves to highlight the latter) are found in Luke's narrative. It is the conviction of narrative critics that, since Luke's Gospel is in the form of a narrative, it is only when we understand how narratives work that we will be able to appreciate its message.

Outline, with examples, the methodology of narrative criticism.

Evaluation

The main contribution of literary criticism in general, and of narrative criticism in particular, to the study of the Gospels has been the focus upon the texts as finished products, rather than on speculation about their pre-history. Thus, narrative criticism is not concerned with the hypothetical pursuits of source and form criticism. Although there is common ground, neither is it concerned with redaction criticism's comparative study of an author's work and his apparent sources. Narrative criticism's sole interest in a Gospel's final form and respect for its literary integrity and independence are seen by many as welcome correctives to the shortcomings of historical-critical approaches to the Gospels. Welcome also is the emphasis on treating a text holistically (the whole work), rather than atomistically (focusing on isolated passages). Again, narrative criticism has drawn attention to the literary character of the Gospels, whose narrative features and dynamics must be appreciated if readers are to get the most from them and interpret them properly. Further, this approach to the Gospels has highlighted the aesthetic and emotional impact they make on readers through their literary artistry – a purely historical or intellectual approach to the Gospels limits their communicative potential. Finally, narrative criticism has demonstrated the weakness of adopting a detached, critical distance from texts. Texts are fully appreciated when the reader

---

[1] Kingsbury, *Conflict in Luke: Jesus, Authorities, Disciples* (op cit)

enters their narrative world and attempts to read them empathetically from the narrator's perspective. One's own intellectual integrity need not be compromised in this process, since it may be seen as a temporary psychological adjustment for the purpose of experiencing the full impact of the text.

However, the following criticisms of narrative criticism should be noted:

Rejection of history

Narrative criticism often regards the historical background and context of a text to be irrelevant to appreciation and understanding of the text. In fact, many deny that texts are referential (refer to a real world outside the text) at all. This self-consciously non-historical or even anti-historical approach tends to treat texts as fiction with no relation to reality. However, this reduction of texts to a merely literary level does not sit easily with Luke in particular who, as we have seen, is the most historically self-conscious author among the evangelists (see pp27–28), not least in his concern with salvation history (see pp229ff). Further, rejection of any historical referents outside the text can obscure its meaning, since some historical awareness is assumed on the part of the reader by the text itself in order for it to be understood (eg Luke's references to the Samaritans). Thus, extra-textual historical information is necessary for accurate interpretation of texts. The Gospels are not merely literature – they are also history and were perceived as such in the early centuries of the Church and beyond.

Rejection of sources

While attempts to reconstruct a text's pre-history can often be speculative, if the reconstruction is plausible then it can assist in understanding and interpretation of the text. Thus, most scholars are persuaded that literary dependence exists among the synoptics and that Luke used Mark. Redaction criticism, building on this, has enriched our understanding of Luke by drawing attention to its editing of Mark.

Use of modern literary criticism

Narrative criticism of the Gospels developed from, and uses the categories of, modern secular literary criticism, particularly in its analysis of novels and short stories. Questions can be raised here about the appropriateness of using modern literary methods to analyse ancient texts. A more historically sensitive and fruitful approach, it could be argued, would be to analyse the Gospels in accordance with known ancient literary genres and conventions. Thus, comparison of the Gospels with the literary genre of ancient Graeco-Roman biography has contributed to our appreciation of their character[1].

---

[1] eg Burridge, RA, *What Are the Gospels? A Comparison With Graeco-Roman Biography,* Cambridge: CUP, 1992

Overinterpretation

In their enthusiasm for literary analysis, narrative critics can sometimes 'find' literary patterns and strategies which are not obvious in the text, or attribute to the implied author conscious literary motives which may not have existed.

Complex terms and concepts

Technical terms and subtle distinctions (eg implied author, narratee) are often obscure and alienating to the uninitiated.

Thus, while narrative criticism is a useful tool for study of the Gospels, it is only one approach to the Gospels which must be complemented by other methods of analysis, particularly if its excesses are to be corrected.

Outline the main strengths and weaknesses of narrative criticism.

1 (a) Discuss Luke's presentation of Jesus in the context of salvation history. (30)

(b) Critically assess the claim that this view of history is outdated today. (15)

2 (a) Discuss the importance of one method of biblical criticism for an understanding of Luke's Gospel. (30)

(b) Critically evaluate the claim that the advantages of biblical criticism are outweighed by its disadvantages. (15)

3 (a) Discuss the contribution of the Proto-Luke theory to the understanding of Luke's Gospel. (30)

(b) Critically assess the claim that Luke's unique source material (L) is especially relevant today. (15)

Religious themes in Luke's Gospel

MERCY

LUKE'S GOSPEL HAS BEEN rightly called a "Gospel of mercy"[1]. In its first chapter we read of God's "mercy" (Greek *eleos*) no less than five times. In her song of praise, Mary exclaims that God's mercy is for those who fear him throughout the generations, and that he has helped Israel in remembrance of his mercy (1:50,54). We then read that when barren Elizabeth bears a son, neighbours and family hear that "the Lord had magnified his mercy with her" (1:58, author's translation). After the birth of his son, Zechariah's song refers to God's mercy shown to his ancestors, and to his "tender mercy" by which the dawn from on high will come to his people (1:72,78). In this very Jewish opening chapter of Luke, "mercy" appears mostly to have the Old Testament sense of God's covenantal faithfulness to his people (eg 1 Kings 8:23). Certainly, as both Mary and Zechariah speak of God's mercy, they relate the events of the infancy narratives to God's ancient covenantal promises to their ancestors (1:54–55,72ff). The emotional expression "tender mercy" (1:78; literally "bowels of mercy") indicates that here we are thinking of divine compassion as well as of covenantal obligation.

As we move on into the main body of the Gospel, we come across other references to God's mercy and compassion. Jesus tells his disciples that the Most High is "kind" to the ungrateful and the wicked, and that "your Father is merciful" (6:35–36). God's "compassion" is also at the midpoint of the parable of the lost son, graphically represented in the actions of the father, as he embraces his returning son (15:20; see pp125–126). The word translated "compassion" here is a form of the word rendered "tender" in 1:78 (see above). Again, in the parable of the Pharisee and the tax collector, the latter, conscious that he is a sinner, appeals solely to God's mercy and is thereby justified (18:13 –14)[2]. We have already studied other Lucan parables of God's mercy towards sinners, including the parables of the father and the child (11:11–13; see Fatherhood and prayer, pp94–95), the barren fig tree (13:6–9; see p109), the lost sheep (15:1–7, see pp122–123) and the lost coin (15:8–10, see pp122–123).

---

1 By Marie Joseph Lagrange, as cited by Fitzmyer, *The Gospel According to Luke I–IX* (op cit), p258
2 The word normally translated 'be merciful' in 18:13 means 'be propitiated, favourable'; see pp141–142.

However, the focus in the Gospel is on the mercy and compassion of *Jesus*, who embodies God's mercy in his ministry. Indeed, Luke has been described as "the scribe of the gentleness of Christ"[1]. On two occasions in Luke Jesus receives specific requests from the needy that he "have mercy" on them, and he responds by healing them – ten lepers (17:13; see p135) and a blind beggar (18:38–39; see p146). Again, we read of Jesus' "compassion" for a widow who is burying her only son, his inward concern expressing itself in the outward act of raising him from the dead (7:13; see pp215–216). The word translated "compassion" in this passage is used elsewhere in Luke of God's heartfelt concern (see comment on 1:78 and 15:20, p266) and, as in the parable of the lost son, is at the midpoint of this passage. Even when there is no specific reference to Jesus' mercy, there are plenty of examples throughout Luke's Gospel of his active concern for those in need. For example, in our study of Jesus' miracles we have considered his healings, exorcisms, raisings of the dead and nature miracles (see Miracles, p206ff).

We have also noted that in Luke the salvation that Jesus has brought is focused particularly on outcasts, the socially marginalised and downtrodden. Thus, we see a special concern in the ministry of Jesus for the Samaritans, the poor, women, children, tax collectors and sinners (for details, see pp36–38, and corresponding sections of Chapter 2 in this book). Further, we have considered (and will return to) Luke's universalism, with its message that the Gentiles are not beyond the scope of God's mercy. Also of relevance to our theme is Jesus' mercy to Peter, despite his failure to remain a loyal disciple (22:31–34,54–62; 24:34; see pp158–159).

In addition to the mercy of God and of Jesus, we find in Luke a requirement that followers of Jesus should also be merciful. Disciples of Jesus are to love their enemies, even as God is kind to the ungrateful and wicked. In short, they are told, "Be merciful, just as your Father is merciful" (6:35–36). Again, in the parable of the good Samaritan we read of his "compassion" (author's translation) for the wounded man, which expresses itself in practical care (10:33ff). This reference to compassion is at the centre of the passage, as it is in the other places where this same Greek word occurs in Luke (7:13; 15:20). After the lawyer correctly states that it was the one who "showed ... mercy" to the wounded man who was acting as his neighbour, Jesus tells him, "Go and do likewise" (10:37). Clearly, to "love ... your neighbour" (10:27) involves showing him mercy, regardless of race or religion. Finally, in Luke, giving to the needy is also an act of mercy. This is clear when we note that the Greek word *elein* ('to show mercy') is related to the word for 'alms' (*eleemosune*), which Jesus expects his disciples to give to those in need (11:41; 12:33; and eight times in Acts).

Outline the theme of mercy as presented in Luke.

---

[1] By Dante, as cited by Fitzmyer, *The Gospel According to Luke I–IX* (op cit), p257

UNIVERSALISM

We have already noted that the universal scope of God's salvation is an important theme for Luke (see p35). Indeed, William Barclay regards this as possibly the most obvious and outstanding characteristic of the Gospel of Luke[1]. This is understandable when we recall that the author of Luke was himself, in all probability, a Gentile (see A Gentile, p12). Certainly, he is concerned with locating the story of Jesus in the context of the wider Roman Empire, as well as part of the history of Israel (see History, pp27–28). He presents Jesus not only as the Messiah of Israel, but also as the Saviour of the world. The message that salvation is for all is highlighted in various places in the Gospel and is particularly prominent in the book of Acts. Even in the very Jewish and nationalistic infancy narratives with which the Gospel opens, the angels speak of peace on "earth" at the Saviour's birth (2:14). Here, Simeon also declares that the child Jesus, as God's salvation, was prepared in the presence of "all peoples" as a light for revelation to "the Gentiles", as well as for glory to God's people Israel (2:29–32). Jesus thus fulfils Israel's calling (Isa 42:6; 49:6), which will be continued by the Church's Gentile mission in Acts (13:47; 26:17–18).

This theme of salvation for all continues beyond the infancy narratives. While each Gospel quotes Isaiah 40:3 with reference to John the Baptist, it is only Luke who continues the quote to include the words "... and all flesh shall see God's salvation" (3:4–6/ Isa 40:3–5, Greek OT; cf Mt 3:3/ Mk 1:3/ Jn 1:23). Here, and later, Luke finds justification for the Church's Gentile mission in the Hebrew Scriptures. Also, Luke traces Jesus' ancestry back to Adam (the father of the human race) rather than, as in Matthew's genealogy of Jesus, Abraham (the father of the Jewish race; Lk 3:38/ Mt 1:2). We note too Luke's unique reference to the blessing of Gentiles rather than Israelites in the time of the prophets Elijah and Elisha (4:25–27) – another Old Testament precedent for the Church's Gentile mission. Again, like Matthew, Luke reports Jesus' commendation of a Gentile's faith as being superior to that found in Israel (7:1–10/ Mt 8:5–13), and Jesus' exorcism of a demon-possessed man in Gentile territory, who is, in effect, commissioned by Jesus to spread his message (8:26–39). Only Luke has the mission of the Seventy (or seventy-two) in addition to the mission of the Twelve (10:1–20), which many take as a symbolic anticipation of the Church's Gentile mission, since there were reckoned to be 70 nations in the world (cf Gen 10). Related to this is the suggestion that the number of the missionaries reflects the traditional number of the scribes who translated the Hebrew Bible into Greek (the LXX/Septuagint) to make it accessible to the wider world. However, there is no indication in Luke 10 that the missionaries went beyond Israel.

Another passage which reveals Luke's universalism states that the Gentile Ninevites and Queen of the South will rise up at the judgement to condemn Jesus' Jewish peers who are unresponsive to his message (11:29–32). There may also be a symbolic reference to the Gentiles in Jesus' parable of the mustard seed, specifically

---

[1] Barclay, William, *The Gospels and Acts, Volume One: The First Three Gospels,* London: SCM, 1976, p216

in its mention of the birds of the air settling in the tree's branches (13:18–19; see pp111–112). In the same chapter we read of how people from north and south as well as east and west (Matthew only mentions the latter) will be in God's kingdom (13:28–29/ Mt 8:11–12), although this may be a reference to *diaspora* Jews (beyond Israel) rather than Gentiles. Again, in the parable of the banquet Luke has servants sent out twice at the end. This double mission is not found in a similar parable in Matthew and may represent the Church's mission, first to Jews and then to Gentiles (14:15–24/ Mt 22:1–10). Also, in the parable of the tenants, the vineyard (ie God's kingdom) is taken from the tenants (ie the Jewish leaders) and given to "others", which may refer to the Gentiles (20:9–19). This would be consistent with Luke's unique reference to the Gentiles trampling on Jerusalem until their time is fulfilled (21:24). The Gospel also ends with Jesus telling his disciples that repentance and forgiveness of sins is to be preached in his name to "all nations" (24:47; see p189), the fulfilment of which is the main theme of the book of Acts. Luke's omission of Mark's story of Jesus' treatment of a Gentile woman (Mk 7:24–30) has been seen as being due to his Gentile sympathies (note v 27). However, this is only part of a large section of Mark (6:45–8:26) that Luke omits and the reasons for the omission are unclear.

However, despite this tendency to highlight the importance of the Gentiles, Luke is careful as a historian not to read the later Gentile mission of the Church back into the ministry of Jesus. In his scheme of salvation history, there does seem to be some distinction between the period of Jesus and the period of the Church, and it is within the latter that the Gentile mission belongs.

Luke's universalism is not only seen in his concern to show that God's saving purpose goes beyond one nation (Israel) to all nations (the Gentiles). We have seen it also in Luke's emphasis on Jesus' interest in outcasts and the socially excluded, particularly the Samaritans, the poor, women, children, tax collectors and sinners (see Mercy, p267, and pp36–38). For Luke, God's salvation in Jesus is available to all, regardless of race, religion, class, gender, age or morality. Thus, as William Barclay graphically puts it, Luke presents God as having arms wide enough to embrace the whole world, and a heart big enough to love all people[1]. Yet, it is also clear that while there is universalism in Luke, he was not a *universalist* – that is, while all *may* be saved, not all *will* be saved (eg 13:22–30; 17:26ff).

Outline the evidence of universalism in Luke's Gospel.

Despite Luke's universalism, he has been charged with being anti-Semitic, in the sense of being anti-Jewish[2]. Evidence for this has been found in Luke's portrayal of

---
[1] Barclay, *The Gospels and Acts, Volume One: The First Three Gospels* (op cit), p216
[2] For discussion of this issue, see Tuckett, *Luke: New Testament Guides* (op cit), pp54–64.

Jewish rejection of Jesus in Nazareth at the start of his ministry, provoked by Jesus' pro-Gentile sermon in the synagogue (4:16–30). Also, attention is drawn to Jesus' severe criticism of his Jewish peers in general and of Jewish leaders in particular (11:29–52), especially the claim that his own generation will be held accountable for "the blood of all the prophets shed since the foundation of the world" (11:50–51). Again, those whom Jesus taught and with whom he ate will be rejected by him as evildoers on the day of judgement and replaced, apparently, by Gentiles (13:22–30). The same idea of Gentiles replacing Jews in God's kingdom seems to be implied in the parable of the banquet (14:15–24). It is also worth noting that, of all the Gospels, Luke has Jesus predict the destruction of Jerusalem in the most detailed and graphic terms (19:43–44; 21:20,24). Finally, Luke's passion narrative appears to make the Jews in general, and not just their leaders, responsible for the death of Jesus (23:13,18,21,23,25,26ff; note "they" throughout), while the Gentile Pilate repeatedly insists on Jesus' innocence and tries to release him (23:4,14–16,20,22). JT Sanders argues that Luke is thoroughly hostile to the Jews, representing them as responsible for Jesus' death and opposed to God's purposes[1].

However, pro-Jewish material is also apparent in Luke. The very Jewish infancy narratives which begin the Gospel root the story of Jesus in Israel's history, and introduce it as the fulfilment of Israel's Scriptures. This latter theme is also found later in the Gospel (4:16ff; 24:25–27,44ff). Jesus has come for "the consolation of Israel" (2:25) and "the redemption of Jerusalem" (2:38; cf 24:21; Acts 1:6–7). Again, more than the other synoptics, Luke mentions Abraham, the father of the Jews (1:55,73; 3:8,34; 13:16,28; 16:22–30; 19:9; 20:37). We have noted too the importance for Luke of both Jerusalem (over which Jesus weeps, 19:41ff) and its temple, with which his Gospel begins and ends (see Geography, p28). Also, the twelve disciples represent the nucleus of a restored Israel (22:30), whose symbolic number is maintained even after Jesus' ascension (Acts 1:15ff). Further, it has been argued by CA Evans that Luke's stress on Jewish responsibility for the death of Jesus is due not to anti-Jewishness on his part, but to his desire to place the cross within the context of Israel's history[2]. J Jervell, at the opposite end of the spectrum from Sanders, emphasises the Jewishness of Luke's work. He maintains that the Church in Luke, both Jews and Gentiles, is not a new Israel but Israel restored[3]. The Gentile mission is due not to Israel's rejection of the Gospel, but to its acceptance of it, at least by some of her people. Israel is not rejected as such, but only those who reject the Gospel. Luke, Jervell holds, regards the Jewish Law to be still in force for the Church as the restored Israel (eg 16:17–18).

Tuckett makes the point that whether or not Luke is to be viewed as anti-Semitic greatly depends on whether Luke himself is regarded as an 'insider' or 'outsider' in relation to Judaism[4]. If he is an outsider (a Gentile), then his attacks on Judaism may

---

[1] Sanders, JT, *The Jews in Luke–Acts*, London: SCM, 1987

[2] Evans, CA, 'Is Luke's View of the Jewish Rejection of Jesus Anti-Semitic?' in *Reimaging the Death of the Lucan Jesus*, ed DD Sylva, Frankfurt: Anton Hain, 1990, pp29–56,174–183

[3] Jervell, J, *Luke and the People of God: A New Look at Luke–Acts*, Minneapolis: Fortress, 1972

[4] Tuckett, *Luke: New Testament Guides* (op cit), p62ff

be interpreted as anti-Semitism – although, due to the emotive character of this term since the Holocaust, a more accurate term may be anti-Judaism. However, even this is too general in light of the pro-Jewish material in Luke. If Luke is an insider (a Jew), then his criticisms of the Jews are to be seen as *self-criticism*, in line with the attacks made on Israel by her own prophets in her Scriptures. Alternatively, as Tuckett holds, it is probably too simplistic to see Luke in such clear-cut categories, and he should perhaps be regarded as a Gentile who is partially committed to Judaism (sometimes termed a 'God-fearer'). This would account for both the positive and negative attitudes to Judaism that are apparent in Luke, both of which must be taken into account to ensure a balanced assessment of the issue[1].

Assess the claim that Luke is anti-Semitic.

Following on from our discussion about Luke's attitude to the Jews and the issue of responsibility for the death of Jesus, it is perhaps appropriate at this point to consider the influence and role of the Pharisees, Sadducees and the Roman governor at the time of Jesus.

The Pharisees

The Pharisees belonged to a Jewish religious party with which Jesus often came into conflict in the Gospels. According to the first-century Jewish historian and Pharisee Josephus (*Ant* 17.41–42), there were about 6,000 of them towards the end of Herod the Great's reign (ie near the time of Jesus' birth). There is currently scholarly disagreement concerning a range of issues relating to this group, including their name, origins, history, and influence at the time of Jesus. The last point is particularly a matter of vigorous academic debate. The current tendency is to play down Pharisaic influence at this time, in contrast to earlier scholarship which held that the Pharisees dominated Jewish society through the Sanhedrin and the synagogues. This makes it very difficult to speak with anything approaching certainty on these key areas. The uncertainty arises from differing estimates and interpretations of the three main sources relating to the Pharisees:

> Josephus, in his *Jewish War*, his autobiographical *Life* and his *Antiquities of the Jews* (all written in the later first century)
> the New Testament (second half of the first century)
> rabbinic literature (third to sixth centuries AD)

---

[1] A range of scholarly views on the issue are available in JB Tyson (ed), *Luke–Acts and the Jewish People: Eight Critical Perspectives*, Minneapolis: Fortress, 1988.

Steve Mason notes that while all these sources present varying pictures of the Pharisees, they appear to agree that they were a non-priestly group who were regarded as experts in the Jewish laws; functioned as social power brokers between the ruling elite and the general public; promoted traditions additional to biblical laws; were concerned with matters of ritual purity and tithing; and believed in the existence of an afterlife, judgement and a spirit world[1]. However, as Mason goes on to point out, scholars are generally not confident concerning, among other things, the meaning of the sect's name (whether, for example, 'separatists', 'consecrated' or 'Persians') and the time and context of their origins (Mason favours an origin in the second century BC, in the turmoil after the Maccabean revolt).

JB Green notes that Luke is clearly interested in the Pharisees and that in his Gospel they have two main character traits[2]. First, they are interpreters of the Jewish Law, who are concerned with its observance in daily conduct. This brings them into conflict with Jesus because of his association with tax collectors and sinners (5:30; 7:39; 15:2), his Sabbath practice (6:2,7; 14:3), his failure to observe ritual handwashing before eating (11:38), and the failure of his disciples to fast (5:33). Jesus, however, criticises their focus on outward, ritual purity to the neglect of inward, moral purity, and their focus on meticulous tithing to the neglect of practising God's justice and love (11:37–44; see Criticism of the Pharisees, pp99–100). Second, in Luke the Pharisees are interested in promoting themselves. They love the seat of honour in synagogues and respectful greetings in the marketplace (11:43). Only in Luke do we have the parable of the Pharisee and the tax collector, where the former self-righteously compares himself with others (18:9–14; see The parable of the Pharisee and the tax collector, pp140–142). Pharisees are also portrayed as lovers of money (16:14). Indeed, Green regards the main issue in Luke's characterisation of the Pharisees to be hypocrisy (12:1; see Hypocrisy, pp101–102; cf 13:15), which Green views not as insincerity but as failure to follow God's purposes. To these two characteristics we may add the Pharisees' failure in Luke to recognise the identity and authority of Jesus (see 5:17,20ff; 19:37–40). In short, the Pharisees reject God's purpose for themselves (7:29–30).

Nonetheless, in Luke Jesus is invited by Pharisees to have table fellowship with them in their homes and accepts (7:36; 11:37; 14:1). He is addressed respectfully by them as "Teacher" (7:40; 19:39). Some even warn him of Herod Antipas' threat on his life (13:31). This positive presentation of the Pharisees continues into Acts, where the Christian Paul identifies himself as a Pharisee (Acts 5:33–39; 15:5; 23:6; 26:5). It is notable too that despite Pharisaic hostility to Jesus earlier in the Gospel (eg 11:53), the Pharisees do not explicitly feature in the passion narrative which recounts Jesus' trial and crucifixion – the last mention of the Pharisees is in 19:39. Certainly, in Luke the Pharisees are characterised as distinct from the Jewish leadership, and are

---

[1] Mason, Steve, 'Pharisees' in *Dictionary of New Testament Background*, eds Craig A Evans and Stanley E Porter, Leicester: IVP, 2000, p786

[2] Green, *New Testament Theology: The Theology of the Gospel of Luke* (op cit), pp72–75

portrayed sympathetically in Acts[1]. However, against the views that Luke has removed the Pharisees from his passion narrative to clear them from responsibility for Jesus' death, and that he wants in his positive view of the Pharisees to emphasise the continuity between Judaism and the Church (both Pharisees and Christians believe in resurrection), JD Kingsbury makes several points[2]. For example, Luke does connect the Pharisees with Jerusalem (5:17; 19:39), whose leaders rejected Jesus; the Pharisees are linked with the scribes/teachers of the law and through them with the chief priests (eg 5:21,30; 23:10), and in Acts Luke regards all the Jewish leaders as being guilty of the death of Jesus (Acts 3:17; 13:27).

Discuss what we know about the Pharisees and Luke's characterisation of them.

The Sadducees

Josephus tells us that this Jewish group existed in the second century BC, during the Maccabean period. Unfortunately, we know little of any certainty about the Sadducees, despite certain beliefs and characteristics that are often confidently attributed to them[3]. Along with Josephus, the New Testament and rabbinic literature are our sources of information. The origin of their name is unknown, although it has been connected by some with the Hebrew word for 'righteous' (*saddiq*) and the priest Zadok at the time of David (eg 1 Kings 1:32). Josephus says that they did not believe in an afterlife or rewards or punishments beyond death, and that they believed in human free will. He also states that they followed only the written Law, rather than traditions (unlike the Pharisees). Thus, they are characterised as being religiously conservative. Again, he associates them with the wealthy and higher class, noting that they did not have the support of the general public. The high priest Ananas is identified as a Sadducee. The rabbinic writings record disagreements between Sadducees and Pharisees over matters of ritual purity, civil law and the Sabbath, and there is reference to Sadducean denial of belief in resurrection. In Luke's Gospel, we read of them in one place where they pose a question to Jesus which is motivated by their rejection of resurrection (20:27–40). This attitude to resurrection is noted again by Luke in Acts, along with their rejection of belief in angels or spirits, in contrast to the Pharisees (Acts 4:1–2; 23:6–8). In Acts, they are also associated with the priests and the temple, as well as the Sanhedrin (4:1; 5:17; 23:6). Matthew often links Pharisees and Sadducees (eg 3:7; 16:1), implying that they had much in common, which Josephus also claims.

---

[1] Gowler, DB, *Host, Guest, Enemy and Friend: Portraits of the Pharisees in Luke and Acts,* New York: Peter Lang, 1991

[2] Kingsbury, *Conflict in Luke: Jesus, Authorities, Disciples* (op cit), pp22,148

[3] See 'Sadducees' by Gary Porton in *Dictionary of New Testament Background* (op cit), pp1050–1052.

NT Wright has drawn attention to the political usefulness of Saducean beliefs[1]. Their belief in free will was compatible with maintaining a position in power. Conservative rejection of new laws and traditions was a safeguard against the destabilising influences of innovative revolutionaries who would threaten their position. Also, since resurrection was used as a metaphor for the restoration of Israel to power, which would again threaten Saducean power, it was advantageous to reject any belief in resurrection. Furthermore, rejection of the afterlife in general suited their focus on the affairs of this world. Whether or not this is an unwarranted politicisation of Saducean theology, it reminds us that religious beliefs and practices are not totally isolated from their political context.

Discuss what we know about the Sadducees and their role in Luke.

Pontius Pilate

Pontius Pilate was the Roman prefect of Judea (AD 26–36/37; cf Lk 3:1), in whose jurisdiction and under whose authority Jesus was crucified. In 1961 archaeologists uncovered in Caesarea a stone partially, yet indisputably, inscribed with his name and that of the Emperor Tiberius, along with Pilate's title 'prefect'. Our sources for Pilate, in addition to the New Testament, are Josephus and the Jewish writer Philo of Alexandria (around 20 BC to AD 50). Thus, we have Christian and Jewish perspectives of Pilate.

His insensitivity to Jewish religious concerns is apparent in the Jewish sources. Josephus reports (*Ant* 18.55–59; *Jewish War* 2.169–174) that Pilate brought into Jerusalem Roman standards bearing images of the emperor. The soldiers would have given divine honours to the standards. Jews went to Pilate's residence in Caesarea to protest. His threat of military force against the protesters was ineffective, since they showed their willingness to die over the matter. To prevent an uprising, Pilate withdrew the images from Jerusalem. He also took money from the temple treasury to build an aqueduct in the city, and provoked Jewish protests. Pilate's soldiers moved among the crowd in civilian dress, armed with clubs (rather than swords) which they used on the people with fatal consequences (*Ant* 18.60–62; *Jewish War* 2.175–177). Philo mentions that Pilate placed votive shields bearing the emperor's name, although not his image, in Herod's palace in Jerusalem (*Embassy to Gaius* 299–305). Jewish protesters, including Herod's sons, were ignored by Pilate. They appealed to the Emperor Tiberius himself, who was furious with Pilate and ordered the removal of the shields. Finally, Josephus recounts (*Ant* 18.85–89) the incident which led to his dismissal as governor of Judea. In AD 36 Pilate's soldiers engaged in battle with followers of a Samaritan prophet who were gathering at Mount Gerizim. His brutal

---

[1] Wright, NT, *The New Testament and the People of God*, London: SPCK, 1992, pp211–212

treatment of this group led to complaints against Pilate before his superior, Vitellius. Pilate was sent to Rome for trial before the emperor, but arrived after Tiberius' death.

Both Philo and Josephus characterise Pilate as a cruel, greedy and oppressive ruler. His disregard for Jewish religious beliefs is evident too in the pagan symbols on the coins issued during his reign. While other governors of Judea generally had inoffensive images such as grapes or trees on their coins, Pilate had a ladle used by Roman priests for wine in honour of the gods, or a curved staff which was the symbol of the Roman official (augur) who predicted the future.

Luke also refers to Pilate's brutality when he records that he had mingled the blood of some Galileans with their sacrifices (13:1; see p109). This incident is not mentioned in any other source, unless it refers to the deaths that followed Jewish protests at Pilate's seizing of temple funds (see p274). All the Gospels and Acts state that Jesus was crucified under Pontius Pilate, as does the Roman historian Tacitus in about AD 115 (*Annals* 15.44.3) and, possibly, Josephus (*Ant* 18.63ff; however, there is debate about the authenticity of this passage). A contrast is often drawn between the Christian portrait of Pilate in the Gospels and the Jewish characterisation of him in Philo and Josephus. While the latter portray him as strong-willed, aggressive and unconcerned about offending the Jews, the former present him as a weak, indecisive leader who is easily manipulated by Jewish leaders. It is often held that the Pilate of the Gospels has been so portrayed in order to maximise Jewish responsibility for the death of Jesus, while at the same time minimising the embarrassment of the fact that the founder of the Christian movement was executed by the Romans (cf Lk 23:1–25; Acts 3:13–15; 13:28–29). However, Helen Bond has argued that this contrast is too neat and simplistic[1]. She maintains that the characterisation of Pilate in Philo and Josephus is shaped by theological concerns, and that the portraits of Pilate in the Gospels are more complex than the traditional view assumes. In this view, Pilate was not as harsh as the Jewish sources imply, but sought to maintain a balance between his accountability to the emperor and the concerns of the Judeans. A contrasting view of Pilate, however, has been presented more recently by Warren Carter[2]. Carter asserts that, far from portraying Pilate as weak and indecisive, the Gospels, as well as the Jewish sources, present him as an astute and arrogant agent of imperial power, who manipulates events in the interests of that power and its allies (the Jewish leaders). However, even if the Gospels do appear to have a weaker Pilate than that of the Jewish sources, it may be because Pilate had to tread more carefully at the time of Jesus' execution due to wider developments, such as his provocation of the emperor (see p274).

No one in the New Testament has more references to Pontius Pilate than Luke (Lk 3:1–2; 13:1; 20:20; 23:1–25,52; Acts 3:13; 4:27; 13:28; on Lk 23, see p165ff). Bond sees Gentile Luke's characterisation of Pilate as shaped by his desire to relate the story of Christian beginnings to Roman history, and to present the Romans as divine agents in the history of salvation (cf Acts 4:27–28). Despite the imperfections of Rome's

---

[1] Bond, Helen, *Pontius Pilate in History and Interpretation*, Cambridge: CUP, 1998

[2] Carter, Warren, *Pontius Pilate: Portraits of a Roman Governor*, Collegeville, Minnesota: Liturgical Press, 2003

governors, such as Pilate and Festus, they did not regard the early Christian movement as a political threat. Luke's picture of Pilate, according to Bond, served a wider aim – namely that of defending the Roman Empire in the eyes of the early Christians.

Tasks

a Discuss the claim that our sources for Pontius Pilate present contrasting portraits.

b Comment on the role of Pilate in Luke.

DISCIPLESHIP

The word traditionally translated "disciple" in the New Testament (Greek *mathetes*) means 'learner', 'pupil', 'apprentice' or 'adherent', and is found almost 40 times in Luke's Gospel. The term and its equivalents were used in the first century to refer to the students and followers of various philosophical and religious leaders. Thus, 'disciple' assumes the existence of, and a relationship to, a 'teacher' (cf Lk 6:40). Early in Luke, Jesus himself is apparently portrayed as a disciple, listening to and questioning teachers (2:46–47,52). We read in the Old Testament of disciples of the prophet Isaiah (Isa 8:16; cf 50:4), and other prophets and teachers in Israel had their adherents as well (eg 2 Kings 4:38; Prov 22:17). The Gospels refer to the disciples of Moses (Jn 9:28), of the Pharisees (Lk 5:33), and of John the Baptist (Lk 5:33) as well as, of course, to the disciples of Jesus. While Matthew and Mark usually reserve the term 'disciple' for the Twelve, Luke uses the word also of many other followers of Jesus (6:13,17; 19:37–39). The corresponding term 'teacher' is used of Jesus most frequently by Luke in the Gospels, although it is applied to him by those who are not his disciples. While the title 'rabbi' is not used in Gentile Luke's Gospel, it is clear that Jesus is perceived in the Gospels in general as a Jewish teacher with disciples who followed him around (cf Mt 23:7–8; Mk 9:5; Jn 3:2). In addition to 'disciple', the word 'follow' is also used in the Gospels, with reference to the call of Jesus and its accompanying response (eg Lk 5:11,27–28).

Discipleship is the positive response of one's whole life to Jesus and his teaching. This involves both initial and ongoing commitment; that is, we may distinguish broadly between *becoming* and *being* a disciple of Jesus, although, as we shall see, how one commences the journey is also how one must continue it. Indeed, in Luke 'journey' is a metaphor for discipleship. He refers to "the way/path" (author's translation) in his Gospel (1:79; 3:4–5; 7:27; 20:21) and in Acts (9:2; 19:9,23; 22:4; 24:14,22). Jesus' own long journey to Jerusalem at the heart of the Gospel, accompanied by his disciples who are taught by him "on the road", is symbolic of the journey of discipleship. This theme is intensified in the climactic chapter of the Gospel (24:13,15,17,27,32,35). One begins the journey by becoming a disciple, and one must continue it by being a disciple.

Becoming a disciple

The start of the journey involves the following:

The call of Jesus

In Luke we read of Jesus calling people to "follow" him, which initiates the journey of discipleship. This initiative of Jesus in summoning individuals to follow him stands in contrast with the disciples of Greek philosophers and Jewish rabbis who volunteered their allegiance. Peter is called to a new vocation and he, along with James and John, responds to the call (5:10–11). Later in the same chapter, Levi is also called ("Follow me") and responds similarly (5:27–28,32). However, Luke presents us with examples of people who do not understand what is involved in Jesus' call to follow him, or are not willing to meet its demands, as in the cases of the three would-be disciples at the start of Jesus' journey to Jerusalem (9:57–62; see Would-be followers of Jesus, pp78–81) and the rich ruler near the journey's end (18:22–25; see The rich ruler, pp143–144). This leads to another important element in becoming a disciple of Jesus in Luke.

Counting the cost

Large crowds accompany Jesus on his journey to Jerusalem, but they have not begun the journey of discipleship. By means of two parables of discipleship, Jesus urges them to 'count the cost' of discipleship before committing themselves to it (14:25–33; see Conditions of discipleship, pp120–122). The threefold use of the phrase "cannot be my disciple" in this passage spells out the cost of becoming Jesus' disciples – allegiance to him above one's own family and life (v 26), carrying the cross of suffering, even to the point of death (v 27), and renunciation of all one's possessions (v 33). As noted above, some of the people Jesus meets have not considered the cost or are not prepared to meet it (9:57–62; 18:22–25). It is a "narrow door" leading to salvation and God's kingdom, which one must "strive" (*agonizomai*) to enter, for many will be unsuccessful in their attempts (13:22–30; see The narrow door, pp112–113).

Repentance

The call to discipleship is a call to repentance – that is, a call to "sinners" to turn from sin to God and his ways (see 5:32; 13:1–5; 15:7,10,18ff). This is the call that John the Baptist makes, spelling out the ethical nature of repentance to the crowds, some of whom will become his disciples (3:3,7–14). Repentance is the appropriate response to Jesus' ministry (10:13; 11:32), and is to be part of the Church's universal message (24:47; cf Acts 2:38; 17:30).

Faith

In the Gospel, faith is an essential part of a proper response to Jesus, and is regularly linked with salvation in its broad Lucan sense (5:20; 7:50; 8:12,48; 17:19; 18:42). This continues into Acts, where faith *in Jesus* is more explicit in the initial response to the Christian message (eg 10:43; 16:30–31).

> **Tasks**
>
> **a** Outline the background and meaning of the term 'disciple'.
>
> **b** According to Luke's Gospel, what is involved in becoming a disciple of Jesus?

Being a disciple

Becoming a disciple is but the beginning of *being* a disciple. Having started the journey, one must continue it. Indeed, Luke implies that being a disciple is becoming a disciple over and over again with each new day. We have seen that counting the cost involves realising that a cross must be carried (14:27), but only Luke tells us that this cross must be taken up "daily" (9:23; the word is not in Mt 16:24/ Mk 8:34). Being a disciple is following Jesus in response to his call to do just that, but this means continuing the journey beyond the first steps with which it began (5:11,27–28; 9:23; 18:28). Being a disciple of Jesus is multifaceted and all-embracing, since it covers everything that Jesus teaches his followers to do. According to Luke's Gospel it includes at least the following elements:

Self-denial

Followers of Jesus must "deny" themselves (9:23) or, more starkly, "hate" their own lives (14:26; see p120). Jesus' words here do not deny that there is a proper love of self (10:27b–28); rather, following Jesus must take priority over one's own life.

Bearing the cross

Discipleship involves carrying the cross (14:27) and taking up the cross on a daily basis (9:23). The context of the latter statement indicates that discipleship will involve suffering, persecution and possibly death, since Jesus has been speaking of his own impending death (9:22; cf 6:22; 12:4,11; 21:12,16–17). What Simon of Cyrene will do literally (23:26), Jesus' disciples must do metaphorically.

Priority of Jesus

Jesus and the kingdom of God that he brings must be given priority over everyone and everything else. Neither family nor possessions can have a higher claim on one's allegiance (9:59–62; 14:26; 16:13; cf 12:51–53; 14:15–24). The issue of possessions in relation to discipleship is not a clear-cut matter in Luke and needs to be considered separately (see pp280–281).

Faith

As well as the initial faith which marks the beginning of discipleship, there must be an ongoing trust, particularly in the fatherly goodness of God to provide for his children's physical needs (12:22–31, especially v 28; 11:3). In response to the apostles' request that their faith might be increased, Jesus speaks of the power of faith as small as a mustard seed (17:5–6; see Faith, p134).

Learning from Jesus

A disciple is a learner and Mary, in contrast to her sister Martha, is characterised as the model disciple who sits at the master's feet, listening to his teaching (10:38–42; see Martha and Mary, pp88–89). Most of Jesus' journey to Jerusalem in the central section of Luke is also taken up with the teaching of his disciples.

Obeying Jesus

In the parable of the two builders (6:47–49; see p299), Jesus underlines the importance of not merely calling Jesus "Lord", but also of doing what he says. A disciple must put his master's teaching into practice.

Service

Jesus uses the master–servant analogy to teach his disciples to be faithful servants in his absence, humble and ready for their master's return (12:35–38,41–48; 17:7–10, see Readiness for the master's return, pp105–107, and The parable of the unworthy slave, p134).

Worship

We have already noted that the worship of God is an important theme for Luke (see p39) and, along with the worship of Jesus, it is certainly a characteristic of Jesus' disciples (19:37; 24:53).

Prayer

Again, this is another important Lucan theme. In this area the master sets an example for his disciples to follow, as well as teaching them on the matter (see pp38–39). Through prayer, disciples receive God's assistance and Spirit to enable them to meet the demands of discipleship (11:4,9–13; cf 3:21–22).

Love

Love for God and for one's neighbour (10:25–37; see The parable of the good Samaritan, pp85–88), and even love for one's enemies (6:27–36; see p294ff), are essential to discipleship.

Forgiveness

Jesus taught his disciples to be forgiving, rather than fault-finding, particularly towards their fellow disciples (6:37–42, see p296ff; 11:4; 17:3–4; see Fourth petition, p92, and Sin and forgiveness, p133).

Witness

Jesus' disciples are called to bear witness to him and his message, to engage in mission to others (5:10; 9:1–6; 10:1–16; 12:8; 21:13; 24:45–48). This they can do by the power of the Holy Spirit (12:11–12; 21:12–15; 24:47–49; Acts 1:8).

Perseverance

Disciples must persevere through trials and temptations, since the possibility of temporary or failing faith is real (8:13–15; 11:4; 18:8; 21:19; 22:3–6,28,31–34,40,46).

Likeness to Jesus

Disciples will be like their teacher (6:40; see p298), in that they will follow his example as well as learning his teaching.

Reward

Discipleship will be rewarded in this age and in the age to come (6:22–23,35; 18:28–30).

Task

Outline the main elements of being a disciple of Jesus in Luke.

As mentioned earlier, Luke's presentation of the issue of possessions in relation to discipleship is complex. On the one hand, discipleship seems to demand total renunciation of possessions; on the other, it is assumed that disciples of Jesus will have personal possessions, which they must make proper use of. Thus, as JA Fitzmyer characterises it, Luke has both a radical and a moderate attitude toward possessions[1].

The radical demand of total renunciation is seen most clearly in the uniquely Lucan statement of Jesus, "... any of you who does not give up all his possessions cannot be my disciple" (14:33, author's translation; see p120). The words "any" and "all" (the same word in the Greek) are comprehensive, indicating that no person or possession is exempt from this condition of discipleship. This demand that "all" be given up is a particular emphasis of Luke's picture of discipleship. The word is found in discipleship passages relating to Peter and his companions, Levi, and the rich ruler, but not in the parallel passages in his probable source, Mark (cf Lk 5:11/ Mk 1:20; Lk 5:28/ Mk 2:17; Lk 18:22/ Mk 10:21; but, cf Lk 18:28/ Mk 10:28). We note too Jesus' command to his disciples to sell their possessions and give to the needy (12:33). Again, the Twelve are instructed to take nothing on their mission and, unlike Mark, Luke makes no exception (cf Lk 9:3/ Mk 6:8). Similar instructions are given to the Seventy on their mission (10:4). We have also already considered Luke's special concern for the poor and critique of the rich (see pp36–37). This rejection of possessions appears to have characterised the early Church in Jerusalem in the opening chapters of Acts (2:44–45; 3:6; 4:32ff; but note 5:4).

However, evidence in Luke may also be found for the moderate attitude, which does not regard ownership of possessions as inconsistent with discipleship, but does require proper use of such possessions. While the rich ruler is required to sell "all" and

---

[1] Fitzmyer, *The Gospel according to Luke I–IX* (op cit), p249

give to the poor, the same is not true of Zacchaeus, who experiences salvation even though he gives "half" of his possessions to the poor (19:8–9; see p148) – although he may have used the other half to make generous restitution to those he had defrauded (19:8). Again, Luke's regular emphasis on the need to give "alms" (ie give to the poor) assumes that followers of Jesus will have some money, with which they can help the needy (6:30; 11:41; 12:33; cf Acts 9:36; 10:2,4; 20:35). The good Samaritan was able to help one in need because he had personal resources, and is presented by Jesus as an example to follow (10:29–37). We note too that some women who accompany Jesus and the Twelve provide for them out of "their possessions" (8:3, author's translation). Further, Jesus himself revises his instruction to disciples that they should take no possessions on their mission, advising that they should acquire possessions (22:35–36). Certainly, after the opening chapters of Acts we find that early Christians apparently did not regard renunciation of possessions as essential (cf Acts 16:14; 17:12).

However one tries to resolve the tension between the radical and moderate attitudes to possessions in Luke, several parables make important points about wealth and possessions relevant to discipleship. The parable of the rich fool and its context (12:13–21; see The parable of the rich fool, p103) highlights the dangers of greed and of being rich materially, but not towards God. The parable of the rich man and Lazarus (16:19–31; see The rich man and Lazarus, pp131–133) contrasts the postmortem destinies of rich and poor, which are a reversal of their condition on earth. The parable of the shrewd manager and its context (16:1–15; see The parable of the shrewd manager and The hypocrisy of the Pharisees, pp127–129) teaches the need for prudent use of wealth to secure future spiritual security and reward. Likewise, the parable of the pounds (19:11–27; see The parable of the pounds, pp148–150) makes the quality of one's spiritual future dependant on the faithful use of one's resources in the present. Finally, as noted above, the parable of the good Samaritan (10:25–37; see The parable of the good Samaritan, pp85–88) commends the use of possessions to help the needy (see also 14:12–14). It may be that it is not so much possessions as *possessiveness* that is the problem highlighted in Luke. Indeed, it has been argued that possessions in Luke's writings act as a symbol of one's inner response to God (12:34)[1].

Discuss Luke's view of possessions in relation to discipleship.

The disciples

We noted earlier that Luke uses the word 'disciple' to refer to a wider group of followers of Jesus than the Twelve, whom he chose from this wider group and named "apostles" (6:12–16). However, these twelve disciples have a special place and role

---

[1] Johnson, LT, *The Literary Function of Possessions in Luke–Acts,* Missoula, Montana: Scholars Press, 1977

in Luke, as they do in the other Gospels. More than the other synoptics, Luke refers to them as "apostles" – those whom Jesus specially commissions as his authoritative representatives (see p134). Luke stresses that they are Jesus' regular companions (8:1; 22:14,28).

Andrew Clark sees the Twelve as fulfilling four main roles in Luke's writings: they are the nucleus of a restored Israel, witnesses to Jesus' resurrection, authoritative teachers, and missionaries to Israel[1]. The first two of these roles are most relevant to Luke's Gospel. The idea that the Twelve are the nucleus of a restored Israel is most apparent in Jesus' saying about the apostles sitting on thrones judging the 12 tribes of Israel (22:28–30; see p158). Just as the 12 sons of Jacob/Israel were the founders and nucleus of the 12 tribes of the nation of Israel (Gen 49, especially v 1–2,28), so the twelve apostles are the founders and nucleus of a renewed Israel that Jesus is forming. Indeed, they may be the "others" to whom the owner gives his vineyard (God's kingdom), after removing its previous tenants (the Jewish leaders; see 20:16,19). While Jesus' statement about the 12 thrones may point to an eschatological fulfilment at the end times, its fulfilment appears to have begun already in the opening chapters of Acts. In these chapters, the importance of the symbolism of the number 12 is maintained (1:15–26; cf 26:7), and the Twelve are presented as the new and legitimate rulers of the renewed Israel, in place of the Sanhedrin (2:42; 4:35; and chs 3–5 in general). The second role of the Twelve in Luke is their place as witnesses to Jesus' resurrection. In the Gospel, this is highlighted in the commission of the apostles and others by the risen Jesus (24:33,44–48; cf 21:12–13). This witness to Jesus' resurrection becomes an important role of the apostles, particularly in Acts (eg 1:8,21–22; 2:32; 3:15; 4:33). Thus, they are a bridge linking the ministry of Jesus (Luke) to the mission of the Church (Acts). Clark's third and fourth roles of the apostles are relevant to Acts, where the Twelve are authoritative teachers and missionaries to Israel. While they are missionaries to Israel in the Gospel as well (9:1–6), this role is not exclusive to them (10:1ff).

Turning from the roles of the Twelve to their characterisation, JD Kingsbury states that disciples in general, and the Twelve in particular, are presented by Luke as having two main and contrasting character traits: loyalty and immaturity[2]. Their loyalty to Jesus and God's purposes is apparent, for example, in:

> their positive response to Jesus' call (5:11,27–28)
> their mission as Jesus' commissioned representatives (5:10; 9:1–6; 24:44–48)
> their obedience to Jesus' instructions (eg 9:14–15,21,36; 19:28–35; 22:7–13)
> their solidarity with Jesus in the face of opposition (eg 5:29–35; 6:1–5; 22:28)
> their worship of Jesus (24:52)

---

[1] Clark, Andrew, *Parallel Lives: The Relation of Paul to the Apostles in the Lucan Perspective*, Carlisle: Paternoster Press, 2001, pp116–125,326–327

[2] Kingsbury, *Conflict in Luke: Jesus, Authorities, Disciples* (op cit), pp18–21,109–139

As his specially selected inner circle (6:13), they are privileged with knowledge of the mysteries of God's kingdom (8:1,9–10; cf 10:21–24). However, Luke also presents a negative picture of the Twelve. Their immaturity – specifically spiritual immaturity – is apparent, for example, in:

> their lack of faith in testing circumstances (eg 8:25; 9:13; cf 24:8–11,41)
> their failure to comprehend Jesus' mission and God's purposes (eg 9:44–45; 18:15–17,31–34; 22:49–51)
> their ineffective ministry (9:40)
> their self-importance (9:46–48; 22:24–27)
> their narrow sectarianism (9:49–50,52–55)
> their lack of spiritual vigilance (22:45–46)

In the passion narrative, the failure of two disciples in particular is underlined – Judas' betrayal (22:3–6,21–22,47–48) and Peter's denial (22:33–34,54–62). Having said that, as we noted earlier (p16), the disciples appear in a more favourable light than in Mark's Gospel. Most notably, Luke alone of the synoptics does not have all the disciples deserting Jesus at his arrest (Mt 26:56/ Mk 14:50/ Lk 22:53–54; cf 23:49).

Tasks

a What roles do the twelve disciples have in Luke?
b Discuss Luke's characterisation of the Twelve.

Peter

In his discussion of the roles of Peter in Luke's Gospel, Andrew Clark observes that Luke portrays Peter in representative and personal ways[1]. First, Peter acts as a representative of the Twelve. Indeed, he is their chief representative and spokesman, named first in Luke's two lists of the apostles (Lk 6:13–16; Acts 1:13), as he is also in the other synoptics' lists (Mt 10:2–4/ Mk 3:16–19). Like the other synoptics, Luke also notes that the name Peter was added by Jesus to his Jewish name Simon. However, unlike Matthew (16:17–18), Luke does not explain the significance of the new name (meaning 'rock') for Peter's role among the apostles. We find Peter as a representative of, and spokesman for, the others:

> in the story of the haemorrhaging woman (8:45; see p221)
> in the account of Peter's confession of Jesus as Messiah (9:20)
> in the story of the transfiguration of Jesus (9:33)
> in the midst of Jesus' parabolic teaching (12:41; see p106)
> after Jesus' conversation with the rich ruler (18:28; see p144)
> at the Last Supper (22:31; the word "you" is plural, referring to all the apostles; see p158)

---

[1] Clark, *Parallel Lives: The Relation of Paul to the Apostles in the Lucan Perspective* (op cit), pp125–128,327–328

Peter is associated with John and James in particular (5:10; 8:51; 9:28), as in the other Gospels. Only in Luke's account of the preparation for the Passover are Peter and John specified as the disciples who are sent to make the preparations (22:8), an association that will be found frequently in the earlier chapters of Acts.

However, it is Peter's role as an individual that is most prominent in Luke. The first time we read of Simon in Luke is when Jesus heals his mother-in-law in Simon's own house (4:38–39; see Simon Peter's mother-in-law, p208). He is mentioned here without any introduction. A little after this passage we have an account of a miraculous catch of fish, which has Peter as the main character and climaxes with his personal commission by Jesus to catch "people" rather than fish from that point on (5:1–11; for detailed comment on this, see The miraculous catch of fish, pp209–210). Peter's personal role is also seen at the Last Supper, where he is singled out as the one for whom Jesus has prayed, even though the satanic threat is directed at all the apostles (22:31–32; see p158). He is the one who, when his faith is restored, must strengthen his brothers. He performs this role in the earlier chapters of Acts. In the passage, Peter affirms that he is ready to accompany Jesus to prison and death, but is instead told by Jesus that he will deny him three times before the night is out. The fulfilment of this prophecy is recorded, with Luke's unique reference to the Lord turning and looking at Peter (22:33–34,54–62; see pp158–159, and Peter's denial, pp162–163). Finally, in Luke's resurrection narrative Peter is the only apostle to visit the empty tomb in response to the women's claims, and the remaining apostles and others report that the risen Lord has appeared to Peter (24:10–12,33–34; see pp180–181,187). Peter has seen the empty tomb and the risen Lord, and this role of Peter as the main apostolic witness of Jesus' resurrection will be highlighted in Acts (eg 2:32; 3:15; 5:31–32).

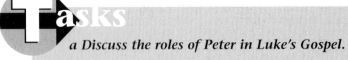

a Discuss the roles of Peter in Luke's Gospel.

b Evaluate the claim that Luke characterises Peter as a mixture of strengths and weaknesses.

WOMEN

A long recognised characteristic of Luke's Gospel is the prominent place it gives to women (see Women, p37), a prominence unmatched by the other Gospels. This concern for women is remarkable, when set against the generally patriarchal, androcentric (male-dominated) and, at times, misogynistic (woman-despising) cultural background of its times. For example, the Jewish writing Ecclesiasticus or Sirach, written about 180 BC, states that sin began with a woman and because of her we all must die (Sirach 25:24; Adam is not mentioned!). Also, if a wife does not obey her husband, he should get rid of her (25:26). Again, a man's wickedness is better than a woman's goodness, for she brings shame and disgrace (42:14). We find a similarly negative view of women in the first-century Jewish writers Josephus and Philo of Alexandria. Philo often characterises women as weak, and Josephus states that woman is inferior to man in every respect (*Against Apion* 2.201; although some doubt the authenticity of the text here). Various sayings of rabbis in the Talmud, written in the centuries immediately following New Testament times, also reflect a low view of women. One rabbi says that a man ought to thank God each day that he was not made a woman (Tosepta, Berakot 7.18), and another that the only wisdom woman has is with the spindle (Babylonian Talmud, Yoma 66b). However, there is some evidence that women did hold responsible positions in Jewish society, including ruler of the synagogue, and that they could be perceived as effective leaders, such as Judith in the late second century BC (see the Apocrypha). Despite such exceptions, in a context of general cultural sexism, apparent in literature over which males had a virtual monopoly, Luke's Gospel appears to be female-friendly and pro-woman. Having said that, we shall see that feminist scholarship has argued Luke is not entirely free from the gender bias of his cultural context.

Luke's concern for women is evident in a number of ways. In his Gospel he names or includes at least 12 women not mentioned in the other Gospels. Apparent too is Luke's special concern with widows. Again, Luke likes to pair men and women, often in near context, to create a male–female parallelism which implies their equal dignity before God. This is seen in the table below.

Angelic announcement to Zechariah (1:13–20)	Angelic announcement to Mary (1:26–38)
Mary's song of praise (1:46–55)	Zechariah's song of praise (1:67–80)
Simeon in the temple (2:25–35)	Anna in the temple (2:36–38)
The widow in Zarephath (4:26)	Naaman the leper (4:27)
Healing of a demon-possessed man (4:31–37)	Healing of Simon's mother-in-law (4:38–39)
Jesus forgives a man (5:20)	Jesus forgives a woman (7:48)
Healing of a centurion's servant (7:1–10)	Raising of a widow's son (7:11–17)
The Twelve accompany Jesus (8:1)	Women accompany Jesus (8:2–3)
Healing of a demon-possessed man (8:26–39)	Restoration of a woman and a girl (8:40–56)
Jonah (11:30)	The Queen of the South (11:31)
Parable of the mustard seed (13:18–19)	Parable of the yeast (13:20–21)
Healing of a woman on the Sabbath (13:10–17)	Healing of a man on the Sabbath (14:1–6)
Parable of the lost sheep (15:1–7)	Parable of the lost coin (15:8–10)
Parable of the widow and the judge (18:1–8)	Parable of the Pharisee and the tax collector (18:9–14)

female discipleship and restricts female roles, with the result that some read it as liberating and others as oppressive in relation to women[1]. In the same work, Mary Rose D'Angelo argues that Luke is more concerned with maleness than women, indeed more so than other early Christian writings[2]. Stories about women are paired with stories about men, with the former being often briefer and the women usually given no voice (eg Simeon and Anna, 2:25–38). This, she maintains, is Luke's attempt to legitimate the gospel before Roman society by reflecting its gender values. Consequently, exclusively positive and optimistic interpretations of Luke's presentation of women are viewed as neglecting evidence that Luke still largely keeps women in the traditional roles of his own social and cultural world[3].

On the other hand, Robert Karris argues that Luke does enhance the role of women in comparison with their place in his own culture[4]. Luke should not be held accountable for the fact that his readers' views have developed over time while his text has remained the same. This point comes into focus in Carol Schersten LaHurd's 'Reviewing Luke 15 with Arab Christian Women', which reports interviews with women in northern Yemen concerning their perception of particularly the parable of the woman and the lost coin[5]. Living in a society today where the genders are often separated, the women approved of the woman's gender-specific sphere in the parable and viewed her role positively. Thus, it is the social and ideological location of the reader that determines evaluation of the text. LaHurd maintains, therefore, that the cultural presuppositions and values of Western feminist readers require more scrutiny than does Luke's text. Certainly, one must be aware of how much a reader's own context can control interpretation, even to the point where cultural and ideological arrogance can simply assume that all other readings are inferior.

Positive and negative readings of the place of women in Luke will continue, but what does seem indisputable is that women have a more prominent place in this Gospel in comparison with the others, and that Luke has a more positive view of women than many in his contemporary, male-dominated culture.

---

1 Levine, Amy-Jill, and Marianne Blickenstaff (eds), *A Feminist Companion to Luke*, Sheffield: Sheffield Academic Press, 2002, pp1–22

2 D'Angelo, Mary Rose, 'The ANHP Question in Luke–Acts: Imperial Masculinity and the Deployment of Women in the Early Second Century' in *A Feminist Companion to Luke* (op cit), pp44–69. (ANHP is Greek for 'MALE'.)

3 See also BE Reid, *Choosing the Better Part? Women in the Gospel of Luke*, Collegeville, Minnesota: Liturgical Press, 1996.

4 Karris, Robert, 'Women and Discipleship in Luke' in *A Feminist Companion to Luke* (op cit), pp23–43

5 LaHurd, Carol Schersten, 'Reviewing Luke 15 with Arab Christian Women' in *A Feminist Companion to Luke* (op cit), pp246–268

a Outline views of women in Luke's cultural context.
b Summarise evidence which shows the importance of women in Luke.
c Discuss the claim that Luke's presentation of women is not entirely positive.

ENTHALPY
VIRTUE ETHICS
RELIGION + STATE SYNOPTIC
KINGDOM OF GOD

Gospel. (30)
relevant today. (15)
for all people. (30)
wish. (15)
Luke's Gospel. (30)
on possessions is

present an entirely

Theological significance of Jesus' words and deeds

THE SERMON ON THE PLAIN

LUKE'S SERMON ON THE PLAIN (6:20–49) is so called because Jesus is standing on a "level place" (6:17) as he delivers it. This distinguishes the sermon from Matthew's very similar but much longer Sermon on the Mount (Mt 5–7), which Jesus delivers on a mountain (Mt 5:1). We will not study the whole area of the source-critical relationship between these two sermons, but before we get into the sermon itself we will consider its setting and structure.

As regards the setting of the sermon (6:12–20a), Luke locates it just after Jesus chooses his twelve apostles, following a night of prayer on a mountain. Jesus comes down the mountain with the apostles and gathered on the plain where he preaches the sermon are two groups – a "great crowd" of his disciples and a "great multitude" of people. The latter have come from a wide area, ranging from Judaism's capital, Jerusalem, to Gentile Tyre and Sidon. Luke says that they have come for two reasons – to hear Jesus and to be healed by him. After recounting that Jesus heals them, Luke then records the teaching that they hear (the sermon). It is clear from the editorial note immediately preceding the sermon (6:20a) that the sermon is directed at Jesus' disciples – that is, at those already committed to him. However, it is apparent too, from a similar note immediately following the sermon (7:1), that it is preached in the hearing of the people generally (cf 12:1; 20:45).

This setting that Luke provides guides us in terms of the focus and interpretation of the sermon. It is Jesus' first major discourse to his disciples, particularly to the twelve apostles as the newly-appointed leaders of the renewed Israel that Jesus is forming (cf 22:29–30). The reference to Jesus coming down the mountain with the apostles to address the people, after being in fellowship with God, recalls Moses with the elders of Israel on Sinai and his descent to teach the people (eg Ex 19:23–25; 24:1–3; 32:15). Thus, in Luke we may have the new Moses descending from the new Sinai to deliver the new Law to the new people of God. The setting also provides part of the *inclusio* or frame for the sermon which indicates one of its key themes – they have all "come to hear him" (6:18) and the sermon climaxes with Jesus speaking about someone who "comes to me, hears my words" (6:47). Jesus' concluding point is that hearing the sermon is not enough – it must be put into practice.

IH Marshall refers to the lack of agreement among commentators concerning the structure of the sermon due to the absence of clear divisions and its diverse themes[1]. Also, different sections may be linked by a passage which both concludes one part and commences another (eg v 36). However, most divide the sermon into three sections containing the following verses: (i) 20–26 (ii) 27–38 (iii) 39–49. These sections are variously characterised, as the sample of analyses of the sermon in the following table indicates.

	ELLIS[2]	MARSHALL[3]	NOLLAND[4]	BOCK[5]	GREEN[6]
6:20–26	Promises of the kingdom	Two kinds of men	Beatitudes and woes	Prophetic call: blessings and woes	Blessing and woe
6:27–38	Principles of the kingdom	Love and mercy	Call to love of enemies and nonjudgemental generosity	Paraenetic call to love and mercy	On giving and receiving
6:39–49	Meaning of discipleship	Inward character of disciples	Importance of what Jesus teaches and need to act upon it	Parabolic call to righteousness, fruit and wise building	Measure of a disciple

---

1 Marshall, *Gospel of Luke: A Commentary on the Greek Text* (op cit), pp243–244
2 Ellis, EE, *The Gospel of Luke*, London: Nelson, 1974, p111; as cited by Marshall, *Gospel of Luke: A Commentary on the Greek Text* (op cit), p243.
3 Marshall, *Gospel of Luke: A Commentary on the Greek Text* (op cit), Contents
4 Nolland, *Luke 1–9:20* (op cit), pvi
5 Bock, *Luke 1:1–9:50* (op cit), pp557–558
6 Green, *The Gospel of Luke* (op cit), p26

All of the headings for the sections of the sermon in the table are attempts to describe the content and main theme(s) of each section. However, Bock has combined this with an identification of the literary genre or form of each section, noted by earlier German scholars[1]. Finally, it should be noted that some commentators do not divide the sermon between verse 38 and verse 39, noting that verses 37 to 42 deal with the one main theme of judging others, in the context of leadership[2].

Tasks

a **Comment on the title 'The Sermon on the Plain'.**

b **Discuss the setting of the sermon and how it can assist with its interpretation.**

c **Explore the structure of the sermon.**

Blessings and woes (6:20–26)

Looking towards his disciples (v 20a), Jesus begins his sermon with four beatitudes ("blessed"), followed by four matching woes. These statements concern four pairs of contrasting situations (poor/rich; hungry/full; weeping/laughing; persecuted/popular). Jesus states that the apparently worse-off are "blessed" (happy, fortunate, favoured), while the exclamation "woe" (an expression of displeasure) is directed against the apparently better-off. Elsewhere in Luke's Gospel and in the Old Testament are other examples of statements which similarly begin with the Greek or Hebrew word for "blessed" (Lk 7:23; 10:23; 11:27–28; 12:37–38,43; 14:15; 23:29; Ps 84:4–5, etc) or "woe" (Lk 10:13; 11:42–52; 21:23; Isa 5:8, etc).

In the second and third beatitudes and woes there is a direct reversal of the fortunes of the contrasted pairs – the hungry will be filled/the full will be hungry; those who weep will laugh/those who laugh will mourn and weep. This reversal theme is found elsewhere in Luke, such as in Mary's song of praise (1:46–55; especially v 52–53, and note "blessed" in v 45,48), Jesus' statement about the last being first and the first last (13:30), his teaching at the table in the home of a Pharisee (14:7–24; note v 11), the story of the rich man and the beggar called Lazarus (16:19–31; especially v 25), and the parable of the Pharisee and the tax collector (18:9–14; especially v 14). In these second and third beatitudes and woes, there is also a contrast between the present (the word 'now', a favourite of Luke's, is found in each) and the future (a future verb in each and two in the third woe). Thus, the unfortunate are "blessed" because of the promise of eschatological blessings – their present adversity will be reversed in future prosperity. Similarly, those who are presently prosperous will experience future adversity at the eschatological judgement – 'woe' oracles by the

---

[1] As cited by Marshall, *Gospel of Luke: A Commentary on the Greek Text* (op cit), p243. 'Paraenetic' is related to the technical term 'paraenesis', referring to exhortations, particularly ethical instructions.

[2] eg Morris, L, *Luke*, Leicester: IVP, 1988, p145

prophets often anticipated coming divine judgement (eg Isa 5:8–23). The implication is that God will bring about this future reversal of fortunes, vindicating the needy and judging the prosperous.

Unlike the second and third in the series, the first and fourth beatitudes and woes do not contain direct reversals of fortune (eg the poor don't become rich and vice versa). Nor do they contain contrasts between the present and future. Rather, the poor are blessed because of their present possession of God's kingdom, and the rich have already received their comfort. Similarly, the persecuted are blessed because they are receiving the same treatment as the prophets of the past, while the popular are receiving the same treatment as the false prophets of the past.

The first beatitude and woe contrast the "poor" and the "rich", poverty and wealth being important themes throughout Luke (see pp36–37). While the corresponding beatitude in Matthew (5:3) has "poor in spirit", Luke seems to refer to the literally poor, just as the matching woe relates to the literally rich. Jesus' ministry begins, uniquely in Luke, with his announcement that he has come to preach good news to the "poor" (4:18; cf 7:22), and now he begins his first major discourse by declaring their blessedness as possessors of God's kingdom. Since discipleship in Luke, in some cases at least, requires total renunciation of possessions (see pp280–281), the reference to the poor would have been particularly appropriate for the disciples, to whom he is primarily addressing his teaching. We should note, however, that the respective financial situations contrasted here reflect, and are often associated with, corresponding religious and moral attitudes. That is, due to their poverty the poor are often humbly dependent on God (cf Mt 5:3), and are regularly characterised as such in Jewish literature (eg Ps 86:1ff; Ps Sol 10:7; and in the Dead Sea Scrolls). Early churches were largely made up of such people (eg Jas 2:5; 1 Cor 1:26ff). In contrast, the rich are associated with attitudes such as self-centred, materialistic forgetfulness of God, heartless disregard of the needy and preoccupation with social recognition (Lk 12:13–21; 14:12–14; 16:13,19–31; 18:23ff). The poor are blessed by God since his kingdom, with all its blessings, is theirs in the present as well as in the future (on God's kingdom, see pp80–81). The rich, however, have had their comfort already (see 16:25), and the woe against them implies that God's coming judgement awaits them (cf 16:22ff). The hunger of the poor will one day be satisfied in the messianic age of salvation (Isa 25:6–8; 49:10–13; cf Lk 13:29; 14:15ff), which has already begun with the arrival of God's kingdom in the ministry of Jesus (9:10ff; thus, poverty is not idealised in the teaching of Jesus). On the other hand, the presently overfed rich will finally be hungry – shut out from the messianic banquet of the coming kingdom (13:26,28–30; 14:24). Similarly, the weeping of the poor in their present destitution will be reversed in eschatological joy (cf Ps 126 on restoration from exile), already begun in the ministry of Jesus (v 23; 1:44ff; 2:10; 15:6, etc). In contrast, the present laughter of the rich will be reversed, turning to mourning and weeping at the future judgement (13:28).

The final beatitude and woe are distinct from the others both in form and content. Their position (last in each case) and length (especially the beatitude) imply a certain amount of stress on their theme. The paradox and irony of the beatitudes in general is heightened here. The persecuted are the blessed, while the popular are under God's judgement. The forms of the persecution, described in four ways, and its cause ("because of the Son of Man", author's translation; cf p79 for details on 'Son of Man') are both indicated in the beatitude. It is the disciples' allegiance to the Son of Man which invites hostility (cf 5:21,24,33; 6:1–2,5,7,11; 9:24ff; 21:17). However, this persecution should be a cause for animated joy (v 23; cf 1:41,44; a Lucan theme), for that is how God's messengers, the prophets, were treated in the past (eg Acts 7:52; Neh 9:26; Ezek 2:1–7). Thus, the persecution of the disciples apparently authenticates their status as genuine messengers of God. They share the fate of worthy predecessors. Consequently, a great reward awaits the disciples in heaven (cf 12:8). In their present persecution for the Son of Man, they can gain encouragement by looking back to the prophets in whose footsteps they follow, and by looking forward to the reward ahead of them in heaven. Conversely, the popular, by their very popularity, indicate that they are the successors of the false prophets of old. These prophets enjoyed similar popularity because they did not deliver the unpopular messages that God's faithful messengers brought (cf Jer 5:12–13; 6:13–15; Mic 2:11).

In summary, Jesus begins his sermon with a series of paired beatitudes and woes which challenge and subvert social norms with a radical reversal of values – blessed are the poor, the hungry, the weeping and the persecuted, but woe to the rich, the full, the happy and the popular. God's blessing is for the former, while God's judgement awaits the latter.

> **Task**
>
> Outline and discuss Jesus' teaching in the beatitudes and woes with which he begins the Sermon on the Plain.

Love and mercy (6:27–38)

The beginning of the second and central section of the sermon is signalled by the words, "But I say to you that listen ..." These words recall the earlier note that those now present "had come to hear him" (v 18) and anticipate the end of the sermon, with its emphasis on hearing Jesus (6:46–7:1). The present section may be divided broadly into two parts – love (v 27–36) and mercy (v 37–38). To be more specific, the first part is about love for one's enemies and the second concerns mercy towards the failings and needs of others.

The passage about love for one's enemies begins with four parallel commands (v 27–28), followed by four parallel illustrations (v 29–30), relating to the theme. It continues with the so-called 'golden rule' (v 31), followed by three parallel rhetorical questions and comments (v 32–34), a restatement of the theme (v 35a), a promise of

Theological significance

great reward (v 35b), and a statement and command concerning the example of God (v 35c–36). The frequent use of parallelism in the passage was a common feature of Hebrew poetry. Jesus has already spoken of the blessedness of those who are hated, excluded, insulted and defamed because of the Son of Man (v 22), and now he speaks of the enemies of his disciples as those who hate, curse and abuse them. He calls on his disciples, as citizens of God's kingdom (v 20), to respond positively to the negativity of persecution. They are to love their enemies, and the practical expression of this is spelt out in the three commands that follow this opening demand – they are to do good to those who hate them, bless those who curse them, and pray for those who abuse them. Jesus calls not for a grudging endurance of hostility, nor for a mere refusal to retaliate, but for positive goodwill and kindness in response to ill will and cruelty. This teaching of Jesus is reinforced in letters to early Christian churches (Rom 12:14–21; 1 Pet 3:9). The requirement to show kindness to one's enemies is found before Jesus in the Old Testament (Ex 23:4–5; Prov 25:21–22). Similar sentiments are also found in the Dead Sea Scrolls and in pagan writers such as Seneca (*c.* 5 BC – AD 65) and Epictetus (*c.* AD 55–135), although the usual view in antiquity was to be hostile to one's enemies.

The four illustrations (v 29–30) provide specific and personal[1] examples of positive responses to one's enemies. Even the beggar may have been considered an enemy in social terms, an outsider who kept company with other beggars[2]. Since the literal application of these four commands would leave Jesus' followers bruised, bare and broke, it has been argued that the spirit of this teaching, rather than its letter, should be followed[3]. Certainly, in Luke's sequel we find Paul apparently not literally following the command to offer the other cheek (Acts 23:2–3). Also, these commands have been interpreted as relating to a very specific setting that Luke was addressing in his time; namely, the passage is a challenge to rich Christians to be generous to poor Christians who despised them[4]. However, DL Bock argues for a more literal and general application which neither weakens the force of Jesus' teaching here nor limits it to a specific church setting in Luke's time[5]. Rather, Jesus calls for a love which does not protect one's rights, but which is willing to help others even in the face of repeated abuse and persecution. However, it may be that these demands need to be balanced by Jesus' teaching elsewhere in this Gospel, which seems to assume the right of the individual to protect one's property and resist those who threaten it (12:39, unless we regard this as a reference to what generally happens).

Next comes the 'golden rule' (v 31) which does not relate easily to what is before or after it. In particular, it has been viewed as at least being in tension with the immediately

---

[1] Personal, since unlike the preceding and following verses, v 29–30 have singular verbs and pronouns in the Greek.

[2] Green, *The Gospel of Luke* (op cit), p272

[3] eg TW Manson, as cited in Marshall, *The Gospel of Luke: A Commentary on the Greek Text* (op cit), p261

[4] So L Schottroff and W Stegemann, as indicated in Bock, *Luke 1:1–9:50* (op cit), p591

[5] Bock, *Luke 1:1–9:50* (op cit), pp591–592

following verses (v 32–35), which speak against acting in accordance with the treatment received from others. It has therefore sometimes been taken not as a command, but as a statement of what normally happens ("You are doing to others ...", as it may be translated), which Jesus immediately goes on to criticise (v 32–35)[1]. However, it is more likely that it *should* be taken as a command (as in Mt 7:12). Similar rules, in the negative ('Don't do to others what you would not want ...') as well as in the positive form found here, are found in Jewish and pagan literature before the time of Jesus. However, Jesus does not appear to be teaching that good should be done to others in order to gain similar treatment from them as is often the case in the other literature, but rather because we have put ourselves in their place and know how we would like to be treated.

Three parallel rhetorical questions and comments (v 32–34) about loving, doing good and lending recall earlier instructions in this section of the sermon (v 27,30). The basic point that is underlined with each question and comment is that there is no credit for Jesus' disciples if their practical love to others is based on reciprocity (only being kind to those who are kind to them), since even sinners do that much. Rather, Jesus calls them to the higher and more demanding ethic, with which he began this section (v 27ff) and which he now repeats as he starts to bring it to a close (v 35a) – love for one's *enemies*. These verses (v 32–34) subvert and challenge the generally accepted principle of reciprocity that operated in society at the time of Jesus – the principle that favours were done in order to get favours in return, with the result that apparent kindness was actually self-serving (cf 14:12–14). The citizens of God's kingdom were to be countercultural in their behaviour – loving, doing good, and lending with no expectation or hope of reciprocation – since these actions were done to one's enemies. Thus, in acts subversive of the social norms, enemies were to be treated as one's friends and family.

Jesus then offers two motives or incentives for love for one's enemies. First, a great reward from God is promised (cf v 23; 14:14). This seems to be an affirmation of the self-serving reciprocation that Jesus has just urged his disciples to transcend (v 32ff), rather than goodness for goodness' sake. However, Jesus appears to be saying that while the disciples' enemies will not reciprocate their love, God himself will reward them at the End. Second, love for one's enemies demonstrates one's relationship with God, since it is God-like behaviour. While "you will be sons of the Most High" (author's translation; cf Ps 82:6; Lk 1:32) could be read as the outcome of God's future judgement based on present treatment of one's enemies, the end of verse 35 points to the idea of showing that one is a child of God by behaving like God, who himself is kind to his enemies (the ungrateful and wicked). In this way, Jesus urges his disciples to be merciful, just as their Father is merciful (v 36). The example of the Father is to be imitated by the children.

The central section of the sermon concludes with verses 37 to 38, which still bear some relationship to the theme of love for one's enemies that has dominated the section thus far. However, the instructions now seem to be more general, following

---

[1] So A Dihle, as noted by Nolland, *Luke 1–9:20* (op cit), p298

Theological significance

on from the reference to God's kindness and mercy in the previous verses. Four parallel commands – two negative (v 37) and two positive (v 38), each with an added statement – require the disciples not to judge and condemn, but rather to forgive and give. The one basic point is that the way they treat others is the way they will be treated by God at the judgement. Critical treatment of others (cf 5:30) should be avoided, while generous treatment of others should be practised. The word translated "forgive" means 'release', indicating that Jesus' disciples are to free others from debts and obligations. Indeed, giving to others (cf also v 30) will be generously rewarded by God, as the illustration which Jesus adds to this fourth command underlines. The picture is of a merchant selling grain who fills the container to overflowing, pressing down and shaking together its contents in order to give as much as possible. This is put into the "lap" of the customer, possibly the fold of a garment near the waist or the skirt of the garment, in which grain could be collected (eg Ruth 3:15). Jesus drives home the point of the illustration, and indeed these two verses, by stating, "with the measure you use, it will be measured to you" (author's translation) – that is, be generous to others and God will be generous to you.

Tasks

a Outline the structure and contents of the central section of the sermon (v 27–38).

b Discuss the view that Jesus' teaching about love for one's enemies is not to be taken literally.

c How did Jesus' expectations of his disciples differ from normal practice (v 32–35)?

d Explain how Jesus makes the character of God the model for the disciples' conduct.

Discipleship (6:39–49)

This third and final main section of the Sermon on the Plain consists of parabolic material which is broadly united by the theme of discipleship. Teaching about teachers and disciples (v 39–40) is followed by instruction about hypocritical fault-finding (v 41–42), about how outward conduct reflects one's inner nature (v 43–45), and about the necessity of putting Jesus' teaching into practice (v 46–49).

It is not clear who Jesus is referring to in his little "parable" of the blind leading the blind (an image used widely in ancient pagan and Jewish literature) and both falling into a pit (v 39). It may be that he is warning his apostles (v 12ff,20), as leaders of a renewed Israel, that they will not be able to provide moral instruction to the people if they themselves lack the insight that he is seeking to give them (eg v 37ff). If this application continues into the next statement (v 40, the disciple and the teacher), which seems to be closely connected with the little parable, then the point may be that disciples of the apostles will not rise "above" the blindness of their teachers but, in fact, will be just like them. This idea of the blindness of the apostles as leaders may continue on into the passage about someone hypocritically trying to correct a minor lack of sight in another person, while the teacher cannot see at all (v 41–42). However, the parable can be interpreted in other ways, such as it being a reference to the Jewish leaders (as in Mt 15:12–14) or erroneous teachers in the Church. Nolland believes that the parable is being directed at those who are led, rather than leaders, urging them not to follow blind leaders (those who teach differently from Jesus in this sermon)[1]. If such leaders are followed then their disciples will share their blindness (v 40). However, Jesus' words about a disciple being like the teacher may have a more general application – will Jesus' disciples become "fully qualified/trained" (author's translation) and, therefore, be like their teacher[2]?

Jesus' humorous, even grotesque, illustration of hypocrisy as similar to someone noticing a speck in a brother's eye and offering to remove it, while oblivious to the plank in their own (v 41–42), is paralleled in both pagan and Jewish literature. The word "hypocrite" focuses on the problem at hand here, namely the insincerity and play-acting (as the Greek word implies) often involved in the correction of others. The problem is not the attempt to assist in the moral improvement of others (see the end of v 42), but the failure first to see and correct one's own (greater) faults. The illustration develops the earlier call to avoid judging others (v 37). If Jesus is still thinking of teachers (the disciples or others) at this point (as in v 39–40), then it is a challenge to them to practise what they preach before they make demands of others.

The illustration of trees and their fruit (v 43–44) and its application (v 45) make the point that one's outward conduct reveals one's inner nature – "each tree is known by its own fruit". What we *do* is what we *are,* and what we *are* is what we *do*. As with the speck and the plank, so Jesus creates ridiculous images (figs on thorn bushes and grapes on bramble bushes) to drive home the point that a bad person cannot live a good life. The image of trees and fruit was used by John the Baptist in his preaching on repentance (3:8–9). Here, Jesus may still have teachers in mind (v 39–40) and, indeed, in Matthew (7:15–19) the illustration is applied to false prophets. On this reading, the reference to the mouth and speaking in the application of the illustration (v 45) becomes particularly appropriate. However, the passage may have a more general reference – as the fruit reflects the tree, so the mouth (speech) reflects the heart.

Having said that, what the mouth says may not always agree with the life lived. As Jesus brings his sermon to its climactic conclusion, he challenges the disparity between verbal confession and practical behaviour (v 46–49). He addresses this question to his disciples, to whom the sermon has been primarily directed (v 20). Their words of address to Jesus ("Lord, Lord") give the impression that he is the teacher they follow, as his disciples, but their actions deny this because they do not

---

[1] Nolland, *Luke 1–9:20* (op cit), p307

[2] Green, *The Gospel of Luke* (op cit), p278

obey him (v 46). To reinforce the necessity of *doing* what he says, Jesus provides similitudes that contrast two types of people. Jesus compares the person who "comes to me, hears my words" (cf v 18) and *does* them to the builder who dug down deep and laid the foundation of his house on rock. When the river flooded and burst against that house, it stood firm. On the other hand, the person who *hears* without *doing* is compared to the builder who laid no foundation and whose house collapsed when the river burst against it. Both *hear* Jesus, but only one *does* what he says. Thus, when the flood of God's judgement comes (cf Ezek 13:10–16), only those will survive who *do* what Jesus says, rather than those who merely *hear* Jesus or only *call* Jesus 'Lord'. The importance of *doing* (Greek *poieo*) is seen in the frequent use of this word throughout the sermon (11 times: v 23,26,27,31,33,43,46,49). In addition, 'doing good' (Greek *agathopoieo*) occurs three times (v 33,35). The Sermon on the Plain, then, ends with Jesus insisting that it must not merely be listened to, but also be put into practice, if one is to experience a favourable verdict at the future judgement of God. That Jesus makes the outcome of God's judgement dependent on response to his own teaching in this way reveals that he is self-consciously God's agent.

Tasks

a Discuss Jesus' teaching in the opening verses of the final section of the sermon (v 39–40).

b What main point is Jesus making in each of the following passages?

(i) the speck and the plank (v 41–42)   (ii) trees and fruit (v 43–45)

(iii) the two builders (v 46–49)

Interpretation of the sermon

Different interpretations of the Sermon on the Mount/Plain have developed throughout the history of the Church, not least because many have regarded its teaching, and Jesus' ethical teaching in general, as containing unrealistic and unachievable moral ideals (eg Lk 6:27–30). A distinction was made in the medieval period between commandments or precepts that all Christians are required to keep and 'counsels of perfection' which apply to more dedicated people such as clergy and monks. Another view, often termed the Lutheran view, holds that much of Jesus' ethical teaching consists of an impossible moral idealism, which is designed to make people aware of their moral imperfection and move them to trust in Jesus for forgiveness of sins. In this view, the sermon prepares people to believe the Gospel for salvation; it is not a code of conduct to be followed, for this would lead to legalism. A further approach, sometimes called the *Liberal view*, maintains that the sermon contains not a set of laws but general principles relating to attitudes rather than actions. What is important is an attitude of love to others, rather than literal obedience to specific commands of Jesus. Again, it has been argued that Jesus' idealistic teaching was intended only for the short time that he thought would elapse before the coming of the kingdom of God and the end of the world. In this view, Jesus was mistaken since history has long since continued, and now people are trying to apply his teaching in a situation for which it was not intended. Yet another position holds that this teaching is not for the present but for a future millennial reign of Jesus upon the earth (Rev 20). The utopian view argues that all of Jesus' teaching should be literally followed so that, for example, love for one's enemies and turning the other cheek prohibits retaliation or the use of force in all circumstances, including military service.

The context of the Sermon on the Mount/Plain indicates that Jesus expects his disciples (a group wider than the Twelve; cf Lk 6:17) to put his teaching into practice (cf Lk 6:46–49). Matthew's Gospel expects that future disciples will also follow all of Jesus' ethical teaching (28:20) and much of it is urged upon early Christian churches elsewhere in the New Testament (eg Rom 12:14–21, and throughout James and 1 Peter). As for its apparent unrealistic moral idealism, it should be noted that literal readings of Jesus' teachings can fail to take into account the figurative and rhetorical character of at least some of it. However, the opposite error would be to interpret figuratively or rhetorically what should be read literally. More important is the observation that Jesus' ethical teaching in the sermon is addressed to those who are already committed to Jesus (v 20) and who are in or possess God's kingdom (v 20, the first line of the sermon). God's reign in the lives of disciples of Jesus provides the dynamic that enables them to fulfil its demands in some measure. Further, the sermon also begins with a series of beatitudes indicating that those in God's kingdom are blessed by him – it is this blessing of God which enables them to realise to some degree the demands of the kingdom outlined in the rest of the sermon. Yet, as the beatitudes reveal, the blessings of the kingdom will only be fully enjoyed when the kingdom comes finally in the future. In Luke's thought, the kingdom is already present and is also yet to come; its demands, therefore, may be met now, even if moral perfection awaits the kingdom's future consummation. Another factor which needs to be taken into account in terms of the apparent idealism of Jesus' teaching is his insistence that character precedes and determines conduct (v 43–45), which assumes that a change is required at the level of one's attitude and nature before behaviour appropriate to the kingdom can be manifested (cf 5:38, and Luke's emphasis on the need for repentance). Finally, just as Jesus in Luke lives his life and carries out his ministry in prayerful dependence on God and in the power of the Holy Spirit, so Jesus' disciples are urged to pray to God and to rely on the Spirit in their efforts to live as citizens of God's kingdom.

Discuss the claim that Jesus' teaching in the Sermon on the Plain is too difficult to live up to.

PARABLES

We have already studied the origin, type and purpose of parables, with special reference to the parables of God's mercy (see Parables, p194ff). We noted there that while some have categorised the parables of Jesus topically, there is among New Testament scholars no generally accepted classification of the parables. Some regard all the parables of Jesus as parables of the kingdom in its different aspects (see pp200–201), while others would include in this category only parables which specifically use the term 'kingdom'. Thus, the following classification of parables of the kingdom, crisis and discipleship which I propose is not prescriptive. Cross-referencing is provided for parables that we have already studied, and students are advised to revisit the relevant pages.

Parables of the kingdom

The new patch and the new wine (5:36–39; see p302)
The sower (8:4–8,11–15; see pp303–305)
The strong man (11:21–23; see p96)
The mustard seed (13:18–19; see pp111–112)
The yeast (13:20–21: see p112)
The banquet (14:15–24; see pp118–119)
The budding fig tree (21:29–31; see pp305–306)

Parables of crisis

The rich fool (12:13–21; see p103)
A returning master and alert slaves (12:36–38; see pp105–106)
A thief and a householder (12:39–40; see p106)
A returning master and faithful/unfaithful slaves (12:42–48; see pp106–107)
The barren fig tree (13:6–9; see p109)
The narrow door (13:22–30; see pp112–113)
The rich man and Lazarus (16:19–31; see pp131–133)
The pounds (19:11–27; see pp148–150)
The tenants (20:9–18; see pp306–307)

Parables of discipleship

The two builders (6:47–49; see p299)
The good Samaritan (10:29–37; see pp85–88)
The friend at midnight (11:5–8; see pp93–94)
The tower builder (14:28–30; see p121)
The warring king (14:31–33; see p121)
The shrewd manager (16:1–9; see pp127–129)
The worthless slaves (17:7–10; see p134)
The widow and the judge (18:1–8; see pp139–140)

The new patch and the new wine (5:36–39)

I have classified this as a parable of the kingdom (on the kingdom of God see pp80–81). Jesus' message has been summarised in the recent context as "the good news of the kingdom of God" (4:43), and in this "parable" (5:36) he now appears to be teaching something about the nature of this kingdom. The twin similitudes of the new patch and the new garment make the same essential point – the new is incompatible with the old. In the context, the old garment and the old wineskins seem to represent the Pharisees and the scribes, who accuse Jesus of blasphemy because he declares forgiven the sins of the paralysed man (5:17,20–21); who criticise Jesus' disciples for having table fellowship with tax collectors and sinners (5:30); who question Jesus as to why his disciples eat and drink while the disciples of John the Baptist and the Pharisees regularly fast and pray (5:33); and who would, immediately after our present passage, enter into conflict with Jesus over the Sabbath (6:1–11).

The kingdom of God in the ministry of Jesus is something new which cannot be patched onto the old garment of Pharisaic traditions or contained within their old wineskins. Garments and wine (and wedding feasts, v 34–35) were symbols of the expected age of salvation (eg Isa 61:3,10; 62:8–9). Wineskins were animal skins which were sewn to form containers for wine and water. Old, brittle and rigid wineskins could not withstand the pressure of new, fermenting wine and would burst. Thus, as the punch line of the second metaphor makes clear, "new wine must be put into fresh wineskins" (v 38). That is, "repentance" (v 32), a change of attitude and orientation, is needed if one is to receive the new wine of the kingdom of God. Luke is clear about the continuity between the coming of Jesus and Israel's history and Scriptures (eg chs 1–2; 4:16ff), and presents Paul simultaneously as a Jew, a Pharisee and a Christian (Acts 22:3; 23:6), so the "old" here is not to be viewed simply as Judaism or Pharisaism, but rather as what these had become in the hands of their leadership (cf 11:37–54). Overinterpretation of parabolic details in the passage has misled some into trying to provide a symbolic reference for the damage of the new garment and the new wine.

After the two similitudes, Luke alone of the synoptics adds a proverb familiar in both Jewish and Greek culture (v 39). Following on from the similitudes and their broader context, the point seems to be that just as mature wine is preferred to new wine, some are so wedded to the old ways that they have no desire even to try the new (compare 'You can't teach an old dog new tricks'). However, the second-century heretic Marcion (and others) omitted the proverb in his edition of Luke, apparently because it could be read as an approval of the Old Testament which he rejected. Indeed, some modern scholars have argued that this proverb is Luke's pro-Jewish interpretation of the preceding metaphors.

Task

Outline the parable of the new patch and the new wine and discuss its meaning.

The sower (8:4–8,11–15)

In its present context in Luke, the parable of the sower (8:4–8) and its interpretation (8:11–15) relate to the kingdom of God, which Jesus is proclaiming (v 1) and to which Jesus refers when the disciples ask about the parable's meaning (v 9–10; on these verses, see pp201–203)[1]. While most scholars regard it as a creation of the early Church rather than authentic teaching of Jesus, its authenticity has been defended by others[2]. The imagery had been used before in Jewish writings in relation to God's word (Isa 55:10–11), God's Law and various kinds of people (2 Esdras 8:6,41; 9:31). In the parable itself, we are told four times that the seed "fell" in different places – *beside* the path, *on* the rock, *among* the thorns, and *into* good soil[3]. In each case, apart from the first, we are told that the seed "grew". However, only in the last case was there a successful yield. In the interpretation of the parable, the seed is "the word of God" (a favourite Lucan expression), that is, the message of God's kingdom (v 1,9–10). Further, it is clear from the interpretation that the parable illustrates four different ways of *hearing* the message of the kingdom, since the verb 'to hear' is used with reference to each of the four examples (v 12–15). This emphasis on *hearing* is seen also in the parable's concluding challenge to listen (v 8), and in Jesus' comments between the parable and its interpretation (v 10). This theme also continues soon after our passage when Jesus urges his audience to watch how they hear (v 18), and identifies his family as those who hear the word of God and do it (v 21). Clearly, just as only the seed that fell into the good soil produced a successful harvest, so the message of the kingdom is properly heard (ie received) only by those who "hold it fast in an honest and good heart, and bear fruit with patient endurance" (v 15). This is the key point of the parable.

The parable begins with a sower going out to sow his seed, a common enough sight in first-century Palestine. While the seed is interpreted as a symbol for God's word, no symbolic referent is provided for the sower. However, the implication is that he represents anyone who spreads the message of the kingdom – Jesus (8:1); the twelve apostles (9:1–2); the Seventy (10:1,9,11); or missionaries in Luke's second book (eg Acts 8:12; 19:8), in the Church of Luke's day and beyond. In the first instance, some seed fell beside or along the pathway worn by the sower and others as a right of way. It is not clear whether here, and in the other cases, the sower is being careless since he knows that both the seed and the temporary path will be ploughed in after sowing anyway (as was sometimes, although not always, the case), or simply that some seed falls on the periphery of the field beyond the reach of the plough. Only Luke adds that the seed was "trampled on" (crushing it and preventing germination)

---

[1] Since our focus is on the final form of the text of Luke, we will not discuss the authenticity of the parable's interpretation (v 11–15 and parallel passages in other Gospels).

[2] eg Payne, Philip B, 'The Authenticity of the Parable of the Sower and Its Interpretation' in *Gospel Perspectives*, Vol 1, eds RT France and D Wenham, Sheffield: JSOT, 1980

[3] Luke has four different prepositions in the parable, which I have translated directly. However, in the interpretation of the parable he has *into* the thorns and *in* the good soil.

and that it was the birds "of the air" (ie wild rather than domestic) that ate it up. The birds are interpreted as a symbol for "the devil" (v 12), who earlier tempted Jesus (4:1–13) and will from now on in this Gospel be called "Satan" (eg 10:18; see p84 for details). As the leader of the rival and opposing kingdom (11:18–20), he is here portrayed as obstructing the successful reception of the message of God's kingdom and the salvation that it brings. The message may have reached beyond ears to "hearts" (cf 1:66; 2:19,51), but not beyond the reach of the devil (cf 22:3), who takes it away to prevent a response of faith in the message leading to salvation. Only Luke has this reference to believing and being saved (cf 7:50; 8:48,50; Acts 16:30–31), salvation being a central theme of Luke's. In Jesus' ministry, the Jewish leadership in particular is represented as this type of hearer (eg 7:30), whose unbelieving response to Jesus' message of the kingdom is here portrayed as satanically inspired.

In the second case Luke says that some seed fell "on the rock", rather than "on rocky ground" (as in Matthew and Mark). The meaning, however, is probably much the same – rock covered by a shallow layer of soil. Like the ungodly in the book of Sirach (40:15), the image is of "roots on sheer rock". With little or no moist soil, the growing plant soon withered. In the interpretation, the temporary growth symbolises initial joyful reception of the message followed by temporary faith (only Luke mentions faith at this point). Reverting to horticultural imagery, Luke notes that these hearers "have no root" – that is, their faith is insecure and vulnerable. They therefore fall away from the faith in a "time of testing/temptation" (author's translation). This is more general than the "trouble or persecution" in the parallel accounts and recalls Jesus' testing or temptation (4:2,13). Jesus would later commend his disciples for standing by him in his trials and urge them to pray that they will not enter into trial (22:28,40,46; cf 11:4). In Jesus' ministry, the group of hearers envisaged here may correspond to some of the wider group of followers called "disciples" (eg 6:17), whose commitment to Jesus may have proved to be temporary when faced with temptation and trial. Peter's lapse (22:54–62) may also be represented here, although his faith did not finally fail (22:32).

Thirdly, some seed fell among thorns which grew up with the plant and choked it. Although the biblical instruction is "sow not among thorns" (Jer 4:3, author's translation), it may be that the farmer knew that the weeds would be ploughed in after sowing anyway or that it was not easy to prevent some seed ending up among weeds at the edges of a field. The thorns are interpreted as symbolising this "life", specifically its worries, wealth and pleasures. These things choke this type of hearer and prevent development and maturity in discipleship. This threefold threat to the process of discipleship is mentioned elsewhere in Luke. Later, the disciples are warned not to allow themselves to be burdened by "the worries of this life" (21:34) and are instructed not to worry about its concerns (12:22–31). In addition, Martha is gently rebuked by Jesus for worrying about such concerns, in contrast to Mary who gives priority to "the word" (10:39,41–42, author's translation). The danger of wealth and possessions is a notable theme of Luke (see pp36–37). They can be a barrier to entering the kingdom (cf 14:33; 18:22–25) or, as in our passage, an obstacle to progress in the kingdom. Related to wealth are the "pleasures" that it provides access to, such as the luxuries and indulgences of life (eg 7:25; 12:19; 16:19). Again, this type of hearer may be represented by some of the broader group of Jesus' followers who were distracted from discipleship by these things. Judas' betrayal of Jesus for money may be relevant here too (22:5).

Finally, some seed fell into "good soil" which grew and produced a hundredfold, a generous although not impossible harvest by first-century Palestinian standards. The contrast is between the other cases, where either there was no growth or where the growth was interrupted, and a successful harvest. As in other parables, such as the good Samaritan and the parable of the pounds (19:12–27), earlier characters or examples are foils for the climactic character or example, where the point of emphasis lies (sometimes called the rule of end stress). The seed in the good soil is interpreted as those hearers of the word who have "an honest and good heart" (cf 6:43–45; Acts 8:21). What distinguishes this type of hearer from the previous hearers is that they "hold ... fast" to the message of the kingdom and bear fruit with "endurance" (Greek *hupomone*; only found here and in 21:19 in the Gospels)[1]. The importance of continuing after commencing is highlighted in Luke's second book (Acts 11:23; 13:43; 14:22). While other hearers believe "for a time" (v 13, author's translation) and bear fruit that "does not mature" (v 14), those who hear the word as it should be heard keep the faith regardless of the devil, of testing or temptation, and of the worries, wealth and pleasures of life. Thus, those who spread the message of the kingdom are assured that, despite disappointments, it will yield a lasting harvest, and those who "hear" the message are assured that only those who persevere with it give it a proper hearing.

Outline the parable of the sower and its interpretation and discuss its meaning.

The budding fig tree (21:29–31)

This brief parable (v 29–30) with its application (v 31) comes towards the end of a discourse by Jesus about the coming destruction of Jerusalem and its temple and the coming of the Son of Man (21:5–36). While the other synoptics just mention the fig tree, Luke adds "and all the trees", possibly to show that the point holds good for trees in general or to make it more relevant to his Gentile readers. Without leaves during the winter, the appearance of leaves on the fig tree is a natural signal that summer is near. In the same way, the nearness of the kingdom of God is signalled by "these things" (ie the events of v 5–28: wars, natural disasters, persecution, the fall of Jerusalem, and cosmic signs). For Luke, the kingdom of God is both present and future (see pp80–81),

---

[1] The NRSV translates this word as "patient endurance" in 8:15 and as "endurance" in 21:19.

and in our present passage it is the future manifestation of the kingdom at the End that is in view (cf v 28; 11:2; 14:15; 17:20; 19:11). Earlier in Luke (12:54–56), Jesus made a similar reference to nature as an illustration of understanding God's time.

Discuss the meaning of the parable of the budding fig tree.

The tenants (20:9–18)

In its present form and context, this parable appears to be an allegory, in that several of its characters and details seem to have a symbolic reference. This is suggested to some extent by the Old Testament text which forms the background to it – Isaiah's song of the vineyard (Isa 5:1–7). Thus, the owner of the vineyard stands for God, the vineyard for Israel, the tenants for the Jewish leaders, the slaves for the prophets, and the son for the Messiah/Jesus. The parable, in this view, symbolises the history of Israel and of salvation which culminates and climaxes with the sending of God's son, whose killing by the Jewish leadership results in their judgement and the transfer of the leadership of Israel to "others" – that is to Jesus' apostles.

The present context of the parable provides important clues to its interpretation within Luke's Gospel. Chapters 20 and 21 of Luke relate Jesus' teaching in the Jerusalem temple, framed by the words, "Every day he was teaching in the temple" (19:47; 21:37). He has just 'cleansed' the temple (19:45–46) and this act has provoked an urgency on the part of the Jewish leadership to get rid of Jesus (19:47). Throughout this section, they engage Jesus as he teaches in the temple, their power base, in an effort to lead him into self-incrimination (20:1,19–20,26). Immediately before our parable, chapter 20 begins with the leaders challenging Jesus as to what authority, what right, he has to act as he does (the temple 'cleansing' and his teaching). This is the key issue – who are the legitimate leaders of Israel? Jesus' parable of the tenants follows immediately and, although it is addressed to "the people" in general (v 1), the Jerusalem authorities know that it is an attack on their leadership (v 19). God is the one who had "planted" Israel; he is "the master/lord of the vineyard" (v 13,15, author's translation) who had entrusted the care of his people to the leaders, and they are accountable to him. While some scholars hold that the tenants represent Israel as a whole[1], others note that in the Old Testament (especially Isa 5:7) a vineyard is a symbol for the nation of Israel and also that the context of the parable clearly implies that the tenants symbolise the Jewish leadership (v 19)[2].

God has sent prophets (the slaves) to his people, but they have mistreated them (v 10–12; cf 6:22–23; 11:47–51; 13:34). Finally, God sends his "beloved son" – words used by God of Jesus at his baptism (3:22) and his transfiguration (9:35 in some

---

[1] eg Bock, *Luke 9:51–24:53* (op cit), p1591

[2] eg Blomberg, *Interpreting the Parables* (op cit), p248

manuscripts). These words recall the relationship between Abraham and Isaac in Genesis 22:2 and the description of Israel's king found in Psalms 2:7. While some doubt that Jesus would have implied that he was God's son, since he was reluctant to make any such messianic claims in the synoptics, his messianic consciousness is implied throughout his ministry and particularly in his last week (cf 19:28ff). Again, only a denial of Jesus' prophetic insight requires us to regard the implied reference to Jesus' crucifixion and vindication as a later invention of the Church. The growing hostility of the Jewish leadership in these chapters is enough to indicate that a crisis is imminent for Jesus.

Within the parable, the tenants may have assumed that the father was dead and that killing the son would make them the heirs of the vineyard, or that, in the absence of the natural heir, their possession of it would amount to ownership. The reference to the master of the vineyard destroying the tenants alludes to the coming destruction of Jerusalem (cf 19:41–44; 21:5–6,20–24), and the giving of the vineyard to other tenants symbolises the transfer of the leadership of Israel to the apostles (22:28–30; Acts 1:15–26; 2:42). Thus, this may appropriately be classified as a parable of crisis. After the people respond with shock at the suggestion of such events (v 16), Jesus refers them to Psalms 118:22 (v 17), a favourite text for early Christians in reference to Jesus (eg Acts 4:11; 1 Pet 2:7). It has been suggested that in Jesus' original Aramaic there is an intentional play on words between 'stone' (*eben*) in this verse and "son" (*ben*) in verse 13, strengthening the link between these terms for the Messiah. Psalm 118 was also quoted in connection with Jesus' entry to Jerusalem (19:38), and now it is being used to show that the Scriptures anticipated both the Messiah's rejection and vindication ("cornerstone" – a foundation stone bearing the weight of two walls). Jesus develops its analogy by stating that everyone who rejects the Messiah will experience the devastation of his judgement. As far as the Jewish leaders are concerned, the parable is directed against them (v 19) and Luke finds nothing wrong with their interpretation of it.

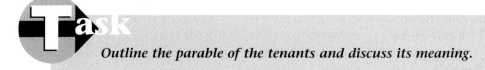

Outline the parable of the tenants and discuss its meaning.

MIRACLES

The theological significance of miracles in Luke concerns their message and meaning – what they teach. We have already studied the function, purpose and characteristics of miracles in Luke (see Miracles, p206ff). Much of this is relevant to our present topic and should, therefore, be studied again. Especially relevant are the studies of individual miracle stories (particular attention should be paid to their theological message) and, above all, the concluding general observations (see pp225–227). In the latter, we noted how Luke's miracle stories are set within the context of Isaiah's vision of "the year of the Lord's favour", the time of God's salvation (Lk 4:18–19/ Isa 61:1–2; 58:6). This has now arrived ("today") in the ministry of Jesus, including, and perhaps especially, in his miracles. Also, we observed the important link between miracles and the kingdom of God, miracles being demonstrations of God's reign which was beginning to be established in Jesus' ministry. Related to this is the theocentric character of Jesus' ministry in general and of his miracles in particular. However, we considered too that Luke's miracles are also Christological in that they, implicitly and explicitly, say something about Jesus himself, not least his concern for the marginalised and outcasts. Further, we noted other characteristic Lucan themes and terms in his miracle stories, including salvation, joy, forgiveness and peace. We reflected also on the role of faith in the miracle stories.

In terms of the theological significance of miracles, we should also consider the parallel that has often been drawn between miracles and parables. Both are powerful pictures of God's kingdom and dynamic illustrations of God's salvation. In effect, miracles are parables in action – dramatisations of the message of the parables. Two of the clearest examples of this involve miracles which are not found in Luke. First, Jesus' miraculous cursing of the fig tree (Mk 11:12–14,20–25) can be seen as the dramatic counterpart of Luke's parable of the barren fig tree (Lk 13:6–9). The point of both is that unrepentant Israel is heading for the judgement of God (cf Mic 7:1–6). Second, Jesus' miraculous turning of water into wine (Jn 2:1–11) can be viewed as the enactment of the parable of the wineskins (Lk 5:37–39). The water and the old wineskins may be interpreted as symbolising Judaism as it has evolved in the hands of some of its leadership (Lk 5:33ff; Jn 2:6), in contrast to the new wine of God's kingdom that Jesus is now bringing. Further, the feeding of the five thousand (Lk 9:12–17) and the abundant catch of fish (Lk 5:1–11) may be seen as miraculous demonstrations of the message of the parable of the banquet (Lk 14:16–24), illustrating the eschatological feast of God's kingdom (cf Lk 13:29; 14:15). Indeed, some scholars hold that certain miracles were, in fact, created by the early Church on the basis of their corresponding parables. This leads us into the area of the historicity and credibility of the miracles of Jesus, to which we now turn.

Discuss the theological significance of the miracles of Jesus in Luke's Gospel.

Miracles and credibility

While many are attracted to and impressed by the teaching of Jesus, many also find difficulty with the idea that he performed miracles and, indeed, with the whole idea of the miraculous in general. This has wider implications in that it raises the issue of the historical reliability and credibility of the Gospels, since each Gospel and each Gospel source presents a miraculous Jesus. One of the problems in the debate about the credibility of the miracles is the matter of definition. Some are prepared to believe in a miraculous Jesus, but only in accordance with a particular definition of a miracle which rules out divine or supernatural intervention in the natural world. However, here we understand a miracle to be an extraordinary event considered to have a supernatural cause (see p206).

CL Blomberg states that the problem of credibility in relation to miracles involves scientific, philosophical and historical objections[1]. The scientific objection, in brief, is that modern science has discovered the physical laws that govern the universe – regular, predictable and unalterable laws that exclude the possibility of miraculous events. In this view, for example, people cannot walk on water or raise the dead. However, in response, it has been observed that people in biblical times knew as well as we do in our scientific world that virgins don't give birth and that people can't walk on water. Thus, it is wrong to give the impression, as some do, that before the advent of modern science people were completely gullible and naive. Further, physics has moved on from the very mechanistic view of the world envisaged by Isaac Newton to quantum theory, in which the 'laws' of nature are provisional descriptions of what normally happens. The confidence of Newtonian mechanics has given way to Heisenberg's 'principle of uncertainty' in relation, at least, to subatomic particles. Again, while nature is regular and fixed, it is not logically impossible to conceive of the suspension (not to say violation) of its 'laws' by their Creator. It may be added that while 'modern' man may find it difficult to believe in miracles, 'postmodern' man has less difficulty, since postmodernism rejects science's claim to have a monopoly on truth. There is a greater acceptance of mystery in the universe and of the possibility of reality beyond the reach of scientific methodology.

The philosophical objection to miracles has been formulated most famously by the eighteenth-century philosopher David Hume. Hume argued that experience teaches that the laws of nature are regular and consistent and that this evidence alone outweighs any claim to miraculous events. However, it may be replied that this argument proves too much, since it rules out the possibility of any exceptional, unusual or unique event occurring. Hume also argued that testimony in favour of a miraculous event has never been sufficient, in terms of numbers of intelligent, honest witnesses, to confirm such an event. It is not clear, however, what criteria must be met before a report of a miracle can be considered sound. Paul certainly felt he could provide numerous, credible witnesses to establish the miracle of Jesus' resurrection (1 Cor 15:3–8). Hume further argued that people are inclined to look for miracles and that this should make us sceptical of miraculous claims. However, this proves the need for caution in assessing miraculous claims, rather than the falsity of all such claims. Another argument by Hume stated that miraculous claims are made mostly

---

1 Blomberg, CL, *The Historical Reliability of the Gospels*, Leicester: IVP, 1987, pp73–80, on which the following is based

among ignorant and uncivilised nations. However, this argument is overstated, since many educated people in developed countries, including philosophers and scientists, believe in miracles. Finally, Hume argued that miraculous claims exist in various religions and, since these religions have irreconcilable beliefs, these claims cancel each other out. This does not, however, disprove the logical possibility that one religion's miraculous claims, or some of them, have a basis in fact.

The historical objection concerns the principle of analogy formulated by the nineteenth-century German historian Ernst Troeltsch. The principle states that historians should not accept as historically valid any claim from the past for which there is no analogy in the present. Thus, since miracles do not happen now, we cannot accept as historically reliable miraculous reports from the past. This argument is similar to Hume's reasoning and, therefore, overlaps with philosophical objections to miracles. However, many would argue that miraculous and paranormal experiences and events *do* occur today.

Staying with historical issues, it has been noted that people in the ancient world in general, Jewish and pagan, believed in the miraculous and attached miraculous legends and myths to people they regarded as significant and wanted to glorify. For example, Alexander the Great was said to have been born of a virgin. It is therefore argued that the miraculous claims for Jesus are not unique, but rather part of a wider phenomenon. In particular, we read of two miracle workers, one pagan and one Jewish, who lived in the same century as Jesus. Healings, exorcisms and prophecies were attributed to Apollonios of Tyana in Cappadocia. Similarly, the Jewish Galilean Hanina ben Dosa was credited with various miracles, including healings. Indeed, one miracle attributed to Apollonios is very similar to Luke's unique account of the raising of the widow of Nain's son (7:11–17). In the account of Apollonios, the funeral of a young girl is interrupted and her life restored. However, quite often it is the case that miraculous legends were attached to individuals long after their deaths, whereas the earliest sources we have for Jesus, written within a generation of his death (eg Q), refer to his miracles. Again, there are significant differences between Jesus' miracles and those attributed to others, leading Anthony Harvey to state that the miracles of Jesus fit no known pattern[1]. Attempts to classify Jesus in the categories of Hellenistic magicians or 'divine men' have not persuaded many scholars.

MA Powell classifies three general positions that scholars investigating the life of Jesus hold regarding his miracles[2]:

- Neutrality: Scholars such as John Meier hold that the historian must remain objectively neutral and silent on the matter of the supernatural and the miraculous, since this is beyond historical investigation.

---

[1] Harvey, Anthony, *Jesus and the Constraints of History*, London: Duckworth, 1982, p104
[2] Powell, MA, *The Jesus Debate*, Oxford: Lion, 1998, pp190–193

- Denial: Other historians, such as Gerd Ludemann, reject the miraculous as incompatible with a scientific world-view and explain the miracle stories in naturalistic ways.
- Critique of methodology: Some scholars, such as NT Wright, criticise traditional methods of historical investigation for being governed by naturalistic presuppositions.

Finally, Graham Twelftree has recently observed that at the start of the twenty-first century there is still a lot of work which remains to be done on the miracles of the historical Jesus[1]. In particular, there is no academic consensus on the basic issue of the place and significance of miracles in Jesus' life.

Task

Discuss the claim that the miracles of Jesus present a credibility problem for many readers of the Gospels.

Practice essay titles

1 (a) Discuss Jesus' teaching in the Sermon on the Plain. (30)

(b) Critically assess the claim that this teaching is morally impractical. (15)

2 (a) Discuss two parables concerning the kingdom of God in Luke's Gospel. (30)

(b) Critically evaluate the claim that the message of the parables has no relevance beyond the ministry of Jesus. (15)

3 (a) With reference to any two miracle stories, discuss the theological message of miracles in Luke's Gospel. (30)

(b) Critically assess the claim that the miracles in Luke tell us little or nothing about Jesus. (15)

---

1 Twelftree, Graham in *The Face of New Testament Studies: A Survey of Recent Research* (op cit), p208

Glossary

A fortiori	argument appealing to a stronger or greater reason
Adoptionism	the belief that the man Jesus was adopted by God, rather than that Jesus was divine in himself
Agnosticism	the belief that certain things (eg the existence of God) cannot be known with any certainty
Allegory	in relation to parables, the idea that several details have symbolic meaning
Androcentric	male-centred, patriarchal
Angelophanies	appearances of angels
Antagonist	leading opponent in a narrative
Anti-Semitism	prejudice and discrimination against Semitic peoples, especially Jews
Antiquity	ancient times
Apocryphal	an adjective used for writings of doubtful authorship or authority, eg apocryphal gospels of the second century AD
Apologetics	defence of a particular belief or position
Apophthegms	term used by Gospel form critic Rudolf Bultmann for sayings of Jesus
Apostasy	falling away from or giving up the faith
Asceticism	severe self-discipline and abstinence
Atonement	the sacrifice of Jesus by which sinners are reconciled to God
Chiasm	literary pattern in which the start and end of a passage are parallel and the parallelism continues inwards towards a significant centre point (eg see p182)
Christocentric	Christ-centred
Christology	the study of the person and work of Christ, especially the former
Countercultural	going against the dominant culture/way of living

Criticism	Biblical criticism is the study and investigation of the biblical texts and related matters. Specific methods of biblical criticism include, for example, Gospel narrative criticism (literary analysis of the Gospels as stories and of stories within them) and form criticism (analysis of literary forms of stories and sayings of Jesus as a guide to their possible uses before the Gospels were written). See p233ff.
Deuterocanonical books/Apocrypha	books not found in the Hebrew Bible/Protestant Old Testament, but found in the Greek Old Testament (LXX or Septuagint)
Diaspora	Jews living outside Israel/Palestine
Docetism	the belief that Jesus only seemed to have a body, but did not in reality
Ecclesiology	teaching about the Church
Epiphany	an event or experience which is a revelation of God, an appearance of the divine or the heavenly
Episcopal	relating to bishops
Eschatology	the last things, the end times
Ethics	concerned with morals, right and wrong
Evangelists	authors of the four New Testament Gospels; or any who spread the gospel message
Foil	in literary terms, whatever functions within the text as a means of enhancing something or someone else
Genre	in literary terms, a style or type of literature, eg poetry, narrative
Gentile	non-Jew
Gnosticism	term for a variety of religious and philosophical movements which flourished in the second century AD and beyond, sharing the belief that salvation came through 'knowledge' (Greek *gnosis*)
God-fearer	Gentile who converts to Judaism, apart from circumcision; or generally someone who reveres God
Hellenism	Greek culture and influence
Hermeneutics	relating to interpretation, especially of the Scriptures

Historicity	historical reality and reliability
Historiography	history writing
Holy Spirit	in traditional Christian belief, the third person within the one being of God (see pp33–34)
Hyperbole	exaggeration for effect
Inclusio	a literary term referring to the opening and closing of a passage by the use of the same word or words (eg see p291)
Kingdom of God	the central theme of Jesus' ministry in the synoptic Gospels – God's saving reign (see pp80–81)
Legalism	strict adherence to law(s)
Liturgy	set or fixed form of worship
Logia	technical term for Jesus' sayings (singular: logion)
Messiah/Christ	a title of Jesus (see p31)
Miracle	an unusual event usually considered to have a supernatural cause (p206)
Misogyny	hatred of women
Modernity	the belief that only science and rationality can be sources of truth, as distinct from postmodernism
Narrative	an account or story, eg Luke's infancy narrative (Lk 1–2)
Naturalism	the belief that the universe operates entirely according to natural, as opposed to supernatural, processes
Novellen	term used by form critic Martin Dibelius for miracle stories of Jesus
Parable	a metaphorical or symbolic story or saying (see p194)
Paradigms	brief stories told by Jesus which make a pronouncement or provide a pattern for conduct
Paradox	something which appears self-contradictory but may not be
Paraenesis	exhortation
Parousia	Greek term often used for the return (Second Coming) of Jesus
Postmodernism	ideology which rejects the belief that only science and rationality (modernism) can be sources of truth

Prayer	addressing or communicating with God
Predeterminism	the belief that events have been planned in advance by God
Proselyte	a convert from one religion to another. The term is often used of Gentile converts to Judaism.
Protagonist	leading character in a narrative
Rationalism	the belief that human reason or intelligence is the only basis for beliefs and behaviour
Reciprocity	getting and giving something in return for earlier favours
Resurrection	rising from the dead, especially in reference to Jesus
Salvation history	a religious view of history as a series of events in which God acts to save people (see p229ff)
Schism	the act of breaking away from the Church, resulting in the formation of a schismatic group
Septuagint/LXX	Greek translation of the Hebrew Bible (Old Testament) from the third and second centuries BC
Son of God	a title of Jesus (see p32)
Son of Man	a title of Jesus (see p79)
Supernaturalism	the belief that there are beings and forces beyond those of nature
Synoptic	term used for the first three Gospels due to their similar view or presentation of the story of Jesus
Theocentric	God-centred
Theodicy	a defence of the justice of God
Theology	religious teaching, teaching about God
Universalism	the belief that all may or will be saved by God
Utopia	ideal or perfect state
Via Dolorosa	the route Jesus took to the site of his crucifixion

Index

A

Aaron 87
Abel 102
Abraham 32, 35, 51, 56–57, 59, 62, 70, 111, 113, 132–133, 136, 148, 268, 270, 307
Adam 35, 203, 268, 284
Advocacy criticism 234
Aesop's fables 195
Ahiqar 109
Alexander the Great 66, 310
Ananias 10, 13, 43, 51
Angel/s 27, 42, 51–53, 55, 58, 60–62, 64, 84, 103, 107, 123, 128, 132, 160, 178–180, 185, 190, 203, 206, 229, 268, 273, 285
Angelophanies 179, 206, 312
Anna 37, 63–65, 190, 285–288
Annunciation 52, 57, 60–61, 190
Antiquities of Josephus 10, 44, 66, 78, 109, 149, 180, 214, 219, 271, 274–275
Apocalypse *see* Eschatology
Apocrypha 65–66, 249, 285, 312–313
Apollonios of Tyana 217, 310
Apostasy 102, 114, 133, 312
Archelaus (son of Herod the Great) 149
Arrest of Jesus 161–163, 168, 172, 175, 283
Ascension 20, 28, 42–43, 49, 76–77, 81, 84, 149–150, 172, 177–178, 189–191, 206, 231–233, 270
Asia Minor 62
Augustine 119, 203, 237
Augustus 27, 43–44, 60–62, 66, 214

B

Baptism of Jesus 29, 31, 33, 48, 66–67, 71, 76, 206, 231, 260, 306
Bar Ma'jan 118, 131
Bar Mitzvah 67
Barabbas 167–168
Barnabas 51
Baruch 96
Basilides 7
Beatitudes 36, 56, 291–294, 300
Beelzebul/Beelzebub 17, 95
Benedictus 58
Bethany 76, 89, 190
Bethlehem 43–44, 60–61
Bethsaida 83
Birth of Jesus 23, 35, 37–39, 44, 48–50, 52–54, 56, 58–62, 64, 66, 71, 151, 190, 223, 238, 268, 271, 287
Birth of John 37, 39, 48, 50–53, 55, 57–61, 266
Burial of Jesus 152, 176–177, 179, 287

C

Caligula 217
Calvin, John 204
Canonical criticism 234
Capernaum 83, 207, 213
Census 43–44, 60
Centurion's servant 17–18, 37, 175, 213–215, 285
Children (excluding Jesus & John) 37, 59, 74, 91, 93–95, 102, 114, 116, 127, 133, 136, 142–143, 147, 169, 197, 199, 215, 220–222, 224, 227, 266–267, 269, 278, 296
Chorazin 83
Christology 8, 13, 29–33, 45, 206, 215, 223, 226–227, 233, 308, 312
Church, the 7–13, 21–24, 27–28, 32, 34, 39–43, 45–46, 49, 56, 82, 84, 90, 97, 106–107, 112, 119, 142, 158, 189, 202–205, 209, 213, 229–234, 237, 240, 244, 246, 248–255, 257–259, 264, 268–270, 273, 277, 280, 282, 287, 293, 295, 298–299, 303, 307–308, 313, 315
Church Fathers 11–12, 24, 56, 237
Circumcision 12, 23, 50, 57, 59–60, 62, 66, 253, 313
Claudius 27
Cleopas 20, 29, 183
Commissioning of disciples 43, 52, 134, 189, 209, 252, 268, 282, 284
Communion 92, 187, 223
Compassion of Jesus & God 29, 126, 153, 161, 215–216, 227, 266–267
Covenant 32, 56–57, 59, 62, 156, 266
Criminals (at crucifixion) 20, 30, 38, 159, 169, 170–173, 175
Criticism, biblical (see also specific types) 41, 205, 233–265, 313
Cross, the 20, 30, 32–33, 72, 76, 121, 153, 169–173, 175, 270, 277, 278, 287
Crucifixion 20, 30, 38, 65, 121, 145, 159, 168–175, 183–184, 188, 229–230, 262, 272, 274–275, 286, 307, 315
Cyrus 60

D

Damascus Road 43, 191
Daniel 9, 52, 79, 192
David 32, 53, 59–61, 80, 146, 229, 273
Day of Atonement 141
Day of Preparation 177
Dead Sea Scrolls 70, 112, 116, 293, 295
Death of Jesus 20, 29, 32–34, 49, 72, 77, 84, 107, 114, 145, 153, 155–156, 160, 169, 171, 173–176, 178, 184, 192, 208, 236, 270–271, 273, 277–278
Deborah 65
Demons 35, 37, 42, 74, 78, 84–85, 95–97, 110, 180, 207–208, 216–219, 222, 224–225, 229, 268, 285

Devil, the 27, 35, 42, 81, 83–84, 92, 95–97, 102, 110–111, 154, 156–158, 160, 162, 172–173, 183, 203, 206, 208, 218–219, 226, 229, 231–233, 257, 263, 284, 304–305

Didache 7, 82, 141

Disciples/Discipleship 8, 16–20, 25, 27, 30–32, 34–35, 41, 43, 51, 53, 55, 67, 72–74, 77–83, 85, 88–95, 98, 101–106, 108, 112, 114, 120–122, 127–130, 133–139, 142, 144–146, 151, 153–154, 158–162, 169, 176–180, 187–190, 199–202, 208, 210, 215–217, 219–220, 222–225, 227, 246, 251, 253–254, 262, 266–267, 269–270, 272, 276–284, 287–288, 290–298, 300–305

Divorce 130

Docetism 108, 313

E

Egypt 56, 131, 153

Elijah 28, 31, 33, 35, 52, 71, 73, 77–78, 80, 215–217, 220, 268

Elisha 31, 35, 80, 213, 215, 223, 268

Elizabeth 27, 29, 37, 50–53, 55–57, 64, 266, 286–287

Emmaus Road 20, 29, 31, 177–178, 181–187, 223

End/End times *see* Eschatology

Enoch, books of 82, 172–173

Ephesus 11

Epictetus 295

Eschatology 10, 13, 23, 39–40, 45, 52, 72–73, 91–92, 105, 118, 149, 155, 158, 165, 174, 195, 231–232, 248, 257, 282, 292–293, 296, 300, 306, 308, 313

Esdras/Ezra 112, 303

Eternal life 86, 143–144

Eucharist *see* Communion

Exodus, the 56, 153, 217, 224

Exorcism 35, 81, 84, 95–97, 114, 206–208, 216–219, 224–227, 248, 267, 268, 310

Ezekiel 91, 123, 148, 185

F

Faith 22, 25, 30, 55, 93, 104, 134, 136, 139, 141, 146, 158, 163, 181, 211, 213–214, 217, 220–225, 227, 244, 268, 277, 279–280, 283–284, 304–305, 308

Family 17, 60–66, 79–80, 91, 93–94, 103, 107, 117, 120, 125–127, 144, 154–155, 210, 215, 224–225, 250, 266, 277–278, 296, 303

Farewell discourse 155, 158, 188

Fasting 65, 72, 141, 272, 302

Fear 17, 21, 53, 57, 61, 87, 92, 102, 104, 147, 153, 162, 172, 179, 187, 214, 216–217, 219–220, 222, 266, 271, 304–305, 313

Felix 27

Festus 27, 276

Forgiveness 18, 20, 32, 35, 59, 69, 90, 92, 133–134, 163, 170–171, 178, 188–189, 199, 205–206, 211–212, 227, 269, 279, 285, 297, 299, 302, 308

Form criticism 41, 205, 234, 236, 245–254, 313

G

Gabriel 51–53, 57–58, 61, 63, 67, 216, 218

Galilee 28, 33, 36, 45, 48, 68, 71, 76–78, 110, 114, 135, 166, 175, 177–180, 209, 215–218, 254–255

Gehenna see Hell

Gentile 8–9, 12, 21, 23, 25, 35, 37, 43, 45, 64–66, 70, 78, 80, 83–84, 86, 97–99, 104, 107, 112–113, 118–120, 145, 147, 151, 153–154, 157, 164, 166–167, 171–172, 175, 178, 184, 189, 213–214, 217–218, 220, 222, 227, 240, 249–250, 253–254, 267–271, 275–276, 290, 305, 313, 315

Gerasa 218

Gloria in Excelsis 62

Gnosticism 24, 313

Gospel, the 24, 288, 313

H

Hades *see* Hell

Hanina ben Dosa 310

Hannah 56

Healing 17–19, 29, 34, 36, 72, 81–83, 95, 110–111, 114–116, 135–136, 142, 145–146, 161, 206, 208, 210–214, 219–220, 222, 225–227, 236, 239, 248, 257, 267, 284–287, 290, 310

Hell 83, 102, 132

Herod Antipas 19–20, 27, 30, 71, 74, 113–115, 163, 166–168, 172, 175, 180, 198, 272, 274

Herod the Great 27, 44, 51, 60, 71, 149, 271

Herodias 22

Herodotus 71

Historical criticism 233–235, 244–245, 250, 252, 258, 263

Holy Spirit 27, 31, 33–34, 36, 40, 52–55, 58, 64, 70–71, 85, 91, 95, 102–103, 146, 178, 184, 189–190, 207, 211, 221–226, 231–233, 245, 279, 300, 314

Hospitality 29, 79, 82, 88, 92–93, 117, 119, 147, 159, 186, 199

Hyperbole 134, 263, 314

Hypocrisy 99, 101–102, 108, 110–111, 129, 141, 161, 272, 281, 297–298

I

Ignatius 11

Infancy Gospel of Thomas 66

Inn 61, 87, 203

Irenaeus 7, 11

Isaac 52, 307

Isaiah 28, 32–33, 35–36, 51, 56, 59, 61, 64–65, 67, 69, 72–73, 83, 109, 145, 156, 159, 167, 171–172, 174, 185, 189, 202, 207–209, 225–226, 231, 268, 276, 306, 308

Israel 22, 25, 27, 35, 40, 49, 52–54, 56, 59–60, 62–65, 69, 72, 82–83, 86, 90–92, 101, 109, 111–113, 115–116, 118–119, 122–123, 125, 132–133, 145, 148, 151, 153, 156–158, 164–166, 170, 174, 176, 178, 181, 184, 188, 192, 195, 198, 202, 213–214, 217, 223–224, 228–232, 253, 266, 268–271, 274, 276, 282, 287, 290–291, 297, 302, 306–308, 313

Israelites 35, 86, 122, 125, 153, 268

317

J

James (brother of Jesus) 6
James (disciple) 8, 36, 77–78, 180, 209, 277, 284, 300
Jericho 86, 145, 150, 203
Jerusalem 7–10, 12–13, 17, 20, 25, 28, 33–35, 37, 45, 48–49, 51, 61–68, 76–78, 80, 86–87, 89, 97, 101–102, 109, 112–115, 118, 120–121, 135–136, 138, 141, 145, 149–154, 158, 164, 166–171, 174, 176, 178–179, 181–184, 186–190, 203, 211, 238 (footnote), 243, 252, 269–270, 273–274, 276–277, 279–280, 286–290, 305–307
  Jesus' entry into 62, 150–152, 154, 176, 252, 307
  Roman destruction of 8–10, 17, 20, 25, 35, 97, 101, 152, 170–171, 174, 269–270, 305, 307
Joanna 20, 37, 180
John (apostle) 20, 36, 77–78, 85, 89, 114, 132, 150–151, 153–154, 161, 167, 169, 176–177, 179–180, 183, 188, 209, 213, 223, 227, 230, 243, 245, 261, 276, 284
John–Jesus parallelism 50–53, 58, 60–62, 65, 70
John the Baptist 17–18, 20, 27, 33–35, 37–39, 48–53, 55–63, 65, 69–76, 78, 82–83, 90, 114, 120, 130, 139, 151, 227, 229, 231–232, 268, 276, 298, 302
Jonah 17, 97–98, 217, 285
Jordan 78
Joseph of Arimathea 176–177
Josephus 10, 14, 22, 44–45, 66, 78, 109, 149, 180, 183, 218–219, 271, 273–275, 285
Joshua 53, 185, 217
Joy 35, 38–39, 52, 55–56, 60–61, 84–85, 111, 122–123, 126–127, 147, 151, 178, 188, 190, 202, 227, 293–294, 304, 308
Judas Iscariot 106, 153–154, 156, 158, 161–162, 231, 233, 256, 283, 287, 305
Judas the Galilean 11, 44
Judea 36, 45, 48–49, 51, 55, 77, 154, 165–166, 216, 274–275
Judgement/Judgement Day 39, 51, 70–72, 77–78, 83–84, 96–98, 100–102, 106–109, 112–113, 115, 132–133, 138–140, 149, 152, 156, 158, 160, 169–174, 200, 202, 210, 230, 268, 270, 272, 292–294, 296–297, 299, 306–308
Judith 65, 285
Justin/Justin Martyr 7, 10–11

K

Kingdom of God 19, 24, 34–35, 39, 73, 75, 78, 81, 83, 85, 90–92, 95–97, 101, 104–105, 107–108, 111–113, 118–119, 126–127, 129–131, 137–139, 142–147, 149, 155, 158, 172–173, 176, 196, 199–202, 204–207, 209–210, 219, 223–226, 231, 244, 249, 269–270, 277–278, 282–283, 291, 293, 295–296, 300–306, 208, 314

L

L 15–16, 18–21, 26, 41, 238, 241–243, 245, 249, 259
Last Supper 32, 155–159, 223, 243, 251, 283–284
Law, the 13, 18, 45, 57, 63–64, 71, 73, 75, 86, 99–100, 115, 129–130, 153, 164, 176–177, 185, 210–212, 220, 231–232, 245, 270, 272–273, 291, 302
Lawyers 73, 86–87, 88, 99–101, 116, 122–124, 126–127, 143, 164, 198–199, 202, 212, 267, 273, 302
Lazarus see Rich man & Lazarus
Leprosy/Lepers 14, 18, 29, 31, 36, 135–136, 210, 227, 236, 267, 285
Levi (Matthew) see Matthew
Levites 87, 203
Leviticus Rabbah 125
Light/Lamps 17, 35, 59, 64–65, 98, 105, 128, 189, 197, 268
Lord's Prayer 17, 19, 30, 90–93, 253
Lord's Supper see Last Supper
Lot 138–139
  wife of 80, 138
Luther, Martin 204, 299

M

Maccabees 182, 272–273
  books of 146, 182, 211
Magnificat 56, 287
Male–female parallelism 37, 64, 111, 123, 183, 215, 220, 285–286
Marcan priority 15, 238–240
Marcion 7, 10–11, 302
Mark 9–10, 14–16, 18, 20, 26, 28–29, 31–34, 36–37, 39, 41, 48, 71, 74, 76, 81, 102, 111, 121, 138, 144–145, 153, 164, 166–167, 175, 178, 180, 202, 207, 218, 221–222, 224, 227, 230, 236–247, 251–256, 259, 264, 269, 276, 280, 283, 304
Martha & Mary 19–20, 29, 37, 51, 88–89, 104, 279, 286–287, 304
Mary (mother of Jesus) 20, 27, 29, 36–37, 43–44, 50, 52–68, 223, 266, 285–287, 292
Mary Magdalene 180
Master–slave relationship 134
Matthew 38, 277, 280
Mercy 29, 56, 59, 88, 91, 126, 128, 132, 135, 141, 146, 199–200, 223, 266–267, 269, 290, 294–297, 301
Messiah/Christ (title of Jesus) 31, 53, 62, 70, 79, 164–165, 172, 185, 227, 314
Miracles 13, 20, 42, 44, 53, 76, 135, 151, 172, 184, 206–227, 229, 247, 248–252, 262, 267, 307–311, 314
Miriam 65
Mishnah 164
Molech 102
Money see Wealth
Moses 28, 33, 66, 82, 120, 122, 130, 133, 153, 156, 184–186, 217, 223–224, 227, 276, 291
Mount Gerizim 78, 274
Mount of Olives 30, 150–151, 159, 162, 190

N

Naaman 37, 135–136, 213, 285
Narrative criticism 234, 236, 257, 260–265, 313
Narrow door, the 17, 112–113, 277, 301
Nazareth 19–20, 43, 52, 55, 63, 68, 146, 184, 207, 215, 226, 236, 256, 262, 270
Nero 7–8
New Testament 11–12, 14–15, 26–27, 31, 33–35, 54, 77, 135, 137, 160, 173, 180, 183, 191, 194 (footnote), 203,

... 211, 217, 229–230, 236–237, 240, 242 (footnote), 257, 261, 271, 273–276, 285, 300–301, 313
Nineveh/Ninevites 97–98, 132, 268
Noah 138–139
Nunc Dimittis 64

O

Old Testament 10, 27–28, 31, 35, 49–51, 56–57, 59, 63, 69–70, 72, 75, 77, 79–80, 84–86, 90, 92, 96, 99–100, 102–103, 107, 111, 114, 123, 130, 135, 140–141, 143, 148, 151–152, 172, 174, 181, 185–186, 189, 192, 194–195, 203, 210, 215, 217, 228, 230–232, 236, 246, 266, 268, 276, 292, 295, 302, 306, 313, 315

P

Parables 17–20, 29, 32, 36–37, 41, 51, 72–74, 76, 81, 85–89, 93–96, 98, 100, 103, 105–109, 111–113, 116, 118–119, 121–129, 131–132, 134, 139–142, 148–150, 184, 194–206, 209, 216, 224, 234, 246, 248–250, 257, 260, 262, 266–270, 272, 277, 279, 281, 285–288, 292, 297–298, 301–308, 312, 314
Parousia 23, 39, 149, 165, 230–232, 255, 259, 314
Passion, the 18, 20, 28, 30, 33, 48, 79, 145, 151–177, 192, 242–243, 247, 251, 257, 270, 272–273, 283
Passover 66–68, 109, 151, 153–159, 164, 167–169, 174, 181, 186, 284
Paul 7–14, 23–24, 27, 32–33, 43, 45–46, 51, 89, 142, 156, 180, 191, 203, 217–218, 230, 241, 243, 251, 272, 295, 302, 309
Pentecost 34, 70
Peter 14, 20, 29–30, 38, 41, 46, 51, 69, 80, 102, 106, 144, 153, 155, 158–159, 161–163, 175, 180, 183, 187, 191 (footnote), 208–209, 221, 239, 252, 267, 277, 280, 283–284, 286, 300, 304
 denial of 20, 30, 80, 102, 153, 155, 158–159, 162–163, 180, 182, 187, 267, 283–284, 304
Pharisees 17, 19–20, 29, 31, 38–39, 44, 51, 72–73, 99–101, 114–117, 120, 122–124, 126–127, 129, 131, 133, 137–142, 151, 171, 198–199, 202, 211–212, 266, 271–273, 276, 281, 285–286, 292, 302
Philip & Ethiopian eunuch 181
Philo 66, 168, 274–275, 284
Philosophy 120, 276–277, 309–310, 313
Pilate 20, 23–24, 27, 30, 109, 153, 163–169, 172, 175–176, 270, 274–276
Plato 54
Pliny 173
Plutarch 66
Politics 23–24, 30, 35, 59–60, 62, 109, 120, 129, 151, 153, 157, 166, 168–169, 171–172, 176, 184, 205, 214, 218–219, 274, 276
Polycarp 7
Poor, the *see* Poverty
Post-structuralism 234
Poverty 20, 36–37, 56, 64, 70, 72, 99–100, 103, 105, 117–119, 128, 131–132, 140, 144–145, 148, 195, 215, 221, 226, 234, 257, 267, 269, 280–281, 292–295
Prayer 16–17, 19–20, 29–30, 38–39, 52, 54, 56, 65, 72, 82, 85, 90–95, 110, 139–141, 153, 158–161, 163, 170–171, 173–175, 210, 214–215, 226, 228, 245, 253, 256–257, 260, 263, 266, 279, 284, 290, 295, 300, 302, 304, 315
Predeterminism 156, 315
Priests 51, 57, 63, 65, 82, 87, 109, 115, 135, 153, 161–162, 164, 166, 168, 190, 203, 210–211, 273, 275
Promised Land 217
Prophecy/Prophet 8, 18, 27, 31, 33, 37, 41, 49, 50, 52, 54, 57–59, 62–66, 68–71, 73–75, 77, 82–85, 91, 100–101, 113–115, 130, 133, 138, 145, 150, 152, 154–156, 159, 162–165, 170, 174, 176, 178, 184–186, 188, 192, 195, 198, 206, 209, 215–216, 218–219, 223, 225–227, 229, 231–232, 234, 246, 248–249, 253, 268, 270–271, 274, 276, 284, 291, 293–294, 298, 306–307, 310
Proto-Luke theory 21, 236, 240–244
Psalms 115, 151, 165, 171, 174–175, 188, 217, 307
Psalms of Solomon 80, 293
Purity laws 100, 122, 216, 220, 222, 272–273

Q

Q 15–18, 21, 26, 41, 81, 238–246, 249, 251, 256, 259, 310
Qaddish 90–91
Quirinius 27, 43–44, 60–61

R

Rabbi Hillel 195
Reader-response criticism 234–235, 260
Redaction criticism 41, 205, 234, 236, 245, 254–260, 263–264
Reformation 204
Registration *see* Census
Remarriage *see* Divorce
Resurrection 18, 20, 24, 28, 30, 32–33, 39, 41, 48–49, 76–77, 79, 84, 86, 97, 114, 117, 133, 145, 173, 176–192, 203, 206, 209, 222, 230, 236, 242–243, 262, 273–274, 282, 284, 286–287, 309, 315
Rhetorical criticism 234–235, 260
Rich man & Lazarus 19, 37, 131–133, 141, 198, 281, 292, 301
Rich ruler 143–144, 147–148, 277, 280, 283
Ritual purity *see* Purity laws
Rome/Romans 7–9, 13, 23–25, 27, 30, 38, 40–41, 43–45, 49, 60, 66, 70, 80, 86, 101, 109, 145, 147, 149, 151–152, 165–166, 168–172, 175, 184, 213–214, 218–219, 241, 264, 268, 271, 274–276, 288
Ruth 57, 297

S

Sabbath, healing on 110–111, 115–116, 207, 212–213, 249–250, 272–273, 285–286, 302
Sadducees 271, 273–274
Salt (parabolic saying) 80, 121–122
Salvation 10, 12, 22, 24–25, 28, 31, 33–38, 40, 49, 53, 58–59, 61, 64, 69, 72, 75, 78, 82, 85–86, 112–113, 123, 136, 139, 144, 146–148, 152, 170, 172–173, 187, 189, 200, 211–213, 218–219, 221–222, 226–227, 229–233, 255, 257, 263–264, 267–269, 275, 277, 281, 286, 293, 299, 302, 304, 306, 308, 313, 315

Salvation history 10, 22, 28, 49, 59, 226, 229–233, 255, 264, 269, 315
Samaria/Samaritans 19–20, 28–29, 36, 45, 49, 76–79, 82, 85–89, 112, 135–136, 141, 198, 202–203, 227, 243, 264, 267, 269, 274, 279, 281, 301, 305
Samaritan Pentateuch 78
Samson 52, 59, 65
Samuel 50, 52–53, 59, 63, 65–67, 185
Sanhedrin 82, 164, 271, 273, 282
Sapphira 51
Sarah 51
Satan see Devil
Science 42, 46, 309–311, 314
Scribes see Lawyers
Second Coming see Parousia
Seneca 295
Sentencing of Jesus 163, 167–169
Septuagint 14, 82, 268, 313, 315
Sermon on the Mount/Plain 17, 36, 90, 238, 290–300
Seventy, the 19, 80–85, 92, 251, 268, 280, 303
Shechem 78
Shemoneh Esreh 90–91
Shepherds 38 (footnote), 58, 60–62, 65, 123–124, 206
Sidon 83, 290
Simeon 33, 35, 37, 59, 63–65, 68, 139, 148, 176, 268, 285, 287–288
Similitudes 197–198, 299, 302
Simon of Cyrene 169, 278
Sin 18, 32–33, 35, 37–38, 59, 69–70, 86, 92, 95, 107–109, 112, 122–127, 133–134, 138, 141, 143, 147, 178–179, 188–189, 198–200, 202–203, 205–206, 209, 211–212, 239, 266–267, 269, 272, 277, 279, 284, 286, 296, 299, 302, 312
Sinai 223, 291
Sirach/Ecclesiasticus 90, 92–93, 103, 114, 125, 158, 188, 190, 195, 284, 304
Social-scientific criticism 234
Sodom 83, 138
Soldiers 69–70, 153, 167, 169–172, 213, 274
Son of God (title of Jesus) 32, 53–54, 60, 68, 79, 165, 175, 227, 315
Son of Man (title of Jesus) 18–20, 32, 34, 74 (footnote), 79, 97, 102, 105–106, 113, 134, 137–140, 145, 148, 164, 179, 185, 200, 212–213, 294–295, 305, 315
Song of praise (Mary/Zechariah) 39, 50, 55–62, 64–65, 107, 216, 223, 266, 285, 287, 292
Source criticism 234, 236–245, 254
Stephen 8, 46, 171, 174, 230
Structuralism 234
Suetonius 66
Suffering Servant (of Isaiah) 32, 56, 65, 145, 156, 159, 167, 171–172, 175, 189
Supernatural 42, 54, 57, 192, 206, 219, 229, 309–310, 314–315
Susanna 37
Synoptic problem 236, 244

T

Tacitus 275
Talmud 118, 285
Tax collectors 19–20, 29, 37–39, 51, 69–70, 73, 112, 118, 122–124, 131, 140–142, 147, 198–199, 202–203, 243, 266–267, 269, 272, 285, 292, 302
Temple 9–10, 25, 29, 35, 50–52, 61, 63–68, 75, 87, 109, 115, 135–136, 141–142, 153–154, 161–164, 166, 174, 178, 181, 190, 270, 273–275, 285, 287, 305–306
Temptation 17–18, 28, 33, 48, 67, 76, 81, 84, 92–93, 138, 158–160, 231, 252, 256, 280, 304–305
Textual criticism 233, 245
Theophilus 12, 21, 24–25, 30, 41, 169
Theudas 11, 44–45
Thucydides 22, 46
Tiberius 27, 168, 274–275
Tithing 100, 141, 272
Tobit 79, 125, 188
Torah see Law
Tosepta 285
Tradition criticism 234
Transfiguration 29, 54, 185, 206, 223–224, 256, 283, 306
Trial of Jesus 23, 30, 153, 163–168, 172, 272
Twelve, the 9, 29, 81–82, 92, 106, 120–121, 134, 154–155, 158, 223–224, 251, 268, 276, 280–283, 285–286, 300
Tyre 83, 290

U

Universalism 12, 35–36, 43, 64, 78, 82, 109, 113, 120, 130, 138, 178, 189, 267–277, 315

V

Valentinus 7
Virgin conception 7, 32, 52–54, 60, 206, 309–310

W

Wealth 20, 25, 36–38, 56, 73, 103, 105, 118–119, 123, 127–129, 131–132, 143–144, 147, 157, 215, 273, 281, 293, 304–305
Widow of Nain 19, 31, 37, 215–216, 220, 222, 267, 285–286, 310
Widow of Zarephath 37, 286
Wisdom, book of 61, 90, 114
Woes 81, 83, 99–101, 131, 157, 291–294
Women 19–20, 25, 37, 52–53, 55, 57, 64, 89, 123, 139–140, 152, 169–170, 175–182, 184–186, 192, 215, 221, 227, 234, 267, 269, 281, 284–288, 314
Worry see Fear
Worship 38–39, 51, 65, 78, 81, 86, 90, 115, 136, 178, 190, 244, 248, 250–251, 279, 282, 314
Writings, the 186, 188

X

Xerxes 217

Z

Zacchaeus 19, 29, 36, 38, 146–148, 281
Zechariah 29, 37, 50–51, 53, 55, 57–59, 61–62, 64, 101, 150–151, 169, 185, 190, 216, 266, 285–286